A DICTIONARY OF
Modern Politics

A DICTIONARY OF

Modern Politics

DAVID ROBERTSON, 1946-

TAYLOR & FRANCIS

Philadelphia

Taylor & Francis Inc
242 Cherry Street
Philadelphia, PA 19106-1906

Library of Congress Catalogue Number
LC 85-2728 10 '85
ISBN 0-85066-320-2

Printed and bound in England by
STAPLES PRINTERS ROCHESTER LIMITED
at The Stanhope Press

for Jessica, Oliver and Giles

Preface

I was originally asked to be one of three co-authors of this work, but ended up as the sole one. Even more than usual, therefore, I must accept that the good belongs to others, and the blame is mine. In fact the need, with such a work, to have drafts read and re-read by as many, and as different people as possible would in any case require total modesty. My initial enthusiasm for the project arose because of the countless times I have given students an essay topic and wanted to tell them to look up some key word in the title before starting the reading, to ensure they at least started off on the right lines. As I worked on it, I came to see a wide potential usage. All political scientists have to live with the fact that any educated person is sure that he knows as much as they do about politics simply because we are all political animals. Perhaps that is true, but it remains the case that we have a professional vocabulary (which is *not* the same as admitting to writing jargon) which is not part of the word-stock of the educated layman. Yet increasingly these words—*charismatic* is a fine example—are expropriated, usually by the media (another good example) and become, with no clarity, part of general discourse. Furthermore there are 'facts', 'ideas', 'ideologies' (a third example), 'doctrines', 'concepts', about which any informed newspaper reader should be aware, but quite bluntly usually is not.

Sometimes these words are highly technical and specialized but become important to a wide public because of a public policy concern. No one ought really to try to form their view on nuclear weapons for example, if they cannot follow what is meant by saying that Trident II has a much smaller 'circular error probability' than Trident I, or why that matters. Sometimes they are terms of art in another discipline which can have an importance in general public discourse about politics, where the full rigour of the professional definition in the original discipline is not needed, but where merely a general education will not, in fact, equip the political animal to

Preface

know what he is talking about. Legal terms are often of this nature—'Civil Law', 'Accusatorial System' are notions that matter, but where intellectual osmosis is inadequate, and a legal dictionary too technical. Economics, even more, produces these—newspapers happily brand this Chancellor a 'Keynesian', that one a 'monetarist'.

Sometimes there is no need, but a high degree of desirability, to know something of the intellectual origin of a belief or concept with which one is adequately familiar in use, but unsure of the reason for its importance—'Polis', for the city state serves as a good example. Appended to this sort of use of the book is the fact that theories often carry a label created by suffixing a person's name with '-ism'—people really do still talk of Augustinianism, Platonism, obviously of Marxism; most of their listeners, for perfectly good reasons, do not know why. Given that I have such entries I have also added brief entries on some thinkers who have been or are highly influential, have given us their '-isms', but without their names actually appearing. There is not, as far as I know, a social theory called 'Nozickianism', but at least in America there are an awful lot of Robert Nozick's ideas floating about in conversations where the interlocutors probably have heard of him—just—but do not realise it is his ideas they are using. Again, there are modern names that ring a bell—Gramsci, for instance, but leave one unsure why.

Finally, and most important, there are the big words; the ones we all use, the ones that are the coinage of political propaganda—'democracy', 'liberty', 'civil rights', 'capitalism'. Here the problem is not that people do not know what they mean when they hear or use the words; the words have too many meanings. When the *Federal* Republic of Germany and the *Democratic* Republic are contrasted with a 'democratic' and 'federal' polity like the USA, whole language-games are being played. Trades Unions want *industrial* democracy; some writers talk of *representative* democracy, others of *liberal* democracy, and Leninists of democratic *centralism*. How many of us can sort these out well enough to know if the four things are compatible? *Participation* is often demanded against an *élite*. It is sometimes granted, too. But one remembers the wall poster in Paris 1968 which conjugated the verb 'to participate'—I participate, you participate . . . we participate, They *control.*

Politics as an art, and political studies as a science are overwhelmingly about words, shades of meaning, ideological linkages often neither grammatically nor logically determined. So this book is for everyone who, picking up a newspaper, doubts his grasp of what a *falangiste* is, or wonders whether anything at all important follows from one country alleging that another is breaking international

viii

law. It is also for students. It is to prevent another student of mine, and I hope anyone's ever again confusing conservatism with classical liberalism, Eurocommunism with socialism, either with social democracy.

The selection of concepts is inevitably partly arbitrary. One starts with a list, conjured up with the help of several people. Writing each entry one uses terms that themselves turn out to require definition, so a chain reaction starts, and it stops when the rate of reaction has slowed down and the sheer length of the book is at a publishing optimum. One really operates with rules for exclusion, not inclusion. No people, unless they gave birth to a creed, belief or ideology. No events—there are many good historical dictionaries. Few institutions—because it is not an almanac. Some political parties are 'defined', initially because many were used as examples in definitions of creeds. It then made sense to add the remaining major parties in the major Western democracies, simply because newspapers are likely, very briefly, to report their electoral successes. Consequently it is not just a dictionary of political ideas. The emphasis is on ideas because those are the enduring elements of political argument. It is 'modern' in the sense that it is meant for those grappling with politics today, but deliberately not contemporary, because there is no point in including an entry for 'wets', for example, because it will probably have dropped out of our political language in another five years. In the end the entry list has to be subjective—based on my sense of what people do not readily recognize but often come across. I have, as best I can, · checked these intuitions on my students and non-academic friends, and the publishers have been enormously helpful in pruning unnecessary, and urging necessary, entries.

To end—how objective is it? I have not sought the impossibility of pure value freedom (a term I define) because there are concepts that are inherently evaluative. Where I have not felt it possible to find one, unarguable, and 'correct' definition, I have to the best of my ability tried to give what I think would be a professional consensus on its meaning, rather than my own preference. It is just as inevitable that I have failed sometimes in this as it is inevitable that my preferences and interests have included material others would have excluded, and vice versa. However I have arranged for every entry to be read by others, and have nearly always altered anything that was objected to. I leave anonymous all those who have helped in this and other ways.

Where, in the text of an entry, a topic or person is given in capital letters, the reader might usefully pursue the subject further by referring to the entry under that title.

There remains only two things I wish to say about the book: I have learned a lot in the process of researching it. I have enjoyed writing it far more than anything else I have written, and even if nobody learns anything from it, I hope someone enjoys it.

David Robertson
Oxford
October 1984

ABM

Anti-Ballistic Missiles (ABMs) are weapon systems developed in the late 1960s and early 1970s by both the USA and the USSR. (The American system was called Safeguard and the Russian one was known to NATO as 'Galosh'). They were intended to destroy incoming Intercontinental Ballistic Missiles (ICBMs), primarily for the defence of either population centres or the country's own ICBM sites. Being essentially defensive, ABMs might seem more innocent than other forms of high technology warfare, but they seriously threatened the balance of power; for if one country could deploy a major ABM system, it might be all the more tempted to take the risk of launching a nuclear first strike. As a result, agreements reached during the early rounds of the SALT (q.v.) talks restricted the USA and USSR to a very limited deployment of ABMs, primarily to defend their national capitals. In any case, there are good reasons to doubt the effectiveness, certainly at any reasonable cost, of these weapon systems.

Absolutism

Absolutism describes a political theory which became popular during the 17th century, its main champions being HOBBES and Bodin. An absolutist system is one in which there is no limitation whatsoever on what a legitimate government may legally do; in which authority is absolute and unchecked. The theory is emphatically concerned with legitimate government and its legal entitlement to do anything whatsoever:—it is not a factual statement (that the powers that be can get away with anything they like), but an assertion that a duly constituted government has a right to absolute authority.

If, as some constitutional experts do, one takes the view that 'the Crown in Parliament' is a single entity, then the UK has an 'absolute' government. The question of absolutism, at any rate in theory, revolves around whether or not there are any powers or constitutional restrictions that can legally prevent a government from taking any action. The United States is not absolutist because Congress and the presidency can check each other, and because the Constitution prohibits certain executive and legislative acts. Britain, however, has no effective Bill of Rights and no separation of powers, and so its government could be described as unlimited and therefore absolutist.

Another approach to absolutism is to ask whether the general ideology or justifying myth to which the government owes its power imposes any limits on its use. One might argue, in the Lockeian tradition (see LOCKE), that as all rule is based on the consent of the governed, there cannot be unlimited and therefore absolute government. Other theories, especially some versions of Hobbesianism, would deny that citizens can regulate government, which must therefore be legitimate and absolutist.

In practice, the reasons for justifying absolutism tend to be fear of the instability that might be caused by having more than one source of authority, or the use of a justifying theory (theocratic or Marxist, for example), in which rival views cannot be tolerated and some body or group has the absolute right to determine truth. Absolutism does not refer to the content of the laws, which could, in principle, be few and extremely liberal.

Accountability

Accountability in the modern state has two major meanings which overlap. First there is the strongly normative meaning, common in democracies, that involves the idea that those who exercise power, whether as governments, as elected representatives, or as appointed officials, are in a sense stewards and must be able to show that they have exercised their powers and discharged their duties properly. Second, accountability may refer to the arrangements made for securing conformity between the values of a delegating body and the person or persons to whom powers and responsibilities are delegated. Thus in the United Kingdom the government is said to be accountable to Parliament in the sense that it must answer questions about its policies and may ultimately be repudiated by Parliament. In 1979, for example, the Labour Government headed by James Callaghan was defeated by a majority of one in a vote of no confidence (see CONFIDENCE, QUESTIONS OF) which precipitated the general election of May 1979. The Parliamentary Commissioner for Administration (popularly known as the OMBUDSMAN) is thought to have improved the accountability of the administration by his scrutiny of administrative methods and his inquiries into complaints against government departments. Ultimately, of course, governments in democracies are accountable to the people through the mechanism of elections.

Accountability is not confined to democratic forms of government, although it is in democracies that demands for greater accountability are generally heard. Any delegation of power will usually carry with it a requirement to report on how that power is exercised, and any institution seen as having power may be required to justify its operations to a superior authority. Thus it would be possible to speak of a dictatorship or totalitarian regime making the press, the universities or the trade union movement accountable to the government.

Administration

This term may be used in a number of senses and the meanings are frequently blurred. It may refer simply to the political part of the EXECUTIVE branch and it is frequently so used in the United States ('the Reagan administration'). In some countries where a sharper distinction is drawn between politicians and civil servants, the word may describe the civil service or bureaucracy alone; this is common usage in the United Kingdom. And 'administration' also relates to the process of implementing decisions and organizing the government of a country; for example, one can talk of the administration of quasi-governmental agencies, nationalized industries and local authorities.

In recent years both active politicians and political scientists have become concerned with the problem of governmental overload and the inefficiencies which result from an executive which has too many responsibilities. One solution which seemed possible for a time in the United Kingdom was DEVOLUTION. In the United States the problem has to some extent been tackled by deregulation, which involves strict reviews of government rules and orders, and efforts to reduce or even remove government intervention and control. Other questions which arise in relation to administration are whether the administrative corps is either competent or socially representative enough, and whether the administration can be effectively controlled by the politicians (see ACCOUNTABILITY).

3

Administrative Courts

Administrative Courts comprise a distinct system of courts which exist to implement and develop public as opposed to private law, and which handle disputes in which the state is a party or has an interest. Many English jurists such as A.V. Dicey once considered administrative courts inimical to traditional ideas of liberty, assuming that they would apply standards unduly favourable to authority. More recently, however, opinion has tended to favour the establishment of such courts, partly because of the rapid extension of governmental activity (for example, the WELFARE STATE) and partly because a need has been felt for distinct principles of law which can be applied to protect the individual when he comes into contact with governmental authority.

Affirmative Action

Affirmative action describes the deliberate policy of giving preferential treatment to some groups in a society on the grounds that such groups have hitherto been disadvantaged either by governmental policies or as a result of popular prejudice. Affirmative action—sometimes also called reverse discrimination—has been used to help ethnic minorities and women (see FEMINISM), and it is sometimes suggested that it should be used to help other kinds of minorities, for example homosexuals or the handicapped. The idea has been most extensively translated into public policy in the United States, where the executive has encouraged the hiring and advancement of minorities by requiring, *inter alia*, that all organizations which have contracts with the federal government employ a given percentage of people belonging to a minority group. A policy of affirmative action has proved extremely controversial in relation to university and graduate school admissions, and one of the most celebrated constitutional cases of recent years (*Bakke* v. *Regents of the University of California*, 1978) set limits to the extent to which the policy could be used. Although the Reagan administration which came into power in 1981 expressed its general dislike for the policy of affirmative action, the courts have not ruled it unconstitutional *per se* and it seems likely that the idea will continue to influence public policy in the USA.

Agrarian Parties

Agrarian parties are political parties chiefly representing the interests of peasants or, more broadly, the rural sector of society. The extent to which they are important, or whether they even exist, depends mainly on two factors. One, obviously, is the size of an identifiable peasantry, or the size of the rural relative to the urban population. The other is a matter of social integration: for agrarian parties to be important, the representation of countryside or peasantry must not be integrated with the other major sections of society. Thus a country might posess a sizeable rural population, but have an economic system in which the interests of the voters were predominantly related to their incomes, not to their occupations or location; and in such a country the political system would be unlikely to include an important agrarian party. As agriculture comes to employ a progressively smaller percentage of Western populations, which concurrently become ever more urbanized, this sort of political party tends either to decline in importance or to broaden its appeal by shifts in its policies. Both of these tendencies can be observed most clearly in Scandinavia, where agrarian parties have perhaps been more important than anywhere else in Europe. However, the same tendencies have appeared elsewhere. The politics of the Third Republic in France were to a large extent based on an urban/rural cleavage leading to at least semi-agrarian parties. These declined rapidly in the Fourth and Fifth Republics as the predominantly rural population turned into a predominantly urban one. In some countries, for example the USA, separate agrarian parties do not exist because loose party structures have permitted the existence of identifiably agrarian wings within parties, developed around other cleavages. (However, in the America of the 1880–1910 period some states did have specific farmers' parties.)

Alienation

Alienation is a very widely, and loosely, used concept, which originates in its modern form with MARX, though he took the term from HEGEL, and a similar usage can be found in ROUSSEAU. In modern sociological analysis it has much in common with the Durkheimian concept of ANOMIE. It is helpful to take an etymological approach in trying to define this important but sometimes obscure concept. In legal terms 'alienation' means giving up rights in property; analogously, political philosophers have used 'inalienable rights' to mean those rights which cannot be given up, and cannot ever legitimately be taken away. But the other derivation, from alien, suggesting something other, foreign, distant, is also helpful.

For Marx, alienation is a condition occurring in pre-socialist societies, where the human nature of man is made other than, alien to, what man is really capable of being. This is also the sense in

5

which Rousseau used it, though his view was that contemporary society had made man other, and more corrupt, than he had once been. Marx had a sophisticated theory of alienation, especially as it occurred in capitalist society. Man could be alienated, for example, (1) from himself (i.e. from his true nature); (2) from other men (absence of natural FRATERNITY); (3) from his working life (because it was meaningless and involved 'alienating', in a legal sense, his labour for the benefit of others); (4) from the product of his labour (because, unlike craftsmen, most industrial workers do not have the satisfaction of lovingly designing and creating an entire product through the exercise of their skills). All of these are interconnected, and for Marx they all stem from the capitalist productive system, and especially from its practice of DIVISION OF LABOUR.

This stress on human nature, and on the way in which man is turned into a wage slave, without respect for himself, his fellows, or his daily work, is much weakened in the later and more economics-oriented work of Marx, but it has continued to be of vital interest and importance in social thought generally. It has often been applied far too loosely so that alienation frequently means no more than unhappiness; but some new applications are obviously legitimate extensions of Marx's usage, as when feminists argue that capitalist society, as part of its generally de-humanizing effect, alienates men from women. However, there are serious objections to the concept of alienation. First, though Marx's writing is often highly persuasive in regard to the existence of the phenomenon, many critics hold that alienation is created by the division of labour endemic to any high-technology economy (perhaps even by the very nature of such economies) rather than by a particular system of property rights; and if this is so, alienation will remain a problem even in full-scale communist societies. Second the concept of alienation relies on the unprovable notion that a basic or true human nature exists. From a philosophical point of view the concept would be useful only if it could be shown (a) that man really would have certain characteristics under a different system, and (b) that these are in some sense 'natural'. Yet Marxists, and most others who make use of the concept, are strongly opposed to the idea that any basic human nature exists independently of social reality. Despite such problems, the concept retains its vigour and is widely used in social analysis.

Amendment

An amendment is a change made to a bill, law, constitutional provision or regulation. The process of making such a change is also known as amendment.

The provisions of some constitutions make constitutional amendment especially difficult, and these are known as entrenched constitutions. In some legal systems certain laws are thought to be of peculiar importance and are similarly protected—for example, laws guaranteeing freedom of speech, freedom of religion or other basic liberties. Where a constitution has been altered or supplemented, the amendments may become almost as important as the original text. This is the case in the United States of America, where the first ten amendments to the Constitution are collectively known as the Bill of Rights. They were ratified in 1791 and have since proved a major instrument for the protection of individual freedom in the USA as well as providing models for other countries (see JUDICIAL REVIEW). Of particular note because they have passed into the general political vocabulary are the First Amendment, guaranteeing freedom of speech, religion and thought, and the Fifth Amendment, which granted the individual protection against self-incrimination. In the period of McCARTHYISM the Fifth Amendment was invoked by a number of witnesses accused of communist sympathies or communist connections, and gave rise to the phrase 'Fifth Amendment communists'. The most important aspects of the Fifth Amendment is its guarantee that no person shall be deprived of life, liberty or property without proper legal process (see DUE PROCESS). Since 1954 the Fourteenth Amendment of the Constitution has been used by the Supreme Court to promote both procedural and substantive equality in the USA in a way which has also served as a model for other jurisdictions (see EQUAL PROTECTION).

Where ordinary rather than constitutional laws are concerned, the general assumption is that the stronger the executive and the weaker the legislature the less likely are amendments offered in the legislature to be successful. Thus in Fifth Republican France it is rare for bills to be changed significantly during their passage through the National Assembly. In Britain, when the government has a working majority, amendments of substance are also rare, although the combined pressure of government backbenchers and opposition parties can sometimes lead to successful amendments.

Anarchism

Anarchism is a political theory based on two propositions: that society does not need government, and that no government is legitimate unless truly, and in detail, consented to by the individuals governed. Its history is long and confused, and the other political attitudes held by anarchists have ranged from far right to far left in the political spectrum.

7

The earliest serious anarchist thinkers were 19th-century writers such as Proudhon and the French theoreticians of SYNDICALISM, who began to develop ideas about founding a society without government. However, anarchist elements can be found in many social theorists. One good example is MARX, whose doctrine that the state will 'wither away' under Communism has clear affinities with anarchist goals.

Theoretically, anarchism rests on the moral assumption that freedom is an absolute value and that no one should ever be obliged to obey authority without having freely consented to do so. Empirically it rests on a set of assumptions about the possibility of organizing genuine voluntary associations dedicated to co-operative work and mutual aid. These assumptions seem more plausible where no great degree of industrial sophistication is involved, and there has often been a rather idealistic aura of peaceful rurality about anarchist theories.

Despite this there are important connections between anarchist theory and the more general theories recommending DIRECT DEMOCRACY and INDUSTRIAL PARTICIPATION. Turn-of-the-century associations between bomb throwing and anarchism are outdated and unhelpful. The sort of commitments to extreme egalitarianism and total liberty that characterize anarchism have been taken over by radical socialist and Marxist groups, or, in more moderate versions by exponents of INDUSTRIAL DEMOCRACY.

Anomie

Anomie is a sociological concept, originated by DURKHEIM, similar in scope to Marx's concept of ALIENATION. Anomie is held to be present in a society where normative regulation, the common acceptance of value and rules, is weak, and it consists of feelings of individual isolation, loneliness and meaninglessness that manifest themselves in social disorder. Though there are many technical definitions, both by Durkheim and in later works, the basic meaning of *anomie* is contained in one of Durkheim's more poetic descriptions: it is 'the malady of infinite aspiration'. What Durkheim meant was that modern industrial society, which sometimes seems to lack any moral or ethical basis beyond utilitarianism or arguments based on rational expectation, cannot offer anyone a reason for not doing or trying to get anything he wants, although ever-growing personal appetites cannot ultimately be satisfied. To Durkheim this state of affairs was the result of the Industrial Revolution, which broke down the traditional pattern of existence that bound man closely to his fellows by deeply accepted cultural norms (see CORPORATISM). The concept can be used to explain unrest and dissatisfaction in any sort of social system, though it is often used either loosely or even tautologously (for example, to mean no more than a state of lawlessness, despite the fact that the term is actually intended to explain the lawlessness). One may question the validity of Durkheim's contrast between anomic industrial societies and traditional societies where the malady is absent because all know and accept their role; but the concept of anomie itself, if used with care, can be illuminating.

Anti-Ballistic Missiles (see ABM)

Anti-Clerical

Anti-Clerical describes a political outlook strongly opposed to the churches wielding any direct political influence or power. Anti-clerical parties or politicians have had an important role in most Western societies at one time or another. Nowadays a clerical/anti-clerical cleavage still exists in Italy and, to a lesser extent, France. In France during the period 1870–1948 important sections of the electorate would automatically back certain political parties because they could be relied upon to oppose any clerical influence in politics. Other electors (nowadays especially the Christian Democrats in Italy) vote as they do precisely because they feel that the Church should play a significant role in the state.

Anti-Semitism

Anti-Semitism, in political terms the discrimination against or persecution of Jews, is nowadays associated in most people's minds with Hitler's Germany. In fact it has a very much longer history, has had some political importance in most Western societies, and is by no means a spent force. The historical origins of anti-Semitism are complex and date back to the Middle Ages and beyond. Most European nations practised some form of discrimination against Jews, more or less intermittently and with varying degrees of clerical approval, for centuries before 19th-century anti-Semites, and later the Nazi Party, changed the emphasis of anti-Semitism from religious to racial hatred. To Hitler, the Jews constituted an international conspiracy and exercised the real power in all the nations opposed to Germany, whether capitalist or communist.

9

Modern anti-Semitism is a common element in right-wing political creeds for a largely functional reason: such creeds base much of their appeal on nationalism and an ideal of national unity that denies the existence of important conflicts within the nation. In order to build this sense of a common national identity, it is extremely useful to have a group of 'outsiders' against whom everyone can unite, and who can be blamed for social ills that might otherwise be attributed to the right wing rulers or the social system. (Other racist 'targetting' of minority groups is usually undertaken for exactly the same reason.) The existence of Soviet anti-Semitism suggests that similar reflexes may exist in a 'left-wing', but totalitarian society. Where a Christian tradition is an important part of the historic national identity, anti-Semitism is a peculiarly, if sadly, apt creed. Thus, for example, American right-wing movements such as the John Birch Society and the Ku Klux Klan have tended to be most popular in parts of the American South where fundamentalist Christianity is very strong; and such movements have never omitted to add anti-Semitism to their anti-black stance, despite the integration of Jews into American society. Again under the Third Republic in France, the anti-republican right, largely aristocratic and clerical, linked republican political power with the Jews, so that the famous Dreyfus affair eventually became a political battle between the Right and Left. In recent years other targets, especially immigrant workers, have replaced the Jews, and anti-Semitism in the West may cease to be common. In the Middle East the clash between Israel and the PALESTINE LIBERATION ORGANIZATION, and anti-ZIONISM in the Arab states and elsewhere, are not primarily anti-Semitic phenomena.

Apparatchik

Apparatchik, properly speaking, means an employee of the Apparat, perhaps best translated into English by the use of the modern Marxist term 'State Apparatus', that is, any institution involved in the running of the state, whether formally part of the state or not. In the Communist countries where the word is used, it means in practice a member of the Communist party who is in some intermediate position in the bureaucracy. It is the *apparatchiki* who form the bulk of Djilas's NEW CLASS. The term is sometimes used pejoratively in the West of administrators and bureaucrats who bully those in their power and truckle to their superiors. It has no necessarily unpleasant connotation when used in, or of, Communist societies.

Aquinas

St Thomas Aquinas, (1225–74), was one of the earliest Western thinkers to re-introduce Aristotelian philosophy into our political and philosophical heritage; the work of ARISTOTLE had been lost in the West since the end of the Roman Empire, though Arab philosophers had long known of it. Aquinas was primarily a theologian, but his writings had political significance since there was no clear-cut distinction between purely theological and political writing during the Middle Ages, when the Church was a major political and social force.

Like Aristotle, Aquinas regards civil society, or the political system as a natural part of life. For Aquinas man cannot be truly human outside some sort of ordered society, and he conceives of the family as the basic political unit. (Aristotle too starts his famous *Politics* with an analysis of the domestic economy.) But Aquinas insists that such small units can never provide an ordered and secure social framework, and therefore sees full-scale political societies built up from the family, as essential. The main purpose of such societies is to provide a framework within which man can develop his reason and moral sense, and thus come to live well and, specifically, to live as a Christian. On the all-important question of who should rule, Aquinas again follows Aristotle, arguing that though the best form of government, given the unequal reasoning powers of men, would be a monarchy or aristocracy, these are too easily corrupted. Hence he too argues for a mixed constitution.

Aquinas's main differences with Aristotle occur where Christian doctrines clash with pagan values. The most important area here is the definition of human nature. For Aquinas there is a crucial difference between the human nature of the Christian, influenced by baptism, and that of the pagan; and for this reason he did not expect that his political theory could be relevant to all men. Now that our culture is fully familiar with classical Greek thought, Thomism (the name for Aquinas's doctrines) is often regarded as superfluous, although much of the political thinking of the Catholic Church even today is based on Thomist principles. Aquinas was mainly responsible for the spread of knowledge of Greek philosophy and, more important, for its acceptance within the Western Christian political tradition. It should be noted that, formulated at a period of increasing monarchical centralization, his doctrine of mixed constitutions, and his stress on reason rather than authority, had a 'radical' aspect. This is one of the reasons why Thomism remains most influential amongst Catholic clergy of a radical persuasion in areas such as Latin America, where elements in the Church take part in opposition to dictatorial régimes.

11

Aristotle

Aristotle (384–322BC) was a thinker of the Classical Greek period whose political theories like those of PLATO, set the bounds of political discourse throughout the Middle Ages; his work still exercises a profound influence on modern political and social thought. Aristotle's political ideas are more immediately acceptable to the modern Western mind than Plato's because he comes closer to approving of DEMOCRACY. But it is salutary to remember that even Aristotle saw DIRECT DEMOCRACY as the least undesirable of existing types of government rather than the best obtainable form. Like most Greeks of his period he would have preferred a mixed government with important elements of aristocracy intermixed by popular rule. (In this context it should be remembered that the original meaning of 'aristocracy' is 'the rule of the best', not 'the rule of the well born'.)

An important aspect of Aristotle's thought, which derives from his interest in marine biology, was his use of biological analogies in discussing social life. Following Plato, he took an essentially functionalist approach to social and political institutions (see FUNCTIONALISM), believing that political life, being natural, takes certain natural forms, and that individuals therefore have natural and fitting places in society from which it would be both immoral and 'disfunctional' for them to depart.

Aristotle's direct impact on European social thought began with his rediscovery, via medieval Arab thinkers, by the Catholic Church at the time of AQUINAS, and Aquinas's development and interpretation of his ideas into the Catholic doctrine of natural law, from which our modern inheritance of NATURAL LAW and NATURAL RIGHTS conceptions derives.

Armies

Armies (used here, for convenience, to include military forces of all types) are amongst the oldest of all organized social institutions, and have a correspondingly long history of political importance. However, this apparently trivial point needs expansion. All societies have had some system for organizing men into military units for temporary or long-term defensive or offensive operations. Nonetheless armies in a politically important sense are, with one exception, products of the post-medieval era. The exception is the Roman legionary army. The point is that a 'real' army is a permanent and bureaucratically organized standing force rather than a temporary and amateur force assembled only during emergencies. As long as a nation relies on temporary, amateur troops, the army cannot be a threat to other social and political institutions. But as soon as an army in the bureaucratic sense comes into being, and with its own legitimacy and power base, it becomes a potential contender for control of the state. Thus the Roman legions came to determine who should be emperor quite early in post-Republican times.

The earliest politically important armies in the modern world included the Cromwellian army in 17th-century England and the Napoleonic armies in France. The politicians' fear of the political power of standing armies is exemplified by British and American policies in the 18th and 19th centuries. As late as 1940 the Americans kept their military establishment as small as possible. Later, after the inevitably huge increase in the size of the military machine during and after the Second World War, no less a person than the President of the USA, Dwight D. Eisenhower (who had been Allied Supreme Commander in 1945) publicly warned the nation to fear what he called 'the Military-Industrial Complex'. In Britain, the army was kept firmly under the political control of the ruling classes by simply restricting membership of the officer corps to those who could afford to buy their commissions from the Crown—a system that survived until a series of military blunders in the Crimean War forced a change of policy.

Nowadays armies tend to be of most importance in the politically undeveloped countries of the Third World, where military rule is a common feature. Though the explanations for any specific occurrence of military rule vary, what such occurrences usually have in common is the fact that the army has a near-monopoly of bureaucratically efficient and disciplined personnel, often trained in the developed countries. As civil services develop and civilian governments acquire an aura of legitimacy, the fear of military *coups d'état* will diminish and armies will become servants rather than masters of the state.

Arms Races

There have been arms races several times in recent history, brought about by the fact that military equipment has become highly dependent on technology. Perhaps the first important arms race was the competition between Britain and Germany at the turn of the century to build bigger and better battleships, the 'Dreadnoughts'. In current terms the arms race refers to the competition between the USA and the USSR to build up more powerful nuclear weaponry, especially INTERCONTINENTAL BALLISTIC MISSILES, in the hope of achieving a position in which they would have a FIRST STRIKE capacity over the enemy. The point is that an arms race is tied to the idea of a BALANCE OF POWER, so that any technological advance by one side threatens the other, which then tries to build better weapons, forcing the first mover to improve his weapons, and so on. Often the arms race may be impelled into a new stage by a relatively small development—for example CIRCULAR ERROR PROBABLE improvements by the USSR led in the early 1970s to extra investments by the USA, and the earlier American development of ANTI-BALLISTIC MISSILE systems, although defensive in themselves were seen as a threat to the balance of power by the Russians, who therefore increased their weapons developments still further.

Assemblies

Assemblies are collections of people who either directly comprise, or represent, a political or social entity. The common idea of a school assembly helps to explain the concept. In this case the entire body of people, pupils and staff, who make up the social group of the school, assemble together to discuss or to hear rules, information, or instructions. In a political sense assemblies are decision-making or rule-passing groups. In many cases there is no real difference between an assembly and a parliament, house of representatives, chamber of deputies, or whatever the local terminology of the political system may be. Thus the French equivalent, and the EEC equivalent to the British Parliament, are known as assemblies.

There remains a shade of difference in the implication, however. Because a full assembly (as in the school example) implies that *all* relevant people are present, calling some body an assembly implies less a meeting of representatives, perhaps with freedom of action, than a direct collection of all parties. In the United Nations, for example, the General Assembly contains all the member states, in contrast to the Security Council which has only a few members. The authority of an assembly is accordingly greater than that of a council or set of representatives. The French case is to the point: the theory of direct representation of the will of the people which permeates French democratic thought from ROUSSEAU onwards leads to a preference for thinking that elected members somehow stand in for the physical impossibility of collecting the whole population of France into a true general assembly. Similarly the EEC uses the title Assembly for its parliament in contrast to the Council which officially represents governments instead of electorates, or the Commission which is a meeting of top civil servants.

14

Association

An association is a group of people united to pursue a common cause. The right to associate politically is fundamental to CIVIL LIBERTIES because without it political activity would be largely ineffective. The rights and capacities of political associations vary considerably from one society to another (see INTEREST GROUPS).

On an international level many countries form associations to advance their mutual interests; the Association of South East Asian Nations (ASEAN), for example, exists to promote co-operation in that region.

St Augustine

St Augustine (354–430) was the Bishop of the diocese of Hippo in North Africa, and one of the earliest systematic Christian theologians. He was certainly the first to grapple with the question of what should be the proper relationship between the state and the Christian religion. In discussing this he was more aware of the value of pre-Christian political philosophy than any thinker before St Thomas AQUINAS, and much of his doctrine, where it is not specifically Christian, derives from classical political thought, especially from PLATO and the Roman orator-writer Cicero. Like his classical forebears, Augustine stresses the 'naturalness' of civil society, which he regards as an association of men united by a common set of interests and a common sense of justice. Indeed, for Augustine justice, which he tends to define in a rather Platonic way as the 'ordering' of men in their proper station and the regularizing of their relations, should be the cornerstone of society. Like many later thinkers he is in fact sceptical about human nature, and believes that this idealized civil society is rather unlikely to occur because of man's innate wickedness. This of course reflects his Christian belief in Original Sin rather than a HOBBESIAN view based on observation. Nonetheless Augustine argues that Christians will make better citizens than pagans.

Like Plato, Augustine sees it as the function of the state to enforce a moral code, but being a Christian he interprets this role in a subtly but significantly different way. For Plato, simply doing what is right is what matters. For Augustine, state coercion cannot really create good men because it can only direct their external behaviour, whereas it is the desire to be good that marks out the Christian. Politics, then, is a necessary but negative force. Hence Augustine's distinction between the 'two cities' in his most famous work, *The City of God*. The earthly city is the actual political system in which

15

a person lives; the heavenly city is the metaphysical unity of all true Christians. The political relations between these two remain unclear. Indeed Augustine never does produce any definite theory about the proper relations between the secular and the spiritual powers in society. As a Roman citizen and one who admired much of the past glory of Rome, he would have found this difficult. Living at a time of political collapse many of his contemporaries believed that the Christianization of the Empire had contributed to its weakness, and Augustine is therefore at pains to demonstrate that a Christian could also be a loyal and effective citizen. Had the power of the centralized Christian church been more assured at the time, and had Augustine not been so keen to use any power, secular if necessary, fighting campaigns against heresy, he might have developed a more satisfactory theory on this matter. But a more 'satisfactory' theory from the viewpoint of the church would not, in all probability, have been well received at this stage by the political rulers. His thought, including both his positive ideas and his omissions was to influence relations between church and state for centuries.

Authoritarianism

Authoritarianism, rather like TOTALITARIANISM is more of a technical term in political science perhaps than one in ordinary political usage, and has no one very clear definition. An authoritarian system need not be a DICTATORSHIP strictly speaking, and may well not be totalitarian. The essential element is that it is one in which stern and forceful control is exercised over the population, with no particular concern for their preferences or for public opinion. The justification for the rule may come from any one of a number of ideologies, but it will not be a democratic ideology, and ideas of NATURAL RIGHTS or CIVIL LIBERTIES will be rejected in favour of the government's right to rule by command, backed by all the force it needs. It is very much tied to the idea of command and obedience, of inflexible rule, and a denial of the legitimacy of opposition or even counter-argument.

Because it is such a broad term, it is, in a way, 'value-free'—one can equally sensibly talk of left and right, of communist, capitalist, even religiously-based, authoritarian governments. (This is also true of totalitarianism). Nor is it limited to describing political sytems or faiths. One of the most influential works ever written on the subject was in social psychology by T.W. Adorno *et al.*, entitled *The Authoritarian Personality*. It is an attempt to discover the personality traits encouraged by, and found amongst those who most readily fit into an authoritarian system. The stress here tends to be on characteristics such as a perfect willingness to obey orders from above, combined with a ruthless intolerance of disobedience from those below, an unquestioning attitude to the justifying ideology, and associated psychological attributes such as 'a low tolerance for ambiguity'. The real opposition to authoritarianism is LIBERALISM, or even PLURALISM. While the Soviet Union and Nazi Germany are clearly authoritarian (at least in intention), so is modern Chile and Iran both before and after the revolution against the Shah. It can also be used as an epithet not only to political creeds, but of a particular politician's assumed character or aims. Like all the most useful terms of political analysis, it can be applied to micro politics as well as macro—thus it can be useful to describe certain industrial managements as more or less authoritarian in nature, or indeed methods of organizing classroom behaviour in a primary school, though clearly it would make little sense to see a voluntary organization in such terms.

Authority

Authority is a word in common usage, but at the same time one the technical sense of which is not easy to define. Basically it means the right to give an order, such that the command will be obeyed with no question as to that right. Or, if not an order, the right in some way nonetheless to evoke legitimate power in the support of a decision. Thus one may have the authority to instruct soldiers to fire on a crowd, the authority to sign a binding legal document, or the authority to pass a security perimeter or frontier.

In the sociology of politics authority is contrasted with mere power; authority is being in a position to give an order that will be obeyed because it is seen as legitimate (see LEGITIMACY) by those to whom the order is addressed, rather than simply being a command which is backed up by coercion, bribery, persuasion, etc. Exactly what it is that gives one authority, what are the sources of legitimacy in politics, is more complicated. The best thinker on the matter is Max WEBER. He distinguished, broadly, three kinds of authority. The most relevant to the modern day is 'Rational-Legal' authority, the authority which stems from an overall social view that a system of power is legitimate because it is justified by a general view that it maximises efficient running of society. A second vital source of legitimate authority is the 'Traditional' mode of 'domination' (to use Weber's own language). This is based on the assumption that citizens learn that there are accepted ways of running a society and any rule enshrined in the tradition should be obeyed simply because

17

it always has been so obeyed. Finally, but seldom of relevance today, is the 'Charismatic' (see CHARISMA) mode of legitimate authority, the idea that a command should be obeyed because of the overwhelming personal attributes of the man who gives the order. Whatever the source, 'Authority' is the use of power that does not require immediate coercion to the majority of citizens brought under the command or request.

B

Balance of Power

This is a concept drawn from international relations and strategic theory which dates back at least to the eighteenth century, though it has become crucial in the nuclear age. It rests on the theory that peace is more likely where potential combatants are of equal military, and sometimes political or economic, power. A number of conclusions follow. One, largely responsible for the ARMS RACE, is that any increase in the military capacity of one side must be met by an equal increase in military expenditure on the other side, else the 'balance of power' will be disturbed. But consideration of the balance of power might also limit a military build-up on the grounds that one's own increased capacity would only provoke an increase in the capacity of the potential enemy, leading at best to a stabilization at a higher, more dangerous and more expensive level.

The doctrine involves several problems, not the least being the question of whom the balance is to be struck between. It makes sense only if one assumes there are no more than two really important sides in any conceivable conflict. In a SCENARIO where the USA and the USSR were the only SUPERPOWERS, there might be a sensible argument for a balance of power approach; but if Western Europe was seen as an independent third force, the doctrine would be hard to apply. A second problem arises through the sheer power of nuclear weapons. The concept of OVERKILL suggests that one country might have fewer nuclear weapons than its rival, but that the system would still be in balance as long as the weaker country retained a guaranteed SECOND STRIKE CAPACITY.

Ballistic Missile Defence (see BMD)

Ballot-rigging

Ballot-rigging describes any fraudulent, illicit or underhand interference with votes after they have been cast, the intention being to

19

falsify the result or to make sure of electoral victory in advance. It used to be common in many countries but systematic attempts to eliminate corruption have generally been successful in most Western states. However, as recently as 1960, during the American presidential election, there was a strong suspicion that illegalities had occurred in connection with the ballot in Cook County, Illinois; and Chicago's mayoralty election of 1983 also witnessed attempts to inflate the number of eligible voters by false registrations. See also GERRYMANDERING.

Ballots

Ballots are votes cast in an election contested by two or more individuals or parties. By extension the *ballot box* is the box into which the votes are put, and *to ballot* denotes the process of voting. There are many different kinds of voting procedure (see ELECTORAL SYSTEMS.) In modern democracies ballots must be cast in secret and an effective and impartial machinery must be established to prevent any tampering with the ballot (see BALLOT-RIGGING.)

Behavioural

This is a term applied to certain schools of thought in the social sciences. Behavioural approaches in POLITICAL SCIENCE became important in post-war America and spread to some university departments in Europe, though a behavioural approach is still a minority one in European political science. Technically a behavioural approach is one that concentrates on explaining overt political or social behaviour in terms of other overt or express phenomena. For example, when considering voting the only part of the process which can be subjected to a behavioural study is the actual casting of the vote which can be observed externally and objectively; the ideology of the voter cannot be studied as here more subjective matters are involved. Other objective factors, such as class, religion/region, age etc. can be taken into consideration when describing the voting process but not so easily policy preferences or attitudes to issues. More generally, however, Behaviouralism has come to mean a rather naive distinction between the more apparently 'science like' part of political science, concerned with measuring and statistical analysis, and more traditional aspects, like political theory or political history, or institutional/descriptive studies. These barriers are increasingly tending to break down, partly as a result of a revival in POLITICAL THEORY, and partly because the skills and techniques used by behaviouralists are coming to be more widely available and to be used by those with no theoretical preference for a behavioural position in general.

Bentham

Jeremy Bentham, (1748–1832), is deservedly known as the founding father of UTILITARIANISM, although its seeds can be found in the writings of HOBBES and HUME. Bentham's work, much of it done in collaboration with James MILL, was wide-ranging, covering political and moral philosophy, jurisprudence, and even practical topics such as prison reform. In jurisprudence he was an early legal positivist (see POSITIVISM); on policy questions he took a Liberal line, but his utilitarian position was most fully developed in his political theory and moral philosophy. His general argument was that pain and pleasure were the two driving forces of mankind, and that moral or political values had to be translated into these terms. Treating man as mainly selfish, Bentham argued that the only way to judge political institutions was to discover whether they tended to produce a positive or negative balance of pleasure over pain. Strongly influenced by natural science, he believed that such things should be capable of precise measurement, and he proposed the construction of measuring devices and their application through what he called the 'felicific calculus' to both constitutional engineering and detailed policy-making. James Mill developed the more purely political aspects of this position into a rather limited defence of REPRESENTATIVE DEMOCRACY with more or less manhood suffrage. He attached great importance to the political role of the middle class (as, for similar reasons, had Aristotle), which he believed less likely to push for policies of extreme self-interest than either the aristocracy or the working class. No separate value was given to any of the now-standard liberal democratic values such as civil liberties; indeed Bentham scornfully dismissed all talk about natural rights as 'Nonsense on stilts'. Bentham and James Mill represent the coldest and least attractive version of utilitarianism, though in practice their basic position was a radical one, far closer to egalitarian and democratic values than any of the orthodox political creeds of their time.

Bentley

Arthur Bentley (1870–1957) was an influential American political scientist of the inter-war period. Methodologically, he was a precursor of the BEHAVIOURAL movement of the post-war period, while theoretically he was one of the founders of PLURALISM. His main contribution to the analysis of political systems was his 'GROUP THEORY'. Bentley held that the traditional distinctions drawn in political science between democratic and dictatorial systems were largely superficial. He argued that all political systems really consisted of a number of separate groups competing with one another for influence over policy. The role of the government was essentially that of political broker, responding to the demands and influence of different groups and distributing 'goods' (in the form of policies) in response. In many respects this approach represented a development of ideas expressed by the European elitist school (see ELITISM), and resembled modifications of such earlier ideas made by people like SCHUMPETER. Like many theories of its period, Bentley's was largely intended to strip away what he saw as an artificial shell of respectability surrounding democratic theory, many elements within which he regarded as no more than myths.

Blackleg

This is a term, widely used in trade union disputes, for a person who knowingly carries out work for an employer while his fellow-workers are on strike. The derivation of the word is unknown, but it was probably first employed in the USA in the 1930s. It has taken on a more general meaning, and may be used to describe anyone who exercises a right of private decision when this, by breaking a collective front formed by his peers, may damage their collective power.

BMD

Ballistic Missile Defence (BMD) is a general term for all defensive weapons systems intended to protect against attack by nuclear missiles. The original systems, known as ABM (q.v.) (for antiballistic missiles) were developed and implemented by the USA and USSR in the late 1960s. These, which were of very dubious efficiency, were restricted by a treaty in the SALT process. The two countries are entitled to two ABM screens each, one to protect their capital, one to protect an ICBM (q.v.) site. The Soviet Union has retained its Moscow shield but not implemented a second base, and the USA decommissioned its only site. Active research and development has gone ahead in both countries. The Reagan administration, following a major speech known as the 'Star Wars' speech has put considerable emphasis on the need to develop the technology for a full blown ballistic missile defence.

Few authorities believe that a very effective defence can be mounted, though limited systems to protect ICBM sites may be possible. Any implementation of such a developed system would be a breach of the SALT treaties. The original ABM screens were politically controversial because it was widely felt that the building of a defensive screen, by reducing the vulnerability of the possessor nation, destabilized the balance of terror on which the nuclear peace of MUTUAL ASSURED DESTRUCTION rested. Since the Soviet Union has developed NUCLEAR PARITY the interest in defence rather than deterrence has grown considerably, and the arguments about stability have come to seem less clear-cut.

Bolshevik

The Bolshevik movement was one branch of the revolutionary movement in pre-1917 Russia. It started after a split at the Second Congress of the Russian Social-Democratic Labour Party in 1903, when the movement broke into two, the Mensheviks arguing for a less violent solution to Russia's problems and hoping to introduce a social democracy after any revolution. The Bolsheviks, from whom came the Communist Party of the Soviet Union (see CPSU), were far more left-wing. Under the leadership of LENIN, the Bolsheviks developed the doctrine of the necessity for the masses to be led by the Communist party (the VANGUARD OF THE PROLETARIAT), and for a more or less lengthy period of centralized state control over the people after a revolution before any democracy could be entertained (the DICTATORSHIP OF THE PROLETARIAT). When the first revolution of 1917 broke out in Russia, the Bolsheviks were not immediately very powerful, and a moderate line, with which the Mensheviks could accord, was initially taken. However, the Bolsheviks were a far better disciplined and organized group, as well as being more ruthless, and before the year was over they had completely taken power in Russia, destroyed the liberals and the Mensheviks, and set about creating the party-controlled and centralized Russian state that we know today. Thus was produced, especially after STALIN took control, the hard-line version of MARXISM that the Mensheviks then, and many modern Marxist scholars now, see as a repudiation of much that MARX himself had argued for.

Over much of this century, and particularly during the inter-war period, 'Bolshevik' was a generic term in the West for all forms of COMMUNISM or for the entire Russian political movement. It also

23

became a common description for anyone who was left-wing or simply 'awkward' about accepting common values, disobedient, or critical of society or institutions. Hence the still common use of 'Bolshie' to describe those who will not readily conform to some generally accepted code.

Bourgeois

All that 'bourgeois' actually means is one who lives in a town, and in its original history in the French-speaking world its primary use was to distinguish the upper classes of the cities from either the urban lower orders, or anyone from a rural background, however noble or lowly. As a consequence aristocratic society, which has tended to have more influence on social attitudes even after their political demise, made the word a pejorative one, precisely because rich town dwellers were aristocratic society's most serious political, economic and social rivals.

Bourgeois has a series of technical or semi-technical usages. The most important is the MARXIST use. Here the bourgeoisie is a specific class, those who rose with and helped develop CAPITALISM and thus took power from the feudal aristocracy. They were, on the whole, urban, and they were rich, but lacked the initial legitimacy of the aristocracy, and indeed were once a revolutionary force. With some authors, arguably MARX himself, the creation of a bourgeoisie is a necessary stage in history – until the bourgeoisie exists and creates the economic and social conditions of capitalism, world historical progress cannot lead on to the ultimate class revolution.

Whether derived from the Marxist tradition or otherwise, the identity of this group has been accepted by historians, novelists and journalists since the early nineteenth century at least. In this more general usage, however, much precision has been lost. For example, in its general usage there is scarcely a more bourgeois figure than the middle class professional, a doctor or lawyer, living on rather less money than he admits to with the trappings, servant etc, of a grander life style, in a suitable suburb. Yet in Marxist theory such people, not being owners and controllers of the means of production, are actually marginal in class relations, and ultimately doomed to be crushed by the true property owning bourgoisie just as are the workers.

So much has been written about this class that an entire essay could be dedicated to the creature. Very roughly the bourgeoisie is a class, partially corresponding with the middle class, or upper middle class of Anglo-Saxon terminology, that is characterized by conservative social attitudes, fear of its own potential political insecurity, but is dominant in both running the economy and polity, and in setting standards of decent behaviour. As such it is aped by the petit-bourgeoisie, those who occupy even less secure positions intermediate between the new capitalist ruling class and the traditional manual workers. These latter, characteristically clerks or others operating in auxiliary positions to the true bourgeoisie, are celebrated in such works as *Mr Pooter's Diary*, with their pretensions and anxieties, bent on social mobility.

Outside a proper Marxist theory, the term bourgeois has little or no value. Sociologists have much more precisely defined categories of the classes, and modern culture lacks the value stock to need the phrase, but it lingers on, almost entirely as a pejorative comment. Some more extended usages of the word as a qualifier have developed, as, for example, with 'bourgeois social scientist', used by Marxists to identify their enemies. About all that can be said about the application of the epithet today is that someone who is bourgeois is neither a manual worker nor one with any overt pretensions to landed aristocratic descent.

Bureaucracy

Bureaucracy, in its most general sense, describes a way of organizing the activities of any institution so that it functions efficiently and impersonally. The major theorist of bureaucracy was Max WEBER, and most subsequent research and theorizing has closely followed his analysis. For Weber, and most subsequent writers, bureaucracy is characterized by a set of basic organizational principles. The most important are: (1) that office-holders in an institution are placed in a clear hierarchy representing a chain of command; (2) that they are salaried officials whose only reward comes from the salary and not directly from their office; (3) that their authority stems entirely from their role and not from some private status, and that the authority exists only in, and as far as it is needed to carry out, that role; (4) that appointments to bureaucratic positions are determined by tests of professional skill and competence and not for considerations of status or patronage; (5) that strict rules exist on the basis of which bureaucrats make their decisions, so that personal discretion is minimized; and (6) that such institutions collect and collate detailed records and operate on the basis of technical expertise. For Weber, bureaucracy, which he saw as a necessary development of the modern world, developed along with the shift from a 'traditional' towards a predominantly 'rational-legal' orientation in all

25

aspects of social life. Institutions as diverse as churches, legal systems and symphony orchestras were becoming bureaucratized, as well as government departments and large-scale industrial concerns. Believing bureaucratic institutions to be uniquely efficient, Weber expected this pattern of organization to become supreme; and because he thought SOCIALISM, with its planned economy, to be essentially bureaucratic, he expected a form of what we would now call STATE CAPITALISM to become dominant throughout the developed world.

The essence of the bureaucratic idea is that technical experts should perform a set of precisely defined roles in such a way that all personal elements in decision-making are ruled out. In his own words, 'affective' or 'traditional' elements in social control were replaced by 'rational' elements. Since Weber's day it has become increasingly clear that this 'ideal' type of bureaucracy seldom exists and is not necessarily more efficient than others when it does. However, Weber's is still the best characterization of how large-scale institutions operate much of the time.

The pejorative sense of 'bureaucracy', describing institutions as full of small-minded time-servers, indifferent to the public and incapable of initiative, was largely ignored by the original theorists of bureaucracy, and indeed refers only to a corrupt manifestation of a useful general principle for organization of efficient goal-oriented human interaction.

The idea that the spread of bureaucracy will produce essentially similar societies regardless of whether they are officially capitalist or Communist has been developed by later writers, sometimes as the CONVERGENCE THESIS, sometimes as a version of class theory (see NEW CLASS). See also BUREAUCRATIC STATE.

Bureaucratic State

Max WEBER and many later social theoriests have argued that modern political systems are becoming increasingly similar because they are all undergoing a process of increasing 'bureaucratization'. According to this theory, the especial suitability of bureaucratic forms of administration for running complex and large-scale organizations makes the development of a bureaucratic state essential, regardless of official ideologies. One famous theory, derived from WEBER, the 'CONVERGENCE THESIS', claims that even such apparently opposed systems as the USA and the USSR are growing increasingly alike as bureaucracy takes over. The special characteristics that are held to maintain bureaucracy supreme include its control and storing of information (magnified by the bureaucrat's 'everything on paper' ethic) and its concentration of specialist and expert skills. In addition, professional administrators, loyal to each other and the administrative system rather than any political party or group, are able to form a united front against any political decision-maker, whether he be a democratically elected cabinet minister or a member of the Politburo. The thesis is a very hard one to test, since the presumed secrecy and confidentiality of the bureaucratic ethic would allow little evidence of manipulation to emerge if it were in fact rife. At a less sinister level, the idea that the state is becoming more and more bureaucratic is undoubtedly true: as increasing areas of social and economic life have been taken over by the state, huge administrative machines have necessarily been created, which do tend to develop a dynamic of their own.

Burke

Edmund Burke, (1729–1797), was a politically controversial writer, a journalist and pamphleteer as well as an M.P., with an Irish background, who more than anyone of his generation, set the philosophical background for modern British Conservatism. Two events stimulated him to write brilliant and caustic pieces which are still widely read today. One was the French Revolution. His tract on this set forth principles of the value of slow and natural political evolution, and the duty to conserve the best (hence *Conservatism*) along with a deep distrust of the capacity of ordinary human intelligence to plan and construct an ideal society. Of his other writings the most important is probably his tract decrying the British war against the American Colonists, for Burke saw a great injustice in the rule of a colony which was denied effective representation. One further work of his is often quoted in modern political theory, a letter of his, published widely, to the voters in his own constituency of Bristol. This set forth his own views of the duties and rights of an elected representative to parliament. Very crudely, it argues that voters should pick the best candidate available, and then leave him alone. What the representative owes his constituents, according to Burke, is his best judgement, not his obedience. It is, thus, an argument of considerable power against the idea of 'DELEGATION' in democracy and often represents the main opposition to the idea that someone who is elected must repeat the views of those who elected him. All in all, Edmund Burke probably created more of the essence of modern British Conservative thinking than any other single individual.

Butskellism

Butskellism was a term coined by British political commentators during the first Conservative government (1951–55) after the Second World War; it merged the names of the previous Labour Chancellor of the Exchequer, Hugh Gaitskell, and that of the Conservative Chancellor, R.A. Butler. The term was intended to indicate the apparent similarity between their attitudes towards economic management and Treasury operations. The point was that until this period it had not been fully apparent that a high degree of consensus existed between the two major parties on the all-important question of economic policy. This had in fact been foreshadowed by common agreement during the 1939–45 coalition government on post-war economic goals and methods, and was a result of the final conversion of political leaders in all parties to KEYNESIAN economic theory. However, 'Butskellism' was a term of abuse for many of the politically engaged, since the 'mixed economy', with government intervention through taxation and manipulation of interest rates, and (on the part of Labour) an acceptance of limited nationalization, was only approved of the by the 'moderate' wings of the parties. This was especially true of the Labour Party, many of whose members believed Gaitskell had 'sold out' by not relying much more on direct controls, coercive economic planning and widespread nationalization. At the same time the right wing of the Conservative Party was dismayed that there was little de-nationalization and no return to the gold standard, and that the government should pursue anything but a totally LAISSER-FAIRE economic policy. Butskellism can fairly be said to have lasted until the Conservative Party's conversion to MONETARISM in the late 1970s.

C

Cabinet

This is the name for the small body of senior politicians responsible for directing the administration of a country which has the form of government known as CABINET GOVERNMENT.

In France the term 'cabinet' is also applied to the small group of politicians and civil servants who act as the personal advisers to a minister.

Cabinet Government

Cabinet Government is a form of government in which responsibility for directing the policies of the country lies (in theory at least) in the hands of a small group of senior politicians. Cabinet government originated in Great Britain, where the cabinet developed from the inner core of Privy Councillors on whom the monarch relied for advice. As the monarch lost power and party government replaced personal authority, the cabinet came to be formed not from the monarch's most trusted advisers but from the most senior members of the dominant political party. In Britain the existence of the cabinet was not constitutionally acknowledged, in the sense of appearing in either legal decisions or statutes, until 1937, when the Ministers of the Crown Act made provision for differentials in the payment of ministerial salaries.

The essence of cabinet government is that it is collective government by a committee of individuals who are theoretically equal and bound by their collective decisions. Fundamental to the way cabinet government operated in Britain until the early 1960s were the dual notions of COLLECTIVE RESPONSIBILITY and secrecy. The proceedings of a cabinet debate were secret and it was not permissible for a minister to publicize his dissent from any decision of the cabinet and to remain a member of the cabinet thereafter. Collective responsibility also meant that if Parliament wished to remove a government from office it had to remove the whole administration; it could not remove part of it or pick ministers off one by one, although individual ministers have resigned for political and personal reasons.

In the 1960s the conventions of British cabinet government began to change. Individual ministers felt freer than before to reveal the substance of what had occurred in cabinet; and this movement towards a more open style of cabinet government culminated in the publication by a former cabinet minister, Richard Crossman, of a detailed set of diaries which revealed cabinet proceedings and many of the aspects of government previously supposed to be confidential. As a result there was a civil action against the publishers of Crossman's three-volume work and the major Sunday newspaper which had serialized it. The peculiar result of the case was to establish the power of the courts to decide whether or not a particular indiscretion or revelation should be restrained.

Similarly, by the late 1970s the doctrine of collective responsibility had been modified by the willingness of cabinets to accept defeats on legislative measures in the House of Commons without feeling obliged to resign; such defeats were now assumed not to be votes of no confidence in the government as a whole (see CONFIDENCE, QUESTIONS OF). In 1975 individual cabinet ministers were even permitted by the Labour prime minister, Harold Wilson, to campaign on different sides of the referendum over whether Britain should remain a member of the European Economic Community—the first time that collective responsibility had been openly abandoned on a major political issue since the agreement to differ in the coalition government of 1931, when the Liberals were allowed to dissent from their coalition partners on the issue of free trade.

The concept of cabinet government implies that power and responsibility will be shared equally between all members of the cabinet. In fact the prime minister, as chairman of the cabinet and, in most systems which have cabinet governments, the person who appoints the other cabinet ministers, wields a power which is generally seen as superior to that of other members of the cabinet individually and even to that of the cabinet as a whole. In the British system of cabinet government a great deal of decision-making and policy preparation is undertaken not by the full cabinet but by cabinet committees which cover specialized areas of policy. Significantly, James Prior openly explained that he had accepted his demotion from the post of Employment Secretary to the Northern Ireland Office only on condition that he was allowed to remain a member of the influential economic committee of the cabinet.

Britain's system of cabinet government has been exported to other countries, notably those of the Commonwealth. However, the norms and practices of cabinet government may vary slightly from one country to another. When the Labour Party comes to power in Australia, for example, it elects the members of the cabinet, thus denying the prime minister one important source of power and patronage.

Capitalism

This may well be the most used (and abused) concept in modern social analysis. At its most simple and value-free it refers to any economic system where there is a combination of private property, a relatively free and competitive market, and a general assumption that the bulk of the workforce will be engaged in employment by private (non-governmental) employers engaged in producing whatever goods they can sell at a profit. Capitalism has its own ideology and economic theory, like all politico-economic systems. The original theory of capitalism was essentially that an entirely free market of small-scale entrepreneurs, hiring individual labourers at the minimum possible cost, would produce the maximum output, at the cheapest possible price given the cost of the other inputs necessary for production. This is often called the 'perfect competition model' of economics.

However valid or otherwise this simple model might be, current notions of capitalism are bound up with two ideas; production for profit, and the existence of private property which is only partially controlled by the state. To believers in Capitalism (which, with some reservations, means all the major parties of the UK and USA, and most parties in Western Europe and the Old Commonwealth), this form of economic organization provides the greater likelihood of maximizing economic performance and defending political liberty while securing something approaching equality of opportunity.

Catch-All Parties

Catch-All Parties are political parties which have no very clear or specific base in terms of the social and economic characteristics of the people who vote for them—unlike, say, most socialist parties with their predominantly working-class base. The phenomenon of catch-all parties was first commented on by political scientists in the late 1950s. Their enemies see them as predominantly motivated by the desire to put together as large a voting support as possible in order to maximize their chances of winning elections. Catch-all parties are unlikely to stand far from the centre of the political spectrum in which they operate, but may well espouse a set of policies which does not fit in with schematic distinctions between 'left' and 'right'. In practice these parties have usually been right-of-centre, standing for support of the economic and social status quo or at least hoping not to have to modify it too much. They have therefore had all the more reason to deny any specific class orientation, since class politics tends to produce natural majorities of working-class voters who are likely to believe that they will gain by radical change.

Typical of parties often defined as catch-all were the GAULLIST parties in post-war France, especially during the early years of the FIFTH REPUBLIC, when they could attract voters of all classes and almost all political persuasions by appealing to the desire for a strong and stable government. Similarly the Italian Christian Democrats have managed to attract considerable working-class support, although they are essentially a moderate conservative party, because they could associate support for traditional conservative and religious values with the defence of democracy, and thus 'catch' almost anyone who felt afraid of radical social change such as might be offered by the Communists. To a lesser extent the British Conservative party, which has always relied on a considerable 'cross-class vote' from working-class electors, and the major American parties, which have no overt class basis, might be categorized as catch-all parties.

Centralization

Centralization describes the concentration of government and political authority in the capital city and at the national level, as opposed to the sharing of powers and responsibilities between national, regional and local authorities. There is usually a strong correlation between centralization and size, so that a small territorial unit such as the United Kingdom will tend to be highly centralized. However, some very large countries, for example France, have also become highly centralized although the 1981 elections brought to power a president (Mitterrand) determined to reduce the degree of centralization by reducing the prefects' powers to overrule local government decisions. (See also ADMINISTRATION: DECENTRALIZATION: DEVOLUTION.)

CEP

Circular Error Probable (CEP) is the usual rough measure of the accuracy of ballistic missiles. It refers to the diameter of a circle within which 50% of warheads can be expected to fall if launched from the same point. In fact it is a less-than-perfect measure, because it refers to the tightness of grouping of a strike, not the proximity to the target, and that latter is affected by a less well understood phenomenon of bias. Nonetheless it is the conventional measurement used, for example, in deciding whether missiles are accurate enough to destroy hard targets. CEP ranges, for current ICBMs, from around 300 to 600 yards. Planned medium-range weapons systems, especially the controversial Precision Guided Munitions with which NATO is to be equipped are hoped to approach a zero CEP. With current generation ICBM warheads, a very small CEP of less than 200 feet is required to destroy a hardened target, though the measure is irrelevant for large and 'soft' targets like cities where a CEP of a thousand yards or more would suffice. Submarine-launched ballistic missiles (SLBMs) in which the US holds about 70% of its warheads have up to now had unavoidably large CEPs in contrast to land-based systems, but the newest generation of US SLBMs will be as accurate as any other missile.

Charisma

Charisma was originally a theological notion, with the literal meaning of the 'gift of grace', an attribute in Catholic theology of Saints. Its career as a political concept stems from WEBER, who used it to describe one of his three principal types of political authority. To Weber charisma was a personal quality of attraction and psychological power capable of inspiring deep political loyalty in large numbers of people. Thus a charismatic leader won sway over his followers for entirely personal reasons rather than because of any specific policies he espoused, or because he was in some way a 'legitimate' ruler, perhaps by virtue of traditional inheritance. It has become somewhat over-worked, with almost any political leader who can project a pleasing personality being credited with this actually very rare capacity to demand unswerving support simply because of his own character. Possible candidates of some plausibility are Gandhi, Nasser, Hitler, who do seem to have been able to command support in this way. The inclusion of the latter indicates how much we are talking of personal magnetism rather than moral force. Politically the great problem with authority is what Weber indicated as the 'routineisation of charisma'; that is, one dynamic leader may build a state or party around his own qualities, but after him, who should command, and why should the inheritor be obeyed? It seems that charismatic institutions can only be long-lived if there are also pragmatic or traditional reasons for support, or if these can be developed.

Christian Democracy

This concept refers to a peculiarly Continental form of political movement, mainly found in post-war politics and typified by the Christian Democrat parties of Italy, Germany and the Fourth French Republic. These are similar in most ways to moderate conservative parties like those of Britain and the Old Commonwealth. Christian Democrat parties are likely to stand for a moderate social LIBERALISM, a mixed economy, an acceptance that there should be basic social welfare provisions, and some degree of commitment to full employment through KEYNESIAN economic policies. The addition of the adjective 'Christian' now has little religious significance but derives from historical factors, notably the emergence of these parties in France and Italy from Second World War religious resistance movements linked with the Church. The Italian Christian Democrats are partial exceptions to this statement since they have always been closely associated with the Catholic Church in Italy. Opposition to the European Communist parties has always been a mainstay of this sort of political movement, and Catholic opposition to communism has given the 'Christian' label a certain utility. The word 'Democracy' serves to identify the parties concerned as being dedicated to the general interest rather than aristocratic and elitist like most pre-war conservative parties.

Christian Social Union (see CSU)

Christian Socialism

Christian Socialism is not an organized movement or a specific ideology or body of doctrine (though there have been groups, for example in the early Labour Party, which adopted the name). It is a broad descriptive term for individuals or groups, or for a general attitude that has appeared from time to time in various European countries. The central argument of Christian Socialism is that both CHRISTIANITY and SOCIALISM share certain basic values, and that the

Christian should therefore give political expression to his religious beliefs by supporting a certain type of socialism. At the same time, it is argued, Christianity gives socialism a moral basis which is lacking in other versions such as orthodox MARXISM. The supposed common values are those associated with equality, communal sharing, peace, brotherhood, an absence of competition and rejection of hierarchy and power.

The Christian aspect of Christian Socialism involves a stress on one side of Jesus's teaching and one image of him as a man—as a simple carpenter with a radical message. It often also draws for inspiration on the life of the early Church, which is interpreted as a communal and pacifistic movement. Clearly this view of Christianity, whether historically correct or not, is at odds with the way in which the institutions and theology of the Church developed in later centuries. It may be for this reason that Christian Socialism is almost entirely a phenomenon of Protestant Christianity, which was in intention a return to the 'primitive, uncorrupted, simplicity' of the early Church. However, there have been political movements within the Catholic Church of a roughly similar liberal-socialist character, for example the MOUVEMENT REPUBLICAIN POPULAIRE in France and the clerical radicalism found in modern Latin America and the Netherlands.

Relations between Christian Socialists and other socialists are not always easy, since left-wing socialists, in particular, often more or less Marxist in outlook, tend towards MATERIALISM and to the overt atheism and antagonism towards religion which occur in Marx's writings. If only for this reason, the socialism of Christian Socialists is generally moderate and non-revolutionary, close to Fabianism (see FABIANS) and/or the British Labour Party.

Christianity

The political role of Christianity has varied greatly from nation to nation. It has steadily become less important in most Western democracies, since voters increasingly support political parties on grounds that have little to do with religion. Where it retains some importance in politics, this manifests itself in two main ways. One is the conflict between clerical and anti-clerical factions (see ANTI-CLERICAL), which used to be fierce in France and is still significant in Italy. The other is the conflict between parties representing different Christian denominations. The denominations are usually Catholic and Protestant, although in some countries, notably the Netherlands, divisions inside Protestantism have given rise to separate political organizations. Even where there are no overtly Christian parties politics and religion may still be linked, and some of these links (for example in the MORAL MAJORITY in the United States), may even be getting stronger. Political parties in countries as different as Australia, Canada and Britain still tend to attract specific religious groups. A majority of Roman Catholics of all classes vote for the Labour Party in Britain, whilst the Conservative Party is especially popular amongst Anglicans. In some countries, the most notable example being Northern Ireland, conflicts between Christian sects are the entire basis for political alignment.

Christianity as such is not usually seen as leading to any particular political position, and despite its sheer numbers world-wide, it has relatively little political force, though institutions like the World Council of Churches may on occasion exercise a good deal of influence. Where nominally Christian parties exist, as for example in West Germany, they tend over time to become fairly orthodox conservative parties.

Circular Error Probable (see CEP)

Civic Culture

Civic Culture is a term, related to POLITICAL CULTURE, that is used in a classic study, *The Civic Culture,* based on research carried out in five countries in the early 1960s. It proceeds from the observation that political cultures vary considerably in the extent to which they encourage a sense of trust in political authority and facilitate political activity on the part of ordinary citizens. The ideal civic culture would be one in which the political ideas and values of the citizenry were attuned to political equality and participation, and where government was seen as trustworthy and acting in the public interest. This comes close in many ways to the classical Greek notion of the POLIS, and to Aristotle's description of man as 'a political animal'. In fact this sense of 'citizen competence' was found to vary very considerably, according to factors such as class and education, even within the countries that most nearly approached the ideal of LIBERAL DEMOCRACY. More to the point, the researchers who wrote *The Civic Culture* found that it varied greatly according to the efficacy and stability of the democratic regimes surveyed. It was high in the USA and the UK, relatively low in Italy, and marginal in Mexico (which is not, however, a democracy, but rather a fairly liberal one-party state). However, as actual POLITICAL PARTICIPATION rates are everywhere extremely low, it is unclear that citizens' perceptions of their political competence mean very much.

Civil Defence

Civil defence refers to any systematic attempts or plans by governments to limit civilian casualties and damage to civil property during a war. The first major civil defence programmes were instituted during the late 1930s, when the danger of air bombardment of European cities became clear. One important early precaution, in the UK, for example was the issuing of gas masks to the entire population at the beginning of the Second World War. As it happens, no gas attacks were ever made, but the idea that civilian populations could and should be protected against weapons specifically designed for indiscriminate mass killing was established. A parallel development was the extensive building of air raid shelters in the towns and cities of all European combatants. It is fairly clear that effective air raid precautions reduced deaths in both Britain and Germany, the two countries to experience serious air raids, and the absence of such a programme resulted in a more severe impact in Japan, which was heavily bombed by the USA. Civil defence, however, is not just a humanitarian activity. It is itself a weapon, or at least has major implications for the military capacity of the country being attacked. Most theorists of air-warfare, including those most influential in the Second World War, supported 'strategic' bombing campaigns on the grounds that the direct attacks on the civilian population would destroy morale throughout the enemy's society, and swiftly bring it to capitulate. The more one can protect one's civilians, therefore, the longer one can fight, and the more direct military or economic superiority will pay off. In fact it is now known from post-war surveys that the Allied bombing offensive did far less damage to German war efforts than had been anticipated, and the morale factor, while perhaps over-emphasized, was the major one.

In the nuclear age civil defence has been a matter of considerable debate, and the Western and Eastern powers have acted very differently on the issue. In Britain the official Civil Defence organisation was wound down in the 1960s as government expenditure cuts reduced all forms of defence expenditure. Although the USA had originally commissioned an elaborate shelter building programme, and had scheduled air raid practices as late as the Vietnamese war period, it too has largely given up serious efforts at civil defence. The argument in both cases is that there can be no cost effective protection against a counter-city strike by Soviet nuclear weaponry, and that any attempt to evacuate the cities, especially in a hurry, would probably lead to a higher casualty rate in the long term. What civil defence precautions are taken, apart from the provision of secure bunkers for regional administrative elites, are largely secret, and seem mainly concerned with controlling and organizing whatever part of the population did manage to survive an attack. Recent attempts by the Home Office to provide advice on private shelter provision have been derided by the media, and often seen by those opposed to nuclear weapons as positively dangerous to world peace, because civil defence measures suggest survivability, and survivability may encourage nuclear risk-taking. Some local Councils have in fact refused to co-operate at all with Home Office civil defence exercises.

Exactly the opposite policy has been adopted in the USSR, where major efforts have been made to ensure that urban populations can be evacuated, and shelter and training programmes have been energetically pursued to minimize the casualty rate. It may be that this is partly a rational difference based on a geographical advantage possessed by Russia, with its much less concentrated urban population. But it is also a general policy difference; indeed it illustrates a difference that permeates all areas of thinking about nuclear war in the West and East. While the USA and the UK basically take the attitude that a nuclear war, if it comes, can have no winners, the USSR argues that even such wars can be won. Soviet nuclear weapons strategy is therefore based on a theory of fighting and winning a nuclear war, and a relevant civil defence strategy supports it.

Civil Disobedience

Civil disobedience is a protest strategy, arguably invented, and certainly popularized, by Mahatma Gandhi during his campaign to persuade the British to give up their Indian Empire. The idea is to urge large numbers of protesters very publicly to break some specific law, or defy official authority in some clear-cut way, in order to provoke the authorities into action, partly with the hope that they will, indeed, over-act. The aim is the dual one of drawing attention to the evil against which the protest is made, and attempting to force the government to take extreme action in defending the object or policy protested at. If the action the government has to take is sufficiently extreme it may assess it as not worth the effort involved, and may even become sickened with its own actions and become converted in attitude. Even if the authorities are neither sickened, converted, nor led to think the policy not worth the cost, the dramatic demonstration of intensity of feeling amongst those who have protested is expected to increase support for the protestors in the population considerably, thus strengthening the campaign. It is part and parcel of this approach that civil disobedience campaigns must be non-violent, and indeed, should be as law-abiding as possible in every way except with regard to the specific law or policy that is the focus of attention. The reasoning is strictly tactical, and does not follow from any implicit connection between civil disobedience and pacifism. It is, indeed, slightly in doubt as to whether even Gandhi was entirely a pacifist. The point is that the moral force of the campaign is very much strengthened when all violence can be seen to be expressly the reaction of the state to peaceful citizen protest. In the same way general law-abidingness may be absolutely necessary. Gandhi's case in India is unusual, in as much as it was the general right of the then government of India to rule at all that was in question. More usually the legitimacy of the government itself is not in question, but rather special laws or policies. Here Gandhi's first experiences, in organizing a protest of Indians in South Africa against the racial discrimination in the 'pass book' laws is a better example. It was an inherent part of the claim he made then that Indians were equal citizens of the British Empire, and entitled to exactly equal legal treatment. Thus it was essential that the protesters accept the consequences of their actions and passively submit to imprisonment, so not to be thought to be challenging the state in general terms. Similarly northern white Americans, fighting against racial discrimination towards the blacks in the southern states in the 1960s, would break specific laws, as law-abidingly as possible. Thus they would, for example, attempt to ride in 'Negro Only' rail cars, but would not attempt to evade arrest or avoid punishment. It was particularly important that they did not allow the dominant southern white conservative establishment to hide behind the claim that the protesters were 'un-American', or were radicals whose views need not be taken into account. Later, when the Vietnamese war was the object of protest, this strategy was crucial. It would have been too easy to brand those who genuinely opposed conscription for what they thought was an immoral war as traitors, and indeed as cowards had they not attempted to act in due submission to the state apart from their direct actions against conscription. (This does not mean that all, or even most anti-war protests in this era were in fact law-abiding or peaceful. The movement might have been more successful had they been.)

As early as the mid-1950s similar tactics were tried in the UK against nuclear weapons policies, by the Campaign for Nuclear Disarmament in its first manifestation. They especially went in for attempting to block traffic routes by 'sit down strikes', thus disobeying the Traffic Acts, and similar manifestations have been used by countless student and worker demonstrations ever since. As far as political theory goes it is entirely unclear whether the concept of peaceful disobedience, or of limited and specific civil disobedience can be handled inside the general theory of political and legal obligation. As long as it is not generally recognized, as it cannot be, that the individual citizen has the right to pick and choose which laws he will obey, or which policies he will pay his taxes to support, it is impossible to take account of motivation when dealing with an illegal act. Most would agree that it is not, in principle, very supportive of democratic government for individual policy choices of governments to be overturned because a minority of citizens are prepared to make the cost of enforcing them very high. In fact there are very few clear-cut cases of success attaching to any civil disobedience campaigns, in part because governments have learned not to react too harshly to such protests, and thus the mass waves of sympathy have not followed. It is important not to confuse the thesis of civil disobedience, however, with the general right, in a democracy, to protest peacefully and in a fully law-abiding way. Such protests may often have much the same impact as is expected of disobedience campaigns, especially in terms of policing them, and in the chance of overreaction by the authorities, but leave the protesters entirely clean-handed.

Civil Law

Civil law can have two distinct meanings. One meaning, in Anglo-American usage, refers to the Continental European tradition of 'code law', which is often called civil, or even 'civilian', law, as distinct from the COMMON LAW so important in the Anglo-American tradition. Here the prime distinction is between law as a gradual accretion of precedents, statutes, rulings and even traditional legal customs, and the civil law approach. This is usually seen, not entirely accurately, as consisting of formal rules deliberately created, codified and passed by a legislative body. In this tradition, which has characterized the entire European legal experience, decisions made by courts in particular cases do not have binding precedential impact on future cases, though 'La Jurisprudence', a series of interpretations, may heavily influence the way the code will be read. In the common law system, courts are legitimate makers of law, and law is seen as evolving continually from a distant past; civil law is static, fixed in the form laid down by the legislature. The sources of civil law in this sense are partly the codified law of the Roman Empire, especially as re-discovered by the European universities after the Dark Ages, partly the canon law of the medieval Church, and partly the laws re-codified under Napoleon after the French Revolution. (Much of European law is still sometimes described as being the Code Napoléon.) Civil law in this sense exists in certain parts of the common law world where a French presence has been important, notably in the State of Louisiana in the USA and the Province of Quebec in Canada. As the law of the common law world is increasingly codified, and as courts are seen less and less as legitimate makers of law, the old distinction between common law and civil law comes to matter less. International tribunals whose deliberations have an impact on national legal systems, notably the Court of Justice of the European Communities and, to a lesser extent, the European Court of Human Rights, tend to operate like traditional civil law courts, but the presence of English judges on them has been effective in diminishing the importance of the old distinctions. These are probably now most significant in terms of the Anglo-American and Continental prosecution systems of criminal law (see INQUISITORIAL SYSTEM).

The term civil law is also used within the common law system, where it denotes a body of law distinct from criminal law. Civil law concerns contracts, torts, property, taxation and other matters which are not necessarily connected with wrongdoing and are concerned less with punishment than with restitution and conflict resolution.

Civil Liberties

Civil liberties are freedoms or rights which are thought to be especially valuable in themselves and vital to the functioning of a liberal and democratic society. Emphases vary, but most lists of basic civil liberties will include freedom of speech, freedom of religion and of thought, freedom of movement, freedom of association, the right to a fair trial and freedom of the person. These rights and liberties are essential protections against the arbitrary acts of government and fundamental to free political ASSOCIATION.

In some political systems these freedoms are enshrined in a written document or constitutional code, sometimes known as a bill of rights, which is enforced by a special court or constitutional

41

tribunal. In the United States, for example, a powerful body of jurisprudence and legal doctrine has been developed around the first ten amendments to the Constitution—especially the first amendment, the fourth amendment, the due process clause of the fifth amendment and, more recently, the equal protection clause of the fourteenth amendment. In other countries, for example the United Kingdom, civil liberties are simply part of the ordinary law of the land. In many democracies a pressure group exists specifically to protect such liberties; the UK has a National Council for Civil Liberties, and the USA an American Civil Liberties Union.

Even in societies which have good civil liberties records, certain groups—ethnic minorities, for example—may find that certain laws operate to their disadvantage, and may press for greater protection. In the United Kingdom there has been concern about the powers of the police to stop, question and detain individuals on suspicion that an offence might have been, or might be about to be, committed because that law operated particularly harshly against black citizens. Similarly, there has been continual concern about civil liberties in Northern Ireland, where many normal features of the British legal system have been suspended from time to time and EMERGENCY POWERS have been exercised.

Civil liberties and human rights are closely related, and all governments pay lip service to their importance; but it remains a fact that real political freedom exists in only a few countries, while in most political systems—most notably DICTATORSHIPS and TOTALITARIAN states—there is no practical manifestation of respect for their value.

Civil Rights

Civil rights are those rights which are, or which it is argued should be, protected constitutionally or legally as fundamental rights that everyone should enjoy, irrespective of his or her status. They fall essentially into two categories: basic human rights to fair and decent treatment for the individual; and political rights which are seen as vital for a healthy and liberal society, whether or not they are actually desired by many people.

The first category includes the right to legal equality and to equality of treatment and provision, the right to a fair trial and the right to be exempt from unjust or inhuman punishment. The right not to be discriminated against because of one's race, whether by the government or a private agent, as well as protection against arbitrary arrest, a biased jury, police brutality and so on, are seen as basic rights that all should enjoy, and which require constitutional protection in any society.

The more specifically political rights include the right to freedom of speech, to form or join a trade union, to worship as one wishes, and to protest in public against government policy. All these are rights taken for granted in a LIBERAL DEMOCRACY, but they are arguably not absolutely basic to decent human life.

Naturally these two categories overlap considerably, and it is increasingly argued that they should be extended to cover more 'substantive' rights. Substantive rights—the right to work, for example, or to minimum welfare and education provision—differ from procedural rights (which only guarantee equal treatment) in that they commit society to an absolute standard of provision. It is clearly a breach of a civil right if state education is given to white children and not to black children, or if welfare provisions are given differentially according to the sex of the recipient. In the past it has been considered less obviously a denial of civil rights if no one is provided with free university education, or if unemployment pay is below subsistence level for everyone. However, the development of civil rights theories and of actual civil rights provision has tended to involve a steady extension from procedural equality to guarantees of minimum standards. Some constitutions, for example that of the Federal German Republic (West Germany), actually list as basic rights things like minimum, or even higher, educational provision rather than restricting the guarantee to fair or unbiased provision of whatever the government decides to make available.

Another tendency has been to increase the number of criteria which are not regarded as fair bases for differential treatment. There has, for example, been steady pressure on the US Supreme court over the last two decades to rule that no policy which distinguishes between people on the basis of sex is constitutional, by analogy with the ruling that any discrimination on the basis of race is a denial of civil rights. Another recent development has been the effort to stop private agents, whether corporations or individuals, from acting in a discriminatory manner. In Britain the Race Relations Acts prohibit the private exercise of racial discrimination, for example by a shop keeper, and in the United States similar measures have been taken in areas such as access to private housing markets.

Civil Service

The civil service of a country is its public administration, the body of men and women employed by the state to implement policy and

apply the laws and regulations made by the EXECUTIVE and LEGIS-
LATURE. It usually also includes a small élite group of senior public
officers who help the official political leaders to draft laws and
translate policies into practical forms. All governments rely on a
civil service of some sort, but finding a clear operational definition
that distinguishes the public administrators from the politicians is
often extremely difficult. The phrase is itself somewhat culture-
bound, since it is used and understood mainly in Britain, the USA
and their ex-colonies. There is no equivalent to the concept of civil
service in Western Europe; the idea that senior officers of the state
are servants of the public, which is one connotation of the English
phrase, has no place in the political culture of, say, the French
Republic. (Originally, civil servants were simply officers of the
Crown who were employed in a non-military capacity.)

In its full sense, 'civil service' is only a meaningful phrase in a
democratic society, where it is possible to draw a clear distinction
between the politicians, who are elected to office and must face
re-election from time to time, and civil servants who are appointed
to offices which they will hold, subject to good behaviour, in the
same way as any other employed person. A corollary of this is that
the civil service itself has no right to issue laws and regulations, or
to make policy: they exist only to advise and carry out the instructions of their political masters, and are usually supposed to be
non-partisan. In practice these ideals are seldom achieved. Civil
services everywhere have a great deal of political power, if only
because governments are often totally dependent on their advice,
and a combination of time pressure and the technical nature of
legislation makes it difficult for politicians to question or check on
the advice given by the civil service. Furthermore, in many countries
there is little or no pretence that the upper levels of the public
administration are non-partisan. In the United States, senior
appointments are used directly for political patronage. In Italy, the
senior officials belong to one or other of the factions in the Christian
Democrat party; and even in Germany government changes usually
involve new appointments in upper-level civil service offices. Nonetheless the idea of a civil service as a politically neutral body,
dedicated to the execution of decisions it does not make, is an
influential one.

Civil Society

Civil society is a concept in political theory which, though useful,
is very seldom employed today, though it was familiar to most
important political thinkers from the seventeenth century onwards.

Among others, HOBBES, LOCKE and even HEGEL distinguished between the state and civil society, that is the organized society over which the state rules. Such a distinction is not entirely valid, since the state is itself part of society. However, we are aware that, as well as institutions bound up with formal authority and political control, there exists a set of interlinked and stable social institutions which have much influence on or control over our lives. The distinction, and the consequent importance of civil society as a concept, originates with the STATE OF NATURE theorists, especially Hobbes and Locke. They held that political authority was at least hypothetically dispensable; that is, they argued as though it was possible not to have a state, and they therefore needed a concept to describe the remaining institutions. Civil society, then, is the framework within which those without political authority live their lives—economic relationships, family and kinship structures, religious institutions and so on. It is a purely analytic concept because civil society does not exist independently of political authority and, it is generally believed, could not long continue without it; so no very clear boundary can be drawn between the two.

The neglect of civil society as a concept in recent decades has two main causes. One is the fact that the state itself has been discussed less often, having been replaced, inadequately, by notions like 'the political system'. The other is that the growing trend towards using sociological models in political thinking has tended to efface the barriers between political activity and social activity; both are treated as manifestations of underlying ideological, cultural or even economic patterns. In fact the question of the interpenetration of state and society in this sense might more sensibly be treated as an empirical question to be solved in each particular case.

Class

In one way or another the idea that social class has a vital impact on politics has always been held, and has never been denied by political thinkers of any persuasion. The classical Greek political theorists, for example, were acutely aware of the need for all social classes to fit neatly into their stations in life, and ARISTOTLE is often pictured as the champion of a society dominated by the middle class.

Nowadays there are two main approaches to the political relevance of class. One is MARXIST, and is therefore involved in actual political debate, while the other is best described as the 'social science' approach to class. For a Marxist, class is fundamental to politics, since historical development is seen as a continuous series of class-conflicts culminating in the final class-conflict between the PROLETARIAT and the BOURGEOISIE. As the lowest of social classes, the proletariat cannot be challenged, after their future victory, by some other exploited class (none will exist) and therefore a classless communism will be the final form of society. Marxism also produces the simplest and neatest of all class definitions. Classes are defined by their relations to the means of production. Those who at any time 'own and control' the means of economic production (factories, mines, farms, etc.) are the ruling class in any society, and those who do not own them are forced to sell their labour power to those who do. This latter group form the proletariat and are ruled and exploited by the owners and controllers. There are very great difficulties in applying satisfactorily this most simple form of Marxist class analysis, and modern Marxists have devised many subtle and more complex theories to take account of empirical and theoretical problems.

The alternative treatment of class, which is to be found in the works of non-Marxist sociologists and political scientists, is stronger on empirical observation than theoretical formulation. Typically a social scientist will use a notion of class which combines elements of social status (often based on unproved assumptions about the status of different occupations), wealth and income, and structural aspects of the economic location of individuals. These definitions of class are made for one overwhelmingly important reason—that quite simple distinctions drawn between occupations lead to categories that do seem to correlate highly with political and social beliefs and actions. Research into voting behaviour, for example, usually employs a simple two-class model. Those who earn their living in non-manual jobs (typically defined as the 'middle-class') do in fact vote for the right-wing parties much more than for the Left, whilst manual workers (the 'working' class) vote far more heavily for the Left. Such models of social structure may be more or less complicated, and may correspond more or less successfully to actual social and political behaviour. There are many difficulties inherent in these models too. For example, in countries with a sizeable agricultural sector, it is very hard to fit farmers and farm labourers into a class model. Another typical problem is in assessing the class position of married women, whether they work or not.

However difficult it may be to construct class models, whether Marxist or otherwise, the brute facts of politics require them. Though not all parties have a class base, most do, and all societies have at least one political party which is clearly supported because it offers special policies in the interest of one class rather than another. Some political parties (notably conservative parties but also some liberal parties) claim as part of their ideology to be classless or to regard class as irrelevant, but this does not necessarily mean that their voting support, or their policies, are any less class-oriented. See also NEW CLASS.

Cleavage

Cleavage, or 'social cleavage', is a vital concept in much political science analysis, especially in relation to voting behaviour or the formation and working of party systems. It designates a division between groups within a society, based on some more or less fixed attribute: one can have cleavages along lines of class, religion, language, race or even, conceivably, sex. The patterns of social cleavages, their interrelationship, salience, number and nature, determine the battle lines of competitive politics, and to a large extent influence the stability and functioning of the political system. In origin at least, most political parties represent a given side as defined by one or more cleavage lines, and are likely to be opposed by parties representing the other side or sides. If the politics of a society are based on certain kinds of cleavage patterns, political life is likely to be more violent, and government less competent, than if other cleavages dominate. For example, racial or religious cleavages, if at all strong, are much harder to cope with by bargaining and compromise than class cleavages, because they tend to produce absolute demands. The interrelationship between cleavages can also be vitally important. If they reinforce each other, so that two people who are opposed along one cleavage are likely also to be opposed along a second, the temperature of political conflict is likely to be high. Where one finds 'cross-cutting' cleavages—where, for example, opponents on religious issues are likely to find themselves on the same side when the issue is language—intense conflict may well be avoided. One reason why the politics of language in Belgium causes such stress, and parliamentary instability, for example, is that the Flemish–Walloon cleavage largely coincides with the Catholic–Protestant cleavage. By contrast, Italy's survival during the extremely difficult post-war years may owe a good deal to the fact that the vital class cleavage in the country does not correspond very closely to the religious–secular cleavage. The Catholic ruling party, the Christian Democrats, attracts many working-class votes that would probably otherwise go to the Communists, while many middle-class voters who rebel against clerical control in politics are led to vote for left-wing parties (including a surprisingly large number for the Communists).

The sheer number of cleavages within any society has a lot to do with whether it is a multi-party system, and thus likely to be governed by possibly unstable coalitions, or a two- or three-party system which may be more likely to produce stable one-party governments. If any pattern exists in the development of cleavages it is probably towards simplification, in particular through a reduction in the importance of secondary cleavages. The Netherlands, for example, used to have a Roman Catholic party and not one but two Protestant parties, in addition to class-based parties and parties which mainly stood for secularization. As religion has ceased to be of such political importance in the Netherlands, all three religious parties have merged into a single Christian party.

Coalition

Coalitions are groupings of rival political units in the face of a common enemy; they occur in situations where protection from that enemy, or the furtherance of some shared goal, overrides differences and potential conflicts between the members of the coalition. Coalitions usually occur in modern parliaments when no single political party can muster a majority of votes. Two or more parties, who have enough elected members between them to form a majority, may then be able to agree on a common programme that does not require too many drastic compromises with their individual policies, and can proceed to form a government.

Coalitions vary in their stability, their life expectancy, and in the way power is distributed within them (which may or may not be related to the relative sizes of the parties involved). Some coalitions are so long established, and so obviously essential if the aspirations of either party are to be realized, that they virtually comprise a new party in its own right. Thus the only hope of being in government for the Liberal Party and the Country Party in Australia is the alliance between them, which is virtually indestructible. However, political change can break up what seem almost totally united alliances. From 1969 to 1982 West Germany was ruled by a coalition of Social Democrats and Free Democrats which many commentators thought indissoluble. Nonetheless the Free Democrats ended the alliance, and Germany is now ruled by a coalition of Christian Democrats and Free Democrats.

Coalitions can occur in any political situation involving several rival forces which are in fairly close agreement on essentials. Sometimes they are only intended to be short-lived, or even concerned with a single issue: voting in the multi-party assembly of the Fourth French Republic always involved the creation of an *ad hoc* majority of deputies who were agreed only on supporting a particular bill; and despite the two-party system the same situation prevails in the US Congress. Though often accused of leading to unstable governments, coalitions are in fact more likely to be the result of political instability than its cause, and occur wherever several political forces, whether because of electoral rules or some other mechanisms, exist in a rough equilibrium. Traditionally Britain has only resorted to coalition governments in time of war, but this is largely because the electoral machinery seldom produces a parliament in which no single party has a majority. When this has occurred, as in the last years of the 1974–79 Labour government, a coalition has been created in fact if not in name.

Cold War

Cold War is a concept which gained popularity shortly after the last 'Hot' or 'shooting' war, the Second World War. It describes the state of extreme hostility between the superpowers, associated with arms races, diplomatic conflict, and hostile measures of every kind short of overt military action. The Cold War started, at the latest, in 1947 with the Berlin Blockade, and remained intense until the middle 1960s, with incidents such as the Cuban crisis and the building of the Berlin Wall. Since then DETENTE has grown, or at least become more fashionable, but the threat of a return to the Cold War is often discussed, and some commentators believed it was occurring during the early 1980s. Like most such concepts, 'Cold War' can only be valid if some 'natural' alternative exists; and it is arguably unclear that relations between the major powers have been any worse during the supposed Cold War period than has usually been the case in the past.

Collective Goods

A collective good is one which, if it is to be provided for anyone in a society (or indeed in any institution), has to be provided for every member; it cannot be restricted to a given group, even if the group is comprised of all who pay for it. The benefits of military defence, for example, could hardly be restricted to citizens willing to pay a special defence tax; and, similarly, clean air programmes give protection against pollution to everyone, not only those who have voted for them. At a lower institutional level, TRADE UNIONS have always recognized that the wage rises they secure will be

49

enjoyed by all the workers in the industry concerned, and not just by members of the trade union; this is indeed the justification offered for the closed shop—that without one, some workers will get the benefit of union action without themselves having to risk the sacrifices entailed in going on strike.

Collective goods are important because they come as near as possible to being genuine examples of the COMMON GOOD or the PUBLIC INTEREST. They also involve a paradox that has long interested political theorists and economists, and has some real political relevance. On the face of it, if a policy is in someone's interest, it must also be in his interest to fight for it, or to pay his share of the cost of getting it. Yet it can easily be demonstrated that this is by no means always so. If some people are in a position to procure a common good, and need it badly enough, they will provide it even if only for themselves. But as it *is* common, everyone can enjoy it; so it is actually in the interest of such others not to pay their share. The financial contributions made by member nations of NATO are a case in point. The smaller nations have seldom paid their share of the costs; they know that the USA needs NATO, and that it can, and if necessary will, provide an adequate defence for Europe even if it has to pay over the odds. Such a defence is believed to be a common good for all the Western European nations, and advantage is regularly taken of the fact. Many other practical examples could be given of this paradox, which illustrates in political terms the proverbial strength of the weak.

Collective Responsibility

Collective responsibility is a constitutional doctrine more or less peculiar to the Westminster, (British) model of government, and of decreasing reality even in the UK. It means that decisions taken by a collective executive such as the British cabinet are collective responsibilities: anyone involved in making the decision is expected to support it without reservation in public, and generally to act as though he was himself solely responsible for the decision. This is supposed to apply even where the individual in question has always opposed the decision and actually voted against it: as long as he is not prepared to resign from the decision-making body, he must shoulder the consequences along with the majority.

In recent years this doctrine has been increasingly disregarded in Britain. On a few crucial issues, notably constitutional questions like membership of the EEC, the prime minister has allowed cabinet members to campaign publicly against decisions taken by the cabinet of which they were, and remained, members. More insidiously, perhaps, the practice of leaking details of cabinet debate has allowed members effectively, if not overtly, to disclaim responsibility for the subsequent decisions arrived at.

Collectivism

Collectivism can, and often has been given a complicated theoretical meaning or meanings, but its normal use today is rather simple. Theoretically, and the main work comes from the anarchist tradition, a collective is any group of cooperating individuals who may produce or own goods together, but which does not exercise coercive force on its members, and thus is not a state or political system. Such voluntary associations are not, however, just groups of individuals who retain their own shares and are tied by no bonds other than individual self interest, for collectivism is used as a theoretical counter to rational individualism, as well as against statism or state socialism.

In practice collectivism has tended to take a much weaker meaning, so that a society is collectivist if it departs in any important way at all from a laisser-faire liberalism in terms of duties, obligations, property rights and economic management. Under this weak sense it is common to describe Britain as a collectivist society, or at least as having collectivist tendencies since the mixed economy and welfare state involve an acceptance of collective responsibilities and rights of the individual against the collectivity (for welfare) which are nonetheless not sensibly characterized as socialist. In some ways the notion of 'the collectivity' is useful in political discourse, because we need a way of referring to the sum of the members of a society, against whom one may wish to assert a right, or to whom one may wish to claim a duty lies, without wishing to involve the notion of the state. As 'society' itself is an abstraction clearly not capable of rights and obligations, the idea of the 'collective' can play an analytic role.

Collectivization

Collectivization refers to the wholesale and drastic reorganization of the agricultural sector of Soviet society carried out principally by STALIN after his coming to power, in the wake of LENIN'S death, at the party conference of 1923, though much of it was not achieved until he launched his series of five year plans in 1929. How to organize agriculture in the new, supposedly communist state had always been a difficult problem for two related reasons. First, according to MARX, the revolution was not supposed to happen until a country was thoroughly industrialized and would therefore have a rather small and dependent peasantry. Consequently the peasantry, as a category, fits badly into MARXIST class analysis, which posits two and only two mutually opposed classes. Secondly, in order to achieve the Bolshevik revolution Lenin had had to lean heavily on the support of the peasantry, in the absence of a large industrial proletariat, yet peasants in Russia, as is almost a universal truth of sociology, were extremely conservative. Their only interest in the revolution had been to gain legal control of the land they had often farmed as tenants, or to gain land from re-distribution of large semi-feudal estates. This tendency had been exacerbated by the relaxation of communist economic rules that Lenin had been forced into in the famous NEW ECONOMIC POLICY, which had considerably increased the size of the class known as Kulaks, rich peasants with considerable land holdings. Because of the general inadequacy of the industrial base there was not enough money to buy for the urban proletariat the foodstuffs hoarded by the agricultural sector. In any case the large scale ownership of private property, and the straightforward profit motivation of the peasantry were embarrassing in a newly created communist society. Stalin's answer was to create vast 'collective farms' on which the agricultural workers would be employed in much the same way as industrial workers were employed in the state-controlled and centrally-planned factories of the industrial sphere. Other benefits were expected from increasing returns to scale, as high levels of mechanization were seen as economically more suitable than on small scale private farms. The peasantry in general, and the Kulaks most of all resented and opposed this appropriation of 'their' land, and the forced change of status from individual owners (and often employers) to mere wage labourers, but Stalin and the party, helped by the Red Army used all necessary violence to overcome the objections. Massive deportations to other parts of the Soviet Union, and the murder of, in some estimates as many as six million, kulaks and peasants produced an entirely transformed agriculture.

There can be no doubt that the overall result of this has been catastrophic, as agricultural yields have fallen, despite later efforts by KHRUSHCHEV to humanise and moderate the system. The Soviet Union, in most years, depends on western agricultural surpluses for as much as 40% of its grain requirements. Some steps have been taken to re-introduce a private incentive, by allowing peasants on collective farms to control small plots of land themselves and sell their produce on a free market, but no major solution to the country's agricultural problems is apparent.

Colonialism

Colonialism is the holding and ownership of colonies, or the treating of another country as though it was in fact a colony. Indeed recently the concept has been extended so that one can talk of 'internal' colonialism where the capital or economic dominant part of a country treats a distant region just as it might a genuinely foreign colony. For true colonialism to exist two conditions are necessary. The land held as a colony must have no real political independence from the 'mother country', but also the relationship must be one of forthright exploitation. The entire reason for having colonies is to increase the wealth and welfare of the colonial power, either by extracting resources, material or labour, from the colony more cheaply than could be bought on a free market, or by ensuring a market for one's own goods at advantageous rates. In this way a set of colonies may be rather different from an Empire. In the latter case the far flung lands that constitute the empire may be integrated equally in economic and political terms with the original homeland, the motive for imperial expansion being the spreading of a way of life or of a political design, or merely the pushing away of borders and thus military danger from the heartland.

In practice there are no pure examples either of colonialism, or of this non-exploitative version of IMPERIALISM. Colonial government has often been justified, sincerely or otherwise, as an attempt to spread 'civilisation' to socially underdeveloped societies, and few empires have not rested, at bottom, on the economic advantage to producers and merchants in the imperial centre of captive markets and resources on the periphery. Nonetheless the essence of colonialism as a concept, and especially in modern pejorative usage, is the idea of deliberate exploitation of another country and its inhabitants. Thus the earliest colonies of the modern world, the British colonies in India or North America, for example, were set up by trading companies operating under royal warrants, with the express intention of making a profit. The earliest colonies of which we have much evidence are probably the colonies set up all over the Mediterranean basin by the Greek city states from around 600 B.C. The original motive for founding a colony in these cases was to handle the population explosion problem as the rural hinterland of the original city could no longer maintain the population. The colonies were not expected to be independent of the mother city, anymore than a new associated village settlement inside the hinterland would be, and like them were intended to ship back food and other resources to the founding city.

Nothing was seen to be wrong or undesirable about the policy of colonialism at a time when the indigenous populations of the mother countries themselves were allowed no political involvement, and the idea that colonialism was politically unacceptable arose with the development of internal democracy in the home countries. In fact the absolute illegitimacy of colonialism is a twentieth century phenomenon. One of the war aims that was expressed by Germany in both world wars was the achievement of colonial territory on a par with Britain's, and few found the demand in principle wrong, but rather objected simply to having to give up their own colonies. Not until the creation of the League of Nations between the wars, and its successor, the United Nations, did it become commonly accepted that only a mandate from the international community to govern in the long term interests of the colony itself could justify a developed land owning and controlling a less developed one. It is still, of course often alleged that the essence of colonialism characterises the relations between former colonial powers and the newly independent states, and indeed between the industrially developed powers and the undeveloped countries of the third world.

COMECON

COMECON is the standard way of referring to the Council for Mutual Economic Assistance, which is very roughly the Soviet Union's and Eastern Europe's equivalent to the EEC, or, alternatively, the economic equivalent to the Warsaw pact. The dominance the Soviet Union has over COMECON makes this latter analogy perhaps the more appropriate. It was founded by Stalin in 1949, and he initially used it mainly as a weapon in his attempt to bring Yugoslavia to heel by economic boycott. The members are Bulgaria, Czechoslovakia, Hungary, Poland, Romania, the Soviet Union, East Germany, Mongolia and, since 1972 and 1978 respectively, Cuba and Viet-Nam. One original member, Albania, was expelled in 1961 as part of the general process by which it was punished for forming too close a link with China when the Sino–Soviet split began to emerge.

After Stalin it came to be seen as a useful way of countering the increasing integration, especially through the EEC and EFTA, of the Western European economies, and above all, as a way of enforcing supranational planning in the interest of the Soviet Union. Little developed in practice until the early 1960s when, despite opposition from some members, a general Eastern European regional plan was enforced at the insistence of the Soviet Union. The basis of this plan was to concentrate industrial production in East Germany and

Czechoslovakia, while Romania and Bulgaria were to remain essentially agricultural. In the event the economies have not been especially tied together, and the plans for industrial development in Germany and Czechoslovakia do little more than accept what would inevitably have happened. The member nations are still crucially dependent on trade with the West, and require Western credits to provide their liquidity, as is demonstrated by Poland's huge debts to Western banks.

COMECON is probably less popular with its members even than is the Warsaw Pact, and rightly or otherwise there is a widespread belief in Eastern Europe that it functions to cream off the best of industrial production, especially in East Germany, as exports to the Soviet Union. In addition, as with Cuban membership, it is used partly as a tool of Soviet propaganda and as support for third world countries whose membership in an international Communist movement is of less interest to East Europe than to the Soviet Union.

Committees

Committees are technically groups of members of some deliberative or decision-making body. They are charged with carrying out preparatory or investigatory work on some issue, or with dealing with matters of detail under broad lines agreed by the whole body. The main justification for committee work is that detailed discussion can best be handled by a small number of people, and also that committee members have more expertise, and more time, to dedicate to specific topics than other members of the main body. As the institution of which a committee is a subordinate part will usually have a much wider remit than the scope given to any one committee, this allows for a division of labour and task specialization which would otherwise be impossible.

A consequence of this delegation of responsibility is that committees *per se* cannot make binding decisions, but can only make recommendations to the main body, or report their conclusions. In practice committees often wield very considerable power precisely because members of the main body, a parliament say, or the governing council of a trade union or a board of directors are much less well-informed, and have much less time in which to consider a matter than the specialist committee. Consequently there is a general tendency for committee advice to be taken, often with little debate. Probably the most influential and famous political committees are the specialist subject committees of the US Congress. In many areas these committees are the effective legislatures, with the full Senate or House of Representatives being in a position to do no more than rubber stamp the committee resolutions. In these cases, and many other political examples, no legislation or initiative that is not favoured by a majority of the committee can hope even to be reported on to the full legislative body, the committee simply refusing to act on it at all.

One particular type of committee, often known as a 'Steering Committee' is often found of particular power. Such a committee is charged with preparing the agenda for the main body, and deciding the rules of debate and timing, and who should be invited to speak to a matter. Again, with a powerful chairman, such a committee can often manipulate arrangements effectively to stifle issues, or to push them through the main debating assembly with little chance for the opposition to make their case or lobby support.

Because of the specific rules of debate and discussion adopted by some parliaments, including the US Congress and the British House of Commons there has also developed a procedural device by which the entire assembly turns itself into a committee, known as the 'Committee of the Whole House', but in such cases it no longer remains a committee in any substantive sense.

Common Good

The common good is an obvious, but also elusive, concept in political theory. It describes a goal or an object of policy that is in the interests of everyone in a society. It is related to such terms as PUBLIC INTEREST, GENERAL WILL and, in a more complex way, to COLLECTIVE GOODS. The greatest difficulty in employing the concept arises from the fact that there are very few things which are equally beneficial, and imply equal cost, to all members of a society. A typical example, though one by no means unproblematic in itself, would be the avoidance of industrial pollution, or the provision of military defence.

Common Law

Common law is the name usually given to the main system of laws and legal practices in England and Wales, most of North America, and other countries that were once part of the British Empire. It is the legal system that developed after the Norman conquest of England, based initially on judicial interpretation of local customs, on judicial and royal decisions in important cases, and on the rare acts of formal legislation contained in royal statutes. The essence of common law is that it relies on the development of legal principles as they are laid down in judicial rulings in particular cases. These rulings are themselves usually developments or reinterpretations of earlier decisions in cases held to be 'binding precedents'. The idea is one of slow growth and development, of a legal system created by the judges themselves during the actual judicial process. This is usually contrasted with the CIVIL LAW system, in which law is deliberately laid down as a complete, codified system by means of legislation. Through much of English legal history the common law was supplemented by another system, equity, in which cases were decided directly on the basis of moral justice; it was introduced because common law, restricted in its scope by previous cases, and by the small number of 'writs' under which one could bring actions, was seen as too limited to give unfailing justice. As the range of common law expanded, and equity itself became more and more rule-bound, the two became merged during the 19th century.

In the present century, an increasing commitment to democratic ideals made the idea of autonomous judge-made law seem improper. This, and the massive legislation required by the modern state, have much diminished the independent creativity of the judiciary. In the early 1960s, for example, the House of Lords announced, in effect, that no judge could contemplate creating a new criminal offence. However, large areas of English law, especially the law of contracts and of torts, are not codified, and principles can only be discovered by identifying significant precedents. In these and other areas there is still considerable scope for judges to develop law without waiting for parliament to legislate. Furthermore, to interpret the meaning of statute law often involves highly creative judicial work, and the real impact of a statute may depend more on what judges have said in a case which concerned it than on parliament's original intention. The common law in other countries has diverged to some extent from English common law, but reference is often made to the decisions of English courts in awkward cases. This is true of the United States as well as countries such as Australia, in which a residual right of appeal to English higher courts still exists.

Commune

Commune has several meanings in politics. The more clear-cut and technical usage is found in Western Europe, where it usually describes the most basic level of local government, roughly equivalent to a British parish or local district council, or an American township. Its more theoretically significant usage is as a description of left-wing or radical experiments in communal living. During the late 1960s in particular, many young radicals and 'drop-outs' formed collective organizations in which a few people lived together and shared everything in an ideal form of communism, with no property rights and a total commitment to one another's welfare. The phrase 'hippy communes' came into common use to describe one form taken by this experiment in collective living. Many communes were modelled on the Israeli KIBBUTZ, with which they share a respectable philosophical ancestry in writers such as ROUSSEAU and other exponents of DIRECT DEMOCRACY or PARTICIPATORY DEMOCRACY, who advocated small, sharing, communal forms of social organization.

The phrase 'the Commune' refers to the revolutionary authority set up in Paris after the Franco–Prussian War of 1870–71 and suppressed by the 'Versailles' government of Thiers. Karl Marx and later writers of the Left have regarded the Commune as foreshadowing modern revolutionary movements.

Communism

Communism can mean one of two things—a theoretical ideal found in the writings of MARX, or the actual governing principles of the self-described Communist states in the modern world. When one finds the label used in a further way, as, for example, in the Communist parties of France, Italy, Britain, etc., it typically refers to a combination of MARXIST ideals and support for the Communist governments. As far as the Marxist ideals go, Communism is a slightly shadowy state in which private property has been abolished, equality reigns, and the State has 'withered away' because all men live in harmony and co-operation, without classes or any social divisions requiring the exercise of authority. Most post-Marxist writers, and especially the leaders of the Russian Revolution, have believed that there had to be an intermediary phase between the overthrow of capitalism and the full realization of communism. This phase is variously described, often as SOCIALISM, but also as the period in which it will be necessary to exercise the 'DICTATORSHIP OF THE PROLETARIAT' or where the Communist party will have to act as the 'VANGUARD OF THE PROLETARIAT'. This intermediate phase is, roughly speaking, where the leaders of the USSR and its Eastern European allies would locate themselves.

When used as a description of the societies of the USSR and Eastern Europe, or, adding yet another complexity, China and its

Asian Communist allies, it is indicating a set of political practices that may not, necessarily, have very much to do with the Marxist theory of Communism. Communism in this second sense is a system where there is little or no private ownership of major property, this being replaced with state-owned and run enterprises, and where the Communist party rules, non-democratically, both in its own right and through its control, *de facto*, of the official state administration. Values of equality and social co-operation are stressed, as opposed to individual self-seeking or betterment. The economy will be entirely a planned one, with no serious element of competition, although, especially in agriculture, this is often relaxed in minor ways. A characteristic feature of Communism as we have seen it develop is an inequality based on position in the ruling party, but a genuine equality, and a very thorough social welfare system, throughout the mass of the population.

Other aspects of a Communist state are incidentals, more or less present in different societies. Thus the Communist attitude to religion, something scorned by Marxist theory, can vary from hostility in the USSR to a major role for the Roman Catholic church in Poland, and the extent of industrial democracy varies from great in Yugoslavia to minimal in East Germany. Since the mid-1950s there has been an increasingly bitter conflict between the Eastern European and the Chinese brands of Communism, first with the development of MAO TSE-TUNG's Communist views. The reason for this conflict, apart from purely nationalistic territorial conflicts, was that the Chinese Communists were, originally, much less prepared to use the techniques, and the associated professional hierarchies, of modern Western industrial production. So while, to take one example, the USSR continued to make steel in huge industrial plants, giving great authority to professional engineers and planning the overall production of steel in a centralized and authoritative way, the Chinese encouraged all their COMMUNES to build their own small-scale steel plants, and treated professional engineers as undemocratic examples of class status. The USSR remained quite strongly hierarchical, even if the criteria for hierarchy differed from the capitalist societies, being based on party or professional rank rather than inherited wealth, but the Chinese Communists, at least under Mao, worked for a much more total equality. During the CULTURAL REVOLUTION this rose to a height in which anyone occupying a professional or technocratic job was in danger of being sent off to work as a peasant, if he escaped, luckily, THOUGHT REFORM. The only generalizations possible about Communism as an actual political and social system are that Communist regimes are totally controlled by an undemocratic party, abolish most inequalities arising from economic differences, and practise a high degree of economic planning with an efficient welfare state but very little freedom of expression.

Communist Party of the Soviet Union (see CPSU)

Community Power

Community power studies were popular amongst academics, especially in North America, during the 1950s and late 1960s. Because power is not only conceptually elusive but empirically hard to study on the national level, it was felt that it could best be investigated in narrower contexts. As a result, a series of studies were conducted into the distribution of power and influence in individual towns and cities. Most of the studies were carried out to test or develop pluralist theories of power and democracy (see PLURALISM). The results suggested that the communities were not fully democratic, but were dominated by élite groups which controlled different areas of policy. However, most of the studies went on to claim that the various élites functioned separately, without the overlapping that might have given one or more of them a wider-ranging power. The studies were subjected to considerable criticism, largely of a methodological nature, since no incontrovertibly right way existed to discover who was influential, or why. Even more disappointing was the fact that it did not really prove possible to extrapolate from studies of local communities to form a picture of power at the national level.

The utility of the studies was even less clear outside the USA. The federal nature of American politics, and the absence of welfare state regulations, did make it sensible to find out who, for example, might be responsible for building a new hospital, or, given the decentralization of education, to enquire into the influence of Parent-Teacher Associations as pressure groups. In countries such as Britain, where most such decisions are either taken or very strongly influenced and closely regulated by central government, there is rather less to study. Very few such studies have been carried out in recent years, and it is doubtful whether they will again be seen as a way round the problems involved in studying power.

Comparative Government

Comparative Government (or Comparative Politics) is one of the main branches of the academic study of politics. The essence of comparative government as a study is to compare the ways in which different societies cope with various problems, the role of the political structures involved being of particular interest. The aim is to develop an understanding of how different institutional mechanisms work within their contexts, and, more ambitiously, to develop general hypotheses concerning government. A typical examination paper in Comparative Government will ask whether the French or American presidencies enjoy the most power, or ask for a comparison of the roles of the legislature in Britain and West Germany.

Though comparative government is nowadays usually clearly differentiated from POLITICAL THEORY, this is a recent and probably unfortunate development. ARISTOTLE, who is normally thought of as a political theorist, certainly also carried out a comparative study of the political systems known to him, though unfortunately his collection of nearly two hundred city state constitutions has not survived. Later theorists such as Bodin argued for comparative political analysis in the hope that it would reveal universally valid rules and values.

In studies of comparative government quite a lot of progress has been made in some areas. For example, the effect of different electoral systems on the party system is fairly well understood from wide-ranging comparisons, and predictive theories have been developed which work quite well in relationship to membership of coalitions in multi-party systems. The main problem for Comparative Government as a science is that it lacks a generally-agreed theoretical framework that would identify what the principal tasks of a political system are, and thereby locate the institutions or structures that should be compared. In other words it is hard to know what comparisons are worthwhile or sensible; and as a result, researchers have tended either to stick to obvious comparisons within a limited range, or to rely on less than commonly accepted theories, usually borrowed from other disciplines, such as FUNCTIONALISM.

Another problem is that a fruitful comparison of two societies involves a very deep knowledge of their history, culture and languages in order to understand the data and avoid inappropriate comparisons between institutions which are only superficially similar. Many university courses are not really comparative at all, but simply entail the separate study of several foreign countries. At the opposite pole are some texts and courses which deny entirely the need for knowledge in depth and involve comparisons of institutions from all the one-hundred and forty-odd independent nations of the world. Somewhere between these positions progress has been, and will doubtless continue to be, made.

Comte

Auguste Comte, 1798–1857, was the founder of sociology and the originator of the concept of POSITIVISM in the social sciences, at least in the sense that he invented both words and was the first more or less academic writer to construct a 'science of society'. Many of his ideas were in fact derived from the early French socialist thinker Saint-Simon, whose secretary he had been.

Comte divided sociology into two disciplines. One, concerned with the structure of societies and the relationships between their constituent elements, he called Social Statics; the other, Social Dynamics, dealt with the development and progress of social forms. It was Comte's Social Dynamics that made most impact in their time, but their interest today lies in the fact that they are utterly at variance with the sociological canon that we take for granted. To Comte the only possible sources of progress or social change were changes in human thought, whereas not only Marxists but most other modern sociologists would give economic factors, or environmental determinants of some kind, an extremely important role. Comte believed he had identified three stages of social development, along with three corresponding modes of thought. During the 'Theological Age' man was quite unable to understand his environment, lacked any conception of causality, and saw every event as the result of divine intervention. In the second, 'Metaphysical Age', man did begin to try to explain the nature of the world, but in a necessarily 'unscientific' way, since the entire intellectual apparatus of modern science (especially the idea of empirically testing hypotheses) was missing. Finally, in Comte's own lifetime, the 'Positivistic' or 'Scientific Age' had arrived, and everything could be understood and explained scientifically in time. Sociology, as the latest and most far-reaching of all sciences, characterized the age. Society could now be properly planned, and institutions consciously devised or retained and modified to serve specific functions. In this belief Comte is not far removed from the advocates of 'scientific socialism', except that he rejected materialism for intellectual determinism and was also more than a little conservative once he got down to details. For example, he attached enormous importance to the family, as conservatives have always done; but unlike earlier conservative thinkers he held that it could now be seen as a rationally functional element in a planned society. Similarly, he attached great importance to religion as a source of social stability; but having dismissed theology as an irrational manifestation belonging to the first age of society, he tried to promote a scientific 'religion of humanity' which functioned like, and indeed resembled in its ritual, orthodox Catholicism without God.

Though it is easy to deride Comte now, the breadth of his vision, his erudition and his developmental approach were quite new, and established once and for all the idea that large-scale theoretical explanations of society were possible. Elements of Comtian thought can be traced to later writers who retain a serious academic standing, notably PARETO and WEBER.

Confederacy

A confederacy, or confederation, is a political system originating in an agreement made between several independent entities that wish to retain a high degree of autonomy. The idea of confederacy is usually contrasted with that of federation, which also involves independent entities but in which the central authority has a considerable degree of power which may be capable of expansion, for example through interpretation of the federal constitution. In a confederacy, by contrast, certain specified powers are surrendered by the component units to the central government, and all other powers remain with the original states. Probably the best known example was the Confederate States of America, 'the Confederacy', formed by the Southern states that seceded from the USA. The name, and the organizing principle, were deliberately chosen to emphasize the difference betwen the Confederacy and the United States, where the growth of Federal power was felt by Southerners to threaten their institutions, above all slavery. The subsequent Civil War resulted in the destruction of the Confederacy.

Confederacies need not be confined to the nation-state level: in Britain the major pressure group for business interests is the CBI, the Confederation of British Industry, so called because it is an amalgam of separate interests.

Confidence, Questions of

In countries where the EXECUTIVE is responsible to a LEGISLATURE rather than elected for a fixed term (as in the United States), the support of the legislature is necessary to sustain a government in office. Such support may be tested by a formal vote of no confidence (see ACCOUNTABILITY). If the vote goes against the government, it will usually resign; and then one of two consequences will follow. Either there will be an attempt to form a new government which can command the support of the legislature (a course which is particularly likely where no party has an overall majority), or the legislature will be dissolved and new elections held to ascertain the views of the electorate.

In the United Kingdom, where a strict system of party discipline prevails, it used to be believed that any major defeat sustained by a government in the House of Commons should be treated a vote of no confidence. In the 1970s this view has been substantially modified, and governments have come to believe that they may be defeated in the House of Commons without necessarily resigning or even placing the measure before Parliament again in order to reverse their defeat. In some countries, matters are organized in such a way that votes of no confidence are difficult for the government to lose; this is the case in Fifth Republic France, where it represents a response to the pre-1958 situation in which stable government became the exception rather than the rule.

Congress

In general terms a congress is a meeting of representatives or officials for debate and discussion. More specifically the term is used to refer to the legislature of the United States of America, which consists of a 435-member House of Representatives (the 'lower' House) and a 100-member Senate. Members of the House of Representatives are elected every two years; members of the senate are elected every six years, a third of the Senators coming up for re-election every two years. Although both Senators and members of the House are strictly speaking members of Congress, it is customary to refer only to members of the lower House as Congressmen; members of the Senate are referred to as Senators.

In India the main political party involved in the struggle for independence from the British Empire was the Congress Party; it has dominated Indian political life since independence was granted in 1947.

Consent

Many political theories, in attempting to answer the central question 'Why should anyone obey the Government?', fall back on the idea that this obligation is based on an implicit or explicit consent to the exercise of authority by the government or state in question. The belief that man is 'by nature' free and independent has led some political thinkers to argue that a free individual cannot be obliged to obey any ruler unless he freely wishes or wills or agrees to do so. This sort of doctrine, perhaps best represented by the seventeenth-century English political philosopher John LOCKE, is usually associated with SOCIAL CONTRACT theories. These picture society as set up deliberately by independent individuals who come to see that their own interests are best served by collaboration, and who therefore freely give up some of their independence to a government so that it can function for their benefit. Clearly, given this position, the right of a government to pass laws and coerce citizens can only stem from the citizens having given their willing consent to obey. However, the theory, though admirable, is riddled with problems which political theorists are still trying to solve. To start with, in reality none of us is ever given a chance to consent or withhold consent. There is, too, the argument that if the government is either looking after your interests, or doing what is 'right', it does not seem to make much difference whether you have consented or not. Locke himself had to stretch his definition of 'consent' so far in order to make his theory work logically that it ceased to have much attraction to most liberals. Nonetheless, the idea that obligation can be incurred only through consent remains very attractive, and is still a powerful force in democratic or liberal political theory.

Conservatism

Conservatism is a political theory which is peculiarly difficult to define because one aspect of conservative thought is its rejection of explicit IDEOLOGY and its preference for PRAGMATISM in political matters. It is also difficult to define because different societies and generations do not necessarily seek to preserve the same things. Although some elements common to conservative values can be traced back to the early history of political thought, conservatism as a distinctive political creed emerged in the 18th century, when it became necessary to present arguments against the rationalist thinkers of the European ENLIGHTENMENT, the utopian states they hoped to create, and the radical forces unleashed by the French Revolution. In Britain Edmund BURKE published his classic work *Reflections on the French Revolution,* which emphasized the importance of traditions, institutions and evolutionary change as opposed to abstract ideas, individualism and artificially designed political systems. In France Joseph de Maistre (1754–1821) provided a more reactionary version of conservatism in essays which defended established authority against revolutionary ideas; he emphasized the need for order and the importance of the specific national traits in a given political system.

65

Conservatives do not necessarily oppose change in itself. But they are sceptical about attempts to fashion a perfect society in accordance with some pre-existing model. They also tend to believe that man is flawed by weaknesses that make certain ideal goals illusory, although not all of the major conservative thinkers relate this view to the Christian notion of Original Sin. They regard their support for tradition as reflecting their humility in the face of the experience of earlier generations—an experience which they believe to be crystallized in institutions.

At the level of political practice a number of conservative parties exist in the political systems of Western Europe and the Commonwealth. The British Conservative Party has been electorally very successful in surviving the advent of mass democracy and has combined a patriotic outlook and support for the status quo with an acceptance of an extended welfare state. It has always placed a strong value on the ownership of property, while accepting since 1945 the existence of a mixed economy. However, two distinct factions have emerged in the party since the early 1970s. One of these advocates a reversal of many of the initiatives undertaken by government since 1945 and a more vigorous form of market economy. To that extent it has much in common with classical 19th-century liberalism. The other faction—very much in the minority under Mrs Thatcher's leadership—invokes the Disraelian tradition of one nation and seeks to preserve the Conservative Party's tradition of social concern and pragmatic solutions to political issues.

In continental Europe the parties which share conservative values have typically not called themselves conservative. Most have preferred to use the term 'CHRISTIAN DEMOCRAT', although in France the Gaullist Party is the main conservative force.

Constitution

A constitution consists of a set of rights, powers and procedures that regulate the relationships between public authorities in any state, and between the public authorities and individual citizens. Most countries have a written constitution or basic document which defines these relationships (the United Kingdom and Israel are notable examples of countries without such a constitutional code). But all written constitutions have to be supplemented in practice from other sources. The words in any document will need to be interpreted, and constitutional practice may well be amended over time. Thus judicial decisions, custom, convention and even authoritative textbooks may provide guidance and regulation, and may therefore be said to be a part of a country's constitution.

It is possible to classify constitutions in a number of different ways: according to whether they are federal (Australia, the USA) or unitary (the United Kingdom, France); according to whether they exhibit a separation of powers (as in the United States) or a fusion of powers (as in the United Kingdom); or according to whether they employ some device for judicial review (as does the Federal Republic of Germany) or have a special procedure for repealing constitutional laws.

One-party states often issue elaborate constitutions allegedly guaranteeing basic freedoms (see CIVIL LIBERTIES); the Soviet constitutions of 1936 and 1977 purport to provide for civil liberties but do not in reality circumscribe governmental power in any effective manner.

Constitutional Control

The notion of constitutional control relates to the ability of a political system to work within the confines set by its constitution, and to the ability of the guardians of the constitution to apply it to those who hold power. In the United States the 'Watergate' affair, which resulted in the impeachment of President Nixon in August 1974, became a constitutional issue because of the way the chief executive interpreted his powers, and because he resorted to political manoeuvres which seemed contrary to the spirit of the Constitution. Nixon's resignation reaffirmed the efficacy of the American Constitution and marked the decline of the so-called 'Imperial Presidency'.

Constitutional control may be exerted in a number of ways, but the most common method in countries with a written constitution is to provide for a constitutional court or council (in the USA the Supreme Court) which is supposed to ensure that political institutions conform to constitutional norms.

Constitutional Law

Constitutional law refers to the part of a legal system and legal tradition which is directly concerned with interpreting and applying the fundamental rules that define and delimit the powers, rights and duties of governments, other organs of the state, and the citizens. In some cases constitutional law is based on the interpretation of a fixed, binding and usually written formal constitution.

67

The Constitution of the United States of America is the most important example of this, because the Constitution is highly concrete and absolutely binding, and because it provides for an agency, the Supreme Court, empowered to rule on the constitutionality of the way in which any other element, even the president, has behaved. Other important formal constitutional codes include those of Australia and Canada, and the West German *Grundgesetz*.

It is not of course necessary to have a single written constitutional document in order to have constitutional law. Indeed, any stable political system must have a set of basic and defining laws or conventions. In Britain, though there is neither a formal constitution nor a court specifically concerned with constitutional matters, there are clear legal rules and practices restricting the actions of political institutions, granting rights and enforcing duties. Habeas corpus, for example, is as much a constitutional law as its rough equivalent in the 'due process' clauses of the US Constitution. There is in fact no clear line between constitutional law and ordinary law. The 1964 Police Act, which governs the structure, rights and duties of Britain's police forces, and also the controls over them, could, for example, be regarded in certain contexts as belonging to constitutional law; and so could the annual Mutiny Acts which give legal standing to the armed forces.

Containment

Containment is or was (the correct tense to use is unclear) the official US foreign policy doctrine, from 1947 onwards, on how the US should react to the expansion of international communist influence. The idea, originating with Truman's approach to problems in the unstable context of immediate post-war Europe, was that America should seek to contain communism within the territorial boundaries it had achieved as a result of the war. Initially this meant the military defence of Western Europe, and American allies such as Turkey and Greece which were under severe threat in the Mediterranean. As such it represented not the aggressive and even arrogant policy revisionists have tended to paint it as, but a more moderate policy, given a considerable feeling in parts of both America and Britain that communism should be fought directly and ousted from Eastern Europe.

Commentators often include the Korean war as perhaps the first major act of the containment policy, though it is unclear why a United Nations police action against massive and direct military invasion from North Korea need be justified under such a doctrine at all. If Korea was an example of containment, then it is again evidence of the moderation of the policy, given the way both Presidents Truman and Eisenhower avoided the temptation to push further in their actions against communist China.

Containment became a more aggressive policy when, as a result of a belief that communism had a natural tendency to spread over borders and infect neighbouring countries, the Americans invested military support in protecting South Vietnam from internal and external communist pressure. Vietnam apart, containment has mainly been a matter of foreign aid, especially in the Marshall plan, and indirect military aid in the form of weapons credits and training help. The policy of DETENTE, developed from the late 1960s to the late 1970s might have been seen as bringing an end to containment, or at least a recognition that there could never be anything more than a struggle to impart a world view between the USSR and the USA on nations that might very well have ideas of their own. However the apparent weakening of detente, as well as the increasing success of Soviet propaganda and aid programmes in the THIRD WORLD, and especially recently in Latin America and Africa may well force the USA back towards containment as a goal, though it is most improbable that this will again be by military means.

The problems, both practical and theoretical, of containment have always been the difficulty for the Americans of distinguishing between genuine 'home grown' socialist or radical-nationalist movements, and Soviet or Chinese-influenced and manipulated expansions. The USA, through a combination of bad luck, poor judgement and lack of choice have too often tended to support regimes of extremely unpleasant character against the populations of the countries in question under the name of containment, thus bringing into disrepute a policy which, in general terms, is probably the inevitable consequence of abandoning isolationism.

Conventional War

Conventional war is war waged only with non-nuclear weaponry. The concept involves ambiguities and even possible dangers, since it makes the distinction between two ways of creating explosions the main criterion of escalation in warfare. In particular, the distinction invests what are often called 'battlefield' nuclear weapons—small-yield nuclear shells and short-range missiles—with a symbolic significance: because they are nuclear rather than 'conventional', they might be felt to entitle an enemy to respond with more powerful nuclear missiles, even though the 'battlefield' weapons

69

might have had hardly more impact than a heavy 'conventional' bombing raid. Contrariwise, if the distinction between conventional and nuclear were regarded as crucial, a heavy attack on a civilian population by conventional bombers would not entitle the defenders to use nuclear weapons in defence. It is unlikely that the distinction is regarded as a vital one by professional military thinkers, though it is of considerable political relevance (some protesters against nuclear weapons appear to have no objection to any degree of conventional military strength). It is publicly acknowledged that NATO planning is based on the use of low-yield, 'battlefield' nuclear weapons within the first few days of any conflict with the WARSAW PACT, principally because of the apparent conventional superiority of the Eastern Bloc. But this has never been taken to imply that the Western powers would be prepared to launch a major strategic nuclear attack first. Nonetheless, the perhaps arbitrary conventional–nuclear distinction is now deeply rooted in the strategic and political vocabulary.

Convergence Thesis

This is the name given to the argument, first formally developed by political scientists in the 1950s but foreshadowed by WEBER and others much earlier, that SOCIALIST and CAPITALIST societies would inexorably grow more and more alike. The reasons for this prediction vary, but they all have to do with a theory of BUREAUCRACY and assumptions about the kind of organization needed to ensure rational policies and efficient decision-making. The basic idea is that planning is paramount in modern societies, and that all forms of planning and administrative control are, whatever their supposed ideological complexion, essentially the same. The Russian Revolution and its supposedly radical 'DICTATORSHIP OF THE PROLETARIAT' led to monolithic administrative and policy control by the Communist Party, while in the West efficient and powerful CIVIL SERVICES have developed and close control is exercised over the everyday activities of businessmen, workers and others. The imperatives of planning, and the responses of bureaucrats and planners charged with achieving particular goals, are seen as transcending overt ideological differences between the two societies. The thesis has its points, but probably ignores the crucial difference between bureaucracies which are, and those which are not, subject to electoral power. It has, however, been very influential, and is a useful corrective to the belief that the means we use to achieve goals must be less important than the goals themselves.

Corporatism

Corporatism has at least two distinct meanings. Historically it has designated a form of social organization in which corporations, non-government bodies with great authority over the lives and professional activities of their members, have played an intermediary role between public and state. In origin this goes back to the medieval pluralism in which the great trade guilds or corporations controlled the activities of craftsmen and traders; at the height of their power the guilds represented a third force in society along with the Church and the nobility.

Although the Industrial Revolution killed off this form of social organization, it reappeared at the turn of the century as a theoretical concept in the work of Emile DURKHEIM. It also found a political expression, more facade than reality, in the fascist institutions of the 1930s and 1940s. FRANCO'S corporatist design for Spanish society was the longest lived and perhaps most genuine, although MUS-SOLINI'S Italy also had serious corporatist elements. In its 20th century version the theory suggested that people engaged in a particular trade—employers as well as workers—had more in common with one another than with people of the same class or status who worked in other trades. In Spain and Italy legislative assemblies and councils of state were therefore organized around such trade corporations rather than around geographic constituencies and the 'capricious' functioning of competitive elections. The convenience of corporatist theory from a fascist point of view was evident: it by-passed both class-conflict and democratic elections. Durkheim had had rather different aspirations, looking to the corporations to introduce the moral training and social discipline needed to overcome modern ANOMIE, since he regarded the state as too distant and emotionally neutral to be able to solve these problems.

The alternative modern meaning of corporatism (the increasing tendency for the state to work hand in glove with major business corporations and trade unions) is usually distinguished from the older meaning by being labelled NEO-CORPORATISM.

Coup d'État

Coup d'état describes the sudden and violent overthrow of a government, almost invariably by the military. A coup d'état tends to occur during a period of social instability and political uncertainty, and is usually the work of 'right wing' elements determined to impose a social discipline and political order that is felt to be missing. It is distinguished from a REVOLUTION, which usually

71

implies a major change in the social structure or political order; coups d'état replace only the ruling group, without necessarily altering the social context in which they rule. Quite frequently the makers of the coup d'état return power to the politicians after a fairly short period, when they believe that their aims of stabilizing and ordering the political system have been achieved. This was true, for example, of the Greek Junta and of various coups d'état in Africa. The sociological conditions in which a coup d'état is possible are fairly specific, combining a widespread acceptance of the basic social order with great distrust of the ruling political groups. The tendency of the military to be involved in coups d'état stems from their virtual monopoly of coercive means and the way in which they are usually, at least in the context of any particular social system, seen as apolitical or even 'above politics'.

CPSU

CPSU are the initials by which the Communist Party of the Soviet Union is often known. The Party completely controls political and social life in the USSR. About ten per cent of the population are members, and membership is much prized and by no means automatic. The principal way the Party exercises control is by what is called the NOMENCLATURA, which is simply a list of jobs which must be filled by party members, and concerning which the Party is given a deciding voice in appointments. As a result nearly all of the most important managerial, administrative and intellectual jobs are filled by loyal party members. In addition the Party organizes most social life, controls the trade unions, and has the sole right to put up candidates in elections. However, because of the sheer size of the Party, the degree of organized and uniform control it exercises is sometimes questionable, although its command over education and the media helps it to prevent any serious and widespread doubts about its legitimacy. Senior party members get many privileges, such as access to imported goods and better educational opportunities for their children, providing yet another incentive to membership. The Party has always been careful to make sure that it can check the power of potential rivals; this is especially true of the armed forces, each unit of which has, in addition to the military commander, a political officer from the Party who shares command.

Criminal Law

Criminal law describes the part of a legal system which deals with illegal actions, performed by citizens against other citizens or against the state, which are so serious, or so associated with moral turpitude, as to warrant punishment by the state rather than a CIVIL LAW judgement involving the resolution of a conflict or some kind of restitution. The state usually monopolizes the right to carry out prosecutions under criminal law, though some systems, of which the English COMMON LAW is the most important, still include residual private rights to prosecute individuals for breaking the law. In all cases the state has a monopoly of the right to inflict criminal punishment. Criminal law is now increasingly used to enforce the performance of duties in highly regulated spheres such as industrial safety or pollution legislation, or in cases where civil action by an individual to protect his rights is unlikely to be effective. The result has been a blurring of the previously quite sharp distinction between criminal and civil actions.

CSU

CSU stands for the Christian-Social Union, which is the Bavarian wing of the CDU-CSU party alliance in West Germany (CDU stands for Christian Democratic Union). The CSU has remained more clearly a religiously based party (or, as is sometimes the alternative technical vocabulary, a Confessional party), than its counterpart in the rest of West Germany, and is basically supported by Roman Catholics, Catholicism being the dominant religion in southern Germany, though Protestant leaders were involved in its foundation. It is also clearly a regional party, expressing the strong sense of traditional autonomy and regional identity that Bavaria has retained much more strongly than the other German Länder. It has been in a permanent alliance with the CDU for most of the existence of the Bonn Republic, and was their coalition partner along with the small FDP (basically the German Liberal party) all the time they were in government. So tight is the alliance that it was the leader of the CSU, rather than of the bigger CDU, who was accepted as the overall party leader and candidate for Chancellor in the 1980 Federal election. The CSU is generally seen as the more right-wing part of the alliance, and therefore the most right-wing organized party in West Germany, but the impossibility of it ever being able to fight elections outside Bavaria reduces its overall influence in German politics. It has usually been dominant in Bavarian politics and government, with little recent challenge from the Liberal or Social Democratic parties.

Cuban Missile Crisis

This occurred in 1962, when the USSR under the leadership of KHRUSHCHEV attempted to gain an advantage in the COLD WAR by placing medium-range nuclear missiles in Cuba, which under Castro had gradually moved into an alliance with the SOVIET BLOC. The missiles would have threatened the American mainland (Cuba is only ninety miles from Florida), and constituted an ESCALATION in international tension. John Kennedy, the President of the USA, risked international opprobrium and even nuclear conflict by insisting on their removal, and used the US Navy to enforce a blockade of all Soviet ships trying to approach Cuba. Some analysts think that this was the nearest the world has come to a global war since 1945. In the event the USSR gave in under the threat, and this retreat finally swung the Soviet military against Khrushchev, enabling his enemies on the Politburo to oust him from power a year later. The political significance of the crisis was considerable; among other things it demonstrated the way in which an American president can ignore the other elected branches of government and commit US forces in a major conflict situation.

Cultural Revolution

Cultural revolution is part of the post-Marx development of MARXIST theory, most importantly with Chinese communism under the guidance of MAO TSE TUNG (Mao Zedong). Roughly the idea of cultural revolution is a corrective to the materialistic assumption that some commentators claim to find in Marx, that only physical or legal restraints have to be changed to liberate the PROLETARIAT. A cultural revolution is a revolution in thought, in ideology, or, more comprehensively, in culture. What might now be called 'mind sets' have to be changed. People have to drop the attitudes, expectations, intellectual orientations of bourgeois society, and these have to be changed separately from the change in, say, the ownership of property.

With some thinkers in this tradition, notably the Italian communist party under GRAMSCI's influence, the stress is on getting the cultural revolution first, as the only hope towards persuading electorates to allow the legal and property revolution. Building a true socialist or communist consciousness however is seen to be a major and very long-term task by leaders in post-revolutionary societies, because the attitudes of capitalist or feudal society have been shown to linger on long after the political death of these structures.

74

It was because of this problem that Mao authorized his Red Guards, revolutionary youth, in the late 1960s to investigate, punish, humiliate and force into 'political re-education' large numbers of the Chinese élite. The victims were accused of wishing to create a new class system, or of desiring privilege and generally setting themselves apart from the masses in a counter-revolutionary manner. The theoretical problem inside Marxism of the idea of a cultural revolution is that it implies an autonomy of thought from socio-economic structure, which does not fit well with the general thesis that thought and attitude are superstructural, dependent on the economic substructure.

D

D Notices

D Notices are part of Britain's security arrangements, like the OFFICIAL SECRETS ACT, which can be used to stifle public disclosure of sensitive information. In fact D Notices involve a voluntary self-censorship on the part of newspapers, prompted by the Ministry of Defence (MOD). If the MOD has reason to believe that journalists have, or might obtain, information that would damage state security if published, it issues a D Notice to editors requesting them not to do so. This is almost invariably complied with, mainly because the issuing committee, itself an unofficial body, is trusted not to abuse its responsibility. Although ignoring a D Notice is not in itself an offence, publication of sensitive information might well leave an editor or a journalist liable to prosecution under the Official Secrets Act.

Dahl

Robert Dahl, (b.1915), a Professor at Yale University, is probably the best known of all the talented and energetic political scientists who appeared on the American academic scene shortly after the Second World War and effected a great development of the discipline that has influenced its practice throughout the Western world. His work covers both political theory and empirical political research, but he is best known as the most important of the pluralist writers on democratic theory (see PLURALISM) who recast the definitions of democracy to make it more realistically applicable to the Western political systems. He produced one of the shortest, clearest, and most original of all these restatements of democracy, *A Preface to Democratic Theory*, in which he developed his idea of POLYARCHY. He also carried out one of the earliest of the COMMUNITY POWER studies. There are few fields of political science he has not touched, and although he has often been criticized by those less convinced of the value of Western political systems, his ideas have not been seriously challenged.

De Facto

De Facto rule or power, against which is contrasted *de jure* rule, simply means that, as it happens, a certain group, class, nation or whatever is in a position to control and order some political system. It does not necessarily mean that the rulers are illegitimate, but its principal use is as a contrast with *de jure* power. *De jure* power means that, according to some legal or political theory, a particular group is entitled to give legitimate orders over some area. Again, the actual coincidence depends on the theory one chooses to apply. To take an extreme example, someone might hold that Britain had *de jure* authority over a long lost colony, or that England only had *de facto* power over Scotland and Wales, depending on the choice of ideologies.

The importance of the conceptual distinction is that it allows a distinction between the actual chance of someone in authority being obeyed (which might be a matter of the number of available machine guns), and the way in which the right to be obeyed is justified, or seen as justifiable by any chosen audience. For example, until the official creation of the State of Zimbabwe, the UK had had *de jure* authority in what used to be known as Southern Rhodesia, although in fact the society had been controlled by white Rhodesians in revolt aginst the UK government from 1965 until the creation of Zimbabwe. The distinction has considerable practical effects in the world order, because most countries would have refused to recognise the *de facto* government of that country, and would have assisted in applying what the UK took to be the legal order, as it was the *de jure* ruler.

De Gaulle

Charles de Gaulle, (1890–1970), was a general, the leader of French resistance to Hitler in the Second World War, and President of the Fifth Republic (1958–69). He gave his name not only to a French political party but also to a whole tradition in post-war French politics that still exercises a very important influence. As a colonel in the French army during the 1930s, de Gaulle was a somewhat unpopular figure who advocated modern doctrines of armoured warfare that were largely ignored. He was the senior French soldier who opposed the Vichy regime after the fall of France in 1940, and for much of the war headed a French government in exile in London. When the Allies liberated France in 1944, de Gaulle became for a while the head of the French government, but his ideas for a strong presidential government were rejected by both the politicians and the public, and he retired from political life. In 1958 the crises in the Fourth French Republic, especially those connected with the Algerian war, led to a widespread demand for him to take power. He accepted, becoming the last prime minister of the Fourth Republic and then the first president of the Fifth Republic. In this capacity he led the party that had fought for his ideas during the 1950s (under a variety of names), and was a highly autocratic ruler of France until he resigned after a referendum defeat in 1969. However, his political position had by then been crystallized into a political ideology supported by his party, and one of his ex-prime ministers, Georges Pompidou, won the resulting presidential election. In modern French politics there is a clear ideological position usually identified as GAULLISM, which to a large extent represents a devlopment of 'the General's' views; it resembles other brands of modern European conservatism, though it places an unusual emphasis on national independence.

De Tocqueville

Alexis De Tocqueville, (1805–59), was a French aristocrat who, while in some ways regretting the passing of the Ancien Régime as a result of the French Revolution, nonetheless became one of the most sympathetic and acute observers of Western democratic movements during the 19th century. His two great works were *The Ancien Régime,* a study of the social and political forces at work in France immediately before the Revolution, and *Democracy in America. The Ancien Régime* is still a valuable contemporary document for historians, but de Tocqueville was too close, chronologically and emotionally, to be capable of the sustained value-free analysis that might have made it a first-class work of political science. However, after he visited America in 1830, and despite the fact that he was there for only eight months and visited only a few Eastern seaboard states, he produced a massive, detailed and analytically brilliant study which can still be read today for its insights into the operation of American political culture. In this work he also develops a political and social theory about the consquences of mass democracy that is similar in many ways to DURKHEIM'S much later thinking. His principal concern was to demonstrate that some aspects of the traditional European aristocracy had been beneficial, and that their absence in modern democracy raised dangers to the very values of democracy itself. Formal political equality, without actual economic equality, put the masses in the hands of those whose wealth gave them power, but who lacked the 'noblesse oblige' tradition of the aristocracy and with it a sense of duty towards those whom they ruled. De Tocqueville also feared the vulnerability of the masses to demagogic manipulation, and regretted the absence of the countervailing influence of some aspects of the feudal world order. He observed very sharply, for example seeing that America was becoming an increasingly litigious society where not only inter-personal conflicts but also general political questions rapidly became entangled with the legal system. His predictions were also extremely perceptive. He was convinced that America would become one of the leading world powers (which was hardly obvious in 1830), and even foretold that its great opponent would be Russia. Ultimately he approved of American democracy much more than he deprecated it. He was perhaps the first real political sociologist in that he sought to explain American culture in terms of its social and economic conditions and political culture.

Decentralization

Decentralization denotes a process or situation in which powers and responsibilities are transferred from a central authority to other, usually more local, organs. The term can be employed in relation to the political decision-making process, to the distribution of powers between elected authorities and to the organization of the bureaucracy. Most federal systems of government, for example the West German Federal Republic, Australia and the United States, exhibit a considerable degree of decentralization, although they may also (as a result) exhibit overlapping authorities.

Defence of the Realm Acts (see DORA)

Delegation

Delegation of power in political discourse has two rather different usages. The first is the idea that a body, a parliament most typically, with constitutional authority to make law may delegate some part of this power to others. Usually this involves the parliament passing a law which sets the major aims and outline shape of a legislative programme. Rather than try to deal with the details, which themselves may have to be altered frequently to accord with changing circumstances, they may delegate responsibility to make regulations under the act to a CIVIL SERVICE body, a minister, or even an independent agency. (In this context, see LEGISLATIVE VETO). The body to which power is thus delegated usually has to pass only rather formal tests of the validity of the subsequent rules and regulations, though these may be more easily challenged in courts or elsewhere than originating legislation.

In the UK, for example, it is not unusual for a court to hold that some act of a minister of state done under the authority of power delegating legislation is *ultra vires*, exceeding what parliament intended to allow him to do. It is, at the same time, impossible to attack an act of the originating body, parliament, as *ultra vires*, because the British Constitution knows no limit to parliamentary power.

The secondary meaning of delegation is almost the opposite of the primary meaning. A delegate is one who is selected to represent a body or group, but unlike a fully free representative under the BURKEIAN theory of representation, is not at liberty to vote according to his own will. Although not as firmly bound as someone seen as mandated to vote in a particular way, a delegate is expected to carry out broad instructions and to refrain from independent policy-making.

Democracy

Democracy is the most valued and also the vaguest of political terms in the modern world. Political systems as diverse as the USA, various one-party states in Africa, and European Communist states all describe themselves as democracies. Indeed it is characteristic of this vagueness that when a UNESCO conference on democracy was held in 1950, more than fifty nations, utterly diverse in political systems, all insisted that they were (and sometimes that *only* they were) democracies.

The ancient Greek word 'democracy' means rule by the *demos*, which can be translated as either 'the people' or 'the mob', depending on one's ideological preference. By itself democracy means little more than that, in some undefined sense, political power is ultimately in the hands of the whole adult population, and that no smaller group has the right to rule. Democracy only takes on a more useful meaning when qualified by one of the other words with which it is associated, for example LIBERAL DEMOCRACY, REPRESENT-

ATIVE DEMOCRACY, PARTICIPATORY DEMOCRACY or DIRECT DEMOCRACY. Those who seek to justify the title 'democracy' for a society where power is clearly in the hands of one section of the population (for example, in many Third World states or Communist bloc countries) mean something rather different. The claim is not really that the people rule, but that they are ruled in their own interests. Defenders of the USSR, for example, have claimed that until economic and social progress has been made, and a true 'socialist man' created by education, that is until the masses have lost their FALSE CONSCIOUS-NESS, democratic procedures would be worse than useless. The argument is that people cannot be left to choose their own leaders, or make their own political choices, until their vision is genuinely free of distortion and they can identify their real needs. This version of democracy has a close connection with the 'Positive' theory of liberty (see LIBERTY, POSITIVE).

Democratic Centralism

Democratic Centralism is the doctrine, espoused by LENIN, according to which the Soviet Communist Party (CPSU, q.v.) and most other Communist parties are run. It lays down that conflicting opinions and views should be freely expressed and widely discussed at all levels of the party hierarchy, and that the central committee should take them into account when making any decision, but once a decision has been made, the policy must be unquestioningly accepted and carried out by all party members. The CPSU is organized on strict hierarchical lines, with considerable control over the committees at each level by the one directly above; so in practice very little upward flow of views and opinions takes place, while the 'centralist' aspect of the doctrine is fully utilised. There is no particular reason why the CPSU, whose authority is justified in terms of its own ideology by the need for a 'DICTATORSHIP OF THE PROLETARIAT' to build communism, should wish to appear democratic now. In its earlier days, however, and especially under Lenin just after the Revolution, central control of the party was more problematic, hence the linking of the two values, democratic participation with central command authority. Were the freedom to argue fully before the policy decision a reality, there would in fact be relatively little difference between democratic centralist Communist Parties and such organizations as the British Conservative Party, where policy is ultimately made by a party leadership which expects to be loyally supported by all rank-and-file members.

Dependency Theory

Dependency theory was a popular radical critique of Western capitalist nations in their relations with the THIRD WORLD during the 1960s and 1970s. The theory still has its advocates. It derives from a theory of economic imperialism, and is also used as a critique of foreign aid programmes. The basic idea is that major capitalist powers like the USA and the members of the EEC have not really given up their colonial power, but in fact exercise enormous political control over Latin American, African and Asian countries. But they do this now by the use of economic pressure and by exploiting their superior market position to extract unfair advantage in international trade. As most of the finance for industrial and agricultural development in the third world has to come from the money markets in the developed capitalist states (the theory goes) the very basic development of these countries is tied to the economic interests of the West.

The theory is even taken by some to the point that outright foreign aid gifts are suspect, because the funding is simply used to develop third world economies further in such a way that they remain totally dependent on markets in the first world. While it is clear that economic power is vital, and that the Western investors will try to maximize their advantage, it is far from clear that poor and over-populated countries have any alternative, at least in the short run, to exploiting their primary products for the Western market. There is, after all, nothing fixed about the terms of trade in primary goods; oil may have once been a matter for exploitation and political control by the FIRST WORLD. It is now clearly a weapon of considerable power in the hands of the oil states against their former exploiters. Nonetheless the theory, by pointing out how irrelevant formal political control may be, does help to show how long lasting are the chains of empire as they were cast during the great development of colonial economic exploitation by the European powers in the nineteenth century. Combined with the spread of multinational companies outside the control of any Western governments, companies who frequently do control the raw resources of poor countries, the general notion of economic dependency cannot be ignored.

Deputies

Deputies are elected members of a legislative assembly. The term is not normally applied to British MPs but is used in connection with members of the French, German and Italian legislatures. The delegate or deputy view of representation stresses the obligation of a member of the legislature to echo the views of his constituents, who are seen as entrusting him with a strict mandate. The opposite view, that an elected member should be able to speak and vote according to his own convictions, stems from BURKE.

The term 'deputy' is sometimes used to refer to a person who is a surrogate for a leader or fills his place when necessary. Thus most political parties have deputy leaders. In Britain in recent years the term 'deputy prime minister' has come into use, although it is nowhere formally recognized in the constitution. The British Labour Party has an elected deputy leader, and in the early 1980s there was heated controversy over the procedure that should be adopted to elect him.

Détente

Since the 1960s the word 'Détente' has crept into our political vocabulary to signify a foreign policy process mainly concerned with an easing of tension between the USSR and the USA. At any particular time the content of policies meant to increase détente may vary widely. Very roughly, any policy which involves self-interested economic co-operation, or steps towards reduction in the level of armaments, is likely to qualify as an example of détente. In many ways the apparent existence of a new and softer orientation of the two super-powers towards each other has more to do with a tendency to use the extreme hostility of the COLD WAR of the 1950s and 1960s as a bench mark than any real reduction in conflict between Western states and the East. The country in which détente has been both most politically important and perhaps most real is West Germany, where a genuine rappochement between the Soviet Union and the Federal Republic seems to have taken place.

Deterrence

Deterrence is a concept much used by defence strategists and military planners and their political allies. Literally, deterrence refers to the capacity to protect oneself from attack by another nation by being able to threaten terrible, or at least unacceptable, reprisals. Deterrence, however, has come into its own in the often bizarre world of nuclear strategy, and highly sophisticated theories have been developed around the concept. Political leaders of both the Western and Eastern powers have argued, ever since 1945, that their countries need nuclear weapons, (or, alternatively, just very

83

strong military conventional forces) (see CONVENTIONAL WAR) so that peace can be maintained. The argument is that, as long as any potential enemy knows that any attack by them would cost them dear, no attack will be made. In terms of nuclear capacity a host of other concepts become involved in detailed working out of this essentially simple notion, especially those of MUTUAL ASSURED DESTRUCTION, SECOND STRIKE CAPACITY, Pre-emptive strikes, MASSIVE RETALIATION, and FLEXIBLE RESPONSE. Perhaps the most significant thing is that military capacity does now seem to be justified every-where in terms of the need to deter others, rather than of having an offensive capacity.

Devolution

Devolution is the process of transferring power from central gov-ernment to a lower or regional level; among the reasons given for doing so are that it will increase the efficiency of government and meet demands from special sections of the community for a degree of control over their own affairs. The word gained great currency in the United Kingdom in the late 1970s, when proposals were made to establish separate assemblies for Scotland and Wales, each with a range of powers over its own internal affairs. However, a referendum held on the proposals revealed that the majority of voters in Wales were opposed to any such transfer of powers. In Scotland, a majority of those who voted were in favour of the proposals, but this represented less than the forty per cent of the total electorate which had been stipulated, and the proposed legis-lation was therefore abandoned. The question had arisen much earlier in the 20th century when the Irish issue had led to calls for 'home rule all round'. The establishment in 1921 of a separate Parliament for Ulster with considerable powers over domestic administration was controversial because the administration were accused of discriminating against the Roman Catholic community. The devolved Ulster Parliament was suspended in 1973, and efforts to re-establish it on a power-sharing basis have since failed.

Dictatorship

Dictatorship is a form of government in which one man has sole and complete political power. In antiquity, temporary dictators were often appointed as an emergency measure by states which were normally organized in some other fashion. The Roman Repub-lic appointed dictators during military crises (the term actually originates from this practice), and the ancient Greek city states sometimes gave supreme law-making powers to individuals like SOLON when civic unity was seriously threatened.

In the modern world many dictators have come to power as leaders of mass movements, and have ruled through their control of such movements or through political parties that have acquired a monopoly of power. Dictators also frequently emerge from the armed forces when a military JUNTA takes over after a COUP D'ÉTAT. An important distinction should be made between the dictator who exercises personal power based on his own popularity or control of coercive institutions, and the apparently dictatorial leader who is in reality largely a figurehead or no more than the 'first among equals' within a ruling clique. HITLER, MUSSOLINI and STALIN were real dictators, whereas more recent leaders of the Soviet Union, who have owed their eminence to their position within the party hierarchy and have had to contend with the rest of the POLITBURO, have probably not managed to become dictators. Of other modern leaders, General FRANCO was certainly a powerful ruler in his own right to the end of his life, while General DE GAULLE came close to being a popularly appointed 'crisis' dictator on the Roman model.

Dictatorship of the Proletariat

This is one of the concepts taken over from MARX's writings by the early leaders of the BOLSHEVIK Party (later the Communist Party of the Soviet Union), especially by LENIN, and used to justify the dominant role of the Communist party in the state. According to the developed Marxist-Leninist doctrine, immediately after the revolutionary overthrow of capitalism there will be an intermediate period during which the Party, as the VANGUARD OF THE PROLETARIAT will have to exercise political and economic control in a 'dictatorship of the proletariat'. This undemocratic and inegalitarian state of affairs is unavoidable because the transition from capitalism to true socialism is impossible until the necessary conditions have been created. These conditions are partly economic, depending on the level of capitalist development that has been reached, but more important is the creation of 'Socialist Man'. This entails the development of a true socialist consciousness amongst the masses. Until they come to grasp the true ideology, it is pointless to entrust political and social decisions to them, since they will still be suffering the ALIENATION and ideological distortion that life in a capitalist society produces. Ultimately, when a true socialist understanding has been developed, not only will the party's supreme

85

power be unnecessary, but indeed the whole state will 'wither away', leaving a peaceful co-operative society. Until then democracy could only hold back this development; in fact selfishness and conflict would be rife unless kept down by forceful central control on the part of those who, having been admitted to the Party, are known to have a proper understanding of scientific socialism. Whilst there are theoretical difficulties in accepting this idea, it should not be taken as nothing but cynical pretence. In many areas of Soviet life one can see serious attempts to build such a socialist man, for example in the ordinary criminal law and, above all, the educational system.

Diplomacy

The idea of 'diplomacy' is used in a variety of rather vague ways in political language, all deriving from the techniques and styles developed by European foreign affairs representatives during the 18th century, though, of course, diplomacy as behaviour and political strategy is as old as politics. Technically the Diplomatic Corps consists of all the men and women professionally engaged in representing the interests of their countries abroad. This activity varies from the gathering of information and evaluation of the politics of the host country, via the direct protection of the legal interests of any fellow nationals who are in trouble in that country (the Consular function) to international negotiations and the delivery of special messages, including threats and bribes, to the host government. Diplomacy has come to mean something slightly apart from this, however. It has come to describe an entire method of resolving international conflicts which, though extremely often referred to in the media, is rather hard precisely to catch. At a simple level diplomacy covers anything short of military action, and indeed it is often alleged that 'diplomacy' has 'failed' when countries do engage in outright fighting. The broadness of the concept is demonstrated by some of the ways in which subcategories of diplomacy have had to be invented to describe more precisely what goes on when diplomacy is resorted to. Thus one reads of 'personal diplomacy', when a particular national leader tries to sort out some international problem on the basis of his own personal relations with, and understanding of, other national leaders. A sub-category even of this is the notion of 'shuttle' diplomacy, engaged in almost exclusively by the USA when an influential or important foreign affairs spokesman will travel backwards and forwards between hostile states trying personally to find grounds for compromise between opponents on the basis of building up a personal connection and understanding with both sides.

Alternatively one reads of 'diplomatic channels', for the delivery of ideas or the collection of information, which essentially means using the diplomatic corps for its proper function, and indeed actually stands in contrast to the amateurishness involved in 'personal' diplomacy. In as much as there is a further real content to the notion of 'diplomacy' *per se* it comes from the idea that diplomats are professional experts in negotiation and information transmission in the international arena. Here it is felt that particular techniques and training are necessary to ensure that no personal emotion or style should colour the message, that two diplomats of different nations have more in common, and are better able to treat the matters they discuss objectively and unemotionally than are two ordinary politicians. As foreign policy is increasingly made, in all countries, directly by the heads of the executive, and as international conferences increasingly depend on direct confrontation between senior politicians, it might be thought that diplomacy as a special technique, and the diplomatic corps as professional experts both in the making and execution of foreign policy is becoming out of date. There is probably a good deal of truth in this. It was noteworthy that the British Cabinet's 'think tank' report on the foreign service some years ago urged its radical cutting, and the replacement of most functions by ordinary civil servants who were technical experts in the area in question. No action was taken on this report, and it caused considerable public debate. In the USA the tendency for foreign policy to be taken out of the State Department and into the White House has not attenuated over the years.

Direct Democracy

Direct democracy is opposed to REPRESENTATIVE DEMOCRACY much as the respective titles suggest. According to the theory of direct democracy, all concerned citizens must directly participate in the making of decisions and the passing of laws, and this function can neither be delegated to others, nor can it be carried out by others chosen to represent the interests of the many. The inspiration for this system of democratic politics comes from classical Greek democracy, especially as it is understood, sometimes, to have worked in 5th century Athens. The earliest, and still most influential exponent in the modern world is Jean-Jacques ROUSSEAU, particularly in his *The Social Contract*.

The arguments given for the advantage of direct instead of

representative democracy are varied. Foremost is the idea that only a genuine majority of the population can make a law which really maximizes the democratic nature of rule, and representative government can only very seldom be seen as fully applying majority rule. Other arguments are equally important. To Rousseau, for example, direct democracy is necessary for true freedom, because a man is only free when he is obeying a law he has himself 'willed'. As, according to Rousseau, one cannot delegate one's will, it follows that no law in the making of which a man has not directly shared can be obeyed without a loss of freedom. A somewhat similar argument is that direct involvement in politics, listening to and joining in debate and voting has an educative influence. People are seen as coming to understand their own and others' needs more clearly, and to grow in personality and morality through direct participation in decision making and law creating. At a less elevated level demands for direct democracy often arise out of a sheer mistrust of putting power in the hands of a few, often because of a feeling that hierarchy, even if it is supposed to be representative, inevitably becomes corrupt. It is not necessarily the case that advocates of direct democracy as a legislative process also insist on full and equal participation in decision-making at the stage of executing policy—indeed Rousseau clearly sees the executive as separate from the mass meeting of all citizens that legislates. On the other hand the only arenas where direct democracy is at all widely practised, say colleges or clubs, usually do not have a clear distinction between legislating and executing.

The problems are fairly obvious. If all citizens are to share fully in decision-making, the society must be very small indeed. Classical Athens could only manage to employ the system because, at its height the free adult male citizenry probably numbered no more than 20,000, and because most people seldom took up their rights. A second major technical problem is that, unless the society is to be very simple, and operate at a very low technology level, the time consumed in policy-making would prohibit all those who had to work full time from any serious use of their rights to participate. No political system today comes anywhere near operating direct democracy at the national level, nor has one ever done so. At times, (the Town Meetings of early New England States are the best example), local government may have approached this system. On the other hand the cry for direct democracy is increasingly heard, and increasingly answered in the running of institutions. Universities, political parties and to some extent industrial plants are subject to the demands for such governance, as part of the more general value attached to participation throughout the developed states.

Directed Democracy

Directed democracy, also called guided democracy, is a term sometimes used to justify the absence of anything remotely resembling Western REPRESENTATIVE DEMOCRACY in developing countries. It was first formulated in the 1960s by the Pakistani leader Ayub Khan, who ruled with the support of the army. It is in many ways analogous to the Marxist concept of the leading role of the Communist Party during the transitional period of proletarian dictatorship. It rests fundamentally on the argument that the people in a newly-independent Third World country cannot be allowed full participation in electoral politics because they are in no position to make rational political choices. For practical reasons such as lack of general education, (if not mass illiteracy), and poor communications, and also because of possible ideological hang-overs from colonial times, it may be feared that the people could be easily led astray by reactionary elements. Alternatively they might demand far more in the way of economic benefits than their country could afford, especially at a time when sacrifices might well be needed to build up heavy industry and to create a capital base for the later consumer industry. The idea of directed democracy does allow for some participation: people may join the one permitted party, or it may even be the case that other parties are allowed to exist and to have views on policy provided they refrain from challenging the decisions ultimately taken in the public interest by those who know best. The stated intention in most directed democracies is that eventually, as barriers to rational participation diminish and economic conditions improve, the people will be 'guided' into a democracy that can function effectively.

Discrimination

Discrimination in politics refers to the practice of singling out—usually for unfavourable treatment—certain groups which are defined by such characteristics as race, language or religion. As a practice it is endemic in most societies; but during the 20th century, especially in the aftermath of the Nazi Holocaust, most democracies have made serious efforts to combat it through legislation and judicial decisions. Reverse discrimination (see AFFIRMATIVE ACTION) has sometimes been adopted, and it has been suggested that in some circumstances (for example in the hiring of academics in the United States) it may actually be an advantage to be a member of a hitherto disadvantaged group.

In non-democratic societies official discrimination is still common. In Iran under the Khomeini regime, for example, many people have been executed simply for belonging to faiths other than the Shi'ite form of Islam. In South Africa the systematic incorporation of racial discrimination into the laws of a state with a tradition of Christian and Western political values has made it an object of widespread suspicion and dislike.

Divine Right

The Divine Right of Kings to rule their realms was a vital political and theological doctrine in medieval Europe, and political theorists as late as Bodin (1529–1596) and Hooker (1554–1600) were more or less committed to the doctrine, which to some extent lay behind the Royalist position during the English Civil War, and was finally killed off largely because of the victory of the Parliamentary forces in that war. The argument, which was useful both to the Churches and to Monarchs, developed as a result of the mutual need of the spiritual forces in European society and the monarchical dynasties for a concordat on their relative positions. In return for the ideological defence given them by the Church's imprimatur, Kings were expected to defend and support the Roman Catholic Church and its doctrine with physical force, and to leave the regulation of religion and morals entirely to the Pope and his Bishops.

The doctrine derived from various theological sources and political occasions, but it is not particularly unusual, in as much as some connection between the right to political power and a religious role is anthropologically common. Indeed, the precedent for the medieval European version stems originally from the dual rule of the early Roman Emperors as both Gods and Rulers, whilst the combination of tribal chief with archpriesthood is a more general example of this political need for a spiritual backing. The problem is simply that there is a very restricted number of ways in which one can justify the right of one man to rule over others, and in entirely non-secular societies, with a united and powerful church wielding vital symbols of eternal life or damnation, no ideological claim exists other than one tied to God's purposes for man. It is notable that the first commonly-accepted political theories to use some other form of justification arose in England after the Reformation and the Civil War had made any appeal to such united and powerful religious symbols more dangerous than useful. Until the Reformation few would have doubted that there were two spheres of influence in a society, the religious power and the secular, and that the secular only gained its authority because it was needed to back up the church, to create the environment in which men could lead a good life. This, the best-argued version of the doctrine, was set out most fully in ST. AUGUSTINE'S *City of God*.

Division of Labour

Division of Labour is the system under which both economic production and other, especially administrative or policy-making, tasks are handled in all modern societies. It is a system contrasted to craftsmanship or to generalized political and social leadership and it involves the splitting up and distribution of different parts of any job amongst several people. In a modern manufacturing enterprise, for example, not only the manufacture of a car, but even of a simple object like a pen, may be subdivided into hundreds of very minor tasks, done repetitively by many men, over and over again, with none of them actually being responsible for creating the whole unit. Many social theorists, but especially DURKHEIM and MARX, notably in his theory of ALIENATION, have attached great importance to the division of labour as a causal factor in social development. Although the division of labour is the cornerstone of modern economic productivity, it is held to have a seriously deleterious impact on human self-confidence and interpersonal relations by such theorists. On the other hand in other theories, it is seen as a necessary aspect of development and modernization and in its political coverage is almost a definitional element of theories of POLITICAL DEVELOPMENT and political modernization.

Djilas

Milovan Djilas (1911–) was born in Montenegro, and from an early age was a senior member of the Politburo of the Yugoslav Communist Party, fighting with it from 1940 when it was an underground organization. He became a minister in Tito's communist government at the time Tito was managing so successfully to develop Yugoslavia's independent position vis-à-vis Moscow. However, Djilas represented just too well the spirit of autonomy inside the liberal communism of Tito's Yugoslavia, and began to be a serious critic of communist governments. His most important work by far is his book, published in 1953, *The New Class*. Here he argues that the sort of BOLSHEVIK revolution carried out in the name of the people by an authoritarian Leninist party, either that of Russia in 1917, or like the communist governments set up by the Soviet

Union in eastern Europe after the Second World War, had a fatal flaw. Instead of producing a classless society, the ultimate goal of communism, by abolishing private property, they had instead developed a new class system, every bit as exploitative and undemocratic as those of the past. The new class consisted of the party officials, the managers of the nationalized industries, and those bureaucrats whom the rapidly growing state planning and administrative machinery has come to require. These people, and especially the ones near the top of the tree, were the only ones in the communist states to have any power. They used the repressive forces of the state, especially the secret police, to ensure total obedience, and their control over education and media to secure much more acquiescence to their version of a ruling ideology than had any previous state. At the same time they enjoyed a standard of living vastly higher than ordinary members of society, and were able to pass on this privilege to their children. Even though they could not legally own much more than any ordinary citizen, access to high quality education and easy entrance to prestige jobs guaranteed their children the same status that they possessed themselves, and denied it to others. Most of his analysis was entirely correct, and would be accepted by modern Western analysts.

His particular prescriptions for solving the problems, which involve a great extension of participation and direct democracy, already more extensively practised in Yugoslavia then elsewhere may, however, be less easily accepted. Soviet critics, and some Western Marxists still refuse to accept that these facts, even if true, constitute a class, on the largely definitional grounds that only outright ownership of the means of production make a society one based on class. Djilas has never given up being a Marxist, and should not be read as saying that a classless communist society is impossible, nor, perhaps, even denying its ultimate inevitability. Rather he was doing no more than extending with hindsight and more experience the criticisms that many of Lenin's contemporaries had made. For this book, and other writings Djilas has received prison sentences, and has been banned from publishing in Yugoslavia. It says a great deal for the liberalism of this regime that nothing worse happened to the author of so trenchant a critique of his own society.

Doomsday

The idea of a doomsday machine is an intellectual construct in modern strategic thinking used to clarify certain points in nuclear war theory. The ideal doomsday machine would be a super-bomb triggered to go off automatically if the country which built it was to suffer a serious nuclear attack. As the name is meant to imply, the destruction caused by this bomb would be so total that the aggressor nation would be eliminated totally (as would all others.) The point is to take Mutual Assured Destruction to its logical conclusion, because a doomsday machine would make it impossible for any nation ever to risk triggering nuclear war.

Although manifestly absurd (though not technologically impossible), the concept acts as a limiting factor in Deterrence theory. Some proposals that have been seriously made approach these limits. An example is a suggestion of how to control the US Navy's strategic nuclear submarine fleet. The technical problems of communication with an under-sea fleet, especially after a possible attack that may have wiped out the national command and control centres have always worried planners. One suggestion is that a continuous signal should be transmitted to these submarines, on the cessation of which their captains should automatically launch an attack on the Soviet Union. This, by making retaliation quite automatic, has the doomsday effect. The phrase was made popular by the famous film *Dr Strangelove*, a biting satire on nuclear strategy.

DORA

DORA is the acronym for the British legislation passed during both World Wars, officially known as the Defence of the Realm Acts. Their most important aspects were the clauses allowing the incarceration of any aliens from enemy countries, and of British citizens, who were seen as a threat to national security. During the Second World War, for example, clause 18B of DORA was invoked to imprison Sir Oswald Mosley because of his leadership of the British Union of Fascists and his sympathy with the Axis dictators. This legislation produced a major decision in British Constitutional Law which has been opposed by Civil Liberties lawyers ever since but not reversed by subsequent precedent or legislation. In this case, *Liversidge* v. *Anderson* (1942), the DORA legislation was interpreted as giving the Home Secretary a virtually arbitrary power to intern anyone he believed to be a threat to security, without being obliged to offer the court any convincing reason for this belief. Only one member of the Judicial House of Lords, Lord Atkin, dissented from this judgment, which has been interpreted not only as a breach of habeas corpus, but as typical of a lengthy period during which British courts gave up any serious attempt to check executive power.

Doves

Doves are those who take a gentle, conciliatory or pacifistic stance on any issue, as opposed to 'HAWKS', who favour an aggressive stance or 'hard' line. The terms originated in the debates over the Vietnam War conducted in the USA, but are now applied to almost any kind of political conflict, however trivial. For example, members of a University staff in favour of supporting student requests to reduce a course work-load might well be called 'Doves' by those who felt that the load was already too light.

Downs

Anthony Downs (born in 1930), was an American political scientist in the 1950s (he has since left academic life and become a millionaire), who was responsible for starting an entirely new promising line of research in politics with just one book, *An Economic Theory of Democracy*. At a time when most empirical research was influenced by sociology and psychology, this argued for the use of models and assumptions drawn from economics in analysing political behaviour. The difference is far from trivial. Downs's approach, which came to be known as the rational-choice theory, is based on taking political man as a creature who seeks to achieve maximum satisfaction through choices based on rational calculation—just as 'economic man' does. This contrasts sharply with approaches that play down the role of rationality in favour of a political model of human behaviour much closer to the psychologist's stimulus response approach view of man. Downs showed that much of the behaviour of voters and political parties in Western democracies could be explained very satisfactorily by a few simple assumptions of this 'rational-choice' sort. Subsequent work, mainly in the USA and Britain, has considerably developed the theory, and has produced formulations which even have a certain predictive value. There are several reasons for this drive to make political science more like economics, not least being the fact that economics is the most successful and highly-developed of the social sciences. Furthermore, many political scientists have disliked the patronising attitude implicit in the assumption that mass political behaviour is a-rational, if not positively irrational. Perhaps most important of all, the Anglo-American tradition of political theory from HOBBES to the UTILITARIANS and beyond has mainly been based on an assumption of human rationality. Turning empirical research and empirical theory in this direction offers the best chance of uniting the two main traditions in political science, divided since the

BEHAVIOURAL revolution which at one time seemed likely to lead to the demise of POLITICAL THEORY.

Due Process

Due process involves a guarantee that an individual who is accused of a crime or faced with legal action will have the opportunity to see that the charges or claims against him are determined by proper legal procedures, without bias, and in open court. The notion of due process may be assimilated to that of procedural fairness, and in the United Kingdom it is implemented by the judiciary who have since the 1960s done much to extend the scope of the doctrine in administrative cases (see ADMINISTRATIVE COURTS). In the United States due process is a constitutional right available against both the federal and state governments.

Durkheim

Emile Durkheim (1858–1917), along with MARX and WEBER, was one of the great founding fathers of modern social science. He took as his main task the explanation of the changes that overcame societies with the development of the Industrial Revolution and the change from traditional or feudal society to the sort of liberal capitalist social systems we experience today. His work covered an enormous range, encompassing sociological theory, research methodology, and empirical observation. Apart from Marxists, it is probable that the vast majority of modern sociologists would accept the label of being essentially 'Durkheimian' in perspective. Although he wrote little that was directly and obviously about politics, most of what he has to say is suffused with political importance. Methodologically his position was that individual motivations and feelings were irrelevent to the social scientist, because society was something with a real existence of its own, over and above the individual members who were largely formed by the social structure. Thus social facts were to be explained by other social facts, not by investigating individual human experiences.

A good example of this was his classic study of suicide in which suicide *rates* in various areas were explained by, *inter alia*, the *rates* of affiliation to different religions. Thus a highly personal act, self-slaughter, was turned into social fact, and explained in a structural manner. Perhaps his most important work, as far as political implications go, was his study of the breakdown of social regulation and normative order in modern capitalist societies characterized by a high degree of DIVISION OF LABOUR. This led both his investigation of 'ANOMIE', (with important similarities to Marx's idea of ALIENATION), and to the development of a theory of CORPORATIST politics which was taken over and misused by later FASCIST dictatorships. He is probably the most important precursor of 'FUNCTIONALIST' social theory which enjoyed a great influence in post-war social science, and he has stamped modern French social science deeply with his views and methodology.

E

Effectiveness of Government

The question of the effectiveness of government has come to worry many Western governments. Many observers (and many Conservative politicians) claim that the modern state is in a parlous condition as a result of what some writers have termed 'governmental overload'. This situation is said to result from government intervention in areas of social and economic life where it is unable to make any real impact on the substantive problems; the negative by-products include increasing public expenditure and a widespread popular cynicism that arises when expectations which have been heightened by the political leadership are not fulfilled. In the United States the period 1964–1968 saw a major expansion of the federal government's role in social policy, but this was followed by a reaction based on the fact that poverty seemed as pervasive as ever and some problems (for example crime) even seemed to have become more acute. The resulting mood of scepticism about the role of the federal government (see NEO-CONSERVATISM) led to an unwillingness to spend public money without good evidence that it would make a measurable difference to the problem involved. In the United Kingdom, as in the United States, concern with the effectiveness of government has also gone hand-in-hand with an anxiety to maintain a proper balance between expenditure on functions which only the state can perform (for example law-enforcement and defence) and the welfare functions of government.

Egalitarianism

Egalitarianism is the doctrine that all citizens of a state should be accorded exactly equal rights and privileges. However, there are many conflicting interpretations of what this commitment means in practice. Three major strands of thought can usefully be identified. (1) Egalitarianism certainly means that all political rights

97

should be the same for all adult human beings. In terms of access to politics, the suffrage and equality before the law, no social, religious, ethnic or other criterion should be allowed to produce inequality. This is the minimum definition of egalitarianism, and is accepted in theory, and usually in practice, in most Western democracies and many other types of state. (2) Egalitarianism may also be held to involve 'equality of opportunity', which implies that, regardless of the socio-economic situation into which someone is born, he will have the same chance as everybody else to develop his talents and acquire qualifications, and that when he applies for jobs his case will be considered entirely on the basis of such talents and qualifications, rather than, say, on the type of school he attended or his father's social status. This requires, at the very least, an educational and social welfare system which will train and provide for the less-advantaged so that they can really compete on equal terms with those from more favourable backgrounds. While no modern state can be said to actually achieve this goal, many seriously attempt to do so, and all would probably pay lip service to the idea. (3) The most stringent version of egalitarianism would require not just equal opportunities, but actual equality in material welfare and, perhaps, political weight. Such total equality is not regarded as even theoretically possible, let alone desirable, by most states. In Communist societies, where it is accepted as an aim, it is conspicuously not the case at the moment. Most non-Marxist thinkers argue that such a situation could only be attained by extensive loss of liberty, and would be economically inefficient since it would provide no material incentives to effort.

Election

An election is a method of choosing amongst candidates for some post or office, and elections have become the only fully respectable method for selecting political leaders and governors throughout the world. Even countries which are universally known to be dictatorships or military regimes use fraudulent elections to disguise their actual mechanisms for political selection.

Elections can be carried out by a wide variety of techniques. Votes can be given to individuals, as in most national elections, to collective entities (national delegations to the United Nations) or to institutional units (trade union branches). The voting procedure may be secret, public or even recorded and published, as is done in many legislative assemblies. Votes may be counted according to any one of a dozen or more methods ranging from varieties of pure

PROPORTIONAL REPRESENTATION to the simplest 'first past the post' plurality system (see ELECTORAL SYSTEM). All that elections have in common is that they are a method of selecting one or more candidates for office from a wider field by aggregating the individual preferences and counting them. Historically, elections have been only one amongst many methods of selection, and they have become the totally dominant method only in this century. There is no necessary connection between elections and DEMOCRACY, for even monarchies have been elective, and the selection of leaders in states like the USSR involves election, though the effective electorate is likely to consist of a handful of leading party figures. In fact elections will occur whenever selection does not depend on the will of a single person, force, or some special concept of LEGITIMACY.

Electoral College

This describes a group of people who have been specially appointed, nominated or elected in order that they should hold an election for a political office. It thus constitutes a way of making election to some significant position of power indirect rather than direct. The most important example of a modern electoral college is perhaps that which elects the American president. A slate of electors tied to a presidential and vice-presidential ticket appears on the ballot paper and once the votes have been counted the slate with the most votes on a simple plurality basis takes all that state's electoral college votes. The candidates with a majority in the electoral college become president and vice-president respectively. If no candidate has an overall majority in the electoral college the vote will be thrown into the House of Representatives, which then determines who is to become president. Many third-party candidates such as George Wallace and John Anderson have run for the presidency not so much in the hope of being elected as of forcing the election into the House, where the voting (by states) might secure a more desirable outcome than the usual system.

The states are not equally represented in the US Electoral College. Each state is allocated the same number of electors as it has members of the House of Representatives, plus two. Thus a state with two House members would get four votes and a state with thirty House members would get thirty-two electoral college votes. This system of course tends to under-represent the more populous and over-represent the less populous states. The US Electoral College never meets as a body, since the electors on each slate assemble at their state capital and cast their votes there.

99

Criticism of the electoral college surfaces regularly in the United States, and two major arguments are frequently levelled against it. First, because it was devised as a method of protecting the presidency from the excesses of popular government it has come to seem anachronistically undemocratic. For this reason many liberals in the United States are in favour of direct election of the president, while many conservatives, who argue that the United States is not a democracy but a republic, are anxious to retain the college. Second, the fact that the votes are distributed on a winner-take-all basis means that a candidate who takes a large state such as California or Texas by the slenderest of margins will gain an enormous advantage, since he will collect all the electoral college votes for the state. There is certainly an element of suspicion of direct democracy in the system, and it does to some extent distort the popular vote. But other aspects of the American system (such as the role of the Supreme Court) underline the fact that the United States is not unambiguously committed to majoritarian democracy (see MAJORITY; DEMOCRACY) and in a rough way the system balances the interests of states and regions against the pure arithmetic of popular votes.

In the United Kingdom an electoral college has featured in a recent and controversial reform of the Labour Party's method of electing its leader. Prior to 1981 the leader was elected by the votes of the Parliamentary Labour Party alone; then, as a result of a concerted movement to give the extra-parliamentary elements in the Labour Party greater control over policy, it was agreed that trade unions and constituency parties should also participate in leadership elections. The electoral college to be established was expected to give the predominant voice to Labour MPs, but in fact the special conference called to set up the new machinery voted for a system which gave MPs thirty per cent of the electoral college vote by comparison with forty per cent for the trade unions and thirty per cent for the constituency parties. The method was first used to elect a new leader, Neil Kinnock, in 1983. Dissatisfaction with this scheme led a group of right-of-centre Labour MPs who had long been dissatisfied with the direction of party policy to break away and form the Social Democratic party.

Electoral Systems

An electoral system is a method used to translate the votes for candidates in an election into an allocation of seats or a decision as to who has won. There are a very large number of electoral systems, and details may vary considerably even within these. However, three broad types of electoral system may be distinguished: the simple plurality system; PROPORTIONAL REPRESENTATION; and majoritarian systems.

The simple plurality system, which operates in the United Kingdom, is designed to find the most popular candidate in a way which is clear and comprehensible. The candidate with the most votes wins the seat and there is no redistribution of votes after the count. Although this system has the benefit of simplicity, it is frequently criticized for its unfairness to minorities, who may be ludicrously under-represented if they consistently come second, or a good third, in each constituency. After the British general election of 1983, for example, the Liberal–SDP Alliance won 25 per cent of the popular vote but gained only 23 seats, whereas the Labour Party, with 28 per cent of the vote, gained 209 seats. Minority parties are thus penalized, and may be squeezed out by the system merely because their supporters give up hope and begin to vote more 'realistically'. Another drawback of the system is that, where there are many candidates, a candidate may be elected on a minority of the popular vote: 30 per cent might suffice to win, for example, if rival candidates collected 25, 25 and 20 per cent each. The simple plurality system can be used with the single-member constituency, as at general elections in contemporary Britain, or in multi-member constituencies as occurs in some local government elections in Britain, where electors have (say) two votes and the two highest-scoring candidates are declared elected.

There are many varieties of proportional representation, but all are designed to ensure that minorities as well as majorities are represented. 'PR' does this by creating large multi-seat constituencies and allocating seats in proportion to the voters' expressed preferences. In an election where the votes in such a constituency were split between the parties in the ratio 3:2:1, six seats might be allocated: party A would receive 3 seats, party B 2 seats and party C 1 seat. If a simple plurality system had been used it would have been possible for party A to win all six seats in the six constituencies, by being 'first past the post' each time with no more than 35 per cent of the votes cast. Systems of proportional representation require large electoral districts to make greater representation of minorities possible, and indeed in some states (for example Israel) the entire country is treated as a single constituency. Usually, however, the difficulty of allocating seats requires that some redistribution of votes should take place, and second preferences must then be counted.

The arguments against proportional representation have frequently been based on the belief that such a system encourages political fragmentation: rival wings of a party are more likely to break away and form their own organizations if their increased minority status is not penalized, as it would be in a plurality system; and therefore, the argument runs, a multitude of parties and a series of unstable coalition governments would become the norm. In reality, while there has been an association between proportional representation and unstable government in some countries (for example in Weimar Germany and contemporary Italy) the system has also worked perfectly well and produced stable governments in countries such as the Federal Republic of Germany and the Irish Republic.

Majoritarian electoral systems are designed to ensure that a candidate can only be elected if he or she wins a majority of the popular vote and not simply a plurality of the votes cast. If no candidate wins such a majority at the first count, the objective can be achieved (as in France) by a second ballot (see SECOND BALLOTS) or (as in Australia) by a second count in which the votes of the less successful candidates are redistributed according to the second preferences registered by their supporters.

Elitism

Elitism (or élitist theory) is a rather loose term used to describe a variety of political theories. What all the theories have in common is the conviction that every political system, whatever its official ideology, is in fact ruled by a political élite or élites. The originators of modern élite theory were two famous late 19th-century Italian social scientists, PARETO and Mosca. (Which of the two devised the éltist theory was a subject of an argument between the two men themselves that was continued by later commentators.) In showing that all societies must be governed by élites, Pareto and Mosca intended to destroy the MARXIST belief that there could one day be a classless society with complete political equality; ironically, writers with a Marxist perspective subsequently used much the same model to dismiss the democratic pretentions of Western liberal societies. Whereas Pareto treated contemporary democracy as a complete sham, Mosca changed his position over time, eventually accepting that democracy was possible in the form of a system in which competing élites submitted to being chosen or rejected by electors. However, he never moved far from his main position, summed up in his statement that a parliamentary representative was not someone the people had elected, but someone whose friends had arranged for him to be elected.

Elitist theories were developed further in the early 20th century by several thinkers, notably SCHUMPETER and one of Mosca's disciples, Michels. Setting out his famous IRON LAW OF OLIGARCHY, Michels tried to show that even the German Social Democratic Party, the oldest socialist party in Europe, was inherently undemocractic, and bound to betray its working-class members. In the 1930s Schumpeter mapped out what was to become, with DAHL and others, the pluralist model (see PLURALISM). He reinterpreted democracy as nothing more than a system in which rival élites of party leaders vied for power through elections; but, far from condemning this state of affairs, he insisted that ordinary people could not, and indeed should not, have any more say in politics than this power of electoral choice. (Much later DOWNS, in his rational-choice model of party politics, tried to show that this did not affect the democratic nature of Western politics.) From the Left, many commentators have attempted to show that Western democracies are indeed governed by power élites, or élites based on a ruling class, and are thoroughly undemocratic; but such commentators of course retain their conviction that an abolition of capitalism will lead to political equality.

The various élite theorists share no common ground when attempting to explain the inevitability of élites. Pareto had a complicated psychological theory, linked with a pessimistic view of the human capacity to exercise reason in social life; Mosca and Michels relied heavily on a theory about the nature of organization and BUREAUCRACY quite similar to WEBER's; Schumpeter believed the masses were bound to suffer from the hysteria associated with crowd psychology; and the list could be extended. There is no general agreement among political scientists about the factual accuracy of élite theories or the desirability of the situation they describe. There are, though, few who would care to deny that there is at least some evidence for the existence of élites, if only the relatively sanitized version developed by pluralists, and the less far-reaching claims of writers like Michels in his classic *Political Parties* find considerable support from much later and less biased research.

Emergency Powers

Emergency powers are special powers (usually granted to a government or executive agency) which allow normal legislative procedures and/or judicial remedies to be by-passed or suspended. In democracies such emergency powers are usually strictly controlled by the legislature and permitted only for the duration of the emergency. In the United Kingdom, however, an Act of 1976 makes permanent provision for the use of the armed forces to undertake work of national importance if, for example, those who would normally carry out such work are involved in an industrial dispute or strike. As this indicates, although the primary association of emergency powers legislation is with a wartime situation, governments in fact retain some such powers for domestic crises. Indeed Edward Heath's Conservative government of 1970–74 declared five states of emergency to deal with industrial unrest.

Northern Ireland's internal conflicts have generated additional emergency legislation which gives the government power to proscribe organizations and exclude individuals from the United Kingdom. In France, emergency powers may be exercised under Article 16 of the 1958 constitution (see FIFTH REPUBLIC) by the President, although the President must consult the Prime Minister, the President of the Senate, the President of the National Assembly and the President of the Constitutional Council before declaring a state of emergency under that provision of the constitution. These powers were in fact used only once, during the period April to September 1961, and this caused considerable political controversy, especially over the powers which Parliament might continue to exercise.

In non-democratic countries emergency powers are frequently referred to as states of siege, and all civil liberties are suspended; one of many examples is the period following the military coup in Uruguay in 1972.

Engels

Friedrich Engels (1820–95), was the son of a prosperous German industrialist whose business interests extended to cotton mills in Manchester, where Engels spent twenty years of his life and witnessed conditions that had a great deal to do with his loathing for capitalism. Although attracted in his youth to the rather vague romantic radicalism of the Young Hegelians, he realized the vital importance of economics and began to think out a materialist conception of history and philosophy somewhat earlier than the man who later became his lifelong friend, Karl MARX. Indeed, Engels introduced Marx to many of the ideas that the latter made so thoroughly his own. So Engels was not only the great popularizer of MARXISM, but should also be recognized as the originator of much that has entered the Marxist canon. In particular, Engels was a first-class empirical observer, and documents such as *The Condition of the Working Class in England* contained brilliant analyses. The most popular and earliest of the great Marxist writings, *The Communist Manifesto*, was drafted by Engels and only revised by Marx. A theoretically more complex work attacking the rest of the Hegelian movement, *The German Ideology*, which is the backbone of Marxist views on social consciousness, was written by Marx and Engels jointly. Late in his life, mostly after Marx's death in 1883, Engels became closely involved with the German Social Democratic Party and fought a bitter campaign against its reformist or 'revisionist' wing. His famous attack on the intellectual leader of that faction, Eugen Dühring, entitled simply *Anti-Dühring*, became perhaps the most important vehicle through which Marxism as a doctrine reached the next generation of young socialists, who included the leaders of the Russian Revolution. Engels had himself been actively involved in revolutionary activities in 1848, the great year of European revolutions, and throughout his life was associated with working-class movements and émigré revolutionary cadres. His intellectual interests were prodigious, and his writings spanned a large number of intellectual disciplines, though Marxists have always considered his greatest service to socialism to be his editing of Marx's last great work, *Das Kapital*.

Enlightenment (or European Enlightenment)

The Enlightenment is a conventional label in the history of ideas used to cover a set of theories and attitudes developing just before and after the French Revolution, though some would date the Enlightenment as occupying the whole period from the middle of the 17th century to the end of the 18th. Its political importance stems from the way it has influenced most subsequent political thought, partly in terms of its actual content, but as much simply by destroying earlier political assumptions that had reigned throughout the early and medieval periods of European political history. Although the Enlightenment was a broad movement involving many strands of thought, it is associated particularly with writers like ROUSSEAU, Diderot, the authors of the French *Encyclopedia*, and, in Britain, with HUME, and, stretching the definition slightly, with HOBBES and LOCKE.

As far as its political influence goes, the Enlightenment creed stressed the possibility of man's own intellect planning a society on rational grounds, and denied, therefore, the traditional authority of Kings and the Church. Freedom, especially of thought, and cooperative human behaviour were the high points of the philosophy, which was, on the whole, optimistic about human nature

105

where the prevailing, religiously-derived, notion of man was pessimistic, accepting the Christian doctrine of original sin. In many
ways Enlightenment social thought was developed on an analogy
with physical science, seeking for almost mathematically perfect
designs for society. The major importance was, indeed, the rejection
of received authority, especially that of the Church, rather than any
particular specific doctrine.

Some have thought Rousseau to be responsible for the French
Revolution, because he argued that men could be, were originally,
but were not now, free, and that this freedom, possible only in an
egalitarian society, could be grasped by modern man were he only
to throw off the chains of traditional expectation. In contrast to the
conservative doctrines that were developed by, for example, BURKE
in opposition to this movement, the Enlightenment put great
emphasis on the power of independent human thought, and may
well be seen as the precursor of modern LIBERALISM and SOCIALISM,
especially in writers like J.S. MILL and other English Utilitarians
(see UTILITARIANS). A later Enlightenment thinker, KANT, summed
up the entire spirit of the movement with his motto, the title of an
article he wrote, 'Sapere Aude' ('Dare to Know'). Kant, HEGEL and
MARX followed the more continental aspect of the theories originating in Rousseau that have led to our contemporary European
socialist position, whilst James MILL, BENTHAM and J.S. MILL developed David HUME's British version of the position into Liberalism.
There was, however, an important Conservative reaction to the
challenges and threats of the Enlightenment, found in Britain with
the moderate conservatism of Edmund Burke, but in Europe in a
more sinister, more reactionary trend of thought amongst those like
De Maistre, and, innocently, amongst social theorists like DURKHEIM
that may be seen as a precursor position to FASCISM.

Entryism

Entryism is a recent acquisition into political vocabulary covering
a far from new phenomenon. It refers to the attempts by members
of extreme political movements to join, and take control of, more
moderate and established political parties. In Britain in the late
1970s and early 1980s some have believed that far left political
activists have 'entered' constituency Labour parties in the hope of
winning control of the local party executives and thus influencing
candidate selection and policy formulation at the annual party
conferences. The phenomenon is not limited to an attempted take
over of the moderate left by the extreme left. Allegations have been
made that some Conservative, and even some Liberal, constituency

parties have come under the influence of 'entryists' from the far right. As a political tactic it is as old as politics.

Environmentalism

Environmentalism is a loose concept to cover a growing, if amorphous, trend in Western politics that only started becoming important in the late 1960s and early 1970s, and whose actual political influence is still very uncertain. Broadly, environmentalism refers to a political stance in which economic growth is regarded as much less important than the protection of standards often referred to as 'the quality of life'. In practice environmentalists tend to be in favour of pollution controls, even if these reduce economic productivity, against developing extractive industries, as, for example, in the Australian environmentalists' objection to uranium mining in the Aborigine territories. They also oppose nuclear power as a major safety hazard, and in general are enemies of large-scale industrial expansion. As a political force environmentalism has had some moderate successes. In New Zealand and West Germany, for example, there are organized parties, the former called the 'Values' party, the latter the 'Green' party, both of which names give an indication of the sort of political position they have adopted. In Britain the 'Ecology' party fought in many constituencies in the 1979 election.

Although a concern for such values in itself hardly constitutes an organized set of policies for governing a society, many other policies which have a psychological rather than logical link to the central concern are espoused. Thus policies like INDUSTRIAL DEMOCRACY, liberalization of laws on private morality, and often a considerable degree of PACIFISM, are associated politically with the main ecological protection thrust. At its most fervent, environmentalism becomes a considered economic-technological policy of opposition to economic growth and commitment to a much simpler and less materially-affluent socio-economic system, through well-argued fears of depletion of world resources. There are several important international and national pressure groups such as the Club of Rome and the Sierra Lodge which may influence government policy rather more than the more widely-based political parties.

Equal Opportunities

This expresses the idea that individuals should not be impeded in their careers by such factors as their race, religion or sex. In the 1960s sensitivity to various forms of discrimination became especially strong in both the United States and the United Kingdom. The UK passed legislation—the Race Relations Act of 1968—making certain forms of racial discrimination a legal offence. The Act was strengthened in 1976, and legislation was added to cover discrimination on the grounds of sex. However, in Britain the issue of discrimination against women has been less central to political debate, and certain other forms of discrimination—for example discrimination against homosexuals—have also remained minority causes.

Equal Protection

This describes the idea that the legal system should protect all citizens from arbitrary discrimination and guarantee them equal rights. Initially it seemed that this idea was very similar to the guarantees of procedural fairness and DUE PROCESS offered in many societies. In the 20th century, however, a distinction has increasingly been made between, on the one hand, equal protection and simple procedural fairness, which offer a formal equality that may mean little where wealth, education and similar factors are unequal, and, on the other hand, substantive equal protection. In the United States in particular, the idea of equal protection has been extended from a procedural guarantee to a fuller conception of equality, albeit in a limited and restricted field.

The guarantee of equal protection in the United States is contained in the equal protection clause of the Fourteenth Amendment—an amendment which was originally passed in 1868 to protect all citizens (and especially former slaves) against the abridgment of their rights by state governments. Since the innovative era of Chief Justice Earl Warren (1953–69), the American Supreme Court has used this constitutional provision to eliminate various forms of racial discrimination and to promote its own view of constitutionally mandated standards in such areas as criminal law and desegregation (see JUDICIAL REVIEW).

Other political systems afford comparable guarantees of equal protection, although the interpretation of the doctrine will obviously vary from country to country; and even in the United States the vigour with which the Supreme Court promotes equal protection will vary according to the composition of the Court at any given time.

Equality

Equality is a doctrine with many ramifications, and though few societies today fail to pay lip service to its political importance, much depends on the detailed interpretations involved. These are discussed under EGALITARIANISM.

Equality of Opportunity

Equality of opportunity is perhaps the most basic of equalities, after equality before the law. It is agreed to be a basic social justice by all ideologies in the modern world. In principle it is simple—any job, post, status, occupation or whatever should be open to every member of society on the same terms. The terms may be stiff—a set of tests and interviews like those used for entry to the higher grades of the CIVIL SERVICE—they may be almost non-existent, as for entry to apprenticeships in the printing trade—but they must be the same for everyone. When exactly the ideal of equality of opportunity came into prominence is unclear, but the Napoleonic reforms of French institutions provide a good starting point. His position is known from two famous slogans. One, that institutions in France should provide a 'career open to the talents' indicates the basic idea, that whatever may be the relevant skills for a job, these skills should be subject to a test, and people appointed on, and only on the basis of these tests. The other slogan, about his armies, was that 'Every private had a Field Marshal's baton in his knapsack.', which well indicates the lesser aspect of equality of opportunity, the possibility of talent being rewarded inside a career track, regardless of starting point.

However obvious and simple these ideas of equality of opportunity may be in principle, they have proved to be very difficult completely to satisfy in practice. Social background, ethnicity, a host of personal characteristics can operate to impede someone's access to a post, even when those in charge of appointment sincerely attempt to free themselves of bias. Often they do not even attempt this. The British Civil Service was notorious for being recruited, despite apparently efficient objective testing, overwhelmingly from arts graduates of Oxford and Cambridge Universities. The printers' unions operated a blatant scheme of nepotism so that no one without a family connection in the trade could be employed. One major consequence of the frequent failure in practice properly to operate equality of opportunity has been the American idea of positive discrimination, whereby those who are known to have suffered less than equal chances at prestigious posts in the past are given extra chances of success now.

Equivalent Megatonnage

Equivalent Megatonnage is one of the indexes used in assessing the relative strengths of Soviet and American nuclear forces. One cannot directly compare, say, a 5 megaton warhead with a half megaton one and say that the former is ten times greater. The physics of nuclear explosions involve relatively greater impact from smaller warheads, and surplus capacity from large ones. Only in special circumstances, the destruction of super-hardened silos, for example, do the very high yield Soviet warheads give an actual advantage over the typically much smaller US missiles. Different megatonnage can be standardized roughly in units of 'equivalent megatonnage' (MTE) by the formula that: $MTE = N \times Y^{\frac{2}{3}}$—equivalent megatonnage equals the number of warheads (N) multiplied by the theoretical yield (Y) raised to the two-thirds power.

Escalation

Escalation is a term in modern strategic thought, especially nuclear war theory, which indicates an increasing violence or force in the response of one protagonist to his enemy. Thus one might start a war with purely conventional weapons (see CONVENTIONAL WAR), and when one side finds itself doing badly, it might 'escalate' by using battlefield, or 'TACTICAL', NUCLEAR WEAPONS. At this stage the other side might move to the use of major strategic nuclear weapons, 'escalating' the war further. The concept is very much based on the image of a ladder, with rungs representing different levels of force. Most strategic thought is concentrated on minimizing the 'escalating' tendencies of any particular policy, which has led to great emphasis being put on the idea of 'FLEXIBLE RESPONSE', as a replacement of the old idea of 'MASSIVE RETALIATION'.

Established Church

Established churches are religious denominations which are given special legal rights and protection by the state, but are also to some extent controlled by the state. The usual example taken is the established church in England, which is the Anglican church, and is formally called the Church of England. The very fact that this title tells nothing at all about its theology or organization, (it is, in fact, Episcopalian) but concentrates entirely on the geographical/political identity demonstrates the nature of established churches quite clearly. In the English case the state is directly involved in

110

running the church, with appointments to Bishoprics being made by the Prime Minister, with the Monarch officially the head of the church, and with any change to the very prayer book requiring Parliamentary approval.

These facts have a perfectly natural political explanation arising from the political context of the Church of England's foundation in Tudor England and the subsequent Civil War and the revolution of 1688, which led to a firm belief that religious orthodoxy was necessary for political stability, a point accepted by many political theorists as different as HOBBES and ROUSSEAU. But the establishment of a religion has equally been seen as highly illiberal, and was one of the first things to be forbidden by the American Constitution, in the first amendment. This quite probably followed the attack on the idea by the other great political thinker of the period, John LOCKE, in his *Letter on Toleration*, for Locke's liberal principles and opposition to strong state power were generally influential in the drafting of the American Constitution.

Most codes of civil rights today mention freedom of religious persuasion, and whilst the establishment of one church does not preclude others, it can be seen as unduly favouring one version of Christianity over others. Certainly a strong minority of priests and laymen in the Church of England feel uneasy and would prefer the church to be disestablished, as it was, long ago, in Wales. Britain is by no means alone in having an established church—the Scandinavian countries have established Lutheranism, and indeed ministers there are actually paid by the state as civil servants, while orthodox Christianity of all denominations has a semi-established place in West Germany, where the state assists them by levying a (voluntary) tax on their congregations. In practice it is not the formally established churches which now exert any important political influence, but those, whether the Roman Catholic Church in Italy, or versions of Islamic religion in, for example, Pakistan or Iran, that have a direct mass support with political overtones.

Ethnicity

Ethnicity refers to a sometimes rather complex combination of racial, cultural, and historical characteristics by which societies are occasionally divided into separate, and probably hostile, political families. At its simplest the idea is exemplified by racial groupings where skin colour alone is the separating characteristic. At its more refined one may be dealing with 'ethnic politics' as where, for example, Welsh or Scottish nationalists feel ethnically separated from the 'English' rulers, as they may see it, of their lands. Almost anything can be used to set up 'ethnic' divisions, though, after skin colour, the two most common, by a long way, are religion and language. Although racial political divisions have always been vital where they exist, it is probably only in the last two or three decades that other forms of ethnic politics have become vital, though this is not to say that the actual divisions have not been long established and of personal importance. There are, for example, crucial ethnicity problems in Belgium and Canada, (mainly language conflicts, but with associated religious splits), Britain (historical-cultural divisions sometimes fought around language politics but also with religious connections), remnants of such divisions in Scandinavian countries (mainly language again), to mention just a very small sample.

Ethnicity raises the whole socio-political question of national identity, which is why ethnic politics are at their most virulent and important in third world countries whose geographical definition owes, often, far more to European empire-builders than to any ethnic homogeneity. Probably one needs to distinguish between the politics of ethnicity in advanced societies, where it is somewhat of a luxury, given the overall strength of national identity and the relative importance of other basic political issues related to organizing a productive economy, and the THIRD WORLD, where ethnic divisions may be absolutely central to the problems of organizing a working political system at all.

Ethnocentrism

Ethnocentrism is a problem arising in much comparative research in the social sciences, and in any study that involves more than one social culture. The problem is one of the researcher, probably unknowingly, reading meanings into the activities of those he is studying that are foreign to them, and which cannot really be their motivation. Another way of putting this is to say that the standards by which we judge and decide are heavily culture bound, and may not be interchangeable between social contexts. One example that is often cited is the tendency of some racial groups to do badly on standard IQ tests, not because they are in fact innately less intelligent than other races, but because the sorts of questions asked, and the imaginary problems set have little or no meaning inside their sub-culture.

While an ethnocentric approach is probably always undesirable, there is in fact a difference between the perhaps inevitable failure to grasp properly the meaning of an action in a foreign culture, and the deliberate use of standards of evaluation from one's own context.

112

An example of this has often been the study of political development. In much of the earlier behavioural research on political
development the progress of a political system was often judged in
terms of its approximation to an ideal type of 'developed' system,
when what counted as being 'developed' turned out simply to mean
'being like America'. Because, for example, it is usual in technocratic
Western societies to expect professional and administrative decisions and appointments to be made on 'universalistic' or 'achievement' grounds, societies where familial relations and emotional
links were more important were judged less developed. Whilst
there may be a possibility of arguing for the superiority of standards
from one's own culture, it is necessary at least to realize that this
is a value argument, and not, ethnocentrically, to see one's standards
as somehow universal. Similarly concepts cannot be expected automatically to translate between political cultures, and thus the very
activity of comparative research, which involves at a minimum the
possibility of taxonomy, involves the danger of ethnocentrism.

For example two institutions can appear to be equivalent, two
pressure groups say, and would be judged, ethnocentrically to be
examples of the same political phenomenon. It might, however be
that in one country the emotional symbolism of what is in another
a mere pressure group transforms its legitimacy in the foreign
culture. To study the French Army in the late Third Republic on
the assumption that armies were the same sort of institutions in
France, America and the UK would, were the judgement made by
an Englishman, involve a serious ethnocentric mistake.

In a less technical context, ethnocentrism is akin to racism, being
the assumption of the innate superiority of one's own culture and
society.

Euro-Communism

Euro-Communism is the new version of Communism espoused by
some Communist parties in Western European democracies. The
two most important parties to pursue this line are the Italian
Communist party (PCI, q.v.) and the Spanish Communist party
(PCE). The root of the development lies in the need of Communist
parties in Western democracies to compete electorally with socialist
and conservative parties if they are ever to gain political power as
a result of an election. During the inter-war years Communist
parties either hardly existed or managed only barely to survive
because they were closely associated with revolutionary politics,
and with the Stalinist (see STALINISM) state in Russia. During the

113

Second World War Communist parties in France and Italy came to be more respectable because they were deeply involved in opposition to FASCISM and in the resistance movements against German occupation. Nonetheless, after the war they were still seen, on the whole, as anti-democratic, even if they fought elections. The doctrines of the DICTATORSHIP OF THE PROLETARIAT and the need to transform capitalist society totally and immediately, as well as their close connection to the Soviet Union, which had by this time become the main COLD WAR threat to Western Europe, meant that the French and Italian Communist parties were effectively excluded from the main arena of democratic politics. Slowly the Italian Communist party broke away from this position, principally under the leadership of Enrico Berlinguer, and followed the theoretical doctrines developed by GRAMSCI while in a Fascist prison. The essence of the new Italian Communism is that democracy is accepted as the only way in which the long-term aim, the transformation of Italian society to communism, can be reached. In its turn it requires at least a temporary acceptance of a mixed economy, where capitalism would still have an important role, and overall a belief in the sort of GRADUALISM that used to be preached by the English FABIAN movement. In more practical terms it has meant an acceptance of the need for Italy to remain in NATO, and a general move away from automatic support for the Soviet Union in preference for backing European institutions like the EEC. The move has certainly helped the PCI, which has been only a few per cent behind the Conservative governing coalitions in recent elections, and which was briefly in support of the Government in the late 1970s. How much Euro-Communism is a purely Italian phenomenon is hard to tell. The Spanish Communist party, only recently free to practise overt politics since the death of FRANCO, shares much of the creed, but the French Communist party, which has done increasingly less well electorally in the last twenty years remains much more staunchly Moscow-oriented, and in the eyes of some, is still fairly STALINIST. So broad is the social backing for the PCI and the PCE, and so moderate many of their policies, that it is sometimes doubted that the 'Communist' part of their labels is really very important. They may be better seen as simply socialist parties somewhat to the left of the British Labour party, but basically accepting a mixed-economy, liberal, society.

European Economic Community

Constitutionally the EEC is only one of three European internal agreements which collectively make up what is properly called The

European Communities, with a set of central institutions. These are the EEC itself, the European Coal and Steel Community (ECSC), and the European Atomic Energy Community (EURATOM). The ECSC came first, being set up in 1951 by the original six members of the EEC, France, Italy, Germany, Holland, Belgium and Luxembourg, to create one common set of policies, tariffs, taxes and to plan the production and use of coal and steel throughout the whole of industrial Europe. Britain was invited to join, as it was originally invited to join the full EEC when that was set up in 1957, but refused. The European political leaders who originated the ECSC, mainly from France, Italy and Germany, intended it from the start as the beginning of a movement to unify all aspects of economic, and possibly political, institutions in Europe, with avoidance of future wars just as much a factor in their plans as the technical economic aspects.

The next move indeed was much more political, with the attempt to set up a united military union, the European Defence Community. This idea was originally floated by the USA and the Churchill government in the UK, partly as a result of fears of escalation of the Korean war. It came to nothing because Britain again backed out, and France then feared the dangers of re-arming Germany so soon after the war, and the French Parliament refused to recognize the treaty, in 1954. However the European integration movement was becoming increasingly popular, and the full EEC, along with EURATOM was negotiated and drafted rapidly, finally coming into being with the signing of the Treaty of Rome in 1957. Once again Britain could have been in and refused. For years after that, as the benefits of free trade and large scale planning were felt, especially in agriculture, efforts were made to get Britain in after all, though this was always a controversial policy in the UK. British requests to join were systematically rejected by the French President, de Gaulle, and it was not until after his death and the election of a convinced 'Europeanist' in Mr Edward Heath as Prime Minister of Britain that the UK was able to negotiate entry, joining in 1973 when the original six members were increased to nine with the additional membership of Denmark and Ireland. Much of the character of policy was set by then, however, to fit the economic, and especially the agricultural, interests of the original members, and no British government has been entirely happy with the UK membership. The EEC was set for another round of expansion with the joining of Greece in 1980 and the likely future membership of Turkey, Spain and Portugal.

The European Communities are governed by a complicated interaction of several institutions, each varying in the extent to which

115

it represents separate national or common European interests and aspirations. Ultimate political power and decision-making rests with the Council of Ministers, consisting of representatives of the governments of the separate states. It is the least 'integration-minded' of the institutions. Council meetings are where the bloodier battles of compromise are fought, and it is essentially an arena for competing national interests. The European Commission is the Civil Service of the EEC, and the nearest thing it has to a unified government. It is not purely administrative, but has the responsibility which it eagerly embraces of putting forth suggestions and originating ideas for greater and greater integration, as well as running the day to day affairs and preparing the annual and always controversial budgets.

The European Parliament is in theory the legislative body of the community with 'Members of the European Parliament' (MEPs) now elected from each country. In practice it is powerless, having no general right to veto the laws drawn up by the Commission. The powers it does have, to refuse to pass the budget, and to force the entire Commission to resign on a motion of no confidence, are actually too strong ever seriously to be used. Until its members are taken seriously in their own countries its demands to be given a greater say in community affairs are unlikely to be granted, and at the moment its reputation as a mere 'talking shop' renders it largely invisible. (The turnout for the first direct election of MEPs in Britain, in 1979, was only 30 per cent). The final institution is the European Court of Justice, charged with hearing cases brought against member states or the Commission, usually by other member states or the Commission, but under certain circumstances by citizens of the community. In doing this it has an extremely important role in interpreting the meaning of the Treaty of Rome, and has slowly extended the influence of the original inspiration. It has also taken important steps in forcing the Commission and the member states actually to implement parts of the original design on which they had found it convenient to go slow, above all in the area of equal pay for women. There are many other European Community institutions and councils with advisory and recommendatory roles, but what actually gets done tends to be the result of interplay between the integration-minded Commission and the national-interest protecting Council of Ministers.

Since its early days there has been a decrease in the intensity of the drive to integration, and there seems little prospect of a full political integration into some form of European Federal State. Indeed, even in terms of economic integration and supranational planning the EEC is less cohesive by a long way than it was before the expansion from six to nine members. Without much doubt this has been because of the dominant role of the major single policy, the Common Agricultural Policy. The vast bulk of the EEC budget goes on subsidizing the production of foodstuffs and shoring up the European agricultural scene. Essentially the problem is the low efficiency of much European farming, and the tendency to produce surpluses of products which, were they to be sold at competitive market prices, would bankrupt thousands of European farmers each year. Britain has been particularly unhappy with this policy, because the agricultural sector in the UK is relatively efficient compared with the industrial sector, whilst the reverse is true for the rest of Europe, and the division of the budget has, in recent years, led to an annual battle between Britain and the rest of the members over UK demands for repayments, on the grounds that the UK budget contribution makes its membership a net loss.

It was inevitable that expansion would reduce the homogeneity, and thus the political consensus of the EEC, and the crucial role of the Common Agricultural Policy can only become more and more of a strain with the addition of further economically backward and agriculturally inefficient states like Greece. But in any case the initial drive towards political integration was largely a product of immediate post-war fears, and the internal political stability of Europe, along with the economic problems of the post-1973 world recession were bound to make national interest and national differences more salient as time went by.

Executive

The 18th-century French political theorist Montesquieu divided the political system into three distinct elements: the legislature, the judiciary and the executive. Each branch performed a different function and, in Montesquieu's view, ought to be kept separate from the other branches of government (see SEPARATION OF POWERS). The executive is defined as the part of a governmental system which takes decisions as opposed to making laws, although modern political systems in fact allow their executives to legislate both in the sense of determining which laws ought to be passed and, as in France, allowing them some autonomous law-making capacity.

In the United Kingdom members of the executive are recruited from Parliament, whereas in the United States and France no one may be simultaneously a member of the government and of the legislature. In many systems the term 'executive' covers both the elected political and the non-elected bureaucratic parts of government.

117

There are various types of executive, but the most important in modern democratic systems are the presidential form (see PRESIDENTIAL GOVERNMENT) and the cabinet form (see CABINET GOVERNMENT).

Existentialism

Existentialism is a rather broad label for a tradition in European philosophy that has influenced political thinkers in various ways since at least the 18th century. Its most nearly contemporary instance is in French politics with the existentialism of Jean-Paul Sartre in the inter-war, and immediately post-war, years. It is unclear whether there are any specific doctrines in existentialism that actually have a direct political consequence, and the philosophy is, in any case, one that Anglo-American culture finds difficult and obscure. Most probably the political influence of existentialism has more to do with the milieu of left-wing café society, or, as in Camus's case, radical anti-colonialism in which it was espoused than with such logical connections as one might find normally between a philosophical tradition and a political doctrine. Sartre himself was for some time a MARXIST as well as an existentialist, and his political positions derived rather more obviously from this. The nearest one could safely come to describing the politics of existentialism is to suggest that the philosophy speaks to those who see modern societies as alienating and de-humanizing, run by bureaucrats hiding behind roles, to those who would wish to destroy these aspects of state power. Indeed a general distaste for organized power, an opposition also to being forced to choose between limited alternatives in terms of organized left- and right-wing parties, a feeling that individual autonomy and creativity are being destroyed by politicians runs through Sartre's work. Especially in his famous four-volume novel of French life from the Spanish Civil War to the fall of France in 1940 *The Roads to Freedom*, Sartre certainly paints a perceptive emotional analysis of the corruption of the French Third Republic, and it may well be in the not strictly philosophical literature that one finds the political theory. This would apply equally to other modern existentialists, especially Camus, who had grown up in French Algeria and developed a hatred for the colonial mentality. In the end there is little more than a politics of despair, and a fear of power to be found as theoretical doctrine in the works. One might well link this political reaction to the politics of Kafka's *The Trial*. This is not to deny the genuine influence on many political actors, especially in the fringe left-wing groups and the militant students, and many serious critics of political theory might well wish to claim a more clear-cut political consequence for existentialism. What would probably not be denied is that its days of influence have been, at least temporarily, dead since the 1960s.

F

Fabians

The Fabian Society was set up in 1884 by a group of left-wing intellectuals in England, and was one of the groups that joined together around the turn of the century to organize the Labour party. Its predominant position has always been one of advocating peaceful political progress towards socialism, through electoral politics. Not only would they not accept the need for revolution, but they would not, as would some other non-revolutionary but left-wing members of the Labour party, accept such unconstitutional acts as the passing of an enabling bill to postpone the next election once the Labour party had won an election. Judged by today's standards there is little to distinguish Fabians from any other Social Democrats inside the Labour party. In the early days the Fabian Society was far more important, representing a powerful non-revolutionary analysis of the need for, and pathways to, socialism, when the alternatives were either pure trade-union politics, or extreme militancy.

As its title suggests, the Fabian society, (named after the Roman general Quintus Fabius Maximus 'Cunctator', famous for his tactics of delay) has always held that the road to socialism is a very long one, and one that must be trodden very slowly—one of the founders, Sidney Webb, used to talk of the 'inevitability of gradualness'. It has very little influence in the Labour party now, though its constant production of very intelligent policy discussion papers makes it a sort of semi-official party think-tank for those on the right of the party. No specific doctrines could be said to underlie Fabianism over any length of time—it does not, for example, have any particular overall analysis of the shape of the economy in a socialist country, for it is not an ideologically-organized group. In the early days important intellectuals, including George Bernard Shaw and Sidney and Beatrice Webb, were members, and it was partly the Webbs' disappointment with the actions of the post-1917 Communist Governments in the USSR that held the Fabians to their gradualist position. Today the membership is very similar, with a considerable sprinkling of senior academics and writers.

Falangism

The original 'Falange' was the Spanish Fascist movement, Falange Española, which brought General FRANCO to power in the Spanish Civil War and which he used to run the country throughout his dictatorship. Subsequent movements of a similar nature have either adopted or been christened 'Falangist' since, and the most important is currently the Christian Falange in the Lebanon.

Like POPULISM, which it resembles in some respects, it is hard to give a tight definition to a falangist movement. It really means a social and political movement in which historical traditions and ideas of national character or destiny are coupled to right wing and authoritarian practices for running a state. The most important of these traditional elements is undoubtedly the church. Not only is the Christian Falange in the Lebanon clearly church-based, but the acquiescence, at times enthusiastic support, of the Roman Catholic hierarchy in Spain was vital to Franco's success. The movement is populist in as much as it aims for cross-class support in which the religious and national identities are claimed to be vastly more important than mere economic status differences. However, whilst populism can be said to be of essence working class, and most probably based on organized labour, a falange rests more on the middle classes, tying the working class in, but depending on other institutional support, especially the church, for its authority, and lacks the minimum degree of economic re-distribution to be found in populism and some forms of fascism.

False Consciousness

False Consciousness is a concept that comes from the theory of IDEOLOGY and especially from MARXIST arguments on this subject. It refers to a state in which people's beliefs, values, or preferences are seen as 'false', that is, artificially created by the culture or society. For example, a conflict between trade unions inside a work force might be seen as false conscience, on the grounds that workers 'ought' to realize that unity in the face of capitalists is in the 'true interests' of all workers. Similarly, affluent workers who see a Conservative government as more in their interest than a Socialist one that might increase their taxes to pay for welfare benefits to the less affluent would be suffering from 'false consciousness', because they should realize that in the long run all workers are exploited by capitalist society and would want to support their less affluent proletarian brothers were they enjoying true consciousness. Clearly it is an evaluative concept, and one that requires a very powerful theory to support it. Otherwise we can all describe anything someone else wants as a 'false' interest. Nonetheless there are clear examples of people suffering false consciousness, believing that some policy will help them when it will not, or holding values and attitudes that one can easily trace to ideological conditioning or media manipulation. The problem, as with all concepts in this area, is to establish ground rules for using the arguments.

Fascism

Fascism is one of the most loosely used of all political terms. In the mouths of modern radicals a Fascist is simply anyone whom they think is fairly right-wing. It has also come to mean anyone of extreme views, especially if verbal or physical violence is used by such a person as a political weapon. Hence one sometimes hears references to 'the fascism of the left' as well as of the right. Technically this latter usage may, by accident, be more correct, because the original Fascist parties, to be found throughout Europe in the 1930s and 1940s, were ambivalent on the left/right dimension. The originally important Fascist parties were those created by MUSSOLINI (the word being of Italian and Latin derivation), FRANCO, and HITLER. As the full name of Hitler's party (the National Socialist German Workers' Party) shows, some appeal to working-class solidarity, of a largely POPULIST nature was common to most Fascist movements. (The creator of the British Union of Fascists, Oswald MOSLEY, had been a junior Labour party minister).

There is no coherent body of political doctrine that can be attributed to Fascism because all Fascist movements were opportunistic, and depended on demogogic exploitation of local fears and hatreds to whip up public support. The most common themes were NATIONALISM, often expressed in essentially racist tones as a way of building national unity in the face of class divisions, and a hatred and contempt for democracy. This latter view was usually linked to a well-developed theme of the need for firm leadership, the appeal being to the strong man who would solve a country's problems as long as he was given loyal and unquestioning obedience. Post-war outbreaks of Fascism have been few, and unsuccessful, and the tendency to assume that any right-wing group,

122

especially if it has nationalistic overtones, is Fascist is a debasement of political vocabulary. Fascism was almost certainly a unique response to a particular historical context, and as a label the word has very little place in our set of political categories.

Federalism

Originally federation indicated a loose alliance or union of states for limited purposes, usually military or commercial; and as such it could hardly be distinguished from a confederation. In the 18th century, however, the newly independent American colonies developed a model of federal government which combined a strong role for the central or national authority with a degree of independence for the hitherto autonomous states. 'Federalism' is now used to describe such a form of government, in which power is constitutionally divided between different authorities in such a way that each authority exercises responsibility for a particular set of functions and maintains its own institutions to discharge those functions. In a federal system each authority is therefore in theory sovereign (see SOVEREIGNTY) within its own sphere of responsibilities, because the powers which it exercises are not delegated to it by some other authority.

Federalism is often seen as a complex and cumbersome method of government because it involves a number of potentially overlapping jurisdictions and the maintenance of similar institutions at each level of administration; in the United States, for example, the presidency and Congress have equivalents in every state in a governor and state legislature. Federation is typically used in heterogeneous societies where it is thought necessary to allow distinct areas as much political autonomy as possible. Switzerland, with its different linguistic and religious groupings, is an example that has a history of federal association going back to the 13th century, although the modern Swiss Federation dates from 1874.

The federal model was much favoured by British governments in the process of decolonization because it allowed small entities to be linked together for defence and foreign policy, and because it seemed an efficient way to protect minorities. Northern and Southern Rhodesia and Nyasaland were federated in 1953; Malaya acquired a federal constitution in 1948; and the Federation of the West Indies was created in 1958. Many of these federations have not survived because some of the component parts wanted complete control over their own affairs; and the existence of a federal constitution has not prevented civil war and general political instability in Nigeria.

Size is also a major factor in determining whether a federal constitution is appropriate, since large areas are obviously more difficult to govern effectively from a single centre. Canada, Australia, India and the USA all have federal constitutions, although Indian federalism is unusual in that the states were redefined after the creation of the federal constitution.

The precise balance of power between the central and local authorities in federal systems will vary between different federations and over time within a particular system. In the United States, for example, powers not originally granted to the federal government (among them the power to impose a federal income tax) have been acquired by constitutional amendment. Less formal methods have also been used to alter the federal-state balance. The courts have on occasion changed their interpretation of the proper spheres of activity of the federal and state authorities, as they did with respect to reapportionment and criminal procedure in the United States in the 1960s. And the increasing dependence of the states on the federal government for financial aid has in many ways enabled the federal government to influence policies which are nominally within the control of the state government.

Two constitutional features are found in most federal systems. There will frequently be an upper house or senate (see SENATES) where the states are represented in their own right and equally, as opposed to the representation proportionate to population allocated in the lower house; and there will usually be an enhanced role for the courts since the judiciary is normally required to adjudicate in disputes between the central and local authorities (see JUDICIAL REVIEW).

Federalists

'Federalist' may be used as a general term for those who favour a federal system of government (see FEDERALISM). More narrowly the term refers to an American political faction or party which emerged at the beginning of the Republic's history and advocated a strong national government for the United States. Its main strength lay in the North, and its emphasis on the need for commercial expansion made it the natural party of the trading and manufacturing classes. Its opponents advocated a weaker role for the national government vis-à-vis the states, and were supported by the agricultural interest. The Federalist Party was dominant during the administrations of George Washington and John Adams (1789–1801), but after Thomas Jefferson's election to the presidency in 1800, the Federalists declined, and the party ceased to be important after 1830.

Feminism

The modern feminist movement stems from the middle of the 1960s in North America, and perhaps a little later in Europe, although important political feminist activities (for example, the Suffragette movement in Britain), long pre-date the contemporary phenomenon. There is no political doctrine of feminism *per se*, and the various groups and currents of thought amongst feminists are often in bitter disagreement. At the root, the movement seeks equal political and social rights for women as compared with men. The main common theoretical assumption which is shared by all branches of the movement is that there has been an historical tradition of male exploitation of women, stemming originally from the sexual differences which led to a division of labour, as, for example, in child-rearing practices.

The actual policies pursued by the feminists vary from the legalistic, in demanding greater equality of opportunity and a ceasing of sexual discrimination in, for example, employment policies and wage rates, via demands for social institutions like free day-nurseries to remove disadvantages to women in the job market, ultimately to demands for positive discrimination. There are many important and successful feminist pressure groups, but no feminist political parties, for the obvious reason that feminism of itself is a reform movement, and not a doctrine for overall government. Feminism has tended to be left-wing in general orientation, if only because it is attacking what it sees as an established power relationship. But there are major theoretical problems along this line because of the way that sexual political divisions fit very badly with the social class divisions around which the left tends to develop its thought. As a reform movement feminism has been rather successful in a short period, with equal rights legislation being passed in many countries, and with female politicians coming more and more into prominence.

Feudalism

Feudalism is one of the most misused of all terms in political analysis, because, while it has a precise meaning when used by historians to describe a particular form of medieval government, it has come to be attributed to a wide variety of modern socio-political systems which share almost nothing in common with genuine feudalism. Crudely, feudalism was the basic form of political organization that had arisen in Europe out of the shattered remnants of the old Roman Empire by the 9th century, and which reached its peak, in England anyway, after the Norman invasion of the eleventh century. It was founded on the principle that the King, or some other overlord, had rights over land that he could grant to his followers in return for services, originally military, on the basis of an oath of loyalty. At its extreme the King was actually held to own all or most of the land. The one to whom estates were granted could in turn grant what might be thought of as a sub-lease to his followers on the same sort of terms. The whole edifice of feudalism was a complex of two-way obligations, firmly set in an unquestioned set of statuses, rather than being based on contractual rights or more vague notions of citizenship or nationality. While there was no pretence of equality of rights and obligations, and no general sense of what would now be called 'social mobility' (one's position in the social order being more or less fixed at birth), the justifying ideology was one of reciprocation of loyalty.

Nowadays societies as varied as Latin American 'Latifundia' (huge estates privately owned by absentee landlords and worked by ruthlessly exploited day labour peasants) and Japanese industrial enterprises are described as feudal. This latter arises simply because some Japanese firms tend to provide homes and social lives for their workers, and because Japanese society is characterized by an unusually sharp sense of status deference. It has no more to do with the theory or reality of feudalism than does plantation slavery in the ante bellum South of the USA. There are almost certainly no genuine feudal systems in the contemporary world, largely because not only has the idea of legal ownership of property completely changed, but also because the organization of a modern state cannot survive on the basis of ties purely of personal loyalty.

Fifth Republic

The Fifth Republic is the present political system of France. It came into being in 1958, when mutinies by the French Army in Algeria proved too much for the weak government of the Fourth Republic and forced the President to invite General DE GAULLE to take office as Prime Minister. De Gaulle made it a condition of his acceptance that he be empowered to write a new constitution and submit it to the public in a referendum. His analysis was that the troubles of the THIRD and FOURTH REPUBLICS had stemmed from strong and undisciplined National Assemblies with a cumbersome multi-party system, and the constitution he designed was close to the one he had advocated for the immediate post-war Fourth Republic, with very strong presidential powers (see PRESIDENTIAL GOVERNMENT) and a much weakened LEGISLATURE. This was approved by an overwhelming majority of the electorate.

There is no doubt that the Fifth Republic has been the most successful French regime since Napoleonic times, although there are still fierce arguments about the extent to which this is the result of constitutional engineering, the General's charismatic authority, the popularity of his party (which stayed in power from 1958 to 1981) or a coincidental upsurge of economic prosperity. Politics in the Fifth Republic have certainly been more stable than in preceding regimes, and the peaceful transfer of power to the socialists in 1981, and their subsequent ability to govern with very little opposition, is in certain respects unique in French history. Coming after nearly ninety years of IMMOBILISME and ten years in which the life expectancy of a government was measured in weeks rather than months, the Fifth Republic has come to be seen by the French as constituting a radical change in the very nature of French political life. Typical evidence of its political durability is the way that the first socialist president, François Mitterrand, himself a past member of Fourth Republican governments, who had attacked the Fifth Republic for years, happily accepted the powers and authority of the presidency, an office more authoritative than France had ever had under a democracy before.

First Strike

This means the use of strategic nuclear weaponry to attack an enemy without their having launched such an attack. First strike, represents a major escalation of any conflict, and is eschewed, officially at least, by NATO forces.

One form of First Strike is the pre-emptive strike, which can be launched with either nuclear or conventional weapons. A pre-emptive strike is one aimed against some specific feature of another power's potential or actual military capacity. The intention is to prevent the other power from using that specific weapon or capacity. It was sometimes argued in the late 1950s and early 1960s, for example, that the USA should launch a pre-emptive strike against Chinese research establishments to stop them developing nuclear weaponry. Israel carried out what they claimed to be such a pre-emptive strike against Iraqi nuclear reactors in 1980, but using conventional forces. The interesting psychological aspect of pre-emptive strikes is that though they are in fact unprovoked First Strikes, they are seen by those who launch them as essentially defensive measures.

127

First World

First World is a seldom used term, though its meaning is no less clear, and no less useful, than the commonly found THIRD WORLD, which describes the underdeveloped nations of Africa, Asia and Latin America. The First World consists of the Western European and North American countries which experienced the Industrial Revolution, plus Australia and New Zealand: in effect, the advanced industrial powers of the period before the First World War. The Second World is the Communist bloc, much of it by now as industrialized as the First World, but on the basis of a different blueprint for economic organization. Membership of the Third World is therefore defined more by the dates at which political independence was achieved and economic growth started than by the actual level of economic development, although in much of the Third World this is in fact extremely low. The classification is very crude, and throws up plenty of problems. Can Argentina, for example, be classified as a Third World country when it has much the same level of economic development as New Zealand, and was politically independent earlier? Did Russia move from being a First World nation to the Second World simply because of its political change in 1917? Like all simple classifications in politics or political science, this one needs to be used very cautiously, but it is certainly a convenient portmanteau term.

Flexible Response

Flexible Response is the strategic doctrine, especially popular in the USA, which says that, in serious war situations, a government should have a whole range of possible defensive and offensive strategies available to it, so that war need not be escalated too fast in response to an attack. It is principally opposed to the doctrine of MASSIVE RETALIATION that was the mainstay of US defence thinking at the beginning of the nuclear age. The main point of the doctrine is that a leader, the US President, for example, should be able to meet an attack with increasing but highly specific degrees of force, and should be able to fire, perhaps, only one or two missiles against purely military targets, working his way up, if necessary, by clear stages to an all-out missile attack against cities. The doctrine calls for far more subtle targeting programmes by military planners, and far more accurate weapons-delivery systems, than a simple notion that, if a single missile lands on one's country, the whole arsenal will be launched against the enemy. It is sometimes attacked, nonetheless, on the grounds that the flexibility simply makes more credible, and therefore more likely, an outbreak of nuclear war.

Force Majeure

Force Majeure is a phrase which indicates that a given political outcome is dependent on the exercise of irresistible force rather than on consent, agreement or legal process. Thus a strike could be settled by *force majeure* if a government sent the troops into a factory to stop it rather than attempting to negotiate with the strikers. Or a government which had no claim to legitimacy or popular support, but simply depended on repression, would be said to rule by *force majeure*. Such a situation may be deemed to have existed in Poland following the suppression of the independent trade union Solidarity in December 1981 and the subsequent imposition of martial law.

Fourth Republic

The Fourth French Republic came into being in 1946 after the newly-liberated French electorate resoundingly rejected a continuation of the Third Republic, which had been in abeyance since the German victory of 1940 and the setting up of the collaborationist Vichy regime. The Fourth Republic was never popular, and never enjoyed the support of a clear majority of the electorate. Designing a new republic after liberation in 1944 was not easy: the first proposals for a new constitution were rejected in a referendum, and the second draft, which became the Fourth Republic, actually differed very little from the discredited Third Republic. Although this draft was given a majority vote in a referendum, nearly 30% of the electorate abstained (mainly under orders from the Communist party) and the final 'yes' vote was actually smaller than the number who had voted 'Yes' in the minority to the first draft. The main reason for this mess was that the leaders of the traditional parties who had governed France before 1940 had no wish for their parties and themselves to lose power, and feared the effects of a strong Presidency and a unicameral legislature without the conservative blocking-function of an upper house. The result was a political system no more stable than the previous Republic, with over twenty governments in its lifetime, many lasting weeks rather than years. In some ways the Fourth Republic did, admittedly, have a harder time than its predecessor. There were overt anti-system parties on both the left and the right. On the left the PCF regularly won nearly a quarter of the votes in elections, at a time when it was much dominated by Moscow and quite unprepared to accept the legitimacy of the Republic. On the right the Gaullists, who had backed a very different constitutional plan, not only opposed it publicly but intrigued against it in private, ultimately bearing a good deal of the guilt for the Army mutiny in Algeria which overthrew the government, and finally also the constitution. Indeed the specific political problems that caused it so much trouble and led to its collapse were the problems of decolonization, the first being the loss of French Indo-China to a guerilla movement, the area then becoming North Vietnam. Given that the much more stable and powerful Americans lost their war in Vietnam, the size of the task for a weakened immediate post-war European nation can be seen. The second and fatal problem was in North Africa, where France was reluctant to let Algeria become an independent Arab state. Algeria is somewhat misunderstood outside France, because to the French it was not, in fact, a colony, but an integral part of metropolitan France, with a huge number of white French residents who saw themselves as actually living in a French state, not as expatriates. This fact, combined with the bitterness of the French army, determined to recover their prestige after the disasters of 1940, and what they saw as a political betrayal in Indo-China in 1954, suggests that few governments could have hoped to resolve the problem. Indeed de Gaulle, brought to power in 1958 as a man acceptable to the army, and to be trusted to maintain the status quo because of his vision of French glory, solved it only by what the army and Algerians were to see as a worse sellout than Dien Bien Phu, the defeat that ended Indo-China. He simply accepted all the Algerian nationalist demands, and gave them independence within four years of taking office. To set against these hardly-surprising failures, one should note the extremely rapid industrialization and economic recovery, influenced largely by the entirely new Commisariat du Plan, set up by the Republic, and their vital role in creating the EEC. The Republic was never, perhaps, properly legimate to the French, hence its inability to control the threat of civil war arising from the Algerian problem, and the lack of support it got from major institutions, including the civil service in 1958, but it was from the point of view of its failure that Gaullists portrayed it. It was ill served by its parliamentarians, and by the numerous centre, centre-right and centre-left governments that ruled it in much the same squabbling fashion that had made the Third Republic a disaster of 'IMMOBILISME'. But at no time has the French parliament had the respect of either Frenchmen or foreign analysts, and the contrasting political stability of the Fifth Republic is often said to follow De Gaulle's emasculation of the national assembly and contempt for political parties.

Franchise

The franchise is another name for the eligibility to vote. Conditions attached to such ability have varied both over time and within countries. In the United Kingdom the franchise was gradually extended during the 19th century until in 1918 all men could vote, regardless of whether or not they were property holders. In 1918 also, some women obtained the vote and all women were allowed to vote by 1928. The age of voting has generally been reduced in Western democracies so that it is now 18 years in both the United Kingdom and the United States; and only Switzerland for long held out against extending the franchise to women.

Some countries place severe residence, nationality and citizenship restrictions on the franchise. In the United Kingdom people deemed to be represented directly elswhere may not be allowed to vote so that peers for example cannot vote, although the public announcement by the Archbishop of Canterbury—Robert Runcie—that he had cast a vote in the general election of 1983 raised the question of whether the prohibition against peers voting extended to the Lords Spiritual. (Peers may vote in elections for local authorities, referendums and elections to the European Parliament.) Criminals serving sentences of more than a year and inmates of mental institutions are also disbarred from voting in the United Kingdom.

Franco

Francisco Franco (1892–1975) was a Spanish army officer, the youngest general in Europe, when he joined a group of officers in rebellion against the short-lived Second Spanish Republic in 1936. During the course of the ensuing Spanish Civil War (1936–1939) he rose to pre-eminence amongst the senior officers of the 'Nationalist' army, and was made both Chief of the army and of the provisional government. His success in these roles, and also his ability to unify the disparate elements made him the supreme power in Spain once the Nationalists won the Civil War. He ruled Spain as an absolute dictator, as head of state, prime minister, head of the only legal political party, and supreme commander of the armed forces until his death.

Although he took increasingly little interest in most detailed policies, his ruthless use of well-picked subordinates, and his skilful control of mass support allowed him to remain virtually unchallenged, and ensured that his ideology prevailed. He was more or less committed to a CORPORATIST state in the style of MUSSOLINI, though much closer both to the Catholic Church and the military which became major supporting institutions to his rule as 'Caudillo'.

Over the nearly forty years of his rule he changed somewhat both the actual policies and the justifying ideology of his system, allowing Spain slowly to modernize economically and, to a lesser extent, to liberalize socially. There was never a clear theory or ideology, never a substantive 'Francoism', but always a firm adherence to a conservative, religious, anti-Communist and authoritarian orientation, with the ultimate appeal being to a glorious Spanish past sanctified by the sacrifices of the Civil War. Largely because of his own preparations, Spain moved easily into a constitutional liberal monarchy on his death.

Fraternity

Fraternity (the better translation of the French Fraternité, the original political occurrence, would be simply 'brotherhood') was one of the three slogans of the French Revolution and subsequent regimes. Although the other two values (Liberté and Egalité) are enshrined in the ideologies of most Western states, fraternity is seldom referenced. Instead the idea of brotherhood, with its implications of communal life and mutual support and respect, is found largely in the propaganda and ideology of Eastern Communist societies, or in the left-wing internationalist movements. It is a value less clear perhaps than the other two, and certainly less commented on and written about in political theory or philosophy. The main reason for its relative exclusion is probably that, while equality and liberty are essentially negative rights, in that they deny the government or others the right to do certain things, or at least place burdens on the state, for example in achieving equality, brotherhood actually demands positive actions from ordinary people. This is not to suggest, cynically, that such a call would fail, but rather that the structure of Western states, and the overall nature of their ideologies, is geared away from such values and towards an individualism and rational self-satisfaction that fits ill with such demands. As a revolutionary cry it was splendid, but as a practical value in the French regimes that followed the revolution it was harder to achieve.

Free Trade

Free Trade is an international economic system in which no country sets tariff barriers or other import controls against products from others, and in which each country has an equal right to sell its own goods in those other countries in the same terms as indigenous producers. There has probably never been a time when total free trade existed since the development of nation states, and indeed not all nations have always had internal free trade between regions. In practice alliances of nations have allowed varying degrees of freedom of trade amongst themselves and put up collective barriers against other countries. Such an alliance has often been known as a 'Custom Union', or by the German equivalent, 'Zollverein.' The most important example today is the EUROPEAN ECONOMIC COMMUN-ITY, where there are no customs barriers or tariffs that allow any discrimination between producers amongst member states on national lines, and where a common tariff is imposed on third-party states. As an example of just how hard it is actually to guarantee equal treatment of foreign and domestic producers even when tariffs are theoretically absent, one has only to see the case load of the European Court of Justice, the EEC's judicial branch, which is largely taken up by complaints that de facto discrimination is going on.

The economic arguments for free trade are complex. In general the economic theory known as the 'theory of comparative advantage' states that the global economic product will be maximized by entirely open international trade competition. However, in the short or medium run it can often be to the interests of some industry or economic sector in a country to be protected. Protection may even be in the whole national interest, though this is less likely. Typically the question of international tariff levels to be applied is a matter of political conflict inside a country, as with the intermittent conflict between capital-intensive and labour-intensive industry over tariff levels in the USA. Whether free trade is a 'left' or 'right' wing issue in a country can also vary from time to time, according to the sorts of political values that might be protected by an economic protection policy. At one stage in Britain, for example it was common for Conservatives to want to use tariff barriers to protect trade between members of the Empire. Over the last decade the left of the Labour party, disenchanted with an EEC they see as essentially capitalist and against the interests of the worker, have urged that the only solution to employment problems in Britain is to protect our domestic producers with high tariff walls.

Whatever the abstract economic theory, policy towards free trade will always be inherently political, and tariff barriers will be set as a political instrument, bringing political consequences and consequences for international politics which will be at least as important as any consequences for international economics. One constant, both historically and geo-politically, has been the acceptance of free trade by 'Liberal' parties, which have indeed at times taken adherence to this position as almost definitional of 'Liberalism', in the way that acceptance of nationalization is partially definitional of socialism. This is explained quite simply by the fact that Liberal parties have always been exponents of capitalism, and have rested on the votes and funds of the rising bourgeoisie rather than either Conservative parties or Socialist parties for whom the economic theory of capitalism does not necessarily have the same importance, even when it is not disputed.

Freedom

Freedom, along with brotherhood (see FRATERNITY) and EQUALITY, was the great rallying cry of the French Revolution, and has been, in one guise or another, an unarguable value of most societies ever since. Inevitably there are dozens of versions of freedom (or Liberty, which we treat as interchangeable) as a supreme political virtue. At its most basic, the demand for freedom is the claim that every human has the right to do exactly what he wants to do, at any time, provided only that he does not infringe the equal right of every other individual to a similar freedom. There are very few arguments positively to prove this doctrine, because, like equality, it is usually taken as an obvious natural right, the infringements of which require justification.

There are three major aspects of freedom as it has been politically important. Historically the earliest has not been a notion of individual freedom, but of national freedom as endless nations have sought to throw off foreign domination; even today the 'wars of national liberation' are still with us, and the idea of a 'free people' is still a vital coin in political currency. This ideal, of course, says nothing at all about the political and social ties to be found inside the liberated state. The second most important strand historically has been the fight for individualistic, 'legal', freedom, originally the demands of the rising economic bourgeoisie for equal political rights and economic laisser-faire against the feudal aristocracies. This was the essential meaning of 'Freedom' to the French Revolutionaries. Developing from this has been the demand for 'CIVIL LIBERTIES', for specified basic freedoms that are held to be essential to the chance for man as an individual and for mankind generally to develop and progress. Hence come demands for freedom of assembly, of association, of speech and of religious practice. Within the inevitable limits of imperfection, the basic human freedoms of this sort are available in Western democracies, although economic freedom is often held to have been severely limited in the last few decades by the need for state involvement in controlling the economy. The third broad current in discussions of freedom has come from the socialist camp. It is here held that freedom consists not only in legal permission to do or be something, but in the possibility of so doing. Thus, for example, some socialists would argue that we have very little freedom of expression in modern democracies, because while there is no legal censorship, most of the media are owned by capitalist enterprises, or the state, and thus rival, radical, views are prevented from being expressed. Any socio-economic barrier to the carrying out of desires is thus held to be an infringement on freedom, with the obvious consequence that Liberty and Equality, otherwise separate values, are forced to be inter-derived. Much of the clash between these second and third meanings of political freedom relates to deep philosophical divisions in the debate often described as being between the 'Positive' and 'Negative' conceptions of LIBERTY.

Functionalism

Functionalism, or its related theories of STRUCTURAL-FUNCTIONALISM and SYSTEMS THEORY, has been one of the most influential of all social science theories, not only in political science and sociology, but in anthropology (where it originated) and several cognate disciplines. Associated with DURKHEIM it perhaps had its heyday in political thinking within the last two decades, though it is still important. Functionalism is an attempt to find a way of comparing both the structures and the operations of all social systems by finding necessary elements common to any stable social system. Much of its origins depends on analogies with biological systems, and in just the way that a biologist might study the role of some physiological aspect, some set of cells, in the maintenance of life, functionalists have tried to understand what are the necessary 'functions' that must be carried out in any political system if it is to cope with its environment and achieve its goals, and to locate the 'structures' (political parties, socializing agencies like churches, etc.) which facilitate the functioning. The theory, which played a considerable part in the POLITICAL DEVELOPMENT researches of the post-war years, has never been uncontroversial. In particular it has been accused, because of its stress on understanding the sources of stability in political systems, of innate conservatism. However it is by no means dead as a theoretical perspective, and may well be the only large scale theory social scientists have with which to challenge Marxist thinking on its own level.

G

Gallup Poll

Gallup poll has come to be a generic name for public opinion polls, especially if reported in newspapers, in much the way we talk of 'biros' or 'hoovers' instead of ball-point pens and vacuum cleaners. The name arose because the Gallup Organisation, founded by George Gallup, was amongst the first regularly to be commissioned by the media to produce quick and cheap polls, especially in the immediate post-war world. There are dozens of polling organizations, most of which spend most of their time conducting general market research, and which use the survey techniques of market research to estimate public opinion on policies and politicians, and especially report on 'voting' intention during election campaigns. In Britain there are now several monthly series of figures on party popularity, some going back over twenty years, and most newspapers will commission a special poll from time to time on some issue of public debate. The phrase may also be used from time to time to cover other political behaviour surveys, whether commissioned by political parties or by academic researchers, though for a variety of technical reasons it is often unfair to the latter to make this equivalence.

All polls rest on the idea of taking a 'representative sample' of people, asking them a few questions, and then extrapolating the results to the nation as a whole. The idea that reliable estimates can be gained of what literally millions think from asking a few hundreds is one that laymen find very difficult to accept, though in principle the statistical theory on which the method rests is valid. All depends on two crucial matters—the sampling details and the question wordings. Very simply, the bigger the sample, all other things being equal, the safer the results. However, accuracy does not rise anything like as fast as sample sizes. Doubling a sample does not cut the error margin in half, and bigger samples are very much more expensive than small ones. The typical size of a sample

136

used by a newspaper public opinion poll is between 1000 and 2000, and yields a margin of error for any opinion figure of between 2 and 5%. Just as important as sample size is the method used to select the sample, and here 'Gallup' polls are notably less reliable than academic polls and most surveys taken by government departments, because market research firms, accustomed to the lower standards and greater cost consciousness of industrial clients, use what are known as 'quota samples'. These have considerably greater chance of being unrepresentative than fully representational, but more expensive and time consuming sampling methods. Despite these problems media public opinion polls have a fairly good record of reliability, especially when investigating clear cut issues or choices, like which way the public is going to cast its vote. (The idea that polls have a bad track record on electoral forecasting is an error, largely due to the fact that electoral systems themselves so much distort the results when turning votes-cast into seats won.) The problems really arise when subtler questions are investigated, because the wording of questions can have a crucial impact on how the sample answers them. Experiments at the time of the 1975 EEC Referendum in Britain showed that the Yes/No ratio changed violently with relatively small alterations in question wording.

Game Theory

Game Theory is an application of mathematical reasoning to problems of conflict and collaboration between rational self-interested actors. Developed in the 1940s by Austrian mathematicians von Neuman and Morgenstern, it has been applied to dozens of problems in political science, strategic theory, and even moral philosophy. To some extent it has been used practically by defence planners, and has applications within economics. The essence of all game theory applications is to analyse the interaction between strategies which actors, intent on maximizing their welfare, are bound to take, or likely to take, given certain levels of information.

The most crucial distinction probably is between two basic sorts of games, a distinction that so neatly summarizes a recurrent quality of real life politics that the terminology has entered ordinary political discourse. This is the distinction between zero-sum games and non-zero sum. Simply, one might say that a conflict between, for example, an employer and a trade union is zero-sum if there is a fixed amount of profit that the firm can make, which cannot be increased by cooperation between them, or, perhaps, that a conflict between university departments for finance is zero sum if there is no chance that the departments can do anything to increase the total university budget. The technical quality of a zero sum game is that the gains to one player (we assume for convenience that this is a two player game) exactly balance the loss to the other. A non-zero sum version of these examples would allow the total amount available for division to be increased by cooperation between the players—profits might actually go up given good labour relations, or the university budget might be increased by an Education Ministry impressed by altruistic university departments, and so on. Most political situations are probably not in fact zero sum, but most are 'played' by their actors as though they were.

By examining the likely choice of strategies of independent players it is often possible to show not only what the outcome will most likely be, but where apparently rational interest-maximizing choices, if taken by independent actors, will produce a sub-optimal pay-off for both! This is characterized by the most famous of the simple game analyses in game theory, the Prisoner's Dilemma. One assumes that two prisoners are held in separate cells, accused of a crime they committed together. To each is made the offer of turning state's evidence against the other, or remaining silent. If a prisoner gives evidence against the other, implicating himself, he will receive a minor prison sentence; if he stays silent, but is convicted on his partner's evidence, he will get a major sentence. But if both remain silent, there being no other evidence, they will both be acquitted. What do they choose? Social psychology experiments have given empirical confirmation of the theoretical prediction that they will both confess, rather than trust the other to cooperate and remain silent. Thus a sub-optimal result arrives, in the absence of malice, out of rational calculation.

One point about the prisoner's dilemma game, and it has many real political applications, is that the results depend crucially on the surrounding context, which changes the effective pay-off matrix. Suppose, for example, that both the accused are members of a criminal gang which ruthlessly punishes informers, once they are let out of prison. In this context the prediction changes. The more complicated the game, and to model any important political situation obviously requires vastly more complicated games, the more unexpected become the predictions, but also the more uncertain. One general result is to show how little our major political actions depend ultimately on rational choice, or how limited is the possibility of rationality, even on major issues, given likely information levels.

Game theory is one branch of a whole development of public-choice theories that are said to shed increasing light on social interaction, and they occupy a curious halfway house between being moral philosophy and purely neutral predictive theory. However, the great promise they appeared twenty years ago to have has not been realized, largely because of the difficulty of building sufficiently accurate empirical assumptions into the models. Where they do work, for example in predicting coalition formation in multi-party governments, the results are often intuitively obvious in any case.

Gaullism

Gaullism is a post-war French political movement originated by General Charles DE GAULLE, but by no means limited to his own views, or parties founded by him. It nowadays represents the main conservative force in French politics. There have been several Gaullist parties, the names of which change from time to time, starting with the party de Gaulle founded at the end of the Second World War, the RPF, with the current version, the Rassemblement pour la République (RPR), headed by a man, Jacques Chirac, who never held an important office during the General's life. As an overall movement it has no particularly distinctive ideology except its adherence to some of the views that were dear to de Gaulle. Of these the most important is a belief in the importance of a strong centralized state, with a powerful executive and without France's traditional burden of a powerful but anarchic parliament, which had weakened and made ineffective all governments during the Third and Fourth Republics. This had been de Gaulle's aim at the beginning of the FOURTH REPUBLIC, and it was what he created in the FIFTH REPUBLIC. Even this, though, is by no means new as an ideal in French politics, being a re-interpretation of the JACOBIN tradition. The other vital element of de Gaulle's thinking accepted by modern Gaullism is the importance of French national independence and a suspicion of internationalist movements. Thus de Gaulle partially took France out of NATO (q.v.), and the Gaullists are still lukewarm to France's membership of the EEC (q.v.). This position went hand in hand with a stress on France's own military forces—de Gaulle created a nuclear deterrence force, and the Gaullist parties have always been determined to keep up such independent military strength. De Gaulle himself had a more complicated political philosophy built round a distinction he drew between 'Noble' and 'Base' politics. Noble politics, which he felt he practised as President of the Republic, had to do with uniting the nation and leading it in crucial areas of the PUBLIC INTEREST, being a non-partisan activity. Indeed de Gaulle derided political parties as divisive and often corrupt, and his personal relations with his own political parties (they never, in fact, had 'party' in their titles) were always distant and aloof. In contrast 'base' politics were the politics of haggling and compromise on private or sectional interests, which he felt were best left to others, especially parliament, in the day-to-day running of society. Politically the Gaullists are now a fairly orthodox conservative party, with a predictable support amongst the middle and upper classes, the religious, the older, and, often, women. Originally it had been an ideologically diverse movement, united above all by a commitment to de Gaulle as a national saviour, and to the need to fight for the stability of the Fifth Republic. Now de Gaulle is dead and the Republic safely entrenched it has narrowed its ideological and voting base, but remains well organized and politically the main opposition to the united French left.

General Will

The General Will is a political concept that originated, in its most detailed form, with J.-J. ROUSSEAU in his *Social Contract*, although similar ideas have always existed in political thought. For Rousseau the General Will meant the collective decision of all the people in a state when they tried to consider only what was good for the whole society rather than what they wanted as individuals. He contrasts the General Will with 'the will of all', which is merely an aggregation of the separate desires of selfishly-oriented individuals. Rousseau believed that the supreme political value, liberty, could only be assured when each man only had to obey those laws he himself created and accepted. It was his theory that, if a society could be organized so that it was ruled by the general will, by this collective view of what was best for all, then in a fundamental way everyone would be free, because no one could oppose such a decision, and would therefore only be bound to do what he believed in. Hence would follow total freedom but without anarchy or licence.

Clearly much depends in such a theory on the design of the society and the state, in order that the general will, if indeed it exists, can emerge. Much of Rousseau's profounder social theory is addressed to the question of how to get such an organization. The first vital part was a commitment to small-scale societies with full political participation in all decisions by every citizen. While not historically particularly accurate, Rousseau's admiration for the classic Greek city state, and for some small and apparently partici-

patory contemporary societies such as Geneva, led him to believe
that it was possible under such conditions for sectional interests
and political self-seeking to be banished, and for this drive to decide
only in the public interest to be victorious, thus achieving the rule
by General Will. He was aware of much that would be needed
sociologically before this could happen—advocating, for example,
a high degree of economic equality, a great emphasis on collective
activities, a ban on parties or cliques. Although few today are quite
happy either with the slightly metaphysical undertones of the
General Will, or the feasibility of organizing small face-to-face
societies with total political participation, his ideas are still the
motivation for much of the interest in PARTICIPATORY or 'DIRECT'
DEMOCRACY. The General will as a doctrine relates to similar concerns
that have become, if anything, more rather than less popular
recently, such as the COMMON GOOD and the PUBLIC INTEREST, which
remain both matters of common political parlance, and topics of
fierce academic debate in political theory.

Gerrymandering

Gerrymandering is the deliberate drawing of electoral districts or
constituencies—whether at the national or local level—in such a
way as to secure a partisan advantage and to distort the outcome of
the election. The term is of American origin and derives from the
name of Governor Eldridge Gerry who, as Governor of Massachu-
setts, in 1812 created abnormally shaped constituencies which
looked like salamanders. Gerry plus mander thereby produced the
word gerrymander.

It is probable that all democratic systems indulge in some kind
of gerrymandering but in most political systems the worst excesses
of gerrymandering are reduced by making the electoral districting
or redistributing process placed in the hands of some neutral
officials. The machinery varies from country to country but however
hard most systems have tried there is almost always a point at
which political self-interest can still enter the constituency drawing
arrangements. In Britain the task of redrawing constituencies is
performed by the Boundary Commissioners, although there are still
opportunities for the government in power to affect the timing of
the implementation of any report. Thus in 1970 the Labour Home
Secretary James Callaghan was thought to have delayed implementation of the Commissioners' recommendations, fearing that redistribution would aid the Conservatives and harm Labour.

In the United States since 1962 the courts have played an increasingly important role in ensuring that congressional state, and local districts are of equal or nearly equal size, although the standards for estimating this 'equality' have varied considerably (see also JUDICIAL REVIEW; EQUAL PROTECTION). The move towards a strict interpretation of the 'one man one vote' injunction of the constitution also reflected an appreciation of the fact that under the existing pre-1962 practice urban areas were under-represented by comparison with rural ones and that hence many urban based minorities (especially blacks and chicanos) might be unfairly treated in the legislature. However, despite the decisive moves of the American Supreme Court, it would be a mistake to see the gerrymandered district as having disappeared from American political life. Each reapportionment exercise is permeated by partisan manoeuvring and the simple elimination of numerical inequalities between constituencies has not prevented the construction (often with the aid of very sophisticated computer techniques) of constituency units designed to favour one party over another.

Government

The term 'government' is a general one used to describe both the body that has power in a given unit—whether national, regional or local—and the whole constitutional system. There are many different forms of government such as DEMOCRACY, autocracy and DICTATORSHIP. The first systematic study and classification of the methods of government was probably that undertaken by ARISTOTLE and since that time political scientists have been involved in distinguishing the different features of government and politics.

Gradualism

Gradualism is, very broadly, a version of socialism which denies the need for revolution, and argues instead that the ordinary and 'slow' means of competitive democratic politics can, in time, produce the needed changes in social and economic organization. Thus gradualism is the creed of SOCIAL DEMOCRAT parties, and of all socialist and communist parties which are prepared to compete against Liberals and Conservatives in normal elections. The Italian Communist Party (see PCI) and the British FABIANS, from rather different positions are gradualists, whilst the French communists (see PCF) and extreme left splinter parties everywhere would despise them as 'selling out' socialism or being REVISIONIST. Theoretically the difference hinges on arguments about the possibility of teaching the public to want socialism by example, by minor changes when a socialist government can get elected, or forcibly creating a socialist society as soon as power can be won, peacefully or otherwise, and producing immediately the sort of state that people 'ought' to want.

Gramsci

Antonio Gramsci (1891–1937) was the founder of the Italian Communist Party after it split from the Socialist Party. When the party had to go underground during the Fascist period, Gramsci underwent a long term of imprisonment, and died in prison. During this period, however, he laid the foundation for the specifically Italian brand of communist tactics and thought which later, under the post-war Republic, allowed the party to attract the largest support of any European communist party. His major work in this area, the famous *Prison Notebooks*, are the source for much of this inspiration and indeed for the whole EuroCommunism movement.

Although Gramsci never dropped the theoretical basis of communism, remaining always committed to the doctrine of historical materialism, he did drop the insistence on a violent proletarian revolution. He made a distinction between tactics for the socializing of a state between the 'tactics of siege' and the 'tactics of movement'. The former was the traditional notion of building class consciousness inside a working class ideological ghetto, ignoring all reformist movements, and waiting (as though besieged by an enemy) until the final moment of the 'true revolutionary situation'. This, the working doctrine for example of the French communist party, and the one that had been forced on the Russian Bolsheviks by their situation and the nature of the Tsarist regime, he felt was quite out of place in Italy. Instead he wished to adopt a much more flexible approach by which the communist movement would seek to ally with progressive forces, and seek to win to its cause those members of the bourgeoisie who had no long term reason to support the capitalist state. At the same time the party should try, by its allies in the media and educational structures to propagandize the whole society, to win a willing acceptance of communism, rather than try to enforce it by a dictatorship of the proletariat. This flexible and non-violent tradition of Italian communism has enabled the contemporary party to advocate the 'Historical Compromise', by which it can hope to join the ruling Christian Democrats in power.

143

Green Socialism

Green Socialism is a name sometimes given to ecological or environmental political parties and movements. The important West German ecology party is actually officially called the 'Green Party'. Green socialism more broadly refers to the concatenation of liberal and socialist values, often attractive to middle-class radicals, which do not form a major part of the class interests of traditional working-class left-wing groups, whose attitudes to cherished values like racial tolerance or freedom of speech is not necessarily very different from orthodox right-wing movements. Rather than a concentration on the entirely pragmatic and materialist improvement of living conditions, Green Socialism is likely to be concerned with more abstract values.

Group Theory

Group theory, in political science, is largely associated with BENTLEY and, in various reformulations, with PLURALIST writers. The central argument is that societies consist of a large number of social, ethnic or economic groups, more or less well-organized, in political competition with each other to put pressure on the government into producing the policies favourable to the relevant group. Versions of this theory can either claim that it is entirely compatible with the aims of democracy, and that group representation satisfies democratic norms, as well as being empirically realistic, or can alternatively be used to argue that all societies have the same true structure, whatever their surface ideology and characteristics. Other branches of political science have taken the nature and multiplicity of groups as vital elements in determining political stability or indeed the liberalness or otherwise of the society.

Guerrilla Groups

Originally guerrillas were unorthodox soldiers fighting behind enemy lines, challenging conventional forces with harrassing actions, and never allowing themselves to be forced into a pitched battle where the conventional superiority would defeat them. The word is of Spanish origin, dating from the Napoleonic Peninsular wars, when some Spanish partisans kept up such unconventional combat. Still in this original sense, the heyday of guerrilla warfare was in the Second World War and after, in Asia. Mao's peasant armies, when fighting the better equipped Nationalist forces in

China, resorted to such techniques, and, indeed, Mao Tse-Tung wrote what is still probably the definitive textbook. Thereafter independence movements elsewhere in Asia, especially in Malaya and what was then French Indo-China used the tactics to try to force out colonial powers. In Malaya the British army managed to develop counter-guerrilla tactics which worked effectively, but Ho Chi Minh's guerrillas ultimately defeated the French colonial forces, leading to the creation of North Vietnam. Subsequently guerrilla warfare contributed to the defeat of the US forces in South Vietnam.

Since the 1960s the phrase 'guerrilla groups' has taken on another meaning, to cover the so-called 'urban-terrorists', the extreme left-wing groups like the Red Army Faction, the Bader-Meinhoff gang, and similar violent opponents of the regime in Italy. The tactics are analogous in as much as they consist of sniping and harrassment raids against the State power, rather than the building of a conventional revolutionary underground intended to fight a pitched battle against police and army. Part of the theory of guerrilla warfare was always to try to force the conventional enemy into repressive actions which would cause those exerting the repression to lose the support of the population, and this is very much the thesis on which Bader-Meinhoff etc. fight.

H

Hawks

Hawks, and their opposites, 'DOVES', came into prominence in America in the days of the Vietnamese War (1962–74). Hawks were those who favoured tough military activities and a general violent solution to problems. Hawks, for example, would be in favour of President Nixon's bombing of Cambodia in 1971, and would be less than interested in Strategic Arms Limitation Talks (see SALT). Since then the word 'Hawk' has expanded its range to refer to any tough approach to almost any problem. One might be, or be seen as, Hawkish, if one supported Israel against the PLO (q.v.), but, to take another example, the stringent regulation of picket lines in industrial disputes could be hawkish. Although it often has overtones of conservative or right-wing political views, the emphasis is more on the use of force and coercion rather than diplomacy and negotiation. Thus a left-wing pressure group might have its hawks and doves, in terms of preparedness to go in for demonstrations or street confrontations with authority.

Heads of Government

The term 'head of government' refers to the person—whether designated prime minister or president or chancellor—who is formally the person appointed to head a GOVERNMENT. Usually the person appointed to be the 'head of government' will be the leading member of his or her party, although sometimes a compromise figure may be asked to form a coalition.

Heads of State

The head of state is the person who exercises a number of formal and ceremonial powers and responsibilities such as receiving visiting monarchs and other heads of state. Usually the head of state will have some residual—almost referee-like political powers—such as the appointment of a head of government or prime minister. In some systems the obvious head of state is the monarch. In others it is a president whose political powers may vary considerably. In some countries such as Israel or Zimbabwe the degree of real political power is very limited except when, as occurs quite frequently in Italy for example, coalition formation requires the exercise of discretion in relation to the selection of a prime minister likely to be able to form a government capable of commanding the support of the parliament. In some systems again the roles of chief executive—with real political power—and head of state are merged and this is obviously the case in the USA. In other political systems—notably France in the FIFTH REPUBLIC—there is an ambiguity surrounding the role of the president whose powers and responsibilities may vary according to particular political circumstances and the personality of the incumbent.

Hegel

Georg Wilhelm Friedrich Hegel (1770–1831) may well be the most influential philosopher and political theorist Germany has produced, with the possible exception of KANT. He follows in a European tradition influenced by ROUSSEAU and having important connections with PLATO and the Classical Greek philosophers. His influence, though often of a tenuous nature, is undeniable across an enormous range of modern social thought, but especially MARXISM, though he would not himself have been in any way a Marxist. No one could reduce the subtleties of Hegel's thought to a dictionary definition. The only approach is to identify a few of his most influential ideas. To start, he argued that human civilization was the story of intellectual and moral progress, and that this was not accidental but the working out of a rational spirit in human perception. This is one of the ways in which he influences Marxists, who also believe in human progress, though they would attach much more importance to material or technological change, whilst Hegel saw the real source and description of progress as lying in our collective intellectual development. Secondly, his detailed account of change and development, the 'Dialectical Argument', has been taken over by Marxists, but also by many other schools of thought. The Dialectic, to Hegel, is the process in which any given social or intellectual state contains an essential contradiction. This contradiction forces a conflict (of ideas to Hegel, of interests to others). As a result we must see human history as a series of conflicts

147

where a 'thesis' (the original state or idea) conflicts with an 'anti-thesis' to produce a result, the 'synthesis'. But the synthesis itself must contain an internal contradiction, and on we go again. Although such ideas usually seem extremely metaphysical, Hegel's writing is often down-to-earth and illustrative, and shows how useful a dialectical approach can be. In practical terms his major importance is as a precursor of Marx, but Marx radically changed Hegel's perspective, by taking material rather than intellectual matters to be crucial. Hegel tended to believe that the STATE was the most important aspect of politics, and much of his more directly political argument was concerned with the development of the State. For Hegel the State, the way we organize our politics and our systems of social coercion demonstrated our degree of rationality, so the State was the best measure of human progress. He raises so many issues that most subsequent political theories can be related to his work. Apart from Marxism the most obvious is the work of another German social thinker, of even more vital modern relevance, MAX WEBER.

Hitler

Adolf Hitler (1889–1945) was the political and military leader of Germany from 1933 to his death at the end of the Second World War, which he caused. He had been a junior corporal in the First World War, a failed artist, a rootless but emotionally and intellectually powerful man who took control of a set of post-war movements of the German right wing in the early and middle twenties. In the chaotic conditions of the WEIMAR REPUBLIC his party, offering a violent and aggressive assertion of nationalism, populism, and racism, and bearing the nowadays self-contradictory title of 'National-Socialist German Working Man's Party', was one apparent answer. Hitler ruthlessly used any phobia he could find in the German population, especially ANTI-SEMITISM, to build up an emotional support for his party against the apparent threat of the Communists, with whom his semi-military party fought in the street demonstrations in German cities. Ultimately he came to power as a result of ordinary electoral politics, and managed to get himself appointed leader, 'Führer', of Germany for life. Once in legal power he and his party took over all aspects of German life, controlling totally the military and police powers, and much of industry, as well as the whole of civil government. There were no elections allowed in Germany during his rule. His aim was the creation of the 'Thousand Year Reich', a new German state that he hoped would cover most of Europe, and which did, for the duration of the Second World War, very nearly achieve this.

Although arguments both about Hitler's personal responsibility for the crimes against humanity carried out by his organizations, and the responsibility of the German people for them, will never be settled, it is undeniable that he was responsible for initiating a movement of fanatical and violent aggression through Europe which took the combined force of the British Empire, Soviet Russia and the USA to overcome. As far as political science goes, Hitler poses two enormous questions. Firstly, how does a movement like his take over a major civilized nation, and secondly, how can one describe the TOTALITARIANISM he represented, or even begin to make such a political system comprehensible inside the usual terms of the social sciences? There are no totally satisfactory accounts of Hitler or his impact, but inevitably parallels are drawn between him and STALIN and Idi Amin as examples of huge and evilly-used political power, the most recent of which is the Cambodian leader Pol Pot. There seems to be an inexplicable tendency for single individuals to wield enormous and catastrophic power at odd times in history, and this (witness, for example, the Roman Emperor Caligula) is not a recent phenomenon. The nearest to an explanation to be offered involves the idea of CHARISMA.

Hobbes

Thomas Hobbes (1588–1679) is perhaps the most famous English political theorist. He wrote during the time of the Commonwealth and the Restoration, and his whole political theory is deeply influenced by the English Civil War. His most famous book, *Leviathan*, tries to present a blueprint for a social system which would be stable and minimize the dangers of anarchy and lawlessness, which Hobbes thought threatened all societies. He is one of the earliest users of the SOCIAL CONTRACT approach, and its associated concept of 'the STATE OF NATURE'. His thought is very complicated, and can only be summarized at great risk of misleading, but the central point is a very deep distrust of human nature, which he held to be fixed and unchangeable. To Hobbes all men, left to themselves, were predatory, greedy, cruel and frightened of others. Thus he argues that only the toughest and most draconian of states, with supreme power, can possibly hold them under control and allow the development of civilized life. Above all he is concerned to remove all sources of competing political authority in the state. There are no rules governing what the sovereign can do to a citizen, because to have such rules would imply some qualification to one's absolute duty to obey. If such a limitation existed, who would judge it? A court? But that would set up a rival authority. Similarly he insists that his sovereign have the right to rule on religious truth, because to allow the church to do that might again set up challenges to authority. Although it can make dreary reading, the development of his argument is subtle and powerful, and Hobbesian ideas permeate many thinkers who would not accept the label. His intellectual commitment was to produce a true 'science' of politics, and he was particularly influenced by the developing mathematical sciences of his day, trying to produce a social science with the same logical certainty.

Human Rights

Human Rights, one of a family of concepts like CIVIL RIGHTS or LIBERTIES, or NATURAL RIGHTS, are those rights and privileges held to belong to any man, regardless of any legal provision that may or may not exist for them in his legal system, simply because man, as man, may not be forbidden certain things by any government. Exactly what the list of these rights is, or why we are entitled to them, varies from thinker to thinker. Since the Second World War there have been several quasi-official listings. The two most prominent are probably the United Nations Charter of Human Rights, and the European Declaration on Human Rights. This latter is actually partially enforceable, because it forms the legal basis for the European Court of Human Rights, to which citizens of subscribing nations may bring cases against their own governments. Typical elements on any list of basic human rights will be, for example, the right to freedom of speech, religion, the right to family life, the right to fair trial procedures in criminal cases, the right to be protected against inhumane punishment, the right to political liberty, and so on. Philosophically all these lists and institutions derive from a long-developed notion of NATURAL LAW or NATURAL RIGHTS, but the modern applications can often be quite mundane, if still important. As examples, cases to the European Court of Human Rights have varied from complaints against court-martial procedures in the Netherlands Army, restrictions on press freedom in English cases arising from contempt of court orders, to the validity of corporal punishment in Scottish schools, and the access to lawyers of German suspected terrorists. Human rights are aspects of the permanent fight of citizens against the power of the state, and are to be found, in some language or other, as a working part of most legal systems and most political theories.

Hume

David Hume (1711–1776) was a philosopher and political thinker of the Scottish part of the ENLIGHTENMENT. Although he is principally famous as a philosopher, his importance as a political thinker is still considerable, and perhaps too often disregarded. As a philosopher he was noted for his defence of empiricism, and this resoundingly common-sense approach spread over to his political theory. In some ways he can be seen as a precursor of two vital movements in social thought, the creation of a UTILITARIAN approach to political and social philosophy, and as an instigator, also, of a 'value-free' political science based on the idea that one must build up scientific generalizations from observing actual social behaviour rather than deducing them from any notion of innate norms or moral truths. His major political works consist of a section of his principal work, the *Treatise on Human Nature,* and a collection of essays on political topics. A good example of his approach to political questions comes from his treatment of property law. Hume argues not that any particular set of laws about rights to property have any special rectitude but simply that, in order to have an organized and efficient social system, there must be some set of fixed rules. Thus for him NATURAL LAW is a highly pragmatic set of rules fitting particular circumstances. Similarly he provides a defence for Aristocracy (which would hardly be accepted today) not on some special, even 'divine' right of the landed gentry, but simply in terms of the likely commitment to social stability and sensible long-term policy-making of those with a permanent, but self-interested, reason to wish for the best return on their investments.

I

ICBM

ICBM stands for Intercontinental Ballistic Missile—the huge nuclear weapons systems, almost unstoppable, that are the core of the nuclear stalemate existing between the USSR and the USA. There is a broad distinction between SLBMs, (submarine-launched ballistic missiles, such as the American Polaris and Trident) and land-based systems. Much of the effort in the SALT (q.v.) and START. negotiations is involved in trying to reduce the number of ICBM systems. There exist also IRBMs (intermediate range ballistic missiles), which are important in arguments about limited wars, because they could hit Russian targets from Western Europe, or vice versa.

Ideology

Ideology may be the most difficult, but the most often used concept in the social sciences, and one that has endless submeanings in both academic and every-day discussion. The simplest definition is probably given by a translation of the German word *Weltanschauung*, which is often used as though intertranslateable with 'ideology'. This translation would render 'ideology' as 'World-view', the overall perception one has of what the world, especially the social world, consists of and how it works. An ideology, and most students of ideology would want to say that we all had one, though often without realizing it, is a complete and self-consistent set of attitudes, moral views, empirical beliefs and even rules of logical discourse and scientific testing. The point is that ideologies, which tell us what we should or do want, and how to achieve these goals, are often held to be highly relative, even purely subjective. Thus a 15th-century Bishop, 19th-century mill owner and 20th-century Russian soldier are all expected to see the world in crucially different ways that might not ever be capable of reconciliation. Not only would they all have different values, they would have different and

152

incompatible explanations for why they valued what they valued. In the MARXIST and HEGELIAN traditions of social thought these 'world-views' are supposed to be related to one's social, and particularly to one's class, position. In this version, factory owners and factory workers actually understand their society in quite different ways, although it is also held that the ruling class of any society permeate their own ideology into all other classes. Very simply, a capitalist will see his profit as the necessary and valid return to his investment of money and effort, while the worker *would* see it as an unfair result of exploitation, unless he has been ideologically manipulated into accepting the owner's own views, and into acquiescing into a FALSE CONSCIOUSNESS, which leads him wrongly to see the capitalist's version of reality as inevitable and true. There are major theoretical problems with such a full version of the idea of ideology, especially the obvious questions about why one rather than another world-view should be given more credence. There are also many much weaker versions of the word 'ideology' current in both real political argument and academic political discourse. Often an ideology means nothing more than a particular set of beliefs and values, with no particular view about which set is correct, nor any special theory on how they come about. Some modern social scientists of the Political Behaviour (see POLITICAL SCIENCE) tradition would even wish to deny that ideologies are commonly-found phenomena at all, believing instead that only a minority of the population have any coherent and logically-consistent views on any social matters.

Immobilisme

Immobilisme is a French term, especially applied to the politics of the Third and Fourth Republics (1870-1940, 1946-1958). Under these systems France had no strong central executive government. Instead all power was vested in the National Assembly, from and by which governments and Prime Ministers were elected. Because of the multiple divisions in French society, and the complex multi-party system that emerged from these cleavages (much helped in the Fourth Republic by a proportional representation Voting system) cabinets were extremely unstable coalitions. At times the life of governments was measured only in days, and few lasted more than a year. In consequence, especially as fellow members of the same coalitions were often in deep disagreement about policies, no coherent and lasting set of governmental priorities and policies could be developed. The consequence was that very little was ever achieved as a result of government initiative. Hence the system came to be seen as 'immobile', as incapable of doing anything to adapt France to changing socio-economic trends. In fact, in many ways, the Fourth Republic did adapt fast, with rapid growth rates and increasing affluence. This however was almost entirely due to the efficiency and power of the administrative civil service, who came to be undisputed masters of the departments of state, no political minister remaining long enough to take control. Certainly almost nothing of value came from the politicians themselves, many of whom, on both the left and right, were in any case mortal enemies of the regimes. Thus such a political system has come to be called 'immobiliste', referring above all to the absence of democratically inspired political leadership. Most commentators would see contemporary Italy in the same light, and it is arguable that, though for different reasons, the enervation of the Eisenhower Presidency with a hostile Congress produced an 'immobiliste' government in the USA during the 1950s. Though with no precise referent outside France, the term remains both vivid and useful.

Imperialism

Imperialism is the policy or goal of extending the power and rule of a government beyond the boundaries of its original state, and taking into one political unit other nations or lands. There can be some variation whether the states that make up the empire retain some degree of independence and identity, or are all swallowed entirely into the administrative and political institutions of the original imperial state. Nor is it necessary that an empire has any specific form of central government, though there must be one central and ultimately overwhelming force otherwise it is more likely to be an alliance or league or loose federation. The British Empire at its height was a constitutional monarchy, but Victoria had lost most of the power of the previous English monarchs, and the empire was essentially a parliamentary one.

In fact though there have been many empires in world history, few have lasted as long as the modern nation states of Europe, and most have collapsed either because of political disunity at the centre, or because of the enormous difficulty of exercising central rule over long distances and against the instics for local autonomy that always spring up. The motives for creating an empire vary greatly, but imperialism in itself should not be confused with COLONIALISM, which is a specific form and motive for holding political control beyond national boundaries. A crucial aspect of imperialism, and one of the best aids to categorization, is the way in which imperial citizenship is handled. If only citizens or subjects of the original 'homeland' can be seen as citizens of the empire, and the rest of the inhabitants are no more than subject peoples with no hope of political power or legal protection, the empire is likely to veer towards the principally exploitative version that is better thought of as colonialism. On the other hand, and the later Roman Empire may be the best example, citizenship, with its legal rights and duties, may be extended to the entire population, or some part of the population, of the whole empire, rather than just the descendants of the nation that built it. In this case the empire is more in the nature of a supranational state which, given the artificiality of national borders in many cases, need be no less legitimate than any nation state.

Independent Republicans

The Independent Republicans are the French political party organized and led by Valéry Giscard d'Estaing while he was a minister under DE GAULLE. They were continually a part of the Gaullist ruling coalitions until the defeat of Giscard in 1981. In the ensuing National Assembly elections, though they lost seats as did everyone but the left, they remained a serious political presence and not one to be dismissed by the Gaullist RPR as unnecessary to their future hopes of a return to power. It is, in fact, difficult to assess the true popularity of the party in recent years in France, because the IR and the RPR had an electoral pact by which only one or other party stood in each constituency. They probably have potentially not much less support than the RPR. Politically they are difficult to categorize, though their centre of gravity lies somewhere on the left, or liberal, side of conservatism. They are, however, in some ways a throwback to old THIRD REPUBLIC traditions in France. Their deputies are mainly local notables, with established positions in their constituencies, interested more in the traditional French parliamentary game of looking after the constituency as a sort of ambassador to Paris rather than ideologically-driven representatives of class or other social group interests. The profile of their voters shows them typically to be older, more often Roman Catholic, more frequently female than the norm, and this to some extent belies the liberal part of the liberal-conservative programme their original leader tried to work for when he was President.

155

Industrial Democracy

This is a theory capable of more or less dramatic and general application. At its more limited it often means no more than that workers should be given more say in the detailed organization of their working lives, or that the profits of a firm should be ploughed back into wages for those who work in the firm. Limited experiments have been carried out in this way, often at the instigation of industrial efficiency experts. Some firms in the UK are actually owned by their workers, though this often results in a management structure indistinguishable from an ordinary capitalist enterprise. In a similar way some countries, notably West Germany, make legal provision for the representation of the unions on the boards of directors.

A more full-blooded version of the theory seeks to replace ordinary REPRESENTATIVE DEMOCRACY with a system in which industrial enterprises constitute the state, and wherein each productive unit is controlled democratically by the workers who will make all production, pricing and pay decisions. The plans for the integration of these multiple productive units are various, though they all seem to require some further degree of representation, or federal organization via inter-industrial councils. Yugoslavia is often (and rather optimistically) cited as a real example of workers' democracy, though in fact this country seems only to practise a limited degree of practical decision-making on the shop floor, rather than a replacement of ordinary political and administrative machinery. Some of the more creative thinkers in modern socialism, however, have toyed with the idea of industrial democracy, as in the case of William Morris and Ruskin.

Industrial Participation

Industrial participation, or industrial democracy, are political goals, covering a wide range of detailed alternatives, and espoused by a suprisingly wide range of ideological positions. At the core all the variants aim to break down the line of command hierarchy which characterizes modern industry, and in particular to remove the class/power distinction between workforce and management. The motivation for such plans can be the elimination of work alienation, a desire to link the interests of the workforce more clearly with the interests of the industry or firm, the increase of overall human freedom, or more far-reaching intentions to restructure either just the economy or the whole polity on egalitarian and democratic lines. Just as the motives vary considerably in ambition, so do the techniques suggested. At the lowest level of ambition, industrial democracy may mean nothing more than profit-sharing schemes, an encouragement and facilitation to workers owning shares. It may imply, instead, trade union representation on boards of directors, as is the case in Germany and was planned by the Bullock report for Britain. Some firms are in fact entirely owned by the workforce, and have management decisions made by meetings of the worker-owners, though these are rare and have seldom proved successful in capitalist societies. The full-blooded theory of industrial democracy, however, is an entire rival theory to capitalism or the communist system of state ownership. Developed by such thinkers as, in Britain, Cole, it imagines the replacement of ordinary REPRESENTATIVE DEMOCRACY with DIRECT DEMOCRACY, not only in the commune but in the individual factories and firms. In these workplaces the workers would be entirely independent and would make all decisions of production, pricing, sales, as well as salaries, themselves. The firms would only loosely be grouped in representative bodies, and there would be no more state control of the economy than of any other aspect of life. The problems of co-ordination raised by such theories are legion, and the whole approach belongs inside anarchist theory generally. Much of the enthusiasm for varieties of worker-control is fuelled by an admiration of the Yugoslavian experiment along these lines. This, though in many ways successful, is by no means as widespread or radical a departure from orthodox management as is often believed. Despite the theoretical difficulties and scarce experience, industrial participation remains for many political activists an attractive alternative to the two major ideologies of industrial organization.

Initiative

The initiative, which is found largely in the United States, is a method whereby a group of citizens can put a legislative proposal before the electorate directly for determination in a REFERENDUM. The proposal may be to enact a new law, to repeal an existing law or to amend the constitution. It became popular in the late 19th century when criticisms were voiced of the party machines in the United States. The initiative, referendum and recall thus appeared a way of by-passing the parties which controlled the legislatures of the states and proved successful as a method of obtaining progressive reforms. It remains important at the state level in the United States, although the advent of such techniques as direct mail have meant that it can be manipulated both by political parties and interest groups. It also remains important in countries such as Switzerland where the REFERENDUM is a significant institution.

Inquisitorial System

The Inquisitorial system is a version of criminal law systems, and is common everywhere in the CIVIL LAW world. It describes the mode of trial in criminal cases, where the court, either a single judge or a bench of judges and assessors, seeks directly to ascertain the truth of the charges brought. The court will interrogate witnesses, call for evidence, perhaps require the counsel for prosecution and defence to answer certain points or make certain arguments, and will not be satisfied until it believes it has itself found out all that can be found out about the case. In contrast the mode of criminal trial in the COMMON LAW systems is known as the accusatorial system. Here the jury has the job only of deciding between the cases put forward by the prosecution and the defence, on the terms they choose to present. The judge has only the duty of seeing a fair trial, of ensuring that the rules of evidence are obeyed, and summing up impartially to the jury. Thus in the latter case no pretence is made that the whole intricate truth will be found out, but only that the prosecution will do its best to convict, and the defence to acquit, and that the better arguments will prevail. For this reason the accusatory system has to load the odds against prosecution, ensuring that their cases must be extremely powerful, in order to ensure fairness, which the inquisitorial system does not need to do. Consequently there has grown up a false simplification that a man is innocent until proved guilty in the common law world (which is, roughly, true), and guilty until proved innocent, (which is not true) in the inquisitorial system. What is true is that the latter, whilst probably the more efficient, gives the court, and thus the state, far more power in the trial procedure.

Intelligence Services

All nations, of course, have both intelligence and security services of a more or less secret nature. The Soviet Union's principal organization, the Committee for State Security (KGB) grew out of LENIN's original internal secret police, the Cheka, and is huge, with a major para-military role as well as an intelligence function. The USA, which had had almost no intelligence gathering machinery before the Second World War, developed rapidly the Central Intelligence Agency, modelled on the British services, though there are many other intelligence analysis organizations. In America, as in most Western countries, the external intelligence and internal security or counter-intelligence operations are divided between different organizations to minimize the risk to democratic institutions of covert forces. So in America the FBI is responsible for internal security, although scandals in the early 1970s suggested that the CIA had breached this restriction from time to time. Britain operates two principal services. The Security Service (sometimes called MI5), in cooperation with the Special Branch of the ordinary police is responsible directly to the Prime Minister for internal security. Britain's external intelligence gathering activities are the responsibility of the Secret Intelligence Service (SIS, sometimes called MI6) which operates mainly under Foreign Office control. Amongst other major examples, France has the Service de Documentation et Contre Espionage Exterieure (SDECE) and a host of internal security organizations, West Germany the BundesNachristenDienst, (BND), and Israel what is arguably the most efficient in the world, in Mossad. The most important point, however, is that traditional espionage activities are very largely superceded by electronic intelligence gathering, from radio intercepts. Far more important in real terms than the CIA and the SIS are the Americans' National Security Agency, and Britain's somewhat gnomically named Government Communications Headquarters (GCHQ). These, combined with satellite reconnaissance, are crucial for defence analysis and planning required in the nuclear age. Nor is intelligence gathering automatically a hostile act, because the balance of power, and the credibility of deterrent forces paradoxically requires that the enemy should know at least quite a lot about one's own capacity.

Intercontinental Ballistic Missile (see ICBM)

Interest Groups

Interest groups are associations formed to promote a sectional interest in the political system. Thus trade unions, professional associations, employers' organizations and motoring organizations are usually referred to as interest groups. The term has a degree of overlap with pressure groups and with voluntary organizations although it is frequently restricted to groups which have organized to promote, advance or defend some common interest—most often of an occupational kind.

A variety of tactics may be used to pursue the aims of the group. Thus trade unionists may threaten to withdraw their labour and to strike; while professional groups typically try to advance their cause by more indirect methods such as contact with government bureaucrats, propaganda and publicity. Interest groups have been seen by such 20th-century writers as BENTLEY and Truman as a key element in understanding the political system, and interest groups are often described in terms of the motor or input side of government. Many interest groups therefore develop close—even formal—ties with political parties. Thus Britain's trade unions and the Labour Party are constitutionally linked—although in that case the unions existed prior to the labour Party and were responsible for its establishment. Similarly close links may exist between interest groups and the bureaucracy or the executive generally. In the USA the 'military industrial complex' with its Pentagon links has shown a high level of political cooperation and interaction as has the National Union of Farmers and the Department of Agriculture.

Interest groups with fewer overt powers of sanction or persuasion often resort to such direct action as mass rallies, marches and demonstrations; intensive publicity and lobbying may also be used to advance their cause. This pressure has been especially evident with regard to such sensitive issues as abortion and the politics of the Middle East.

International Monetary Fund

The IMF is a specialist agency of the United Nations, set up after the war mainly as a result of bilateral agreement between the USA and the UK at the famous Bretton Woods conference in 1944. It was intended to be a means of producing stable international economic relations and, above all, a stable international currency and set of exchange rates. In a sense it was a replacement for the old gold standard which had finally been abandoned almost everywhere by 1931. The trouble with the gold standard, under which all currencies had to be directly backed by equivalent amount of gold held by central banks, was that although it produced stability of currencies, its effect was automatic and often very harsh. Thus a country with a balance of payments difficulty would find its unemployment rate shooting up without being able to do anything to control it. In addition, as the supply of gold was not variable by direct political decision, an essentially arbitrary physical restriction was placed on the amount of money available in the world, reducing the possibility of economic growth. Yet when the gold standard was abandoned, anarchy reigned in the international money markets, with instant devaluations or revaluations, and great instability, which itself acted as a restraint on international trade and economic development.

What was needed, it was felt, was a form of international currency which could support national currencies, reduce uncertainty and bring stability, but which would not be automatic in the way gold was. Thus it was a vital aspect of the arrangements for the IMF that it should allow countries undergoing a balance of payments problem to be much more moderate in their internal economic regulatory moves than had been possible in the past. Essentially the IMF worked like a supranational central bank, with member countries paying in an initial deposit (part of this still had to be in gold), and then being allowed to draw out more than they had put in, as a debt to the Fund, when in balance of payments or currency crises. These debts had to be repaid, usually within five years, and rates of interest, varying with the amount borrowed, had to be paid. The arrangement allowed a country to pay its international debts without having to slam on internal deflationary controls to reduce demand and thus possibly increase unemployment. In addition the total funds in the international economic system could be increased by the Fund simply announcing that each share held by member countries was increased by a certain percentage, as has happened on several occasions to meet the permanent pressure for increased international liquidity. This, of course, could not happen before with a physically limited gold stock.

If the IMF system was to avoid the anarchy of the period after the abandonment of the gold standard, however, its automatic control had to be replaced with some form of international political authority. Thus the IMF was given the power to impose economic policy restrictions on member countries wishing to borrow large amounts, and these controls, which have often been imposed, usually take the form of requirements to reduce inflation, especially by cuts in government expenditure and tax increases. Originally it was also intended that no member state should be able to devalue its currency without consultation with the Fund, but this has never been observed, partly because devaluation decisions are usually taken in great urgency and secrecy. Assessing the impact of the fund is much too technical a task for this book. It would probably be agreed by economists that it has not been the great breakthrough in terms of international economic management that was hoped for, though it has certainly produced stability without the harshly automatic consequences of the gold standard. Probably its greatest drawback has been its failure to expand international liquidity to meet demand. In part this comes from the initial unwillingness of the USA at Bretton Woods to agree to the British idea that member nations who were enjoying a long-term and strong balance of payments advantage should be required to increase imports, thus easing the debt problem for the rest of the world. As the USA was in such a position from 1944 until at least the mid-1950s, this was not surprising. The absence of this restriction, however, has allowed countries like West Germany and Japan to benefit from economic strength without regard to their impact on the rest of the international economy.

As the IMF is inevitably linked to capitalist economic systems and theory, it has been spurned by most members of COMECON. More importantly, perhaps, the IMF restrictions on credit have often been seen by left-wing parties, and even by sections of cabinets which have borrowed, as involving undue interference with more socialist-oriented economic policies, and have thus been blamed for preventing the growth of welfare state policies in nations with economic problems.

International Socialism

Socialist and communist doctrines have always had, as an important element, the idea of the international brotherhood of the working classes, in part because the nation state has been seen as the prop used by exploiting capitalists. In addition the revolutionary years of the 19th and early 20th century seemed to require world wide revolution rather than what Stalin was to call 'Socialism in one country.' Consequently there have been numerous attempts to set up international co-operative organizations of the separate national socialist, communist and revolutionary groups. The two most important are the Second International and the Third, (also known as the Comintern). Briefly, though, the First International was created in 1864 by MARX, inspired by the *Communist Manifesto*, which he and ENGELS had been asked to write on behalf of a German emigré workers group in 1848. Largely because Marx tried to dominate it, and because of disputes with anarchists and syndicalists, this international was so ineffective that it was dissolved in 1876. The Second International was formed in Paris in 1889, and though weakened by the First World War (when socialist parties who had sworn to oppose capitalist wars all rallied to their respective governments), it was reformed in 1923 and still survives. This International was reformist and social democratic in nature, and had nothing to do with revolutionary doctrines. It has had no appreciable effect on either international or domestic policies, and, indeed, given its ideological nature, has no obvious role to play. Part of the reason for its uselessness is that from 1919 it had a serious and much more powerfully radical rival in the Third International.

162

The Third International was founded at LENIN's instigation by the newly victorious BOLSHEVIK government in Moscow to organize and control communist parties throughout Europe. Indeed the formation of the two most important Western communist parties, in France and Italy, stems directly from splits in their respective socialist parties, who were members of the Second International: in both cases the hard-core revolutionary Marxist elements left to join Lenin's Comintern. This body exercised the same autocratic centralized discipline over the foreign members of the International, under the label of 'DEMOCRATIC CENTRALISM', as the Central Committee of the Soviet Communist party did over its subordinate bodies. Its deliberate revolutionary and Moscow-inspired temper probably did more to prevent serious united left-wing governments from coming to power in inter-war Europe than anything else. Electorates and the Second International parties could not trust members of the Third International to take proper care of national interests, and the Third International rejected any reformist road to socialism. It had to be abolished by Stalin in 1943 to placate his Liberal Democratic allies, and has never been replaced by anything equivalent. There was, briefly, an attempt by TROTSKY, by then in exile, to create a Fourth International in the 1930s to unite all left-wing parties in an anti-Fascist popular front, but this came to nothing, in part because the Third International itself gave orders in the mid-1930s to forget ideological purity in the face of Russian fears of a German invasion, and to link up with other left parties. An example of how strong was the control of Moscow over the members of the Third International is the way in which the French Communist party would not oppose German invasion of France, nor join the resistance until Hitler's invasion of Russia in 1941 broke the non-aggression pact between Germany and the USSR.

Iron Law of Oligarchy

This phrase comes from the work of one of the pioneers of political sociology, Roberto Michels, in his famous study of the internal politics of the German Social Democratic Party, *Political Parties*. It is part of his general thesis that all organized groups, whether states, political parties, trades unions or whatever, are inherently undemocratic. His argument is that organization is necessary for any effective action in society, that organization inevitably requires bureaucracy, and the bureaucracies equally inevitably concentrate power in the hands of a few at the top of a hierarchy. The reasons he gives for these assertions are multiple and not always compatible, but the general theory is powerful. Briefly, only those at the top of a bureaucracy have the information, and control of internal communications and funds that effective propaganda requires. As a result any organization, even the German Socialists, the earliest effective socialist party in Europe and externally dedicated to democracy, equality and freedom, will not exhibit these characteristics itself. He saw the wishes of the mass membership as being systematically ignored or distorted by the private interests of those who, though officially only civil servants of the organization, actually controlled it. Much of Michels' thesis is simply a development of WEBER's more general account of bureaucracy, but Michels also thinks that the inevitability of oligarchy inside all parties means that democracy in the political system as a whole is thereby made impossible of attainment. A similar analysis, if slightly less pessimistic, is found in what is still the leading text book on British political parties, Robert Mackenzie's *British Political Parties*. It is however questionable whether an oligarchic leadership must necessarily stray from the preferred path of the mass members, or whether internal democracy in political parties is necessary for external democracy in the system. As long as voters can choose between teams of united politicians freely, it may in fact be an advantage that the parties should be internally oligarchic, if only to ensure the unity necessary before a voter can make a rational choice.

Irredentism

Irredentism referred originally to an Italian political movement in the late 19th century, but has come to be a general label for a common political cry. The word is derived from the phrase *Italia irredenta* (literally unredeemed Italy), a slogan for the return to Italian control of lands they thought of as naturally Italian and lost to Italian rule by the past aggression of their neighbours. Parts of Austria, for example, had once been Italian states, as had Nice and parts of South Eastern France, and in the new spirit of Italian unity the demand for the integration of the whole Italian linguistic region was politically emotive. As a movement in Italy it collapsed after Italy was forced into an alliance in 1881, with two of its previous enemies, Germany and Austria, but it gave its name to any similar situation where the return to their rightful home of long lost lands become a rallying cry. In this way the French policy of 'revanche', the retaking of Alsace and Lorraine lost after the Franco-Prussian war, which was so vital a force in French politics during the early

Third Republic could be described as 'irredentist', as could Hitler's demands for the Third Reich to control German-speaking Czechoslovakia, or, for that matter any long-standing territorial claims based on a largely linguistic claim to national sovereignty.

Islam

Islam refers to the Mohammedan religion, to those usually called Muslim, but it also has a geographical sense as in the phrase 'The Muslim World'. This 'world' is very large: a 1971 estimate put it at perhaps 400 million, containing Arabs, Turks, Persians, Indo-Pakistanis and Indonesia-Malayans, spread, of course, over even more political frontiers. Theoretically there is no divide between the state and the faith, because, according to the Muslim religion, the state is a religious institution, guided by the Prophet's words in the holy Koran, and expected to legislate by the moral and practical precepts therein. Indeed rather more than Christianity, Mohammadism is a complete socio-economic and political theory, although, naturally, much developed and modified over the centuries. Two examples may suffice:- in economics there is a strong belief in equality which leads, in theory at least, to forbidding usury (a doctrine the Roman Catholic church gave up even in theory in the middle ages). The theoretical equality of all Muslims (or all Muslim men, at any rate), has prevented anything like the creation of an elite of institutionalized clergy, which is not to say that individual spiritual leaders have not held great power. But they have done so on the basis of their own talents, reputation or, in Weber's over-used phrase, for once properly relevant, 'CHARISMA'.

Though Islam was a major force in world politics until the middle of the 19th century, it had declined to a colonial status as a result of European expansionism and imperialism until the recent post-war decades. Since then, in several Middle Eastern and Asian countries Islamic power, and the desire to create a truly Islamic state has been resurgent, causing no little trouble on the world scene. Libya, under the militant leader Colonel Gaddafi was the first state to make Islam into a 20th century revolutionary creed, partly in an effort to unify the whole Arab world against Israel and its Western allies. At roughly the same time Pakistan, which had been split off from the rest of the Indian sub-continent in 1949 specifically to make a home for Muslims, began to take this position as well. Although earler signs, like the symbolic naming of the new Pakistani capital Islamabad in 1959 had not appeared to mean much, later events have proved this wrong. There is an increasing tendency to replace Westernized law, especially in criminal and family law areas, with the often barbaric Koranic law, and some moves have even been made to operate the economy as nearly as possible on Islamic lines.

There have been two recent examples of the tremendous ideological power of Islam. The first was the sudden and shattering overthrow of the Iranian state by militant and right-wing Muslim political groups and its subsequent violently coercive rule under the direction of Muslim holy men. The second was the fear of dissension amongst Muslims in the eastern USSR, which led the Soviet Union to invade Muslim Afghanistan in 1980. The guerrilla warfare by primitive Muslim peasant armies has continued to tie down thousands of Soviet troops in their equivalent of the American morass of Vietnam. It is possible that Islam may grow to be as powerful an international creed as either Chinese or Russian versions of communism, or liberal capitalism. Certainly it is equally hostile to all three, and represents, though no doubt a legitimate aspiration for self rule, also a de-stabilizing force in world politics.

Isolationism

Isolationism is a foreign policy strategy in which a nation announces that it has absolutely no interest in international affairs, or the affairs of other nations as long as they do not affect any vital interest of its own. It is a form of avoidance of entanglement, and implies a neutrality in most possible conflicts. The most famous example is the foreign policy of the USA, where isolationism as regards any part of the globe other than the western hemisphere was a corollary of the Monroe doctrine enunciated in 1823.

In practice the USA only followed isolationism when it was in its interest, and became heavily involved in Asian affairs, as well as finding the definition of 'western hemisphere' extensive enough to include both Hawaii and the Philippines. At its most effective, American isolationism operated during the inter-war years to keep it out of the League of Nations, and to prevent it becoming involved in the Second World War until attacked by Japan at the end of 1941. Whatever the balance of advantages to the US may have been, the policy was disastrous for Europe, where the rise of the dictators was helped by their confidence in American neutrality and isolation from European affairs. Although isolationism is still attractive to many Americans, the Truman Doctrine of 1947, when America pledged to help all peoples fighting for freedom against 'armed minorities or outside pressure', spelled the end even to a pretence of isolationism, which would, in any case, be incompatible with its obligations under the UN Charter.

In effect, of course, isolationism is practised by most small powers most of the time, and only becomes an obviously deliberate strategy where a real choice is available. When Britain was still powerful there sometimes existed a strong isolationist element under the title of 'little Englanders', who wished to give up imperial responsibilities and concentrate effort on protecting the direct interests of the homeland itself. Where there is an apparent choice nowadays the complexity of international politics and the intermixing of the alliance lines of the superpower blocs in a nuclear context makes isolationism scarcely feasible.

J

Jacobins

Jacobins were the revolutionary party in the French Revolution of 1789 onwards, and their principal fight was for the creation of a single national parliament, democratically expressing the will of the people and solely symbolizing the sovereignty of the state. Its modern use, especially in French politics, derives from this early concern with central authority, the objection to what they called 'pouvoirs intermédiaires', the feudal idea of a hierarchy of levels of authority, with legitimate foci of power and citizen-loyalty between the individual and the state. In its modern guise this becomes an insistence that all important decisions be made centrally in a state, and that only the official central government should in any way express sovereignty or be seen as entitled to legitimacy and loyalty. Thus politicians in France who are regarded as Jacobin deny the need for semi-autonomous regional governments, and would also oppose any hiving-off of decision-making power to other national institutions. France is, in fact, famous for the degree of centralization of policy-making, as much on minor as on major issues. Thus decisions as trivial as the re-naming of a tiny commune, or as important, but elsewhere non-standardized, as what textbooks should be used in schools are entirely controlled from Paris. It is interesting that this Jacobin position cuts across ordinary party ideological gulfs. In the 1970s the two most Jacobin parties in France were from the extreme left and right of orthodox politics, the PCF and the Gaullist RPR. Both insisted on the primacy of central government, while the Socialists and, to only slightly less an extent, the Giscardian Independent Republicans were committed to regionalism and decentralization. There is no reason why the label Jacobin should not be used of politicians in other countries, but it has its particular importance in France simply because the Jacobins were so successful for so very long, to the almost total exclusion of real local government even until recently.

168

Judicial Review

Judicial review is a method whereby a superior judicial body may decide whether an executive or legislative action is constitutional. It is most frequently used when a court decides that an act of the legislature is unconstitutional and hence void, as in the USA where the US Supreme Court has over the past two hundred years struck down some significant acts of Congress as well as pronounced unconstitutional certain congressional procedures such as the LEGISLATIVE VETO. For example a large portion of President Roosevelt's NEW DEAL legislation was struck down by the court in an orgy of judicial review which led to a major confrontation between the president and the court. Judicial review was not, however, written into the constitution of the United States but was inferred from its provisions in a major case of 1803—*Marbury v. Madison*—in which the Supreme Court took the view that its own interpretation of the constitution had to take precedence over other interpretations including the views of the popularly elected legislature.

Judicial review need not always be as dramatic as in the USA. The more common form of judicial review—which is found in almost all countries where the judiciary enjoys some independence—involves the application by the judges of their own standards and values, their understanding of the constitution and their interpretation of the law to the acts promulgated by the legislature or committed by the executive. Sometimes this process will simply produce a pattern of statutory interpretation which was not necessarily envisaged by the legislature or the executive; sometimes it will result in an actual conflict between the judiciary and the other elements in the system. It is therefore a mistake to see the existence of judicial review as being confined to those countries with written constitutions and countries which recognize the practice. Rather, judicial review is a feature of any system in which the judges can control legislative and executive acts by reference to broad constitutional, political and legal principles.

Judiciary

The judiciary is the body of judges in a constitutional system. The powers and role of the judiciary will vary from country to country but there will always be some, albeit indirect, significance both in the doctrines used by judges to interpret the law and in the *ex cathedra* statements of individual judges. The scope for judicial review in the policy-making process will be greatest where there is a written constitution with ambiguous provisions and, as in the

USA, the institution of JUDICIAL REVIEW. However, even in systems such as the British legal system where the judges are traditionally reticent about their law-making as opposed to law-finding fuctions there may be great scope for judicial policy-making and for judicial intervention in the political arena. Thus in the United Kingdom in the 1960s the field of administrative law was elaborated by a series of judicial initiatives and the courts have found themselves in conflict with governments of all parties over the interpretation of statutes.

The recruitment pattern of the judiciary is of political interest because it has frequently been assumed by critics that the law has an individualistic and conservative bias which, when combined with a socially unrepresentative judiciary, militates against collectivist policies. For this reason early experiments with extended welfare provision in Britain—for example by the Liberal governments of the early 20th century—provided that tribunals rather than the ordinary courts should resolve disputes about such matters as workmen's compensation and old age pensions. In some legal systems (e.g. in England and Wales) recruitment to the higher judiciary is almost entirely from the senior branch of the legal profession (the bar); in other systems (e.g. France) the judiciary is a career for which the lawyer opts at the very beginning of his professional practice. In many jurisdictions—including a number of states within the USA—judges are elected.

Because of the danger of corruption and undue or improper influence on the judiciary, most democracies make it difficult to remove judges, although where they are elected (as for example in California) they may be subjected to RECALL and are therefore subjected also to direct political constraints.

Junta

Junta is the Spanish word for a council or board, but its general use in politics, for which the full Spanish phrase would be *junta militar,* is 'military government'. But military government comes in several forms, and the particular form for which junta is shorthand is indeed most frequently found in Latin American countries. The point is that a junta is composed of several officers, of essentially equal political rank, drawn from all the services. The resulting government is direct military government by the whole military machine, balancing the interests of the various services according to their relative power inside the military apparatus. No one man will usually dominate a junta, though this is not invariably true, (for example in Chile), and thus the Presidency, or whatever it is called, can often change hands frequently as rivalries between the services and between members of the junta fluctuate. In contrast is the form of military government more commonly found outside Latin America, where one man dominates as a dictator, using the military to keep him in power, but probably governing mainly by civilian institutions, and not acting simply as *primus inter pares* amongst a group of brother officers. Thus in Pakistan, which has been governed by generals for most of the period since 1962, there has never been a junta, but rather a series of strong men for whom the military forces were no more than tools.

Just War

The theory of when it is just to fight a war, and how to fight justly comes from medieval Christian thought and from the great development of international law that followed. Public interest in just war theory declined considerably in this century with a growing realization of the horror of total war. This emotional reaction not only led to a spread of semi-pacifism, but to the position that war could not be just, and had to be renounced by all civilized nations as an instrument of policy.

Yet largely as a result of the American involvement in the Vietnam war the topic has come to be of increasing interest again, and as public debate heats up on all defence matters in the Western societies, just war theory has started to be developed in the context of nuclear war.

The traditional argument on just war (and modern versions have so far added very little indeed to the well worked out theory of the past) distinguishes two questions. Usually referred to by their associated Latin tags, the distinctions are between *ius ad bello* and *ius in bellum*. The first raises the question of when it is just or right to go to war at all, the second considers what methods may be used in warfare. Historically there has been little debate about the first, but the canons derived have been very much ingored. In contrast arguments over what warlike actions are permissible have been more heated, less consensual, but probably more influential. At least throughout this century, and probably increasingly, most soldiers and politicians have made serious efforts to limit the barbarity of war, through mechanisms like the Geneva Conventions. Acts of atrocity, though they have happened often enough, have not always gone without punishment, and would be more frequent and worse were it not for a general attempt to abide by *ius in bellum*, even when one could not claim by traditional understanding that one's side enjoys *ius ad bello*.

To simplify enormously, most arguments on the justice of going to war at all boil down to the idea that only defensive war is just, though one can claim justly to go to war in defence of a weak third party, and is not limited only to defending one's own territorial integrity. A basic doctrine that runs through both halves of the theory of just warfare is the idea of proportionality, which roughly means that the action one takes must not cause suffering vastly out of proportion to the harm you suffer from the attacker. Thus for example even defence of one's own land might be unjust were it a case of reacting to the invasion of some arid and useless land on one's borders, with little strategic value by taking out an enemy city with a nuclear missile. Similarly though there might be no doubt, as some have argued, that the USA was behaving justly in going to war in Vietnam to protect the weak state of South Vietnam from aggression on the part of China-backed North Vietnam, the search and destroy missions, or declarations of huge portions of the country as free-fire zones were disproportional to the military utility and constituted a breach of the *ius in bellum* side of the argument.

In the context of nuclear warfare it is very difficult to see how the theory can be developed in any useful way, but such a conclusion should not lightly be accepted, if only because of the morale effect, and thus the effect on the credibility of deterrence.

Justice

Justice as a political value is perhaps the oldest of all, forming the main preoccupation of both PLATO'S *Republic* and ARISTOTLE'S *Politics*. It can most conveniently be divided into two aspects, procedural justice, and substantive, or 'social' justice. Procedural justice is considerably the easier to deal with, involving as it does, relatively technical questions of DUE PROCESS, fair trials, equality before the law, and so on. Substantive justice refers to the overall fairness of a society in its division of rewards and burdens. Such divisions can be made on the basis of social efficiency (for example, incentive payments), merit, desert, need, or several other criteria. Probably the mainline meaning of 'social justice' is a matter of giving people what they are 'entitled to' in terms of basic social rights, to food, clothing, housing, etc., and thereafter distributing any surplus in a fair and equitable way. Although it is clearly a matter of great importance, probably 'justice' as a political value can be no further analysed than by saying that it requires a 'fair' distribution of goods. It is, in fact, often described as 'distributive' justice, and the criteria which count as 'fair' depend on previous ideological judgements.

K

Kant

Immanuel Kant (1724–1804) was a German philosopher of enormous influence in every area of philosophical, political and moral thought. In political terms he is especially important as a writer in the ENLIGHTENMENT tradition and a successor to ROUSSEAU and an influence on HEGEL. No very specific political doctrine can be derived from Kant, but without his intellectual groundbreaking many modern political philosophies, including not only MARXISM but also EXISTENTIALISM, would be poorer. In his own times, and in terms of his own orientation, we should probably see Kant as a Liberal, but the complexity and power of his thought makes him vital for far more wide-ranging theories.

Two arguments of Kant's are especially significant. One is that all moral and political judgements should be 'Universal', that is, they should abstract from any particular case and set out only the general moral or policy rules that one could 'universally' wish to obey. Ths is the Liberal element, supporting as it does the idea of the RULE OF LAW. Secondly Kant was acutely aware of the way our concepts and categories determine our social thought, and even the categories into which we distinguish the world. This suggestion that our social perception is not autonomous observation of what acutally exists absolutely, but is conditioned by what we think exists, has had much to do with the development of the theory of IDEOLOGY, especially Marx's reinterpretation of HEGEL and subsequent Marxist thinkers like MANNHEIM.

Keynes

John Maynard Keynes (1883–1946) was a Cambridge economist who was closely involved with practical politics in the 1920s and 1930s, especially with the Liberal party and their senior political leaders both at the Versailles peace conference and later during the inter-war slump. In his economic works, particularly his classical *General Theory of Employment, Interest and Money*, he advocated a theory of how governments could control and manipulate the economy to avoid the worst of slumps and inflationary booms. This involved the idea of using budget deficits or surpluses to counter cyclical trends in the economy by pumping money into the economy during a slump, thus increasing purchasing power and raising demand, or raising taxes during an inflationary period in order to take excess demand out of the economy. During the 1930s and 1940s these ideas rather slowly became accepted in government circles through much of the Western world, eventually forming the basis of government policy in post-war economic debate.

The main points of this position were a commitment to full employment, to stable currency, and above all the idea that economic performance was controllable without recourse to socialist methods of nationalization and direct state control of economic decisions. Instead governments could leave all detailed decisions in the hands of individual firms, and operate through setting tax levels and interest rates to 'fine tune' the overall economy. Until the 1970s this was a more or less consensual policy amongst most important political parties and the vast majority of professional economists. Thereafter the ideas came under more and more pressure from 'right wing' alternatives, especially MONETARISM associated with American economic theorists like Friedman.

Keynesianism

Keynesianism refers to the economic theories and associated government economic policies originated by the English economist John Maynard KEYNES from the 1920s onwards.

Khrushchev

Nikita Sergeyevich Khrushchev was the first overall leader of the USSR to have risen entirely within the ranks of the organized party apparatus, being the generation below the original leaders who had organized the machinery of the Soviet Union. Having fought, as a young man, with the Red Army in the Civil War that followed the Revolution, he rose rapidly in the party, reaching an important post in the Moscow region in 1935, and moving later to the senior post in the Ukraine during and after the war years, As he managed not only to survive the STALIN purges, but even to be trusted by Stalin in the late 1940s to re-organize agricultural production, he must have been a very safe and orthodox APPARATCHIK. His rise to overall command after Stalin's death was delayed by the introduction of collective leadership, as a result of a fear of another period of STALINISM, though he held one of the two most important posts, as First Secretary of the party from the beginning of this phase. Only in 1958 did he collect enough power and backing to depose Bulganin and make himself also premier, though he had an ascendancy over Bulganin from much earlier. His supremacy lasted for only six years, being himself ousted in 1964; the fact that he was allowed to live peacefully in retirement rather than being executed in itself showed that the Soviet Union was beginning to develop a more routine method of political change.

Khrushchev had, in part, come to power as an agricultural specialist, and tried to re-organize the party to give more freedom and influence to agricultural interests, so the continued failure of the agricultural sector went against him. This was by no means his only failure, however. He tried a complicated balancing act in which, as well as agriculture, military investment demands were supported and an attempt to increase the consumer production side of industry, to win public support, was also made. These mutually conflicting demands could not be satisfied, and he gradually lost the support of all the sectors that had helped put him in power. Almost certainly it was his foreign policy failure that finally cost him is position. The most notorious of these was his entangling the Soviet Union in the Cuban Missile Crisis, against the advice of the military, who held him responsible for their embarrassing inability to frighten the USA because he had failed to back them earlier in their demands for weapons development. At much the same time his intransigence to Mao's China brought fears that he would spark off a Sino-Soviet war. He was deposed, ironically on the same day as the British general election brought the Labour party back into power for the first time in thirteen years. On his removal the Soviet Union reverted to a collective leadership again, with Kosygin and Brezhnev holding the posts of Prime Minister and First Secretary. The agricultural system was put back into the orthodox party model, consumer investment decreased, and a major arms programme started. Khrushchev had, however, presided over a slight liberalization of the society, and had never attempted Stalinist tactics. However tolerant he may have been internally in Russia, he had fiercely crushed any moves towards liberalization in Eastern Europe, especially in Poland and in the draconian crushing of the 1956 Hungarian uprisings.

175

Kibbutz

The Kibbutz movement developed in Palestine during the 1930s as part of the Jewish struggle to establish a Jewish State and Homeland, and became a vital part of Israel's early agricultural expansion after the state was established. It is simply an agricultural settlement, originally on virgin and usually inhospitable territory. However the Kibbutz movement was highly 'communal' in orientation, with all work being rationally planned and shared, and with little or no private property, the profits of the enterprise being used communally. Often the Kibbutzim adopted other policies that contrasted sharply with ordinary nuclear-family based economic life in capitalist societies. A famous symbol of this was the communal rearing of children, intended not only to free most women for productive work along with the men, but also deliberately to create a spirit and psychology of communalism, and to downplay individualism. As perhaps the only successful communal organizations in the West they have been a source of inspiration for many Western intellectuals, though in Israel itself they are not necessarily admired particularly today.

L

Laisser-faire

Laisser-faire is the doctrine that the government of a state should have no control at all over economic matters. It is especially associated with 19th century liberalism, but is by no means absent from the modern world. In origin it was a liberal opposition to traditional, semi-feudal, monopolistic patterns in which the state involved itself in direct control of aspects of the economy for general purposes of policy. It came to mean an absolute opposition to any governmental infringement on the absolute freedom of contract, because it was believed that maximal economic performance was only possible where everyone, entrepreneur or unskilled worker, would be better off if the sheer power of market forces of supply and demand were left to work themselves out. Thus no controls, not even minimum wage laws or controls over child labour hours, were seen as acceptable infringements on total economic freedom. The political theory of laisser-faire was buttressed by adherence to the early versions of professional economic theory, the 'Perfect Competition' theories of writers like Marshall and Ricardo, who tried to show that an economy consisting of many equally small units of production would automatically work to maximize social value. For a long time the common law doctrines of contract also operated to support this position, despite the fact that both legal and effective monopolies were distorting the perfect competition model, and inequalities of bargaining power, especially between workers and employers, were reducing the theoretical fairness of laisser-faire policies. Although laisser-faire claimed to require a total independence of the economy and the political system, it was in fact dependent on political support for established power relations. Nonetheless advocates of laisser-faire economic policies are still occasionally influential in policy-making in modern societies, and there are certain connections between this doctrine and other conservative economic policies, especially MONETARISM.

Language Groups

Language groups are often of vital importance in politics. It is not just that which language one speaks, or is forced to speak for social advancement, is of great practical significance, but, even more, that the recognition of a language is a major aspect of the legitimization of a culture and history. Very frequently, where language is politically relevant, one language group is an ethnic minority suppressed by what they see as an alien conqueror or oppressing elite. Here having to speak the language of the rulers is not just a practical difficulty, but a violently-charged symbol of unfreedom. In many cases languages will turn out to be correlated with other social symbols, of which religion or ETHNICITY are the most potent. As a result, language groups can become important centres for the focusing of revolutionary, or at least protest, politics on modern societies, often keeping alive CLEAVAGES which might otherwise have died away. After class and religion, (with which they are, in any case, often interdefined) linguistic cleavages are the most important source of conflict in modern politics. Britain, Canada, Belgium, Norway and Sweden, France, the Soviet Union and Ireland amongst European nations alone have political movements or conflicts based mainly on language groups. In the THIRD WORLD the situation is even more complex because language may be a vital element in the attempt to construct a national unity out of a political system that is really only the result of imperialist map-makers. Unity can, indeed, sometimes only be hoped for by getting agreement to common use of a foreign, formerly Imperialist, language, as with the Indian need to operate in English because of the multiplicity of local languages. Language probably has its deep political significance because of the way in which our thoughts, stock of concepts, and very self-image are reflected by language and restricted by it. Thus it is more rational, perhaps, to define political culture around language than most other cleavage patterns, and this may account for the virulence of language-group politics.

Law

Law is any system of widely recognized and compulsory regulations that govern the behaviour of citizens or political actors, either between each other, or between actor and some overall power or authority. So complex is the theory of law, and so hotly debated its philosophical nature that one cannot easily go beyond that statement without risking contention. It may be generally accepted, however, that there are two broad schools of thought about the nature of law. On the one hand there are those, especially from the Anglo-American legal tradition, who see all law as positive, as direct commands from someone or something able to enforce them. This school tends to differentiate sharply between law and morality, and to treat any command from a *de jure* power as lawful and legally binding, whatever its character. They also wish to deny the status of 'law' to non-enforceable rules, such as those otherwise recognized as making up the body of conventions and expectations known as 'International' law.

On the other hand there is the school often called the 'Natural law' school, and more commonly though not uniquely continental in origin, which sees law as somehow representing binding obligations arising from a prior moral sphere, to which the actual positive laws merely give effect (or ought to). Other basic characteristics of law, as for example, whether or not they must always be universal in character, what authorities in a society may promulgate them, or when if ever they may legitimately be denied, are bound up with these broader theoretical problems. Until relatively recently the 'positive law' tradition was dominant in American and English legal thinking, and most common amongst practitioners of law, if not theorists, everywhere, but this position is increasingly challenged, especially by writers in the new liberal tradition following RAWLS and NOZICK.

Law and Order

Law and order refers to a state of society in which there is a regular process of criminal and civil law and in which certain agencies, such as the police, are responsible for maintaining domestic tranquillity. Law and order is generally seen by most conservatives and many liberals as the basic requirement of a state since without these conditions civil society, political freedom and civil liberties are impossible. Law and order in common parlance has also come to mean the provision of a strong police force and a concern with reducing crime and vandalism. Hence law and order issues are often held to relate to such matters as police pay and punishment. As such, law and order may become an election issue in democracies concerned with rising crime rates. George Wallace in 1968 mounted a presidential bid in the USA which was heavily tinged with concern for law and order; and the 1979 Conservative Party campaign in the UK laid considerable stress on this theme.

Law, Rule of

The Rule of Law is a vital idea in both political and legal debate in the Western world. Its direct technical meaning is fairly simple, but its application can often lead to considerable problems. What the rule of law means, strictly, is that the political decision-makers of a society express their decisions in terms of general rules or principles, which are then applied automatically and indiscriminately by courts, police and administrators to anyone who comes within their ambit. The stress is on the neutrality and generality of such decision-making. ARISTOTLE, in his *Politics* was perhaps the first to recognize that individual human judgement on each and every case of social conflict that came before a judge was not likely to produce fairness and equity, and thus recommended that judges should be no more than appliers of previously fixed rules to factual cases. Following this idea, the rule of law has come to be seen as a major contribution to equality and liberty. It requires legislatures to look only at the abstract feature of a problem, and to promulgate a general rule, and judges to look only at relevant characteristics, under the immediate rule, in deciding cases. It should be noted that the idea of judges here refers to anyone with decision-making powers on particular cases—a judge might, for example, be an employee of the Department of Employment deciding on an unemployment compensation case, or even a county librarian deciding on the fine someone should pay for keeping novels out longer than the appointed period. The essence is that they should decide only according to the rule laid down, not according to their own sense of justice or personal preference. The rule of law is contrasted with arbitrary power, as happens in a POLICE STATE, or the personal whim of a dictator, however enlightened. It is celebrated in the American constitution which specifically calls for 'the rule of law and not of men'.

Leadership

Leadership is a quality which in theory signifies the ability of a person or (more rarely) a group of persons to persuade others to act by inspiring them and making them believe that a proposed course of action is the correct one.

Leadership is generally thought to be a desirable property except when a leader becomes too conscious of his or her position and refuses to be controlled by the rank and file of the party or by the electorate (see ACCOUNTABILITY). Leadership may, in certain romantic or fascist philosophies take on a special role but in normal democratic politics it is seen as a routine feature of the political process (see FASCISM).

By extension, the post of leader when it is an office filled according to certain rules may be known as the leadership; and sometimes the ruling elite of a party may be known as its leadership (see ELITISM). In the Soviet Union, for example, the Communist Party stresses its 'collective leadership' as a basic principle of government in contrast to the STALINIST period when one-man leadership was the order of the day. In many countries—especially newly independent countries with a recent history of nationalist struggle—the leader is seen as the embodiment of the people and the nation, as for example Dr. Hastings Banda of Malawi. However, leadership in Third World countries is often difficult to sustain over a long period of time in the absence of durable political institutions and economic progress.

Left

The term left, or left-wing, to signify socialist or radical political tendencies dates as a symbol from the days immediately preceding the French Revolution. At this stage the French Estates-General (roughly equivalent to a Parliament) was so ordered that those supporting the King and the traditional social situation sat on the Right of the assembly, and the opponents sat on the Left. But in fact the association of 'left' or 'lefthandedness' with those less than totally orthodox is a much deeper element of European culture—the left hand has always been connected with the supernatural or with the socially unacceptable. The 'bend sinister', a left-slanting line on a heraldic device, indicated a nobleman born out of wedlock. Left, and 'Right', its obvious opponent, are tremendously useful, but ultimately empty, slogan-words in modern politics. The most that can be safely said is that those on the 'left' wish to change things, and to do this in the direction of more equality and less tradition than those on the right. The whole idea of the Left/Right dichotomy assumes one can put political life onto a one-dimensional framework, and reduces judgements to a simple schema. In the most basic terms, a 'left-wing' position in modern politics would involve leaning towards such positions as the following, in some mix or other: nationalization of industy; state control of the economy; highly re-distributive tax policies; pacifism or arms reduction; egalitarian policies in education; a preference for ecological rather than industrial expansionist policies; positive discrimination towards minority groups; and so on. There is no logical, only a psychological, linkage here. These terms, in order to retain their utility, have to be highly relative. Thus it makes every sense to ask which is the most left-wing member of the Soviet Government, or who was the most left-leaning General in some right-wing military junta.

Legislative Veto

The Legislative Veto is a legal device adopted by the US Congress to give itself the power to control the behaviour of the vitally important regulatory agencies which govern so many areas of American policy-making, but one that is often seen by the executive as a trick to get round the constitutional SEPARATION OF POWERS which forbid the legislative branch to exercise direct control over the execution and application of laws.

The technique involves writing into any legislation which sets up or grants general powers to agencies the right of Congress to pass, by resolution, a motion forbidding the agency to go ahead with any particular policy or regulation that Congress does not favour. The important point is that resolutions of Congress, unlike acts, are not subject to Presidential veto. In this way Congress can try to by-pass the President's control over the executive side of government. Although they were first used in the 1930s, legislative veto provisions proliferated in the 1970s as part of the general resurgence of congressional power *vis-à-vis* the Presidency.

Many people had argued over the constitutionality of this technique, but until recently there had been no full legal test. In 1983 the Supreme Court, in *INS* v *Chadha* heard a case in which a specific decision by the Immigration and Naturalization Service not to deport an allegedly illegal immigrant had been overruled by the House of Representatives using a Congressional veto provision written into the INS authorizing legislation. They ruled that, once Congress had made a general grant of delegated authority, they had no further right to interfere with its execution, thus at least narrowing, and possibly overruling the purported Congressional power. Further cases will be needed fully to clarify the situation, and Congress is still passing legislation which contains legislative veto provisions, in the hope that the rulings will not be effective in enforcing this aspect of the separation of powers.

Legislatures

Legislatures are the official rule-making body of a political system, as opposed to the institutions charged with applying the rules, or with judging those alleged to have broken them. There is an entirely erroneous tendency to equate legislatures with elected parliaments, but there is no theoretical reason why, even as an ideal, the legislative function should be carried out by such a body, unless a prior commitment has been made to democracy as the source of legitimate rule making. The essence of the distinction lies in the idea of the SEPARATION OF POWERS, so that it is entirely proper to ask of a non-democratic state what body is the legislative one.

Usually we do mean an elected chamber, parliament or assembly when talking of legislatures, though the entities we then identify, the American Congress, or the British Houses of Parliament are not usually pure legislative bodies, having some residual control over the executive. As a vast amount of the material that serves to lay down binding and legally enforceable rules in any modern society does not originate in, and may hardly have been seen by the Parliament or legislative body, but is instead created by the executive under relatively light legislative powers of overview, the distinction is rapidly losing an empirical referent. Nonetheless the idea of the legislative function, even when there is no one body that uniquely serves the function, is an important conceptual distinction.

Legitimacy

Legitimacy is both a normative and an empirical concept in political science. Normatively, to ask whether a political system is legitimate or not is to ask whether the State, or government, is entitled to be obeyed. As such the idea of legitimacy is connected with the legal concepts of DE JURE and *De Facto* power. Whatever the accepted grounds of POLITICAL OBLIGATION may be, legitimacy refers to these. Its more interesting application may be in the empirical usage it has in political science, especially in POLITICAL SOCIOLOGY. Here the concentration is principally on how any given political system comes to be seen as 'legitimate' by a majority of its citizens. Why do most citizens of the USA and the USSR see their governments as entitled to require their obedience when, presumably, people are much the same in both countries but the policies and structures of the state are very different? This is the question addressed by those who study legitimacy as an empirical fact rather than a philosophical problem. As well as being a major question in such research, the bases of legitimacy, a categorization of systemical grounds for obedience that actually work, can give us most useful rules for grouping different sorts of political systems. Many of the classifications of political systems found in the modern study of COMPAR-

ATIVE GOVERNMENT or Comparative Politics rely on typologies based on the various grounds of political legitimacy. Thus democracies tend to argue for their legitimacy in terms of actually delivering the goods, giving voters what they immediately want, whilst other sorts of political system may offer other general principles to support their right to command. Socialist states may focus on the ultimate benefit to workers, right-wing JUNTAS on some sense of traditional national identity.

Lenin

Vladimir Ilyich Lenin (1870–1924, originally named Ulyanov) was, like his younger revolutionary colleague TROTSKY, a revolutionary before he was a MARXIST, both chronologically and intellectually. Probably his lifelong passion for revolution, and his total dedication to politics and nothing else stemmed from the execution of his brother for complicity in the assassination of Tsar Alexander II in 1887. After being exiled to Siberia, he left for London in 1900 and set about helping to organize, and then take over the rather heterogenous collection of emigré Russian left-wing movements that made up the Social Democrat party. He rejected the view of many that Russia was too under-developed economically to undergo a full Marxist revolution that would lead to socialism, and finally managed to win a majority of the Social Democrats to his side, to form the BOLSHEVIK party. (The word actually only means 'majority' i.e. the majority of the social democrats, whose more reformist opposition was known simply as the Mensheviks, the 'minority'). Lenin, though accepting much of Marx, added two vital ingredients to make up what is now the official doctrine of the Soviet Union, under the label of Marxist-Leninism.

The first point, which caused conflict not only with the 'right' wing Mensheviks but also other equally radical Marxists like Trotsky himself and Rosa LUXEMBURG, was a very strong stress on the need for an organized, full-time professional revolutionary cadre. This was not just a tactical point. Lenin never accepted that the Russian masses could be allowed much say in the revolution or its aftermath, and continually stressed the need for elite leadership and highly authoritarian control of the party central committee. This later became the official doctrine of 'DEMOCRATIC CENTRALISM', and is held by many to have paved the way for the totalitarian rule of the Stalin and later periods. It is significant that Lenin was quite open in insisting that this leadership should come from the left-wing bourgeois intellectuals, and never allowed workers' movements like trade unions any important role. Left to themselves, he argued, the masses could not rise beyond a 'trade union' mentality, could never really throw off the chains of CAPITALISM.

The second point, again contested by Trotsky, was that, knowing the Russian industrial proletariat was too small and too new to carry out a successful revolution itself, he advocated an alliance with the peasantry, despite their traditional conservatism. What he then expected to happen, and did in fact start to happen under his rule after the 1917 revolution, was that the Soviet state itself, denying democracy and industrial participation, would complete the process of industrialization until, at a later, perhaps much later, date, full communism would be possible. He expected, in other words, that the revolution would stop short of the full change of society. When, in 1917, he staged a coup d'état against the moderate and moderate-left government that had taken over when the Tsar fell, he lost little time in abolishing all other parties, even though it was possible to have created a broadly based left wing government with the participation of the Mensheviks. Because of the rigours of the last stages of the world war, followed rapidly by the civil war between the 'White' and 'Red' armies, the Russian economy nearly collapsed and he had to accept a considerable weakening of the early socialist economics, in a policy known as the New Economic Policy (NEP, q.v.).

He died in 1924, without naming an heir to his autocratic power, and the ensuing in-fighting amongst the Soviet leaders led ultimately to STALINISM. Lenin, more than any other single man, could have changed the nature of Russian communism, but his real talents lay as a tactician, rather than as a strategist or ideologue. Nonetheless, at least two of his many writings continue to be of vital influence in the communist world. The first, the essay *What is to be done?* set the blueprint for democratic centralism. Secondly, his analysis of imperialism offered an explanation of why Marx's economic predictions that capitalism would collapse of its own internal contradictions had not held, and why, as a result, the revolution could not be a spontaneous rising of the real proletariat, but had to be managed and created by the vanguard party (see VANGUARD OF THE PROLETARIAT).

Leninism

Leninism is that part of modern Soviet doctrine, and to a lesser extent part of the official ideology of Western communist parties that alters MARXISM to fit the perceptions of organized communist movements. It consists mainly of a justification for a strong, auth-

185

oritarian and essentially undemocratic party as necessary for social-ist revolution. Leninism claims that the ordinary industrial proletariat cannot of themselves become revolutionary, cannot per-ceive their true interests, and must be led by a vanguard of intel-lectual revolutionaries. While Lenin himself believed this strongly, his position was relative to the historical conditions of Russia in the early decades of this century, and to the period of massive imperial control of the third world by Western nations, and was probably never intended to be a permanent doctrine. Nonetheless, communist and extreme left movements today can be usefully characterized by whether they adopt a Leninist version of Marxism, or some other. The two most usual alternatives to Leninism are either a tendency to follow TROTSKY or MAO TSE TUNG.

Liberal Democracy

Liberal Democracy, which is what most developed Western nations would claim to practise, is actually a combination of two values which do not necessarily go logically together. As far as the democ-racy aspect is concerned, liberal democracy is a form of REPRESEN-TATIVE DEMOCRACY. Thus the usual system is the election by the whole electorate of a small number of representatives, probably organized in political parties, who form a legislative assembly. The majority of this assembly makes the law, and may, in parliamentary systems like those of the UK, Canada and Australasia, select some amongst themselves to form the executive. It is thus a rather indirect form of majority rule. The liberal aspect refers to a set of traditional values, drawn from the basic stock of CIVIL and NATURAL RIGHTS which the system is expected to enshrine. Thus values like 'due process of law', equality before the law, freedom of speech and assembly, protection for minorities, equal opportunities and so on are seen as central to the political culture, and may indeed be enshrined in a constitution and protected by the courts. The inner logical problem is that there is no particular reason to believe that the majority of the population will necessarily wish to uphold these values. Indeed social research has often shown that a majority of the electorate of Western democracies are, under certain conditions, hostile to, say, aspects of the due process of law. Thus the empirical will of the majority may conflict with the vital system values. As a result Liberal Democracy cannot be a full-blooded majoritarian system.

Furthermore, because those elected to the assembly are usually seen as unbound representatives along Burkeian lines, rather than as bound delegates, legislative assemblies often thwart the desires of those who elect them. A classic example in Britain is the question of capital punishment. Ever since its abolition in 1967 there has been a strong majority of the population in favour of its return, yet several times votes in the House of Commons have rejected the policy by sizeable majorities of the representatives. Similarly certain rules developed by the US Supreme Court to protect the rights of those accused in criminal trials are seen by a majority of American citizens as hampering the police in dealing with the crime problem, yet the unelected court, in what claims to be a democracy can and has prevented the popular will. Liberal Democracy can be seen as the answer to the traditional fear, as expressed by DE TOCQUEVILLE and J. S. MILL, of the 'tyranny of the majority', the fear that unhampered majoritarian democracy could be more dangerous to liberal values than many ordinary tyrannies.

Liberalism

Liberalism can mean either a particular party creed in a particular time period, especially the late 19th century (the hey-day of Liberalism), or a general social and political attitude and orientation. Historically Liberalism represented a move for freedom from remaining feudal and monarchical control, and was thus a middle-class or BOURGEOIS movement, associated, *inter alia*, with economic theories such as LAISSER-FAIRE. As part of this general tradition it tended also to be associated with the support of freedom of membership in groups of all sorts, freedom of belief and speech, even freedom of action in any area that did not obviously hurt another. From this position of supporting basic civil liberties or human rights Liberalism has developed a modern political creed in which the independence of the ordinary man against any powerful body, whether the state or, for example, organized labour, is taken as vital. Modern Liberal parties, and they exist in most democratic states, although not necessarily under that title, tend to argue that traditionally-organized class politics, with an apparently insoluble conflict between CAPITALISM and some form of SOCIALISM or MARXISM is misplaced, and that a greater concentration on the talents, capacities and needs of actual individuals rather than systems of social composites is possible and desirable. Liberals are one of the best reasons for doubting the suitability of the standard LEFT/RIGHT model of politics because they contain both the commitment to equality by the Left and to approval of individual human effort and freedom by the Right. In this sense they are often seen as being 'in

187

the middle' of the spectrum, but most Liberals would argue that, far from being 'centre' or 'moderate', they are in fact radical, wishing to change much in society. Their particular practical political position is indicated by the following fact: in British elections in the 1970s the Liberal party gained almost exactly the same percentage of the votes (around 14%) from *all* social classes. This would be roughly true in most other Western countries.

Libertarianism

Libertarianism was, even as recently as 1960, a somewhat fringe political theory holding extreme versions of liberal capitalist beliefs. There has been a considerable upsurge in interest in libertarian thinking in some quarters, especially in the United States, most probably because of the bankruptcy of most other non-Marxist political theory in the post-war world. Modified versions of libertarian positions have been set out, especially by NOZICK and in some aspects of RAWLS's work, and the old masters of the tradition, especially the Austrian economist von Hayek have come back into fashion.

Libertarianism holds basically that all men have a certain set of rights, which are indefeasible, cannot be given up, and may not be taken away in the interest of the collective. Where these rights come from is uncertain, but they are definitely seen preceding political life, and not being the product of the state itself. Nor may the state intervene to balance rights, to ensure, for example, that someone who is starving is given welfare payments by breaching the property rights of another. The essence is LAISSER-FAIRE and a deep distrust of government intervention. With some thinkers, notably Hayek, state intervention is opposed not only because it involves reduction in rights, but because it threatens human autonomy, which is taken as the basic value. In addition, and this line could come from a much more moderate liberal like J. S. MILL, state intervention, in the social sphere (education, or medicine, say) as much as in economic organization, prevents experimentation and the development of human ingenuity and is thus likely, in the long run, to reduce rather than increase the sum of human happiness. The latter argument, though, is very much an auxiliary, because the maximization of happiness, the old utilitarian aim, is as much opposed by libertarians as is socialism. The resurgence of libertarianism in political thought precedes, but is not unconnected with, the MONETARIST and laisser-faire approaches of some Western governments in the late 1970s and early 1980s, and they both represent a breach with a long term concensus in the non-socialist academic and political worlds of the developed West.

Liberty, Negative

Liberty (or freedom) is often divided by political theorists into two types, for analytic clarity. Negative liberty refers essentially to 'absence of external constraints'. Thus, as long as there is no law or social practice preventing me from doing something, or forcing me into some course of action, I can be seen as free in that respect. This is the idea of liberty most commonly found in modern Western democratic societies and in classical Liberal social thought. The emphasis is on what other people might do to stop me carrying out my will. But what I choose to do is taken as outside the bounds of the concept. If I choose to be a drug addict, I am either free or not depending on what society does to stop me buying my preferred drugs. Often, though not invariably, this will be linked to the idea that the political system is only entitled to infringe on someone's freedom when it is preventing actions that would hurt another person, and that what an individual does to himself is his own business. This concept of liberty is the basic one found in English social thought from HOBBES and LOCKE through the UTILITARIANS onwards. It is opposed by a concept with a more continental European heritage, often referred to as 'POSITIVE' LIBERTY.

Liberty, Positive

Positive Liberty, as opposed to the English tradition of 'NEGATIVE LIBERTY', finds its roots originally in classical Greek thought, and later, in European Idealist philosophy like that of HEGEL or KANT. Nowadays it is found particularly in some MARXIST thinkers, especially those like MARCUSE. The stress here is on actual internal freedom of choice, rather than, as in the English Liberal tradition, external constraints on putting a choice into action. Basically the argument rests on the idea that, left to himself, man's essential human nature will produce freely rational and good choices. But this inner human nature can be warped by social forces and ideological manipulation so that the individual does not realize what he truly wants, and makes false choices. Ultimately it goes back to the Platonic doctrine that no man can ever freely choose what is wrong, and that evil is a fault in understanding, not a weakness of will. In the hands of later theorists it becomes the doctrine that society, especially capitalist society, alienates man from his true nature, and produces apparent needs and desires which are convenient for the rulers of that sort of society. Sometimes the doctrine has obvious sense: those addicted to dangerous drugs can, perhaps, be said to be unfree in pursuing their desires. But often the theory depends on a specially privileged position by which those who are ideologically sound are allowed to stipulate what other people would really want if only they realized it existed. Thus the argument is used to invalidate, for example, election results in modern democracies, on the grounds that the working-class would actually vote for communist parties if they had not been 'tampered' with by the media, and are suffering a lack of 'positive' freedom in voting because of their deluded notions. Neither positive nor negative liberty concepts are as simple as these accounts, and it is unlikely that any single political thinker will hold entirely to any one. But the distinction is an important one, identifying as it does a long-term conflict inside Anglo-European social thought, and relating to real clashes in modern political positions.

Limited War

Limited war, an idea found in modern strategic thought, is one of the apparently simple, but actually quite complex, ideas that characterize contemporary international relations and strategy. The 'limitation' in Limited War is that the war in question should not spread to involve the SUPERPOWERS in an all-out nuclear confrontation. But inside these limits there are enormous variations. Thus both the Arab-Israeli wars and the Argentinian-British conflict in the South Atlantic are limited wars. But in the former case the entire existence of a nation-state was in question, whilst in the latter no actual threat was posed to either of the combatant nations.

Lobby

Lobby, which is very much a term of art in political discourse, can function either as a verb or noun, and under the latter, has two quite distinct meanings. As a verb, 'to lobby' means to apply pressure, present arguments or other incentives to try to make a political decision-maker favour one's position. It can be used either in an institutional setting, where a representative of a pressure group may 'lobby' a parliamentarian, minister, or civil servant to further his group's interest. It may also be used amongst equals, where, for example, one member of a committee, interested in a forthcoming issue, may lobby his fellow members to seek their support, or even where the President of the United States may have his executive assistants attempt to lobby congressmen to seek their vote on some impending legislation.

As a noun the word 'lobby' refers to established institutional arrangements for such transmission of information and pressure on issues. There is, in the United States, for example, an official register of lobbyists, men whose full time occupation it is to represent the arguments of their clients, whether they be the armaments industry or some fund-starved university, to the Federal Government. In Britain, uniquely, the noun 'lobby' has an alternative meaning, referring to the established and accredited group of media correspondents who are made privy to government secrets as a means for ministers to communicate discreetly with the public. They are often given highly confidential briefings on the understanding that they will exercise very great discretion in what they print. In all meanings the word derives from the 'lobbies' in parliament or congress where politicians meet after votes to discuss affairs.

Local Government

Local government is a system of administration for small political units—towns, counties, and rural districts for example. It operates within a larger governmental framework and unlike a federal system (see FEDERALISM) the powers of the local government are usually delegated by the national or central government. Local councils which are traditionally democratically elected administer such matters as local environmental health, refuse collection, parks and recreation, traffic regulation and matters to do with town and country planning applications.

The powers of local government vary from country to country and have varied considerably within Britain over time. In federal political systems the local units may possess considerable powers on such important matters as education; in unitary states the degree of real power of educational policy may be limited. In France before the election of President Mitterrand (see FIFTH REPUBLIC) the government appointed prefects from Paris who possessed the power of financial veto over the mayoral decisions in the provinces (see DECENTRALIZATION). In Britain the powers and responsibilities of local government have become especially controversial in the 1970s because of the desire to keep an overall control of public expenditure at all levels. The Conservative Party introduced major reforms of the local government system in the period 1972-1974 but Mrs.

Thatcher's government has promised to make further amendments by removing the metropolitan councils.

Locke

John Locke (1632–1704) may be one of the most famous political theorists in the Anglo-American world, not so much because of the quality of his thought as for his impact on world events, since many of his ideas were taken as models by the founding fathers of the US Constitution. Like his great rival HOBBES, though slightly later, he was writing against the background of the English Civil War, and his own political connections are vital in the development of his political theory. Like Hobbes he used much the same theoretical methodology, the discussion of a hypothetical STATE OF NATURE and the idea of a SOCIAL CONTRACT or compact to get out of this state into CIVIL SOCIETY. He was very much in the natural law tradition, but, unlike Hobbes, his perception of natural law was much more orthodox. His main aim in his theories, set out in the *First and Second Treatise on Civil Government*, was to draw a blueprint for a political system in which the government would be severely limited in its role, and subject to control and even abolition by the citizenry were it to exceed the tight bounds he put on it. As with ROUSSEAU later, he argued that sovereignty lay with the people, not with a monarch, and governments had their authority only because the citizens consented to their rule to achieve specific benefits. Only the need for a greater protection of certain natural rights could be a good reason for leaving the total liberty of a state of nature for member-ship of a state where some liberty would be lost, and hence only consent to the state could give it authority.

At the same time, because he feared the growth of executive power, he insisted on a SEPARATION OF POWERS between the legislative, the representative of the people's sovereignty, and the executive. Although he hinted at the further separation of the judicial system from the executive, this model of the separation of powers and of government acting in a trust capacity to achieve limited objectives went to the hearts of the newly-independent American politicians in the Constitutional Convention,—(so did similar arguments by MONTESQUIEU, though his were later than Locke's),—and his influ-ence is beyond doubt. Though his theory is, in its end result, an encapsulation of many modern liberal values, Locke himself was neither a democrat, nor an advocate of equality. Indeed the principal value he wished the political system to preserve was the right to private property, which he defends with an odd but ingenious theological argument. He is quite clear in the *Second Treatise* that he does not expect the ordinary people to play any role in the running of the state, and his famous reliance on free consent to create authority in fact ends up, by sleight of hand, as being very much less liberal than it seems. Politically he was on what would pass as the left-wing of the period; his family had fought for Parliament in the Civil War, and his patron, the Earl of Shaftesbury, was implicated in an attempted revolution against the restored monarchy. Some critics, indeed, regard the *Second Treatise* as, in part, an attempted justification of Shaftesbury's position, and he certainly was unusual in writing into his theory a defence of the need occasionally to rebel against government. But the left-wing position of his day can more easily be seen as the intellectual support for the rise of the bourgeoisie, and his advocacy is indeed for the form of government and ideas of property particularly convivial to the development of LAISSER-FAIRE economies. Probably his better intellectual work was as a philosopher, and in that capacity he is studied today almost as much as he is analysed as a political theorist.

Luxemburg, Rosa

Rosa Luxemburg's reputation and ideas still play a vital, if controversial role in modern MARXISM. She was involved in the BOLSHEVIK movement and the development of Marxism into an active revolutionary movement and creed from the beginning, helped build a post-war attempt at revolution in Germany, in 1918, and was murdered by soldiers when the uprising was crushed. Her real importance, apart from being a romantic martyr symbol, was that she repeatedly criticized LENIN and his Russian version of Communism, especially after their coming to power in 1917. Although in many ways she was a perfectly orthodox Marxist, stressing the inevitability of a proletarian revolution, she was seen very much as an advocate of much greater democracy, both in the movement itself, and in the post-revolutionary regime. For this reason her theories and herself as a symbol have been of great inspiration to most breakaway communists and Marxists. In particular the German SPD, which was until the early 1960s defiantly Marxist in theory, was infused with her spirit, because it seemed a way of being non-revolutionary, democratic, and yet still true to Marxism. Whilst debates about what 'true' Marxism is are necessarily sterile, it does tend to be forgotten that she was only one of many leaders of the communist movement in the early part of this century who had disagreements with Lenin, and she was, nonetheless, an economic

193

determinist who cooperated in a violent revolution. An example of how her importance probably is more symbolic than theoretical is that another anti-Lenin Marxist revolutionary, TROTSKY, completely ignored her while she was alive. Only years after her death, when founding the 4th International did he suddenly 'discover' their similarity of position, because his 4th International was itself an attempt to wield together all the dissident Marxists, for many of whom she had become a patron saint.

M

Machiavelli

Niccolo Machiavelli (1469–1527) was a Florentine diplomat and civil servant whose writing included not only political theory but also plays. He is famous more for attitudes somewhat unfairly associated with him than for anything that he really wrote. The work of Machiavelli's most often quoted is *The Prince,* dedicated to Machiavelli's patron, Duke Lorenzo di Piero de' Medici. It is a short analysis of how to rule an Italian city state successfully in the late middle ages. He also, however, wrote a much more solid study of early Italian political history, usually known as *The Discourses.* In both works he presents a tough and practical view of politics, in which questions of how to achieve desired ends as a ruler, by the use of any and every technique and resource available, are seen as vastly more important than moral or philosophical questions about the desirability of such strategies. He is often seen as the originator of the argument that 'the end justifies the means', although it must always have been a very attractive doctrine to any political leader—as Lenin said, 'What else could?' Machiavelli's claim to fame, however, comes from the apparently cynical and 'cool' advice he offers to any potential Italian political leader in *The Prince,* and his name has become code, as 'Machiavellianism', for highly manipulative and cynical political activity of a self-seeking nature, especially when totally devoid of general principles. This is actually most unfair to a man quite dedicated to the welfare of his native city state, and whose other works are an outstanding plea for Italian unity, which aim was indeed the inspiration of *The Prince* itself. However, as a label for a common syndrome in political life it is very useful, and there have even been successful political attitude scales developed by social psychologists based on his prescriptions.

Majority Systems

A majority system is one in which a full arithmetic majority of voters (50% + 1) are required before an act or rule can be passed, a decision implemented, or a motion accepted. As such, majority systems can exist in committees, legislatures, electorates, and anywhere where some process of head counting is required to elect or confirm some candidate or motion. Majority vote has a hallowed, if theoretically insecure position in democratic belief, resting on the argument that a decision accorded to by more people than oppose it is politically legitimate. In practice there are very few majority systems fully fledged, and the logic of majority voting is seldom fully applied or thought out in decision-making arenas.

There are a host of theoretical problems—does a majority involve, for example, all those entitled to vote, or only those who appear and cast a vote? Further problems occur when one considers whether or not a vote really represents a clear majority preference for an act, or simply the preference for one rather than another of the set of unpopular alternatives. As far as elections to office go, this is particularly troublesome, because a complicated set of rules is required with several ballots to ensure that the winner is actually preferred to all alternatives by a majority of voters. Nonetheless the idea of majority rule is firmly entrenched in political attitudes. Varieties of the system occur, the most important being a 'qualified' majority, that is, a requirement that more than 51% of an electorate support an issue or candidate for a valid result. Thus constitutional amendments both in political systems and other organizations often require a two-thirds vote (66%) for passage. Again the logic is slightly hazy—if 51% is not sacrosanct, why fix on any other figure, specifically, short of absolute unanimity?

Managerial Capitalism

Managerial capitalism is a name sometimes given to a brand of what is normally thought of as Conservative party ideology in British politics, and which has some resemblance to a right-wing form of LIBERALISM. The trouble is that much of what has traditionally been seen as Conservatism is not found as part of the working ideas of those actually in the Conservative party, and vice versa. Managerial capitalism is the ideology of those, mainly from the centre or left of the modern Conservative party, whose overwhelming aim is the efficient running of the existing mixed economy, more probably on KEYNESIAN than MONETARIST lines. While they do not wish to see any development of the economy towards a socialist position, and believe in the need for inequality as an incentive mechanism, and are prone to object to trade unions as damaging to economics, they retain very few right-wing beliefs. Nor, however, do they share any of the traditional 'Noblesse Oblige' notions of the aristocratic Disraeli wing of the party. The old term from the 1950s in British politics, BUTSKELLISM, might equally well suit them. In terms of personalities the phrase covers especially well the Prime Minister from 1970–74, Edward Heath, whose personal style and political interests contrasted equally with the patrician Disraeli politics of his predecessors and the abrasive right-wing positions, with their slightly populist undertones, of his successor as Conservative leader, Margaret Thatcher. It is typical, and illustrative of this position, that Mr. Heath's government showed little interest in defence or foreign affairs, but was extremely keen, and successful, in getting Britain into the EEC, with no residual worry about sovereignty. There are so many strands of thought in the Conservative party that such labels are invaluable, though little can be said of their central ideology, and one must rely on indications of a syndrome of attitudes. Managerial capitalism can perhaps best be described negatively—it is not right-wing in social terms, not TORY, and may well be a variant of SOCIAL DEMOCRACY, though with a much more pragmatic approach to welfare style policies.

Mandate

Mandates are typically claimed by successful parties in national elections even when they have actually gained only a smallish plurality of votes. Technically there are two meanings of mandate, though they are interconnected. One meaning is that if a party, or a candidate, has stood for election on a particular set of policies, then, if he wins the election he has a 'mandate' from the people to implement those policies. Thus governments often claim they are 'mandated' to carry out some action even if there is no good reason to believe the policy in question had very much to do with their electoral victory. The alternative, and original, meaning is where some body, perhaps a constituency division of a political party, on being required to send a representative to a national conference, gives the chosen representative binding instructions to argue or vote in a fixed way on some particular issue. The question of mandating a representative is a vital one in democratic theory. One view holds that those who elect a representative are entitled to mandate him to cast specific votes so as directly to represent the majority view in the body that selects him. Alternative to this is the theory, most forcefully put by Edmund BURKE, that selecting a representative, (who may in fact be an authorized candidate at a subsequent public election, perhaps as a Member of Parliament) is a matter of selecting the best person one can find, and then trusting that person's judgement on any issues that come up. Questions of whether a mandate does or could exist, how much anyone is bound by it, and when an election result would certify such a mandate are hotly-contested matters of modern arguments about democracy both in parliaments and parties.

Mannheim

Karl Mannheim (1893–1947) was a German sociologist and theorist who, both before and after the Second World War, developed some of the most penetrating ideas on the problem of IDEOLOGY in society yet to be published. Although there are MARXIST overtones to his theoretical writing, he was not a Marxist in any orthodox sense, and provides us with the only powerful non-Marxist analysis of the social conditioning of thought, and the consequences for political life of socio-economically derived ideologies. His classic work, *Ideology and Utopia,* distinguishes with great care the various ways in which men all suffer from viewing the world through categories, values and assumptions that owe more to their own location in the socio-economic system than from any really clear observation of reality. It is part of Mannheim's corrective to Marxism that he insists that all those with clear socio-economic interests are liable to a distortion in the way they see the world and understand, for example, the workings of the economy. Thus there cannot be some especially privileged class, as some Marxists want to regard the proletariat, who perceive things truly whilst the bourgeoisie are blinkered by FALSE CONSCIOUSNESS. He does, however, grant to one sector of society a greater chance to see clearly. These are what he calls the 'free floating intelligentsia', who, because they have no clear economic interest, being neither properly workers in the Marxist sense, nor capitalists, can hope to synthesize the conflicting world pictures of the two opposing classes. It was this social group on whom Mannheim placed his trust for the creation of a new and peaceful Europe after the Second World War. Not only has the intelligentsia come to be more and more influential in post-war countries on both sides of the Iron Curtain, but also they fit very badly into most orthodox Marxist class analyses.

Mao Tse-tung

Mao Tse-tung (1893–1976) can best be characterized with an aphorism that suits well his own literary style, unusually erudite amongst modern communist leaders. He is the man who ruled a quarter of the world's population for a quarter of a century. The son of a peasant farmer he discovered MARXISM while in Peking (having already broken with Chinese tradition in disobeying his father and leaving the peasant life). He was one of the founders of the Chinese Communist party, in 1921, and from then until the setting up of the People's Republic of China in 1949, of which he became Chairman, was fully engaged in revolutionary and military activities. He proved a great guerrilla leader and military tactician, fighting successively the established Chinese authorities, the Japanese, and the nationalists of Chiang Kai-shek. His most important contribution was the radical re-thinking of Marxist-Leninism to suit the overwhelmingly agricultural and traditionalist societies of Asia, and his insistence on finding his revolutionary elite from the peasantry rather than the urban proletariat. This alone, and his success in achieving the theoretical goal would have made him a master tactician of Marxism. But he went much further in his thought, continually trying to make a communist regime much less dependent on the bureaucratic elite of the party than any other leader in power (as opposed to the outsiders like ROSA LUXEMBURG or the later TROTSKY). In a series of radical attacks on the institutionalized 'cadres' of the party and state he fought, often alone amongst his elite, a battle to keep close contacts with the actual aspirations of Chinese peasant life. Classically educated himself (he was a poet of considerable distinction), he tended to express his ideas in the idiom of classical Chinese tradition rather than the jargon of Marxist-Leninism, and indeed Stalin, amongst others, felt that he either actually did not know, or did not wish to know, very much about the 'scientific socialism' of the orthodox canon. Certainly he appears to have used Marxism simply as a handy weapon to fight the encrusted tradition of Chinese feudalism.

Three of his great campaigns against institutionalized and undemocratic party elitism are characteristic. In 1956, when the Communist world was rocked by the Hungarian uprising, and when its repercussions were met with extra repression in Eastern Europe, Mao reacted in quite the opposite way. Launching a campaign he called 'The Hundred Flowers', he urged the Chinese actively to criticize the shortcomings of party leaders, insisting that any injustices must be brought to light, and that no party that was vulnerable to such attacks deserved to rule. The campaign was brought to a rapid halt, demonstrating what was little realized in the West at the time, that Mao had far from perfect control over his own party leaders, and was often without a majority in the Politburo. A few years later he ignored the arguments of technicians and economists and tried to rush China's economic development, to build true communism, in a massive and short term plan. Typical of this (he called it The Great Leap Forward), was his plan to push Chinese steel production to 30 million tons a year by urging the building of thousands of tiny 'backyard' steel furnaces. As with most of his economic plans, it was a disaster, completely ignoring the need for massive capital injection and large plants with increasing returns to scale. Again it was stopped short, after little more than a year, by pressure from his fellow leaders.

The final push by Mao to stop the development of a new party-based ruling middle class was the famous 'CULTURAL REVOLUTION'. This he launched in 1965, fearing, quite correctly, that he was losing all control of the party. The movement urged the forming of radical 'Red Guards' who would go into the countryside and raise what was very nearly a populist revolution against the communist state. His commitment to the peasant life was so strong, and his dislike of the whole principle of division of labour was so great that he tried to force all technocrats, students, party bureaucrats to be made to work in the countryside along with the peasants and to give up, not only their privileges, but their technical authority. Thousands were killed, and hundreds of thousands forced to give up their specialities, confess their 'revisionist' thoughts, and do penance. Though the cultural revolution only lasted, at its height, for a year, it did massive damage to China's economic and technical development. After his death most of those associated with this movement were purged as thousands of much needed technicians streamed back to the cities, discipline was restored in the universities, and the post-Mao leadership struggled to return China to a more ortho-dox approach to socio-economic modernization. His political thought, neatly expressed in a small book called, officially, *The Thoughts of Chairman Mao,* and more popularly, *The Little Red Book* became the unofficial bible not only in China, but world wide. His insistence on Chinese autonomy was in part responsible for the widening gulf between Russia and China which has led, especially since the rapprochement between the USA and the People's Repub-lic, to a serious ideological split in the communist world. Mao so totally rejected the cooperation of the USSR that he even tried to stop Soviet military supplies getting to the North Vietnamese, whom he was supporting in the Vietnamese war. Though a brilliant, if idiosyncratic leader, it is unclear whether his leadership, so opposed in style and ideology to European communism, helped or hindered China. What is not in doubt is his popularity amongst third world radical movements, which still poses a problem for Moscow.

Maoism

Maoism, largely a matter of following the ideas set forth in the famous 'little red book', technically *The Thoughts of Chairman Mao,* is a radical version of communism, owing rather less than might be expected to Marxist-Leninism which held sway, on and off, in China during his years in office. It also caught the attention of radicals world wide, and much of the French, German and even American far left are still influenced by it. The point behind Maoism is a total rejection of the immunity of the official communist party to criticism, and the need directly to work with and listen to 'the people'. As a doctrine it is completely anti-elitist, rejecting not only hierarchy in organization, but even the authority of technical expertise. Thus Maoism represents a sort of 'populist' MARXISM, a direct opposition to DEMOCRATIC CENTRALISM, and urges a permanent rejection of authority. It also stresses communalism and the small scale organization of social and economic units, rather than large scale organization with more 'privatized' individual life. It is a doctrine attractive to the impatient and anarchist, rather than the gradualist and ordered aspects of revolutionary expectations, which was why it was so popular, for example, amongst the student revolutionaries in Paris in 1968. From the viewpoint of orthodox communism it is extremely dangerous, and the current Chinese leadership is doing as much to eradicate it in China as are leaders of Western and Eastern communist parties in their own countries. Technically it can only be described as utopian, but its form of expression, by a man who wrote naturally in the classic aphorisms of Chinese culture, makes it eminently more readable than the turgid jargon of much modern Marxism. Because Mao organized his revolution, and directed his thought, to communism in predominantly agrarian and non industrialized societies, Maoism has heavily affected communist movements in the THIRD WORLD, and especially in Asia.

Marcuse

Herbert Marcuse (1889–1979) was one of the German emigré intellectuals who came to America between the wars, settling ultimately in California where he taught and wrote political and social theory. Although his scholarly reputation was founded at least as early as the 1941 publication of his major study of Hegel, *Reason and*

Revolution, his real fame came in the 1960s when he was taken up as an intellectual leader by the radical student movement in the US.

A MARXIST of sorts, Marcuse was always more interested in the 'humanist' or 'early' MARX, whose concern for the alienating impact of modern society was much nearer Marcuse's interests than the 'economist' Marx of *Das Kapital.* The books that earned Marcuse his role in the American radical movement were those like *One Dimensional Man* and *Eros and Civilisation* which concentrated more on the emotional and ideological constraints of modern mass society than the straightforward analysis of class struggle and economic exploitation.

In fact Marcuse early realized the great difficulty of fitting a Marxist class model to American society, where the relative affluence of blue collar workers, especially if they were white and northern, and their conservative and racist social views made them, for him, poor material for a proletarian uprising. He was concerned for such status groups, but more because he felt they suffered a FALSE CONSCIOUSNESS, and were caught striving to satisfy false needs implanted by the media and advertising agencies in the interests of an inhuman and over-materalist economy. Marcuse's own hopes were for a new form of revolutionary class, forged out of those, blacks, students, ecologists, any one who was cut loose from the basic acquisitive economic structure and who would fight for human liberation from both capitalist and state socialist systems. His own work on Russia, *Soviet Communism and Russian Marxism* had convinced him that the Marxist revolution as practised in Eastern Europe was every bit as de-humanizing as capitalism, and this semi-anarchist position was perfectly fitting for the Vietnam-anxious radicals of the period. In some ways his work is almost more LIBERTARIAN than Marxist, and despite the death of the cause that made him famous, still stands close reading as an alternative radical critique of high-technology society.

Marshall Plan

The Marshall Plan was the economic aid plan for the recovery of European economies instituted by George Marshall when he was Secretary of State in the Truman administration in the US. He first suggested the plan in a famous speech at Harvard in June 1947. The idea was that a very large dollar programme of aid would be provided for post-war reconstruction on condition that the European powers first started by indicating a serious intent to collaborate rather than compete against each other. Warmly welcomed by France and Britain the plan was bitterly opposed by the Soviet Union, which saw it as an attempt to exert American influence on post-war Europe, and thus as a threat to their own control. Despite this the Western European nations rapidly set up the Organisation for European Economic Cooperation (OEEC, which later became the OECD), and by 1948 the dollars started flowing in. In the four years between 1948 and 1952 over US$17,000 million were given, administered through the OEEC, with Britain and France, along with West Germany being the main beneficiaries. Because of Soviet opposition none of the money was available to Eastern European nations, though Marshall would have been prepared to try to get Congress to allow this had the whole plan not been vetoed by the Soviet Foreign Minister.

As well as being the major single cause of the rapid economic recovery of Europe, the supply of these funds during the early days of the COLD WAR (the Berlin Blockade, for example, coincided with the first payments) helped cement together the alliance that later became NATO (q.v.) and, in opposition, to fix the Eastern European/Soviet Union alliance. Britain would certainly have found the recovery even harder had it not been for Marshall aid, especially as the initial post-war defence cuts had to be reversed with the increasing political tension. Other countries, notably France, were able to take advantage of the dollars and the dislocation of social patterns arising from the war not just to repair, but massively to modernize their economy, so that by the late 1950s the French economy was no longer recognizable as a development of the Third Republic economy.

Martial Law

Martial Law is a technical concept in international and domiciliary law. Martial law is a state of affairs declared by the civilian government in which the military forces are empowered to rule, govern, and control some area in a way involving direct force, and without the usual constraints of democratic decision-making or the acceptance of civil rights. When an area, which can vary from a small locality all the way to an entire nation, is under martial law the local military commanders may issue binding edicts, and may instruct their soldiers to exercise 'deadly force' (in the technical legal sense) in ensuring immediate obedience to these edicts. It is always seen as a temporary state of affairs, and is legitimate (see LEGITIMACY), in the way that its cognate, military rule, is often not seen to be, because it should be directly decided upon and granted by the civilian government.

Marx

Karl Marx (1818–1883) is the most famous of all socialist or communist figures. More has been said and done in the name of MARXISM than in the name of any other social thinker in history. By origin he was a German academic and journalist, heavily influenced by German Idealism as a philosophical school, and particularly by HEGEL. He came to Britain when his political activities in Germany became too dangerous, and lived as a writer and revolutionary activist thereafter, in a close association with ENGELS, whose contribution to the Marxist canon is considerable. As befitted one of his theories, that there was a need for a close connection between political practice and political theorizing, Marx was always closely connected with Communist and other revolutionary movements, and much of his more evocative writing consisted either of journalistic analyses of such movements, or historical accounts of would-be revolutions. Modern scholarship has suggested that there are at least two distinct phases in his writing, the 'early Marx', which includes at least the rather humanistic ideas of the *1848 Manuscripts*, and the later Marx of the much more technical and 'scientific' economics of *Das Kapital*, the first volume of which was published in 1867.

The most crucial part of his rich and complex theories is the doctrine that man, as a physical being, must be explained in materialistic terms. To Marx, a man was a being whose identity and nature arose out of his purely practical attempts to make his livelihood in what amounted almost to a struggle against a hostile physical environment. As a result, what man did determined what he became. In practical terms this meant that the conditions under which he earned his living, as owner or proprietor, wage labourer or peasant, formed his ideology and consciousness. But as Marx also argued that man existed only as a member of an economic class, and that all classes were always in competition with others below or above them in an economically-supported power hierarchy, he saw human civilization as characterized by class warfare. That this warfare had an economically-determined course, leading to an ultimate Communist society in which there would be no further class antagonisms, and therefore no inequality, was an absolute article of faith. From it derived all the later Communist hopes for proletarian revolution and the socialist belief in the need to abolish private ownership of property, because, for Marxists, control of property is the very definition of a class system. Marx, in his voluminous writings, touched on endless aspects of social life, but all were ultimately linked to a simple formula: man takes his essence from labour in pursuit of material ends; control of material both creates upper and lower classes and gives the upper class control over politics, including the construction of IDEOLOGIES and social consciousness. But there are implacable economic rules which ultimately determine economic development. These economic laws make it inevitable that, ultimately, capitalist society will collapse because of its own inherent contradictions, and Communism will emerge.

Marxism

Marxism is a general label to attach to any social theory that can claim a vague philosophical derivation from the works of Karl MARX. In fact Marxism as a general position has become so broad that there is often little serious connection, even in theory. When Marxism is taken to refer also to the operating policies of so-called Marxist or Communist states, as with the Soviet Union, the philosophical gap becomes enormous. This is not to suggest that the various branches of Marxism are themselves theoretically incoherent, nor that they do not have all that much in common. But by now the connections between different forms of Marxism can best be described as involving 'family resemblances' rather than a minimal set of necessary common postulates. The Marxism associated with the Second International, for example, is rigorously deterministic in an economic way, whilst the Marxism associated with the French school inspired by Althusser has distinctly 'functionalist' undertones, and that of the other French Marxist leader in the post-war years, Poulantzas, allows considerable autonomous political power to the state. Other brands of Marxist-derived theory may not even have 'Marx' as part of the title—TROTSKYISM and MAOISM, while they are 'deviations' from what many would regard as proper Marxism, have much in common with original writings by Karl Marx that modern developments of his insights lack. As far as the actual doctrines of Communist societies go, it is probably better, for the Soviet Union and Eastern Europe, to talk of Marxist-Leninism, because LENIN, and to some extent still STALIN, left major impacts in the process of turning a general theory into a practical doctrine for revolutionaries and subsequent post-revolutionary governments. The most one could require as a common thread to all forms of modern Marxism would be the following tenets: (i) that economic matters ultimately control political and cultural phenomena; (ii) that abolition of private property is necessary to ensure equality and an end to exploitation; (iii) that the road to such a society must come about by the proletariat, or its (not necessarily proletarian) leaders developing a revolutionary consciousness, grasping power, and acting as a vanguard to issue in the Communist society. Of particular importance in explaining the various splits is the whole question of leadership, and the extent to which there has got to be what Marx called a 'DICTATORSHIP OF THE PROLETARIAT' before true democratic Communism can flourish. Secondly the question of the nature of, and need for, a revolutionary rather than a gradualist road to the abolition of capitalist society has great importance, especially in the thinking of the EURO-COMMUNIST parties and their theorists like GRAMSCI.

Mass Media

The media are the methods of mass communication and entertainment which have developed into vital political forces with more or less total adult literacy and extensive ownership of television and radio. There is no doubt that literacy, with its concomitant development of large circulation newspapers had a major impact on political attitudes, and especially on the fighting of elections. Later the spread of broadcasting and above all of news and current affairs broadcasting which give an immediacy to distant events has produced a mass public much less amenable to political manipulation. At the same time there has grown serious concern that such media can themselves be methods of social control, and of political influence. In fact there is little hard evidence that, for example, election broadcasts much effect political choice in liberal democracies. Nor is the rate of up-take of information particularly high; the mass readership, and the mass television audience are not especially interested in political information or debate, and their greater availability do not seem to have increased the demand.

Nonetheless most countries have set up controls, of varying seriousness and severity on the political bias of the broadcast media, though any extensive control of the print media is usually interpreted as unfair interference, or even as a denial of freedom of speech. There are in fact suggestions from elements of the left in some countries for a greater control of newspapers because they are seen as tools of the ownership, but these arguments are seldom heard in other systems, for example Italy and Sweden where direct party ownership of the press is common. Enormous power is at times attributed to the media, and when they can, politicians spend very large advertising budgets most eagerly, on print space and air time, but the real problem seems largely to be the old one of censorship and detailed control of information. Where this is missing, as with any relatively free mass media system, it is unclear that the media have power over and above the power, or consequences, of the sheer information they contain.

Massive Retaliation

Massive retaliation was the earliest of post-war American nuclear strategy doctrines. It was developed in the immediate post-war days when the USA was virtually the sole wielder of nuclear weapons. It was, very simply, the idea that any aggression by the USSR in Europe or elsewhere would be met by a huge nuclear onslaught on Russia. This was only plausible because, at that stage, there was neither a convincing alternative for the West, given comparative figures for conventional capacity, nor any danger of the East launching any sort of counter-stroke. Slowly this doctrine gave way to the idea of FLEXIBLE RESPONSE, and to an understanding of ESCALATION.

Materialism

Materialism is a philosophical or sociological doctrine that only the material, or physical world need be or can be used in the explanation of social processes and institutions. Most commonly associated with MARXIST theories (though by no means limited to them), materialism is a doctrine that, *inter alia*, denies the meaningfulness of, for example religious experience or consciousness except as projections by men of their physical experience. In one of its forms, Dialectical-Materialism (often abbreviated in Russia to DiaMat) it is the quasi-Marxist doctrine that only technical changes in the modes and means of production cause development and change in societies and economies. Materialism thus insists that social consciousness is the product of the material conditions of life, and therefore that all other human institutions, whether legal and political systems, ideologies, religions, kinship patterns or even art forms are ultimately dependent on the economic infrastructure. ENGELS, rather than MARX himself is largely responsible for the 'Materialist conception of history' which, inverting HEGEL, insists on the physical world and man's struggle with it for survival being basic, rather than human ideas, reason and spirit. It is materialism,

207

whether in Marxism, socialism, or other ideologies that CHRISTIANITY, and especially Catholicism has always sought politically to combat.

Miliband

Ralph Miliband is a MARXIST political scientist who has written, *inter alia*, two very penetrating books on the political systems of capitalist countries, with a major emphasis on Britain. Most of his career was spent at the London School of Economics, thus helping to keep up the tradition of Laski and others, though he has been briefly Professor at Leeds University. His first major book, *Parliamentary Socialism*, was devoted to a theme that recurs throughout his work, his disappointment with the leadership of the British Labour Party. He sees this party (and, on the whole, Socialist parties elsewhere when they get into power) as having betrayed the true interests of the working class, and being almost as keen as the Conservative party to keep a capitalist economic system going. The book he is best known by is *The State in Capitalist Society*, which is a version of an elite analysis of Western democracies, though admixed with a rather weak form of a Marxist class analysis. His conclusion is that the branches of state power are all held by those who have inherited or acquired a middle class perspective, that the media is almost entirely biased against true socialism and the interests of the working class, and, as suggested above, that the Labour party is involved in this capitalist web. Though the work is powerfully argued and well documented, it has suffered by falling between two stools. Whilst the PLURALISTS have, not surprisingly, rejected it on both theoretical and empirical grounds, it caused considerable fury amongst Marxist intellectuals, especially in France, for seeming to accept the pluralists' own methodology, and for messing up a proper class analysis. However one ultimately judges it, his work remains a very powerful and informed critique of modern Western society.

Militant

Militant is, of course, a perfectly ordinary English word which means someone who is very strongly committed to, and very active in support of, some cause or other. It could be, and sometimes still is, applied to almost any active supporter of a creed. Perhaps the first common usage like this is, after all, the idea of 'The Church Militant'. However, in British politics in the 1970s and 1980s the word has become almost exclusively the property of the far left. The 'Militant Tendency' is a splinter group of extreme left-wing

MARXISTS who have penetrated the Labour Party, so named after their weekly paper *Militant.* In more general contexts, referring to anyone as politically militant in contemporary Britain would inevitably imply such a political position.

Militarism

Militarism can mean one or other of two empirically related but logically distinct things. When used of the policy of a state it is a claim that the nation in question seeks to gain its ends by overt or threatened use of military force. As such, in the heavily ideologically loaded language that such concepts operate in, the nation would be a threat to world peace, and any armaments increase it carried out would be evidence of its 'militaristic' tendencies. The alternative meaning is to describe a political culture, ideology or idea as militaristic to the extent that it supports or extols military values, patriotism, and the associated group behaviour or symbols. Obviously states that are in fact, militaristic are likely to exhibit militarism in much of the social symbolism, as with the general love of uniforms in Nazi Germany.

Military

Military can be used politically as either a noun or an adjective. As a noun, 'The Military' refers to the whole organization of defensive and offensive armed force in a society. Its typical political use is in some compound, as 'The Military-Industrial' complex, where it means the armed forces and the civil service and political direction of them. The main point of describing this unitary element, in political analysis, is to suggest that they occupy a special set of homogenous related interests opposed to the civil interests of the society, and, in most societies anyway, an illegitimate set of interests, or an illegitimate use of power and influence in their pursuit. The derived adjective is self-evident in meaning. It is worth noting that the words almost never carry, in modern usage, the technical original meaning of relating to land rather than sea forces. Military is not opposed to Naval or Air, but rather includes them all. As such it obscures vital historical and political differences in most countries, producing a false sense of the uniformity of these aspects of social organization.

Military Regimes

Military regimes are very autocratic governments where the MILI-TARY controls the country's political system—usually following a coup d'etat. In military regimes the civil liberties of the subjects and normal political and constitutional arrangements may be suspended. Thus it is unlikely for example that opposition parties will be allowed to operate freely in a military regime. Although military regimes are frequently dictatorial it is not necessarily the case that they will be totalitarian (see TOTALITARIANISM). If they occur because of a national crisis or political emergency (see EMERGENCY POWERS) such regimes may have a degree of political LEGITIMACY. And in some cases the leaders of the regime may intend to restore the democratic system of government as soon as it is deemed safe to do so, although the restoration of normal political life is often difficult.

Military coups and military regimes are most often associated with third world countries though both Greece and Turkey in contemporary Europe have experienced military regimes. In Latin America military regimes have frequently brought experiments with democratic government to an end although their supporters would claim that military intervention in such countries as Chile was necessary to end the spiral of hyper-inflation, urban terrorism and disorder which the troubled democracies were experiencing. In some countries the existence of a military regime is associated with extreme repression such as the so-called "death squads" and torture units, found in El Salvador and Nicaragua. Military regimes are thus a very common form of government but an unpopular and suspect one also.

Mill, James

James Mill (1773–1836), along with Jeremy BENTHAM, was one of the founders of the UTILITARIAN social theories that came to dominate British, and to a lesser extent American social thought during the 19th century. Though less influential than his close friend Bentham, and philosophically much less important than his son John Stuart MILL, James Mill's writings were probably more accessible than those of the other early founders. In particular he wrote more directly about political theory than did Bentham. He advocated an extension of electoral democracy rather before this became generally accepted amongst even radical middle class intellectuals. His theory of democracy was somewhat limited, however, because his distrust of the working class was almost as profound as his contempt for the traditional aristocracy. In a very Aristotelian manner he supported the extra influence for the middle classes, whom he saw as naturally balancing all interests in the state. In many ways he was a brilliant propagandist for selling utilitarian ideals to the rising professional and commercial bourgeoisie (see Bourgeois), rather than an original or creative developer of utilitarianism.

J.S. Mill

John Stuart Mill (1806–1873) was the son of James Mill who, with his close friend and collaborator Jeremy Bentham, entirely controlled his education, with the more or less explicit intention of producing a brilliant successor as an exponent of Utilitarianism. In this they succeeded, although he was to go far beyond them in some respects, and certainly produced a version of utilitarianism more sophisticated and more suited to English Liberalism than we would have had if we been forced to rely on his elders' theories. Through a long career as a writer, though he also had varied practical experience, J.S. Mill worked on a variety of topics. His most famous work today consists of three long essays, *On Liberty*, *On Utilitarianism*, and *On Representative Government*, though his purely philosophical work, especially the *System of Logic*, is also of continued academic interest.

In *On Utilitarianism* he tries to reduce the harshness and hedonism of Bentham's approach, accepting, for example, what Bentham denied, that not all sources of pleasure were equally valid. (He rejected, for example, Bentham's famous notion that it was better to be a pig satisfied than Socrates dissatisfied). The essay *On Liberty* is probably the most read of all his works, arguing for a highly libertarian system in which the only justification allowable for government interference in anyone's life was to prevent them from harming others, and never the claim that a government might know a person's true interests better than the individual. Indeed his great fear, against which the whole essay is directed, was the Tyranny of the Majority, the fear of popular pressure against the non-conformist individual. His justification for such maximum individual liberty, however, is a brilliant thesis about human progress through the discovery of new truths only possible, according to Mill, in a society where no interference in personal belief, or the expression of belief is tolerated. A beautiful stylist, with a wide-ranging scholarship, his major essays remain vital elements in curricula throughout departments of Politics and Philosophy, and much of the accepted values of a Western society still conforms better to his vision than to that of almost any other thinker of his period.

Mills

C. Wright Mills (1916–1962) was an American sociologist, one of few who dominated the field in the 1940s and early 1950s, and unusual, in the American context, for being considerably to the left, though he was never a convinced Marxist (see MARXISM). Though much of his work, for example his superb *The Sociological Imagination*, is of interest only to academics, he produced one of the first, and arguably still the best, radical critique of American politics and the changes in the system that threatened its democratic claims. This, *The Power Elite,* centres on the development from the Second World War onwards of the huge and influential military machine in the USA, an institution that had hardly existed before 1942. By demonstrating the connections between the military and the major industrial corporations, and linking this 'Military-Industrial Complex' to the rising executive power of the Presidency and the top civil service appointments, he painted, early in the 1950s, a picture of decision-making in America that was not to become commonly believed until the days of Vietnam and Watergate. His work has been an inspiration for authors of various political persuasions in the study of American politics, and though he perhaps exaggerated and selected his evidence rather carefully, few deny his perception, or would not admit that he mounts a very powerful and persuasive argument. In particular his attack on the media for turning a once highly articulate and argumentative citizen body into passive receivers of others' views fits all too well with more 'scientific' research on opinion formation, and seems to prophesy the later development of political consultants and the huge impact of media techniques in grooming and selling electoral candidates. It is worth noting, in Mills' support, that his book starts with a quotation by the far from radical President Eisenhower, warning Congress against the dangers of 'the military-industrial complex'.

Minorities

Technically minorities are, obviously, those who are not in a majority in some sense in a political system. In most usages minorities are thought of as having a common positive identity, rather than being united only in their opposition to the majority. Secondly, although it is perfectly proper to refer to a minority existing on only one issue, or by virtue of one single characteristic, this is not usually the most important meaning. The politically important sense of 'minority' is that a group in society has a set of common interests and beliefs over a wide set of issues, which marks it out as needing, deserving or even being given special treatment that the majority of citizens do not. Furthermore minorities are thought of usually as having a permanence, or at least a very long term existence, and requiring the establishment of institutional or structural methods for helping them. The most common politically important minorities are racial or ethnic groups in a society who are seen as suffering across a broad spectrum of disadvantages and needing special legal protection and positive discrimination. Similarly one finds references to sexual minorities (homosexuals), or religious minorities. In all these cases what is at stake is not so much the actual arithmetical minority status, but the fact that the group in question is cut off from, and usually subordinate to a dominant set of interests against which it needs protection. Indeed it would be only partially absurd to regard a group which was, as it happened, in a majority in the population as being nonetheless a minority in this sense. Occasionally one finds women in general described as a political minority, even though they may be statistically in a majority, because of the way in which they have been historically treated as inferior or lacking full rights.

A related use of minority is to refer to a minority party, or minority public opinion where the difference with the overall culture is a major ideological contrast, and not merely a set of specific and contingent policy disagreements. In terms of debates about electoral reform, for example, such political minorities are also often thought of as deserving special legal protection to ensure their views are represented in legislatures.

Modernization

Modernization enters political science and political discourse from sociology, and refers generally to the capacity of countries from outside the European/North American/OLD COMMONWEALTH countries, (the FIRST WORLD, in other words), to develop the economic and political capacity, and the social institutions, needed to support a LIBERAL DEMOCRACY such as is found in parts of the First World. While this approach in political science is obviously at risk of being biased in terms of Western values, there is a strong tradition in social and political theory of studying change in this way, much of it derived from Max WEBER. The main thesis is that a form of political DIVISION OF LABOUR is needed, in which the political system moves from having only a few, all-embracing, authoritative posts, a tribal chieftain, perhaps, to highly specific and task-specialized roles in a modern bureaucratic and governmental system. At the same time changes in social conditions, especially communications and education, are seen as steadily increasing the capacity of a system to maintain and apply complex modern politics oriented to satisfying as many different political interests as possible.

Monarchy

Monarchy means, of course, rule by a single individual who is seen as royal, as especially noble, at the apex of an aristocratic pyramid of honour and authority. Added to this a system, to be truly monarchial, probably has to be hereditary, although not all early monarchies were; now that we have elected rulers of other types, the notion of an elected Kingship seems somewhat otiose. Certainly a monarch is one who rules simply by authority stemming from his position, however this may ultimately be justified, and sovereignty, in such a system, lies in the monarch, not in the people. The most common form of monarchy today, and there are few in modern politics, is Constitutional Monarchy, the phrase having little clear meaning but generally indicating a monarch who has severe limits to his powers, and who must accept the role and power of other bodies, such as Parliaments and Cabinets. In practice Constitutional Monarchs have virtually no powers left, except, sometimes, in periods of great crisis. In Britain, for example, the Monarch technically could refuse royal assent to an Act of Parliament, without which the Act has no legal force, but there is no evidence of this having been done for well over a century.

The monarch typically, as in Britain, has a residual role to play in helping the formation of new governments after an election, or in granting to the government the authority to dissolve Parliament and call an election, much as have many Presidents in systems where the President is Head of State. In some countries, Sweden being the best case, even these residual powers have been stripped away, and, popular though the Swedish monarchy is, there is no mention of the throne at all in the most recent Swedish constitution. It would be wrong to dismiss entirely the potential political significance of monarchy, however. In some countries, Britain and Norway being good examples, the symbolic authority is very high amongst certain sectors. Few military officers, for example, take entirely lightly the idea that their commissions come from the monarch, and might show much more loyalty to a King or Queen than to a government, given the military distaste for politics, were a clash to arise. More generally monarchs as Heads of State serve as a more clearly neutral symbol of national unity, and a focus for citizen loyalty, than do Presidents. Monarchist tendencies have not entirely died out amongst ultra-traditionalist and Conservative elements in European countries that have dispensed with them. Though there remain few monarchies, those which have survived look likely to continue, if only because they provide a convenient way to separate the Head of State role from the Head of Government, and because they remain popular with their subjects.

Monetarism

Monetarism, as used in ordinary political discourse rather than, say, technical economics writing, refers to a rather vague general understanding of certain economic theories, usually associated with Milton Friedman, or the Chicago School of economics in general. It has become rapidly popular with politicians on the right in America and Britain as an apparent alternative to KEYNESIAN economics inside capitalist societies. The Conservative government elected in Britain in 1979 is perhaps the first avowedly 'Monetarist' government in Britain, although many would argue that the economic policies of most governments since the late 1960s, including the Labour governments, have used monetarist policies. The stress of this theory is on reducing inflation at all costs, and its name derives from the fact that the theory claims that the supply of money in the economy is virtually the only factor affecting the inflation rate. At the same time the theory, certainly as understood by most right-wing politicians, argues for a virtual return to LAISSER-FAIRE economics and an abandonment of government control in any direct way, in favour of operating almost entirely on the money market and the rate of interest. One implication of the theory is that inflation is itself the prime evil, and the prime cause of all other economic ills, especially unemployment. As the money supply can only easily be cut either by cutting public expenditure, or by massive tax increases and the restoration of balanced budgets, its application by otherwise laisser-faire politicians can only be by public expenditure decreases. In many ways the theory is not so much new, as a return to what was commonly understood as economic orthodoxy before Keynesian 'demand management' became politically acceptable.

Monroe Doctrine

The Monroe Doctrine is to some extent the major juridical basis for US policy in Latin America, and after decades of irrelevance has become important again in recent years, though it is essentially a unilateral declaration of what America intends to do, rather than a multilateral agreement about how nations on the American continent should collectively act. Announced by President Monroe in a message to Congress in 1823, it states effectively that the US will not allow interference in any country of the American continent by any European power, and that any such involvement will be regarded as a danger to the peace and security of the United States itself.

215

Originally intended to warn off the Triple Alliance of European powers from any attempt to help Spain regain control of its disintegrating South American empire, it was also directed against Czarist Russia, which appeared to have colonial ambitions towards the Pacific coast of the USA. The doctrine was invoked on several occasions during the 19th century, and indeed expanded to mean that any vital interest of the USA anywhere on the continent could and would be protected. As US relations with most Latin American powers grew increasingly cordial during the 20th century the doctrine came to seem both less unilateral and more legalistic, with much of its meaning enshrined in inter-American treaties such as the Bogota treaty which set up the Organization of American States in 1948.

However the increase in radical opposition to the right wing and often corrupt governments of Latin America led after the Second World War to a situation in which the Soviet Union directly or otherwise came to confront the USA as they supported different sides in the civil wars. The doctrine was used to justify the 1962 American action in blockading Cuba to force Soviet withdrawal of missiles, and to justify the intervention by US Marines in the Dominican Republic in 1965 to prevent the election of a Communist government. As the guerrilla campaigns against the traditional ruling classes, especially in Central America increased, with increasing support from a Cuba more and more firmly in the Soviet camp, the importance of the doctrine, and its clear nature as a declaration by the USA of what it would not tolerate became more vital. Although there is no doubt that Cuban aid to left wing movements in Latin America is both financed and encouraged by the Soviet Union, it remains true that the doctrine is actually being used to allow the United States to intervene in purely regional political and social disputes. The US will not readily allow the establishment of any government of a communist nature anywhere in its hemisphere, whether or not this is actually the result of interference from a European power, and this is what the Monroe doctrine has come to mean.

Ironically the doctrine was also the first statement of American isolationism, and indeed part of the justification of the unilateral declaration of hegemony over the American continent was a promise not to intervene or have any interest in matters on the European continent. As the isolationist aspect of the doctrine has now completely disappeared with US membership of NATO, there is no good reason except *realpolitik* for other countries to accept their exclusion, even when invited to help a local State, from the southern half of the American continent.

Montesquieu

The French nobleman Charles-Louis de Secondat Montesquieu (1689–1755) is often seen, along with MACHIAVELLI, as one of the founding fathers of modern political science. His major work, *The Spirit of the Laws* (1734), is an attempt to provide what would now be seen as a cultural and environmental explanation for the legitimacy of different forms of government in different contexts. He held, for example, that climate has a major impact on the nature of social relations, and therefore of political bonds. He tried to identify, at the same time, a particular ideological prop to different forms of government, such as a high value attached to the idea of 'honour' in a monarchical society.

Although his work was influential in helping to develop a more empirical aspect to political studies, influencing future writers as diverse as BURKE and ENGELS, it is his constitutional theory that has been most important in retrospect. Montesquieu, along with LOCKE, developed the concept of the SEPARATION OF POWERS, whereby the executive, legislative and judicial branches of government are independent of each other, and have the power to check each other's actions. This, which he held to be a basic constitutional need if liberty was to be preserved from tyrannical governments, has its most famous expression in the American Constitution, the writers of which were acutely conscious of Montesquieu's ideas on the subject.

Moral Majority

The Moral Majority is an American pressure group founded in 1979 which forms an important part of the new right. Its purpose was to campaign for the election of morally conservative politicians and to alter public policy in a number of areas where it was thought that either the legislature or the Supreme Court had adopted standards that were not consonant with the views of the majority of Americans. Particular issues of concern to the Moral Majority included school prayer, abortion and the tolerance of homosexuals. The Moral Majority became the symbol of two developments in the American political system in the late 1970s which provoked controversy and in some cases the organization of groups to resist the Moral Majority's ambitions. The first was the growing involvement of the religious and the political right in the United States through the mobilization of Christian fundamentalists—mostly independent Baptists in the Moral Majority—in particular (see CHRISTIANITY) around a set of themes known as social issues or family

217

issues. The second was the growth in popularity of a number of television and radio preachers who used their media spots to promote not merely a religious but also a political message. The Moral Majority's head is Rev. Jerry Falwell—a major electronic church personality—although it is clear that much of the initiative for founding the group came from more political new right leaders such as Paul Weyrich, Richard Viguerie and Howard Phillips. (see NEO-CONSERVATISM).

Mosley

Oswald Mosley was the leader of the British Union of Fascists in the 1930s, and was detained under the Defence of the Realm Act (DORA q.v.) in the Second World War. His political ideas were complex, and his career somewhat tragic, because he had been an influential and rising junior minister in Labour governments in the 1920s, being perhaps the first politician outside the Liberal party to grasp the point of Keynesian economics. He entirely miscalculated the reaction of the British electorate to a home-grown FASCISM, and his 'blackshirt' movement, though causing some anxiety, was never strong and vanished totally once war broke out.

Mouvement Républicaine Populaire (see MRP)

MRP

MRP (Mouvement Républicaine Populaire) was an important but relatively short-lived French political party. It was, in essence, a Catholic-based CHRISTIAN SOCIALIST party, built on the Catholic part of the Resistance movement in the Second World War, and was electorally very popular at the begining of the FOURTH REPUBLIC. This was particularly significant because the preceding THIRD REPUBLIC had not entirely accepted Roman Catholics as having a legitimate place in politics, and it was in part the Resistance activity of Catholic groups that made them legitimate, just as happened to the PCF and PCI (qvv). The MRP represented a moderate social democratic position which at the same time tried to deny the significance of class factors, and stressed Christian duty to others and traditional moral values, as in protection of family life. As France modernized and urbanized its social structure during the 1950s this position became less attractive, and once DE GAULLE took power and created the FIFTH REPUBLIC the party all but vanished, though it had been a major coalition partner during most of the Fourth Republic. MRP voters moved, on the whole, to the Gaullist party, and what religious voting still exists in France has continued to benefit either this party or the INDEPENDENT REPUBLICANS of Giscard d'Estaing.

Multi-Party Systems

Party systems tend to be divided by students of COMPARATIVE GOVERNMENT using a slightly unusual arithmetic. Obviously a multi-party system is a political system in which there is more than one political party contesting elections. However the question 'How many is Multi?' is more difficult than it seems. The original divisions were between one-party states, two-party systems, and 'multi'. Even with this simple counting system odd results would emerge. Britain, for example, was seen through most of the early political science work as a two-party system, despite the fact that there have always been at least three political parties represented in Parliament. The point is that some criteria need specifying for the significance of a party before it gets counted. There have always been several political parties contesting the US Presidential elections, yet usually only the Republican and Democratic parties have been seen as sufficiently important to be counted in. Even with recent third party candidates getting several per cent of the vote, America probably remains a two-party system, at least at the Federal level. The continual presence of the British Liberal Party in Parliament but usually unable to alter the balance of power led some commentators, for example, to regard Britain as a 'two and a half' party system. West Germany, on the other hand, though it has since the 1950s also only had three parties in the Bundestag, was seen as a full multi-party system because the small FDP (the German Liberal party) was usually a necessary coalition party. At its most full-blooded a multi-party system is one with at least three and usually more, often many more, political parties, each of them significant. The best test of the 'significance' of a party is that its inclusion or exclusion from government coalitions makes a real difference, and is a real possibility. But even this definition runs into trouble, where one has a party, the French Communist party in the 1950s, say, which has no chance of winning an election by itself, and is excluded as a possible coalition partner by all the parties at all likely to be making up the government, but is nonetheless sizeable. Much of this would be pedantry, were it not that the characteristics of party systems, amongst which, clearly, the 'multi-partyness' or otherwise of them is important, have major consequences for the nature of politics, policy and government. What is most important is to realize that this quality is in fact arrayed on a spectrum from true 'one party' systems to true 'multi-party' systems, with no sharp divisions. Even apparent 'one-party' systems can vary in the extent to which the single party is actually a coalition of competing interests, as opposed to being a monolithic and disciplined entity.

Multilateralism

Multilateralism is a political label that has come about simply because of the need for symmetry in political argument. Its meaning is taken by opposition to UNILATERALISM, the doctrine that a country should abandon the ownership of nuclear weapons immediately, regardless of the actions or intentions of any other power. As such multilateralism can either just mean opposition to this doctrine, or, as is often presented, it can stand for a different policy of reduction in nuclear weaponry. If given this latter meaning, multilateralism means a preparedness to reduce or abolish nuclear arsenals step by step in combination with similar movements by the Soviet Union. It is often said by those who are not of the unilateralist persuasion that everyone is, naturally, a multilateralist. The implication is that no one can actually be in favour of retention of nuclear weaponry if the supposed enemy does not retain them. In fact this blurs a lot of important distinctions, if only because it seems to imply that there can be no rational basis for urging a policy of increasing nuclear capacity. In fact, given some theories of deterrence, and certain assumptions about weapons levels in the Soviet Union, a perfectly intelligent argument can be made for increasing either the US or the UK nuclear arsenal. Thus the 1983 election in Britain was crudely seen to be, in part, fought over the unilateralism versus multilateralism split. In fact, while one party, the Labour party, adopted unilateralist policies, the Conservative party fought on its record of increasing the nuclear capacity of the UK by deciding to upgrade the Polaris submarine fleet. The only genuinely multilateralist arguments put forward were those from Labour leaders who disregarded their party's official stand and interpreted it to mean that a Labour government would dismantle the missile fleet as part of an arrangement with the Soviet Union to reduce its own force accordingly.

Mussolini

Benito Mussolini (1883–1945) was the originator of European FASCISM as Prime Minister of Italy from 1924, and later simply *Il Duce*

220

('the leader'—Hitler's official title of 'Der Führer' meant the same thing) from about 1928, when Parliamentary government was suspended in Italy. He died in 1945 when captured by the Italian partisans, though he had been out of power, except as a puppet ruler in German-occupied Northern Italy, from 1943. Originally a socialist, indeed an influential agitator and left-wing journalist, he left the socialists in the First World War because he supported Italy's joining the allied powers against Austria. From then on he created and led the Italian Fascist movement, which, like the German Nazi (see National Socialism) party, was a curious mixture of right and left attitudes, amounting, in theory at least, to a radical and populist movement. Like the German equivalent, however, very little in the way of redistribution of wealth, or any other socialist policies were attempted, and the capitalist system functioned perfectly happily under him. His Fascist movement was even more corrupt, but considerably less violent, than Hitler's, and the worst excrescences, such as ANTI-SEMITISM, were very much milder. He came to power, as later did Hitler, largely because a civil war between Communists and Conservatives seemed imminent, and, in Mussolini's case, the King made him Prime Minister to avoid this. (Similarly Hitler's first steps to power were more or less legitimate, being based on success in parliamentary elections). His aggressive foreign policy of expansion, and the similarity of creed and practice made an alliance (The Axis) with Nazi Germany more or less inevitable, though ultimately Germany invaded Italy and controlled it directly because the Italian regime had showed, in North Africa especially, that it was incapable of fighting against the Allies. His Fascist movement had reconstructed Italian politics along CORPORATIST lines, and produced a formal one-party state in which only members of the party could stand for office. At no stage did the Fascists very successfully permeate the basic culture of Italy, and they were never, for example, able to defy the Church, with which, indeed, Mussolini signed the Lateran treaty, giving to the Papacy more security than it had enjoyed under the previous regime.

Mutual Assured Destruction

Mutual assured destruction (the commonly used acronym is MAD) is a basic concept in nuclear strategic thought. It refers to a situation where the forces of the opposed countries are equivalent in capacity and invulnerable to such an extent that neither can possibly hope to inflict damage on the other, however great, which would prevent the other imposing an unbearable cost on the aggressor. As such it is a vital element in calculating the requirements for SECOND STRIKE

221

CAPACITY. It should be noted that forces do not need to be equal for mutual assured destruction to exist, as long as the stronger power cannot hope to remove enough of the power of the weaker in a FIRST STRIKE to save itself from prohibitive damage. It should also be noted that unless 'destruction' is taken as very literal and very total, the concept involves an unavoidably subjective element, because how much damage country x is prepared to risk to take country y out of the game is a matter for the judgement of the rulers of country x. It is sometimes argued that only the situation of mutual assured destruction by both the USA and the USSR has prevented war in the last twenty years.

N

Nation

Nation has come to be important in political terms largely through either the idea of NATIONALISM, or as part of the concept NATION-STATE. No obvious technical definition exists, but any working definition in the social sciences would include most of the following criteria. A nation is a body of people who see part at least of their identity in terms of a single communal identity with some considerable historical continuity of union, with major elements of common culture, and with a sense of geographical location at least for a good part of those who make up the nation. The difficulty of definition arises from the way in which all of these criteria may be false in any set of examples. For example, while Belgium is clearly a nation, the sharp, and historically long term, divide along both religious and linguistic dimensions between the Walloon (French-speaking) and Flemish (Dutch-speaking) people, and the fact that Belgium only existed in its present form from the mid-19th century, seem to counter the definition. Similarly nations can exist despite extensive dispersion geographically—there are very many Chinese outside China as well as in it, whilst Poland continued to exist as a nation throughout the several lengthy periods when it had no official political existence on any map of Europe. Usually the political usage of the term does connote the nation-state—phrases like 'The Nations of the World', 'Nation shall speak unto Nation', 'The British Nation', all involve the idea of a political union, and often raise problems inside any straightforward definition of nation itself. The 'British Nation', for example, may well be seen by many as a fiction, standing for the union of three or four separate nations as defined by history, culture and language. But as nationalism is still a powerful political force, the vagueness of the concept itself has a political relevance.

Nation-State

Nation-state describes a context in which the whole of a geographical area that is the homeland for people who identify themselves as a community because of shared culture, history, and probably language and ethnic character, is governed by one political system. Such contexts are the common experience today, but are not necessarily any more natural than other forms that have been common in history. There were, after all, no nation states in Classical Greece, though there was clearly a Greek nation, which sensed that all Greeks had more in common than a Greek could have with a barbarian, and shared language, religion, culture and historical identity. Instead there were a number of, often warring, city-states, and no sense of what we mean by 'civil war' attached, say, to the Sparta-Athens conflicts.

Historically the growth of the nation-state, and its developing legitimacy, came after the collapse of the Roman Imperium and only when its successor in the West, the Germanic Holy Roman Empire, could no longer pretend to rule an international collection of separate sub-states. To some extent the growth of the two or three first and leading Nation-States, especially France and England, were historical accidents, for the seeds of national identity, especially the linguistic and cultural homogeneity, actually came after rather than preceded the political hegemony of the national governments. Later important nation-states, for example Italy and Germany, although clearly possessing many of the characteristics of nationhood, only united into nation-states late in the 19th century. Even more to the point, a large number of nation-states in the modern world are the arbitrary result of external power. Thus Pakistan, as it existed from 1947 to 1972, was almost entirely the creation of the British on leaving the Indian sub-continent, while modern Czechoslovakia was between the wars and after the Second World War the creation of the victorious powers. Indeed the idea of 'nation-building' has been an important topic in the study of political development, where it has been expressly recognized that states come into existence in the THIRD WORLD, and have to create a sense of national identity before they can become sufficiently politically stable to hope for socio-economic progress. As movements for regional autonomy or actual independence continue to grow in political importance even in what might be seen as the historical leaders in nationhood as well as being major problems for many new states, the entire assumption of 'naturalness' of large states ruling over the populations of geographically-identifiable 'nations' seems weaker. National identity remains a powerful political call, though again it has often more to do with manifest absences of nationhood under colonial rule, especially when linked with the idea of a 'war of national liberation' than any genuine community. The need for nation-states has had much to do with assumptions about the desirability of large scale in political systems, and this in turn has tended to revolve round perceived threats from outside by other nation-states. Increasing internationalization of world society may well be leading to a decline in the importance, therefore, of something which would then prove to have been historically artificial and relatively short-lived.

National Socialism

National Socialism was the doctrine of the German Nazi party (the full title of which was the NSDAP, *see* under HITLER), a blend of intense nationalist, even xenophobic, policy with some pretences to be socialist, in at least the sense of representing the working-class (hence the Arbeit in the full German title). It could never in fact be socialist, because it denied the reality of classes and class conflict, arguing instead that there was one true German nation, whose natural unity was threatened only by 'non-German' elements inside the country, and by external enemies. However, as is usually true in Fascist movements, opportunism was rampant, and any symbol that could be invoked to get support was used.

Nationalism

Nationalism is the political belief that some group of people represents a natural community which should live under one political system, be independent of others, and, often, has the right to demand an equal standing in the world order with others. Although sometimes a genuine and widespread belief, especially under conditions of foreign rule, it is equally often a symbolic tool used by political leaders to control their citizens. Nationalism has always been useful to leaders because, by stressing national unity and harping on threats from those who are clearly 'foreign' or 'different', internal schisms can be papered over, or otherwise unpopular policies can be executed. At its simplest nationalism contrasts with internationalist movements or creeds, and means a stress on local, at times almost tribal, identities and loyalties. Whether one sees nationalism as natural and desirable, or as a threat to world peace or rational organization is almost entirely a subjective value, hence the difficulty of giving any clear definition to the concept. As the entries on NATION and NATION-STATE show, the entire idea of such communities is hard to pin down, and often artificial, or at least deliberately created. If, in addition, nationality is to be different from ETHNICITY, and not to be given simply a positive law definition, most concepts built on it are extremely difficult to define, and can seem ultimately vacuous.

Nationalization

Nationalization, which is also sometimes called, especially in America 'socialization', is the policy of taking firms, enterprises or whole industries into public ownership. It has been the official policy of the British Labour party to nationalize the means of production since the adoption of the party constitution in 1918, and is indeed included, as clause 4 of that constitution, in official party documents. The actual amount of nationalization promised in Labour manifestos has, however, varied from almost none to a massive part of the economy at different elections. The theoretical backing for nationalization was originally Marxist, and stems from the idea that classes are formed around the lines of ownership of the means of production. Hence an egalitarian and classless society is incompatible with privately owned industry, and the state should own it instead. A secondary rationale, and one much more important in the post-war Labour party, is that government control and planning of the national economy is vital, and that this requires state ownership of at least the 'commanding heights' of the economy. Yet a third rationale is that some industries, and particularly service industries like transport, are too vital strategically to run under the conditions of competitive profit maximization, and have to be state-owned and run. This latter argument makes nationalization of industry essentially no different from the widespread tendency for vital services, like public utilities, to be taken out of the usual market conditions, or for some, like the Post Office, to be almost everywhere a government monopoly.

In practice there has been a fourth rationale, and one that ironically has often led to Conservative governments nationalizing industries, which is to prevent the total collapse of a major firm that has failed to compete on the open market. Thus it was, for example, that the 1970–74 Conservative government nationalized part of Rolls-Royce in Britain, and the US Federal government created AMTRAK to keep at least some semblance of a passenger railway network going in America.

Forms of nationalization vary a good deal, but they usually

involve the creation of a monopoly run as much as possible on ordinary commercial lines, and with the structure and hierarchy of a commercial enterprise, but with the controlling body (the equivalent to a Board of Directors and Company Chairman) being appointed directly by the Government of the day. The extent of direct governmental influence and control on day to day matters varies a good deal, as does the general remit given to the management. This latter is usually to attempt to break even, but as, as a matter of sheer fact, most nationalized industries, at least in the UK are massive losers, governments usually have to subsidize these public enterprises.

The first wave of major nationalization took place after the Second World War throughout Europe. In the UK this was a direct intention of the 1945 Labour government, but similar or even greater nationalization policies were applied in France and Italy, mainly to facilitate industrial reconstruction after the war. In France, for example, both car manufacture and banking were extensively nationalized by post-war governments, whilst in Britain only the central bank, the Bank of England, was nationalized, and only one automobile manufacturer, British Leyland, has ever been taken into public ownership, and that only to avert financial collapse in the 1960s.

There is a good deal of disillusionment with nationalization amongst European socialists because the form of nationalization does not affect the work conditions or financial rewards of ordinary workers at all, and thus the alienating impact attributed to private ownership is in no way reduced. This in part is why more radical socialists have tended to stress worker-participation or industrial democracy, thus joining radical Liberals who regard state ownership of normally structured industry as simply making even worse a problem that has little to do with formal legal ownership.

Politically nationalization remains a bug-bear to the right and a rallying call to the left, but has increasingly little relevance in its old terms to economic policy.

NATO

NATO (North Atlantic Treaty Organization) is by far the most important of a set of politico-military organizations of co-operating Western states set up after the Second World War, during the early part of the COLD WAR, to protect non-Communist states from a perceived threat from Communism. NATO's membership includes most Western European countries, along with the USA and Canada, and Norway and Denmark. France is only partially a member, having withdrawn its military forces from direct NATO control, although the French military co-operate with NATO, and would almost certainly join fully with the organization in war conditions. NATO works by co-ordinating the military capacities of its member states and allotting specific peace-time and war-time tasks. Under war conditions units of all the member states would come under a unified international command-structure, the head of which is usually an American General in recognition of the huge and disproportionate cost to the USA of NATO membership. Similar bodies, like SEATO and CENTO at one time covered military threats elsewhere in the world, but it is NATO that has survived and is in the forefront of East-West relations.

Natural Justice

Natural justice is an idea which has a long intellectual pedigree and which brings together the belief that there are some qualities and values inherent in the very concept of law, as opposed to arbitrary decision-making, and the notion that individuals should be able to claim certain basic protections in the legal system regardless of whether they are specifically given those protections by statute. The two most common tenets of the natural justice in the British legal system are the doctrines of *audi alterem partem* (which means that each party has a right to be heard in any dispute) and the rule which prevents any person from being a judge of his own case. In the United Kingdom in the 1960s these quite specific principles of natural justice were applied to a large number of administrative as well as judicial decision-making situations and as a result the British judiciary both expanded its own jurisdiction and developed something which it had previously lacked—a coherent corpus of administrative law (see ADMINISTRATIVE COURTS; JUDICIAL REVIEW).

Basically in modern legal systems the idea of natural justice is then the securing of the various rights associated with procedural fairness in a variety of political and administrative controversies and the notion that wherever possible decision-making procedures should not only be fair but be seen to be fair.

Natural Law

Natural law has been a crucial idea in political, social and legal theory from early mediaeval times throughout Europe and, later,

North America. Nearly all the most famous political theorists have had something to say on the matter, starting at the latest with AQUINAS, probably influenced by the rediscovery of analysis of ARISTOTLE, and arguably as early as AUGUSTINE. By no means all those who have used or discussed the concept have seen natural law in even remotely the same light. The contrast between HOBBES' view of natural law and LOCKE's, though they wrote in the same country and only a few years apart, could hardly be more sharp. Natural law is seen, variously, as God's will for the world, moral principles innate in the structure of the universe, the principles of rational self-interest, or the necessary elements logically underlying any legal system. In the latter sense, especially, it is contrasted with 'POSITIVE LAW', those laws actually promulgated by the state. It began to become really important when the European ENLIGHTENMENT, with its faith in the capacity of human reason to solve social problems, and its debunking of the right of the church to teach by authority of its special connection to God's will, simultaneously challenged the legitimacy of both secular and temporal powers. The very thinkers who did this needed some basis for their own views on right and wrong; appeal to moral intuition was not seen as rational enough, reliance on positive law was useless as they were, on the whole, opposed to most of the political authorities, and something had to take the place of these traditional sources of authority. Partly by analogy to what we would today call 'the laws of nature' in their scientific sense, natural law in politics and morals was seen as fixed in the universe by its very principles, and amenable to discovery by rational thought and analysis. Just as there could only be one physical law determining, say, the rate of fall of an object from a tower, there could only be one correct way of organizing a political system, or of acting in a case of moral doubt. To believe anything else would be to accept a randomness about the universe which, in the days long before relativistic and probabilistic models in the physical sciences, was unthinkable. However, what these natural laws that governed political society, which should give answers to all the stock questions of political theory, determine the grounds of political obligation, the balance of power between the state and the individual and so on, actually were was rather harder to discover. The natural law tradition in political theory was not, perhaps, all that long-lived once the idea became common and fell victim, in English political thinking anyway, to attacks by sceptics like David HUME, and the philosophical RADICALS like BENTHAM. Their inability to discover a foundation for natural law led them to resort to human psychological drives as the foundation of political principles, culminating in the UTILITARIANISM so perva-

229

sive today. The tradition never completely died out, even in England, and, often under other names, continues to have some importance. In law it has never been possible to operate only by positive law, and, though they seldom use the language, leading jurists and judges in both America and Britain have to fall back at times on some conception of natural rights to fill gaps and handle problems of discretion, as with the English legal doctrine of NATURAL JUSTICE. In continental Europe the continued importance of KANTIAN and HEGELIAN philosophy has kept the idea alive more obviously, but in a rather changed state.

Natural Rights

Natural rights are those human rights or entitlements which are held to stem from NATURAL LAW, whatever definition may be given to the latter concept. One can probably divide natural rights into two broad kinds, as they are encountered in legal and political theory. One group consists of those rights, seldom specified, that a man would hold, even if he could not enforce, in the theoretical STATE OF NATURE, rights, that is, that are fixed by divine law or by the very nature of man and the universe. These have often been taken over by various Declarations of Human Rights, and include those such as the right to life, to property, to family life, in general rights to do anything one wants, in total freedom, so long as one's exercise of those rights does not hurt or deprive others of their rights. The second group would consist of the more procedural rights that most legal systems find logically necessary if they are to be fair and efficient, as characterized by, for example, the English doctrine of NATURAL JUSTICE, or the American jurisprudence around the notion of 'due process of law'. What is definitional about natural rights is the contrast between their absolute and extra-governmental nature, and other rights which depend only on state policy, as, for example, with welfare rights stemming only from social policy legislation. Whatever natural rights are, they are held to exist independently of what any government does or says, and not to be capable of being legitimately overridden by any government, however often they may be ignored in practice.

Neo-Conservatism

The term 'neo-conservatism' was first coined by Michael Harrington in the United States to refer to a tendency in that country to reject some of the underlying assumptions of American liberalism—

most notably perhaps the optimistic belief that progress is inevitable and that the government can ameliorate various social problems. It has come to be used of a disparate group of writers and academics such as Irving Kristol, Norman Podhoretz, Daniel Patrick Moynihan, Jeane Kirkpatrick, Nathan Glazer and Daniel Bell, although both Bell and Moynihan reject the label. Most of the major figures of American neo-conservatism are former Democrats and some such as Moynihan are still active in Democratic politics. (Mrs. Jeane Kirkpatrick, although the author of an article explaining why she could not become a Republican, joined President Reagan's administration as Ambassador to the United Nations.) Many neo-conservatives are Jewish and the original rather tightly knit group of thinkers and polemicists was very much centred in New York.

Neo-conservatism is not so much a coherent theory as a set of reactions to contemporary politics and especially reactions to the politics of the United States in the 1960s. While it is difficult to summarize the writings of such a diverse and prolific group four themes seem central to neo-conservatism. First, neo-conservatives support Western values and are hostile to communism. Such a position is only surprising in the context of a United States severely shaken by the Vietnam experience (see VIETNAMESE WAR) and because the neo-conservatives have been concerned to make a clear intellectual defence of both capitalism and the policies of the United States.

Secondly, the neo-conservatives have since the 1960s expressed sustained scepticism about the role of government—and especially the federal government—in American life. The magazine edited by Irving Kristol—*The Public Interest*—prides itself on its unbiased assessment of public policy questions and neo-conservatives have been leading advocates of such policies as deregulation and welfare reform.

Thirdly, neo-conservatism has a strongly traditional approach to matters of religion and morality and rejects the trend associated with the 1960s youth movement—especially sexual liberation and the counter-culture. It fears the destruction of the family and in this respect its arguments coincide with those of the new right groups such as the MORAL MAJORITY which became active in American politics in the 1970s.

Finally, neo-conservatism is hostile to utopias and to attempts to promote broad visions of equality. It is wedded to the notion of equality of opportunity and as a consequence has opposed such policies as AFFIRMATIVE ACTION and quotas.

The impact of the neo-conservative movement is difficult to assess. It has changed the intellectual climate of the United States and provided a justification and explanation of trends which were already apparent in its politics. Although its impulses mesh well with those of other forces on the American right—including the new right and the Republican Party—it is, however, a distinct tendency and not to be confused with them.

Neo-Corporatism

Neo-Corporatism is a political theory more or less invented in the last decade as part of a radical critique of the nature of the state in capitalist societies, though some of its ideas would be accepted by less than radical political scientists. The 'Neo' in the title is there simply to distinguish it from the corporatist theories of inter-war European FASCISM, and is sometimes omitted. The essence of the theory is that major industrial institutions, and especially multi-national firms have now entered into a very close alliance with the state, especially with the civil service. Instead of the state controlling and organizing industry as though the corporations were passive, they are seen as being necessary partners. Thus economic and industrial policy is worked out, according to this theory, jointly between industrial institutions and the civil service. Part of the explanation for this move is that the control of information and technical expertise needed for regulating industry is not available to civil services except from the coporations themselves. To some extent the theory is not only true, but not particularly new, surprising, or radical. It has always been the case that governments have relied on interest groups for the information they needed to construct policy. In Britain, for example, the National Farmers Union has long been vital to the Ministry of Agriculture in working out the yearly agricultural subsidy plans. But in this case there are many who feel that the power actually lies with the Ministry, and the Union is forced to co-operate. A better example might be the various Regulatory Agencies in the USA, as, for example, the Federal Communications Commission, or the Federal Food and Drug Agency, where interchange between staff in the regulated industry and the regulatory agencies have tended to make the regulation much more organized around the interests of the regulated than round some notion of the public interest. The implication for those who use the idea as a criticism of modern political systems is that the spirit of Italian Fascism, where industry was directly represented in a legislative chamber is rising again, and the state is no more than a servant to sectional industrial interests.

NEP

NEP are the initials by which is known LENIN's famous New Economic Policy introduced at the 10th party congress in March 1921. It consisted of a considerable relaxation of the strict communist economic policy introduced immediately after the second (Bolshevik) revolution of 1917. The banking system, which had been completely abolished, was re-introduced (though as state, nationalized banks), internal trading was allowed much more freely and without state planning controls on the movement and distribution of goods, and limited private trading for profit was allowed. In other words, it allowed a slight movement back towards a capitalist form of economics, and made sense to many who felt that Russia had to go through the equivalent of a bourgeois capitalist revolution before communism proper would have a foundation to build on. It was largely forced on Lenin anyway, because of riots over food shortages and a fear that the economy, and especially the agricultural economy would collapse, and with it would vanish revolutionary control over the country. It had always been feared by many revolutionaries that, unless the rest of Europe went communist almost immediately, the revolution would not be able to survive alone in Russia. To doctrinaire Marxists, who had wanted to create total communism overnight, abolishing even money, this was unacceptable. But it was not until STALIN developed his five-year plans in 1929, using force and violence to suppress the opposition Lenin had tried to buy off, that the NEP was abolished.

Neutralism

Neutralism is what is often mistaken for neutrality. It is not a term of art in international law, and carries no clear cut meaning. It is the status of many if not most of the THIRD WORLD countries who have decided not to be formally involved in either of the two superpower alliances, and which take aid and support from either or both as offered. Essentially it is the same as 'Non-Alignment', and is practised by an increasingly important element in the United Nations. Unlike the actual status of formal neutrality, which is a breach of the general duty all UN members have to support a UN mandate against an aggressor, it is perfectly compatible with active participation in the world scene and with full membership of the UN.

Neutralism indeed need not at all involve total neutrality, because membership of regional alliances and defence pacts which do not involve superpower relations is perfectly possible. India, for example, is one of the leaders of the non-aligned nations, and yet there is no question of it being neutral in any conflict between, for example, Bangladesh and Pakistan, both of which countries are also practitioners of neutralism.

It is important to differentiate not only between neutrality and neutralism, but also between neutralism and ISOLATIONISM. The latter, famous as the official US policy towards all international affairs outside its own hemisphere from the declaration of the Monroe doctrine in 1823 until its entry in the First World War in 1917, involves a total abdication from international affairs, and a complete lack of any interest in the outcome of any conflict. Isolationism was taken by the Americans, for example, to preclude membership of the League of Nations, yet many neutralist countries (and Sweden, a neutral country) have contributed to UN Peacekeeping forces.

When all is said, however, even neutralism is seldom practised in a pure form as the superpower alliances both offer aid and attach strings to its receipt in terms of general support at least of a diplomatic nature.

Neutrality

Neutrality is often thought of as a rather vague state of non-involvement in international conflict, but it has in fact a fairly precise meaning in international law. If a state wishes to be neutral between two or more others who are at war with each other, it has an obligation under international law to refrain from aiding either party, or to allow either party to use its territory for any warlike purpose at all. In return for this it is to be allowed to continue trading with either or both of the war-making powers, except that they both have the right to blockade and prevent any prohibited trading, though they must exercise care to protect the nationals and ships of the neutral country. At least as far as international law goes, neither party may attack the neutral.

Although the idea of neutrality was at one time, during the era of limited war, perfectly sensible and minimized the impact of war on the rest of the international community, it has not, in the last two world wars, made a great deal of sense. In both wars, for example, protestations of neutrality did not save Belgium from invasion. In the First World War it was to a large extent Germany's refusal to avoid attacking neutral American merchant ships that brought the USA into the war on the side of Britain and France. Only Switzerland, which has been recognized internationally as permanently neutral since the early 19th century was fully able to avoid favouring or being used by one side or another. But there are good reasons of mutual interest even amongst the most bitterly hostile of enemies to have some genuinely neutral intermediary, as with negotiations over prisoners of war.

Legally, in fact, not all nations even have the right to announce a general neutrality. All members of the United Nations, for example, share a common duty to defend each other and to aid in the punishment of an aggressor under certain conditions, and could not claim that their neutrality required or allowed them to be impartial between two parties if one had United Nations sanction. In practice the only effective neutrality is what has come to be known as 'armed neutrality'. This state of affairs, and modern Sweden may be the best example, involves not just the general intention not to be involved in any war, but a manifest ability, at some cost, to defend its own frontiers effectively. The Swedes in fact have an efficient armaments industry and a very effective military capacity based on a large reserve and more or less total liability to conscription for military training. Being able to defend oneself actually comes close to a legal definition of neutrality, because it is always open to a combatant nation to claim the need to occupy a neutral to prevent its enemy from so doing, if it cannot trust the neutral itself to be able to honour its legal obligation not to allow any other party to benefit from its weakness.

Considering the readiness of aggressors to invade neutral countries in the potentially limited wars of this century, the notion of neutrality in any third world war is largely imaginary. Not only are such wars as we may see in Europe inherently likely to be nuclear, but the strategic position of Sweden would make it extremely difficult for either the Warsaw Pact or NATO to respect the neutrality of at least its airspace. Neutrality is, of course, entirely possible in limited and small wars not involving the superpowers or the major alliances, but this is largely the neutrality of those who do not care to be involved, rather than the neutrality of a small nation which fears to be involved. Furthermore there are very few potential conflicts that are not at least on the side lines of the interests of the superpowers, and neutrality in the full sense of giving no aid or preference at all has not been practised by the Soviet Union or the USA in any important post-war conflict.

New Class

New class refers to a theory, usually associated with the Yugoslav politician and dissident M. Iovan DjILAS, to the effect that the supposedly egalitarian and classless societies of the Soviet Union and Eastern Europe nonetheless do have class systems. His argument is that, although major private property holdings have been abolished, and a great degree of equality has been introduced for the mass of the citizenry, those who hold senior positions in the state administration, and even more, in the Communist party apparatus (the APPARATCHIK), have enormous privileges that make them effectively a new ruling class. The control of power, as well as the material rewards, enjoyed by such people is indeed incompatible with a fully egalitarian and democratic society, but it is dubious that they actually constitute anything that can sensibly be called a 'class', mainly because their position is dependent on holding specified offices, and because there can be little or no inheritance of these privileged positions.

New Deal, The

The New Deal was the name given to the peace-time policies of Franklin Delano Roosevelt, who was President of the United States from 1933 to 1945. These policies Roosevelt hoped would end or ameliorate the recession in the USA which followed the Great Crash of 1929 and which threw millions of Americans out of work and into poverty. The phrase was first used in his speech accepting the Democratic presidential nomination in 1932 and it consciously echoed the call by his relative Theodore Roosevelt for a 'square deal' for the American people. Since the New Deal other American presidents have tried to coin similarly resonant terms for their policies so that there has been President Truman's Fair Deal, President Kennedy's New Frontier and President Johnson's Great Society.

The individual programmes contained in the New Deal were very much ad hoc responses to the problems of unemployment and social dislocation experienced in the USA in the 1930s. Only in retrospect did they seem to embrace any coherent political philosophy or underlying economic doctrine. The policies did, however, introduce a significant amount of government intervention in the economy and greatly expanded the role of the federal government generally. As a result, the New Deal proved to be extremely controversial and met with substantial opposition both from businessmen wedded to traditional ideas of LAISSER-FAIRE and from the Supreme Court which ruled many of the key items of Roosevelt's legislative programme—for example the National Industrial Recovery Act—unconstitutional. However, the policies were popular with the electorate as a whole and the New Deal is usually seen as a crucial period in American political history both because it precipitated a party REALIGNMENT and because it greatly changed the nature of the United States' federal system (see FEDERALISM). As a result of the party realignment key groups in American society such as blacks, labour unions, and the poor became linked to the Democratic Party which used this coalition to retain the presidency from 1933 to 1952 and to dominate congressional elections thereafter. Only with the rise of the new politics of the 1960s did the Democratic coalition seem in danger of losing its majority status and even then the evidence of its break-up is ambiguous.

The New Deal is sometimes divided into two periods. In the first period which lasted from 1933 to 1935 the measures were generally exploratory and moderate. In the second period President Roosevelt—assured of electoral support after his re-election in 1936—felt able to act more radically and to confront the Supreme Court over its attempts to challenge his legislative programme.

New Economic Policy (see **NEP**)

Nomenclatura

Nomenclatura, literally just a list of names, is a vital technique for ensuring the control of the Soviet Communist Party (see CPSU) over all aspects of industry, administration and other branches of the state. At every level, from the town up via the regions and Republics to the Central Committee of the CPSU in Moscow, there is a series of posts which can only be filled with the approval of the equivalent level branch of the Communist party. Only candidates whose names are on the local party list, Nomenclatura, may be appointed to such posts. Although it is not necessary to be a party member to have one's name on the list, it is extremely unusual for any appointment above the most junior, at the most local level not to be a party member in good standing. It is by no means easy to become a member of the party nowadays, since a tightening of membership requirements since KHRUSHCHEV'S laxer policies, thus the party officials can rely on obedience from managers and administrators appointed to nomenclatura posts. Good party behaviour, as well as technical efficiency will be required to get on to the nomenclatura for the next rung in a professional career, ensuring tighter and tighter control by the party the more senior is the post.

Non-Proliferation Treaty

One of the early fruits of international attempts to limit the danger of nuclear warfare was the signing in 1968 of the Nuclear Non-Proliferation treaty. This was signed at the time by only three of the five then known nuclear powers, the UK, USA and the USSR, who undertook not to provide the technology for making nuclear weapons to those countries who had not already acquired it. The idea seems to have been that international instability could only arise if some country not locked into the superpower strategic deterrence game was able to make such weapons. It seems also to have been thought that such a new nuclear power, especially if its principal adversary had not yet become nuclear, would be much more tempted to use the weapons than were the existing nuclear powers. The treaty was also available for signing by those non-nuclear powers who wished publicly to state that they would never seek to develop or purchase such technology.

It is unclear whether the treaty has or could have any effect. Not only did France and China refuse to accord to the treaty, theoretically on the grounds that it discriminated too much in favour of those powers who were already nuclear, but the technology cannot easily be constrained. Apart from a real difficulty in distinguishing between peaceful, energy-producing nuclear technology and potentially warlike usage, the scientific mysteries are not so great, and the secrecy so well enforced that a medium-sized nation cannot develop a weapon quite unaided. Entirely non-alarmist estimates suggest, for example, that at least seven nations which were non-nuclear in 1968 are now, or will by 1990, have built and tested such weapons. These include Argentina, Pakistan, Brazil and Egypt, as well as Israel and South Africa which have long been rumoured to be nuclear armed. Whether any breach of the treaty has been involved in this process is unknown. Unlike both the test ban treaty and the SALT and START negotiations, the non-proliferation treaty can hardly be seen as demonstrating international goodwill, but seems instead to function almost entirely in the self interest of the originating nations.

North Atlantic Treaty Organization (see NATO)

Nozick

Robert Nozick, along with John RAWLS, has done more than anyone else to re-create and revive political theory in the Western post-war world. Like Rawls he bases his approach on LIBERALISM and a trenchant defence of inalienable rights which governments may not take away just because to do so might be for the aggregate public good. Also like Rawls, and inevitably for someone who takes this position, he is a violent opponent of UTILITARIANISM and its subdued but definite acceptance by nearly all political actors in the West.

The difference is that Nozick is very much more firm than Rawls in holding these positions, and, because of the particular rights he holds most dear, takes a very much more critical position on the legitimacy of modern government and typical Western welfare state/mixed economy policy. His main work is *Anarchy, State and Utopia*, published in 1974 and still hotly debated and much written about. The theory has three main strands to it. The first is that it is totally individual based—he rejects any idea that societies, states, or collectives of any form can be the bearers of rights or owe duties. They are legitimate only in so far as they are voluntary aggregations of individuals, and not just because they may, as a matter of fact, make most or all members better off. Consequent on this is his theory of the political system, which is semi-anarchist, in that he regards as legitimate only the very minimum state power necessary to uphold the prior existing rights of the individual citizens. The state is, for Nozick, not much more than a police force, and he does, indeed, spend a good deal of time explaining why even this much is necessary, and why private enterprise policing is not enough, in a society of free individuals.

The third main strand is that Nozick's prime human right is the right to property; not only does he take an absolute line on the inviolability of property rights, but his actual theory of how they arise is a strict and limited one. Nozick's theory of property is often taken to be a re-working of John LOCKE's theory, without, as it were, God, because Locke used a theological justification in part. For Nozick, if a man has a right to property, this can come about in two ways—he may have legitimately acquired that property in the first place as an original act, or he may have had it transferred to him by a legitimate process from someone else who had a legitimate entitlement. As long as any distribution of property is entirely covered by such rules, then the distribution is just, however inegalitarian it may be. A major part of Nozick's thesis is that those who concentrate on the justice of an 'end state' as he describes them, that is, a particular distribution of property rights that seems valid in itself are missing the point that actual distributions arise from historical processes that give people entitlements, and justice inheres in the justice of the entitlement chain, not the consequences of the momentary distribution.

239

Because property rights are absolute, and may be highly inegalitarian, one of Nozick's chief features is his rejection of most of the features of a modern welfare state. Nozick regards the taxation inherent in redistributive societies, that is, any taxation above that needed to pay for the minimal state, as a form of forced labour. Few people outside the fringe of radical libertarianism perhaps actually agree with Nozick, but his arguments are mounted with such massive skill, and his analyses so penetrating that he commands, rightly, enormous influence and respect in the development of modern political theory, and he is certainly the foremost modern exponent of the libertarian position.

Nuclear Parity

Ever since the SALT (q.v.) negotiations in the early 1970s measures have been sought to assess the relative strengths of the strategic nuclear forces of the USA and the USSR. No one measure can be very satisfactory, but taking the various measures together, it is clear that by the early 1980s the USSR had redressed America's historic advantage, and achieved, at least, a state of parity. In terms of launchers, missiles, total EQUIVALENT MEGATONNAGE and throw-weight, the USSR was probably ahead, though America retained a lead in actual number of warheads, and probably in the technology of targeting. The main concern of the USA was that the combination of accuracy and explosive power achieved by the USSR had made them able possibly to destroy 90% of the ground-site based American ICBMs, whilst the US could not do the same to the Soviet forces. The arrival of this situation of nuclear parity has thrown doubt on much orthodox strategic thinking and policy making in the USA. In particular the long-established policy of backing NATO's weak conventional defence in Germany with the threat of central strategic nuclear warfare has come to seem highly non-credible.

O

Official Secrets Act

The Official Secrets Act, originally passed by Parliament in 1911, is the main source of state control over secrecy and espionage in Britain. Compared with many Western nations it is very powerful, and can be used to protect sensitive information that the government of the day does not want disclosed, even though the information hardly challenges the security of the state. Once one has signed the Act, and this can be required before quite trivial information is disclosed, one is permanently bound by it. Lengthy prison sentences can, and have been handed down under the Act, and from time to time journalists engaged in quite proper investigative reporting are restricted by it. To some extent it has come under a cloud over the last decade, and several Parliamentary attempts have been made, unsuccessfully, to abolish or amend it.

Old Commonwealth and New Commonwealth

All Commonwealth countries were formerly part of the British Empire but many are now independent sovereign states which adhere to the loose organization known as the Commonwealth whose head is the British monarch. The term old Commonwealth refers to those territories which were settled rather than conquered and which are predominantly of European origin. Thus Canada, Australia, and New Zealand would be referred to as 'old Commonwealth' although all these countries now function as separate political entities despite their strong cultural ties with the United Kingdom.

The term 'new Commonwealth' refers to the countries which gained their independence in the period after the Second World War and which often had to fight to achieve their status as sovereign states. India and Pakistan led the move towards decolonization and in the 1960s most of the African territories—including Nigeria,

Uganda and Tanzania—were granted independence. In the late 1960s and early 1970s immigration from the so-called 'new Commonwealth' became a sensitive political issue because under the British Nationalities Act of 1948 all citizens of the Commonwealth were allowed free access to the United Kingdom. In the period from 1961 onwards successive British governments of all parties have therefore moved to restrict entry to the United Kingdom. The entry of the United Kingdom into the Common Market or European Community has further served to weaken the ties of the Commonwealth and today its symbolism and political significance are limited.

Oligarchy

Oligarchy is one of ARISTOTLE's basic forms of government. His, the first ever, theory of comparative government distinguished forms of government along two dimensions, one dealing with how many people ruled a society, and the other with whether they acted in the public interest or in their own interest. Oligarchy, according to this schema, is the rule of a few, in their own interests. It contrasts on one dimension, for example, with monarchy (literally the rule of one man), and on the other with aristocracy, used to refer to the rule of a few, but where the few are the best of the society (from the Greek 'Aristos' meaning 'the best'). In general it connotes a political system ruled undemocratically by a small group. It is often used of micropolitics, as when one might describe the Professors in a university department as being an oligarchy because they run the department with little concern for the interests of the lecturers and students.

Ombudsman

An Ombudsman is an officer of state appointed to provide an extra check on the rights of citizens against state action. The system, Scandinavian in origin, is not widely utilized, and in many places where versions have been introduced, has proved somewhat of a disappointment. In principle it works so that a citizen who feels he has been the victim of maladministration can make a complaint to the Ombudsman's office. This office will, after ensuring the complaint is not malicious or trivial, call for evidence and files on the matter and investigate the fairness and justice of the administrative action complained against. Where evidence of maladministration is found to be convincing, a variety of remedies is provided. Sometimes no more can be done than the publication of a judgment to the effect of maladministration, though it is more likely that at least some form of financial redress will be given. Whether or not disciplinary or even legal proceedings will be taken against the offending administrator is not usually at the Ombudsman's discretion.

Britain has only limited experience of such a system, and the United States none, at least at the federal level. In Britain the power of the equivalent officer, the Parliamentary Commissioner for Administration is severely restricted, because he is not entitled to accept complaints direct from members of the public, but only on referral from an M.P. More recently a parallel office has been set up for similar complaints against local government administration. Some countries have experimented with ombudsmen for more circumscribed roles, especially to represent complaints by members of the military, where it is felt that there are serious inbuilt difficulties about appealing through normal military justice channels.

Though there are clear advantages to the system, there is also a serious query about why traditional avenues of complaint, either through the courts or through elected representatives should not be adequate. If in fact it is possible for an institutional check to be made on the activities of administrators and policy makers, it is unclear why the older methods of so doing should fail.

Opposition

An opposition is a political grouping, party or loose association of individuals who wish to change the government and its policies.

In democratic states the opposition has a formal position and is expected to present itself as an alternative government both by challenging the government's measures between elections and by offering itself as a potential governing party at an election. In Britain the position of Leader of Her Majesty's Opposition is formalized in statute and the Opposition Leader has certain rights—such as the right of reply to prime ministerial broadcasts.

In SINGLE-PARTY SYSTEMS the opposition may exist as an underground movement as in the USSR where no formal opposition to the CPSU is permitted but dissidents continue to exist. Or an opposition may engage in armed struggle as in El Salvador. Despite the high level of repression in many states it is rare to find no traces of opposition albeit from individuals acting clandestinely.

In some states where party systems are not cohesive, opposition may be effected by institutions so that in the USA, for example, opposition is provided as much by Congress or the Supreme Court as by the party not in control of the White House.

243

Organization of African Unity

The Organization of African Unity (OAU) was founded in 1963 to promote organized and coherent policies amongst the non-aligned African nations, and to help overthrow the remaining colonial traces in Africa. As a result its principal single concern has been with the South African problem and, during the period of UDI, with the Rhodesia-Zimbabwe situation. In neither of these areas has it been particularly effective, nor in dealing with conflicts between black African states or inside them. The OAU was, for example, severely split over both the Angolan civil war and the secession war between Nigeria and Biafra. Its salience in African politics varies from time to time, but it has probably declined generally in importance since its original creation. In part this is because of the greater penetration of influence of the USSR and China into African politics, which has reduced considerably the actual 'non-alignment' of many states. The continued reliance of some ex-colonial states, especially previous French colonies on the former colonial power, and the lack of social and economic homogeneity further reduce the prospects for African states, per se, of building a coherent unity.

Organization of American States

The Organization of American States (OAS) is a regional association supporting the principles of the UN, founded in 1948, but building on earlier pan-American associations dating from the 19th century. It has always been seen as too heavily influenced by the US, although the organization was genuinely unanimous in backing the American action against Cuba during the missile crisis. Its utility has decreased further with the increase in internal violence and guerrilla warfare in some Latin American countries, where the US anti-communist basis makes it less than neutral in the internal affairs of some of its members. During the Falklands conflict of 1982 its weakness and disunity was demonstrated, particularly after the US was forced from its attempted neutrality into moderate support for the UK. The tensions in Latin America, both between states and between the regimes of many and their citizens, are so intense that any overall union is bound to be ineffective. Had Canada not always declined to join, and had Cuba not been expelled at American insistence in 1962 it might at least be able to act as an outlet for the real conflicts, but in its present form it is unable to do so.

244

Overkill

Overkill is a concept in strategic theory, relating to nuclear warfare. It means a situation where one or more nations have so much nuclear weaponry that, whatever the enemy may do, they can guarantee to destroy the enemy's country totally and still have unused capacity. Alternatively it can mean that the combined nuclear capacity of the major states would serve to destroy the entire world and still not be used up. More figuratively it has come to mean using or threatening any force or political option which is stronger than is necessary or appropriate in the context. One might thus use 'overkill' in threatening an irritating neighbour more dramatically than was necessary to stop him doing something you dislike. It arises as an important concept because of the way ARMS RACES can lead to further and further build-up of forces beyond any rationally-needed level.

P

Pacifism

Pacifism is not a particular political doctrine, but the general belief that all war is morally unacceptable, and that there are no adequate justifications for using violence or physical force in pursuit of any end, political or otherwise. Although such beliefs have obviously existed throughout history, it is probable that only in the 19th and 20th centuries have they been at all widespread, organized, or come to be associated particularly with certain political standpoints. Partly the reasons for this are, as it were, historically accidental, because warfare for most of the post-medieval period, until especially the world wars, was largely confined to small and professional military forces. Conscription, practised extensively in continental European armies in the 19th century, and by all important nations during one or both of the world wars, made it hard for those with pacific beliefs to avoid military service. Hence it became both necessary and possible for the collective exposition of the doctrine to develop.

Various other factors have been influential—the abandonment by Christian Churches, for example, of theological arguments that made the notion of a JUST WAR easy to promulgate, and the sheer horror of the First World War which persuaded many who experienced it afterwards to support the various peace movements that were created. Probably the most important political reason for the wider spreading of pacifism is the analysis of the causes of war suggested by much anarchist and left-wing writing, and especially by MARXISM. From this political position wars between nations are entirely prompted by the selfish economic aspirations of the ruling capitalist elites, but the only people to suffer in them are the exploited proletariats of both sides. Thus the spread of the whole idea of international communism, with the idea that workers of all countries are natural brothers and should unite against warmongering capitalists produces an atmosphere in which pacifism can be easily at home.

246

Palestine Liberation Organization (see PLO)

Para-Military Forces

Para-Military forces are those uniformed, armed, and disciplined bodies that exist in most countries to carry out internal security and policing functions which are beyond the capacity of ordinary police forces. There cannot be a very precise definition, and certainly the boundaries between what would be considered an ordinary police force and a para-military force are very blurred. Nonetheless most countries have found it necessary to retain a force to cope with, for example, serious rioting and disorderly demonstrations, equipped for and allowed to use greater force than even police forces that are normally armed. Such forces are usually trained in a very different way, have no responsibility for the day to day police work that requires some degree of acceptability by the citizens, and are often under a different political command structure than the civilian police. In France, for example, where the 'Gendarmerie' are the nationwide para-military police and quite separate from either local or national police, the former comes under the authority of the Minister of Defence, rather than the ministers of Justice or Interior; in West Germany, where the police function is constitutionally the responsibility of the Länder rather than the Federal Government, the latter has created what is technically known as the Federal Border Guard but which not only does that job but acts as mobile and heavily armed riot police under Federal control. Theoretically at least, Britain has no such force, and this is not invariably seen, even by liberals, as necessarily a protection against undue force, because where the police cannot cope, there is then no alternative to the use of the regular armed forces to control widespread outbreaks of disorder.

The political/constitutional heritage of a country has much to do with the presence or absence of such forces. In Britain, Canada, the United States and Australasia there has always been a very considerable fear of centralized police authority, indeed of police power at all, and a heavily armed and centrally controlled para-military force would never have been accepted because of the power it would give to the executive. Nonetheless this constitutional position has not entirely removed the need for the function to be fulfilled, and there are those who would wish to argue that the RCMP, the American National Guard, and perhaps the Special Patrol Groups of English police authorities are little different, and little preferable to a fully fledged Para-Military Force.

247

Pareto

Vilfredo Pareto (1848–1923) was the most important of the Italian political sociologists called the 'New Machiavellians' who started the power elite school of analysis of modern societies, which developed, via the work of people like SCHUMPETER and DAHL into modern PLURALISM. Pareto, who was at least as famous as an economist, attached especial importance to the fact, as he saw it, that the bulk of human behaviour was essentially non-rational, though justified and explained by rationalizations, myths, ideologies, stemming from instinctual drives. These basic drives, common to all societies and all times, which he called 'residues' are masked by the justifying myths, 'derivations', but are the real source of social patterns, rather than the apparent ideologies of the societies.

In a theoretically complex way Pareto links this general proposition about human behaviour to a thesis about the structure of power in a society. According to him all societies have been, and always will be ruled by a small elite governing in their own interest, and keeping the masses in order either, depending on the nature of their 'residues', by force or by guile. These elites arise originally simply because the political talents, just as much as intellectual or musical talents, are unequally distributed in a population, with only a tiny percentage having high 'scores' on the relevant abilities. However, a governing elite naturally wishes to bequeath its position to its offspring, and elites regularly close the entry barriers against those who, though from the masses, have the capacity to govern. Over time the natural inequalities of talent in the population produce a revolutionary leadership amongst the lower classes of greater capacity (and greater preparedness to use force) than the ailing ruling class, and the latter is overthrown. It is replaced though by the new 'elite', which in the long run suffers the fate of its victims. This theory, which has surface resemblances to Marxist views on the class struggle, has been termed the 'circulation of elites'.

Although no one would accept the often curious details of Pareto's theory nowadays, the basic ideas, and the need to combine both a theory of ideology and a theory of social structure to explain power distribution are common to most subsequent work in the field.

Parliament

A Parliament is in general a consultative assembly whose permission may or may not constitutionally be required for the formal passage of binding legislation. The word itself is mainly of English usage, where other languages are liable to use a version of the word simply for assembly. In general parliaments are nowadays elected assemblies with the duty of checking, controlling and sometimes electing the executive power. Their structures can vary, but most are either bicameral or unicameral. A bicameral parliament (the norm in the Anglo-American world) will often have a separate basis for selection for the two 'Houses' of Parliament, and will usually have slightly different powers for the two. A very common difference in the latter case, for example, is the sole right of the 'lower' house to initiate bills that result in the raising of taxation. As far as selection procedures go, the lower house (in Britain the House of Commons, in the United States the House of Representatives) is usually the more clearly democratic. Thus the upper House in Britain, the House of Lords, is not elected at all, whereas the Senate in the US is elected on a basis of equal representation for each state, rather than equally populated electoral districts.

Historically in Europe the development of democracy over the centuries has been largely the growth of power of parliament over the monarchy, and of the lower house over the upper. One can still see this process at work in other institutional contexts, an obvious one being the striving for power of the European parliament over other institutions in the European Community.

Parliamentary Government

Parliamentary government is a system of government in which the EXECUTIVE is responsible to an ASSEMBLY or PARLIAMENT which may be constituted by ELECTION—as has increasingly been the case in the 20th century—or by nomination by some wider body. Parliaments within a system of parliamentary government perform many functions but in most their primary function is to legislate both in the sense of scrutinizing the detail of laws and in the sense of authorizing or legitimizing the passage of laws. In parliamentary government much attention is also given to parliament's right to supervise and control public expenditure and indeed the powers of the original parliaments stemmed from the right to grant the executive money—or as the British terminology has it—to grant supply. Out of this power there developed the more general parliamentary functions of oversight of the executive, the role of representing individuals, groups and classes in any clashes with the executive, and the use of Parliament as a forum in which the great issues of the day may be debated.

The balance between these functions will vary between countries just as the effectiveness of parliamentary government varies between political systems. Implicit in the very idea of parliamentary government however is the notion that the executive will not exercise power arbitrarily and will take Parliament's views into account as representative of the views of the people (see ACCOUNTABILITY). In most systems of parliamentary government the elections to the LEGISLATURE determine the political character of the government but in some systems where the electoral system frequently throws up no clear overall parliamentary majority there may be scope for discretion on the part of the monarch or President in forming a government to reflect the composition of the Parliament. Normally governments must maintain the confidence of Parliament to stay in power, although how this is interpreted varies from system to system (see questions of CONFIDENCE).

In most parliamentary systems the members of the executive or ministers sit in Parliament; in France, however, a curious hybrid system operates so that, while ministers may run for parliamentary seats, if they become members of the government they do not sit within the Assembly or Senate but appoint deputies to perform their functions.

Most systems of parliamentary government make use of a committee system to consider the details of legislation and of the budgetary process (see COMMITTEES). And in many parliamentary systems there are two chambers—a lower house which is directly elected and an upper house which is either appointed or elected on a different principle from that which the lower house employs (see SECOND CHAMBERS.)

Parti Communiste Français (see PCF)

Parti Socialiste

The French Socialist party, under this title and its current form is a relatively new creation, dating from between 1969 when it was first set up to the mid 1970s when it took its final shape. There had been a variety of French socialist parties since the turn of the century, but they were so disunited and complex that they never achieved serious power, and President Mitterrand, elected in 1981, is the first Socialist to hold the Presidency of the Fifth Republic. Originally created in 1905 as a result of the Second International it actually called itself simply 'The French Section of the Worker's International' (SFIO), and continued under this title until 1969. As a result of the dominance in the National Assembly of the Gaullist party, and their proven ability to win elections because of their unity, a feeling grew that the disunited non-communist left had to organize itself properly. The process was slow, starting with an electoral federation of the left consisting of the SFIO, Mitterrand's own party (CIR) and the Radical Socialists, the temporary electoral success of which increased the attraction of some united form of democratic socialism. The CIR (Convention of Republican Institutions) finally joined, along with a series of socialist clubs in 1971, with Mitterrand, who had been the presidential candidate for the Federation of the Left as its first leader. (Technically, First Secretary.) The new party spent most of the 1970s engaged in electoral co-operation with the Communists, even signing a common programme with them in 1972, and this alignment very nearly gave Mitterrand, as candidate for virtually the whole of the French left an electoral victory over Giscard d' Estaing in 1974. However, the very fact of the increasing popularity of the reformist left, now it was united, frightened the French Communist party, who broke off the alignment just before the assembly elections of 1978, almost certainly preventing them gaining an assembly majority. The P.S. continued to grow, both in internal organization and membership, came more and more to look like an ordinary European Social Democrat party (as with the Scandinavian or British Labour parties), and finally ended the more than two decades of right wing rule in the Fifth Republic in 1981. To many political observers this is final proof that the old tradition of multi-partisme in French politics is broken, and the Republic is moving rapidly towards a stable two or three party state, in which the forces of the far left will cease to have any importance.

Participatory Democracy

Participatory democracy is really an alternative label for 'DIRECT' as opposed to 'REPRESENTATIVE' DEMOCRACY. It does however have a slightly wider connotation, because participation need not necessarily carry the implication of ultimate decision-making power. Thus one can argue for a much greater degree of citizen participation in a political system although accepting that the ultimate decision-making and law-creating functions must be handled by a small body of elected representatives. Widespread use of public enquiries, of advisory referenda, of consultative bodies, and similar devices can increase the degree to which ordinary people participate in the forming of policy. (See also DIRECT DEMOCRACY and INDUSTRIAL PARTICIPATION).

Partito Comunista Italiano (see PCI)

Party

A party, in political terms, is an organized group of people sharing common policy preferences and usually a general ideological position. Simply to have such a common view does not make a party—it is necessary also that they seek, or have, political power. The historical derivation of the concept is complex, and party has not always had the innocent sense it has now. Originally, to say of a group that it was a party was to suggest that it selfishly pursued its own collective interest, and that by existing and working towards power it destroyed a true latent unity of interest and opinion in society. Political parties in the sense we know them now did not become important until the extension of the voting right to large sections of the population. In rough outline the sequence of development was for a party, previously existing merely as a group of like-minded men in parliament, to organize nationally in the hope of attracting the newly enfranchised voters and keeping their elective power. Alternatively a party may have grown up from the grass roots, once the vote became widespread, to organize and fight elections to try to get representatives of the newly enfranchised interests into office or the legislature. The two basic modes of parliamentary party are often distinguished as 'cadre' parties and 'mass' parties. They represent no more than ideal types, and there are still examples of competitive parties with virtually no mass organization at all—just as there are mass parties which are really only loose coalitions of separate interests, groups or regions with no central agreement on policy.

Political parties are not necessarily organized or intended to fight elections—the idea of a revolutionary party is an obvious example. Here, though, the aim is still to seek power, if by different means, just as the ruling single parties of, for example, the Soviet bloc countries, though not competing for power, still exist entirely to wield it. Power and its pursuit, for some common purpose or interest, across the whole range of government activity, is the hallmark of a political party. Organizations which exist to push for one single interest or represent opinion on a single issue are not parties if they do not actively seek power for general purposes.

PCF

PCF is the French Communist party, (Parti Communiste Français), set up in 1920 when the Socialist party split, the left becoming the

Communist party, and modelling itself on the CPSU (q.v.). For most of its history, and certainly until the early years of the FIFTH REPUBLIC, it was one of the most STALINIST Communist parties in the West. It was, however, electorally very popular. During the THIRD REPUBLIC it joined in the popular front electoral alliance that won the general elections in 1936, preventing a collapse of the republic in what threatened to be a bitter clash between French Fascists and the left. Significantly it only entered this alliance because Stalin had called for communists everywhere to unite with other left-wing groups, Stalin's interests being entirely to take some of the threat of Nazi Germany away from Russia. Though invited into the post-war government under de Gaulle it rapidly withdrew rather than be tarnished with helping the American-backed French bourgeoisie, and has never subsequently been in office until the Socialist leader, Mitterrand, after his victory in 1981 gave them four places in the first ever left-wing government of the Fifth Republic. During the war the Communist party went underground and formed a vital part of the resistance movement, though as often as not fighting the other, de Gaulle-inspired or Catholic, wings as well as the Germans. After the allied invasion in 1944 elements of the party tried to seize power in the south of France. During the post-war period the PCF had a very strong electoral following, varying between 20% and 25% of the votes in all elections through to the late 1960s. Also during this period it started to cast off some of its STALINISM, and lose its revolutionary fervour—at the time of the 1968 disturbances in Paris the party exercised tight control on its members and refused to see the situation as having any revolutionary potential. This increasing moderation, however, culminating in 1976 when the party officially abandoned the doctrine of the DICTATORSHIP OF THE PROLETARIAT, did it no electoral good. Steadily its votes slipped away to the reformed and re-organized Socialist party which had developed out of the mess of small splinter groups fighting an internecine war. Though the PCF tried to counter this by alliances with the Socialists, they could not quite accept the degree of policy modification required, and the best hope, the common programme between the two parties, collapsed just before the 1978 National Assembly elections, allowing the right to win yet again. By the 1981 Presidential elections the PCF had come to see a possible victory for the Socialists as their biggest danger, but the trend continued, and both the Presidential election and the ensuing Assembly election were won single-handed by the Socialists. Although the President gave them ministerial appointments, there is every chance that the days of political influence for the PCF are over.

PCI

PCI stands for the Italian Communist Party (Partito Comunista Italiano), the largest of all Western European Communist parties. It was founded in 1921 as a result of a split in the then united Italian Socialist Party (in much the same way as the French Communist Party was created). Its early history was largely covert, because the advent of MUSSOLINI's Fascist state forced it underground, and its leader and chief ideologue, Togliatti went to Moscow to work for the Comintern. During the latter stages of the war, when the Germans occupied Italy, the PCI formed the basis of the anti-German resistance and, again like the French Communists, bought themselves a good deal of respectability thereby, as a result of which it was part of the immediate post war government. In 1947 it was expelled from the coalition, dominated by the Christian Democrats, and at first launched a campaign of violent industrial and political opposition to the regime. However the party had always been inclined towards the more 'reformist' versions of communism, partly because of the enormous influence of their intellectual martyr GRAMSCI, and when the 1948 election, giving a huge majority to the right wing showed how little effect obstructionism had, they settled instead for the role of democratic opposition. Slowly over the 1950s and 1960s their popularity grew. By the elections of the 1970s the PCI was not only the second biggest party in the state, but was only a few per cent less popular than the ruling Christian democrats, and seemed to have every chance of overtaking them.

Undoubtedly their popularity and respectability in Italian eyes comes from their deliberate and public split with Moscow, and their avowal of a democratic road to communism. The PCI has indeed become the leading example of 'EURO-COMMUNISM', and maintains a careful distance from Russian communism. They were, for example, amongst the first to denounce both the 1968 invasion of Czechoslovakia and the later invasion of Afghanistan. Though they have never been fully admitted to membership of the governing coalition, their successes in 1976 led to a brief period in which they upheld by active parliamentary support the Christian Democrat coalition government. Their tactical aim, which they call the 'Historic Compromise' is to be accepted into such a coalition fully. Though not yet in power at the national level, the PCI controls many of the Italian regions and cities. At the city government level they have demonstrated, in cities like Florence, their capacity for clean, efficient and uncorrupt government, considerably in contrast to the increasingly decrepit and tainted Christian Democrat city governments. The greatest danger for the PCI comes from the far left of Italian politics, whose revolutionary theories threaten to spoil the image of the party, careful though it is to distance itself from them. The other barrier to final electoral success is the ambivalent attitude of the Catholic Church. In the early post-war days the church opposed them publicly, using the pulpit to warn all Christians away from voting Communist. Nowadays the opposition is much more muted, and indeed radical clergy sometimes openly support them.

Plato

Plato (427–347BC) is the first great philosopher and political thinker of the Western tradition, and the major inheritance by Western political thought of the Classical period. In some ways this is ironic; the usual image of classical Greek politics, or certainly the image of what was best about it is of Athenian PARTICIPATORY DEMOCRACY. Plato, however, was fiercely opposed to democracy, and his most important political writings, known to us as *The Republic,* is in part a vicious attack on democracy and a lengthy and subtle philosophical justification for rule by a small intellectual élite. Other important works, notably *The Laws,* are blueprints for just such a society, which he hoped would stimulate the founding of new non-democratic Greek colonies. Indeed the Greek society Plato most admired was Sparta, the traditional authoritarian enemy of Athens.

Plato's reasons for opposing Athenian democracy can be analysed on at least two levels. For one thing he came himself from an aristocratic family. More important, certainly in his own eyes, was a distaste of the excesses of demagogically influenced masses arising from the execution by the democratic assembly of his friend and hero, Socrates, on a fallacious charge (according to Plato, anyway) of corrupting public morals. At the more theoretical level Plato opposed democracy because of certain conclusions he drew about the capacity of humanity to understand, and therefore follow, the good life. Briefly, human intellectual capacity is not at all equally distributed; knowledge of moral good is just as much dependent on this capacity as knowledge of any skill; indeed 'ruling' is just another skill or trade: only the very most able are capable of seeing moral and political truth properly, hence only they (Plato called them 'Philosopher Kings') should have political power. The theory is subtle and rich, and argues for the rule of the Philosopher-Kings on many dimensions, all infused with very complex general philosophical views. He has been seen by some modern critics as tremendously right wing, even as some sort of precursor to FASCISM, but this is crudely to abstract a powerful and complicated thinker from his context in a quite meaningless way. Plato is hardly less studied than any other major political thinker, and certainly is nowadays more influential than his successor ARISTOTLE, though this was not always so, for the mediaeval rediscovery of classical civilization really started with Aristotle, whose views were powerfully formative on the political thought of mediaeval CHRISTIANITY.

Perhaps the most alien element in Plato's thought is not the undemocratic constitution he advocates, but the way he sees the whole role of the state. To Plato (and here Aristotle followed him) the purpose of the state is to enforce decent living, actively to encourage a morality and religion, rather than to satisfy the demands of the population, or even just to keep law and order to allow freedom. For this reason his philosophical arguments about the nature of goodness and our capacity to perceive it are not so much dismissed, as simply not seen as relevant when a modern thinker of almost any political persuasion considers the constitutional arguments.

Plebiscitory Democracy

Plebiscites are referenda (see REFERENDUM), a system for allowing the whole of an electorate directly to give their opinion on some political question. They have been used in a variety of contexts in twentieth century politics. One quite common use has been to hold a plebiscite for the population of a territory over which two countries have rival claims to sovereignty. Alternatively referenda are used to discover public attitudes to constitutional changes, as in Britain in 1975 (over retaining membership of the EEC), or on many issues of policy at local levels as frequently happens in the USA. The idea that a country might be governed extensively by the use of plebiscites on ordinary policy issues is attractive to some, because it seems to be a way of avoiding the disadvantages of REPRESENTATIVE DEMOCRACY without the impracticalities of DIRECT DEMOCRACY.

To others, however, plebiscitory democracy has often seemed extremely dangerous. The argument against extensive use of referenda in this way is that so much depends on the framing of the question. The proportion of an electorate supporting some proposal can be crucially dependent on exactly what alternative they are offered on a ballot paper. An experiment carried out in Britain in 1975 by a public opinion poll, using a variety of questions about staying in the EEC on different samples produced very widely varying proportions supporting retention of membership. This appears to give far too much power to the political leaders who set the options, and opens up the whole fear of manipulation of an electorate by an unscrupulously demagogic political leadership.

The most recent serious example of the use (or misuse) of frequent referenda to support a political leadership was President DE GAULLE's tendency to put carefully structured options to the French electorate, backing his own preference with threats to resign were the country not to support him. General demands for increased popular participation in government, however, seem likely to extend rather than restrict the use of this form of democracy. The most successful and long term experience is that of Switzerland, where a host of ordinary policy questions are routinely put to the electorate.

PLO

The Palestine Liberation Organization was originally only one of a series of political and activist groups that arose from the plight of the Palestinians expelled from their land when the State of Israel was formed. These refugees settled in UN organized camps in most neighbouring countries, but especially in Jordan and Lebanon. Originally the hopes of the Palestinians were either for re-settlement in Arab countries, or for the then Arab League to win back for them their original homeland. After the Israeli defeat of Arab, and especially Syrian and Egyptian forces in the Arab-Israeli wars of 1956 and 1967 they lost all such hope. Various more or less militant, or political and diplomatic groups were created to try, in their different ways, either through negotiation or through terrorist tactics, to find a solution. The two most important were the *Fatah* organization, under Yassar Arafat, and the PLO itself. The *Fatah* were militant, terrorist, and insisted on a violent means, especially through trying to make alliances with the left wing Islamic co-religionists in the Lebanon against the richer urban Christians. It appears that the revolutionary and terrorist tactics of *Fatah* were more or less consciously modelled on the way the Algerian anti-colonial fighters had forced out the French in the early 1960s. However the analogy was imprecise, at least in part because of the support the Western powers have until recently always given Israel. The PLO, led by a diplomat who had worked in Syria, took a much more peaceful line. As the diplomatic solution systematically failed to win the West away from supporting Israel, it lost credibility, and the masses of Palestinians in the camps swung behind Yassar Arafat, who combined *Fatah* and other extremist organizations with the PLO itself, of which he became leader. Despairing of getting their original land back they ultimately attempted to take over the Jordanian state. Jordan had welcomed, and indeed benefited from Palestinian refugees, and it seemed a suitable society to become the

257

new Palestinian homeland. King Hussain however, finally lost patience with the demands of the PLO, and unleashed his army, which had grown more and more impatient with having to put up with a 'foreign' power inside its own boundaries, especially when terrorist attacks on Israel regularly brought retaliation on to Jordanian settlements. With an incredible fury they expelled the Palestinians, some 10,000 being killed. Lebanon again became the potential homeland, though the PLO, and Arafat himself were steadily gaining international recognition and sympathy. The final stage in the immediate history of the PLO came in 1982 when Israel launched a massive military invasion of that half of the Lebanon effectively controlled by the Palestinians, and drove them out, forcing the dispersal of an increasingly unified movement all over the Arab world. Though no conceivable solution to the problem is in sight at this stage, the PLO is being forced even more on to the political and diplomatic initiative, helped, ironically by the blow to Israeli international prestige occasioned by the very war tactics that seem to have destroyed the military potential of the PLO.

Pluralism

Pluralism is both a technical term in political science, and an evaluative word for a form of government, often used as a defence of what might otherwise be called LIBERAL or REPRESENTATIVE DEMOCRACIES. Technically a pluralist political system is one that has several centres of power and authority, rather than one in which the state is the sole controller of people's actions. Thus medieval society in Europe, where both the monarchy and the church were co-equal rulers in their different spheres, and where craft corporations and feudal landlords also had a claim to the obedience of citizens was truly pluralist. Nowadays the doctrine is slightly more complicated because a modern state will not accept formally that there are rival, equally legitimate, sources of power and foci of legitimacy. But it can be argued that societies like those of the USA, Britain, or Western Europe are effectively pluralist. So, for example, trades unions and industrial associations, along with political parties and perhaps the administrative bureaucracy effectively share power with the official government and legislature. One version of the pluralist thesis wants to attach major significance to the multiple and cross-cutting INTEREST GROUPS and special PRESSURE GROUPS that exist in a modern society, or even the multiplicity of social and ethnic cleavages, to argue that power and authority are widely dispersed in a pluralist Western democracy. In its modern form the theory of pluralism starts with BENTLEY'S thesis of the GROUP nature of society, but it was mainly developed by American political scientists after the Second World War, during the growth of the BEHAVIOURAL movement. Such writers as Robert DAHL undertook studies of power in local communities, and when they were unable to show that effective PARTICIPATORY DEMOCRACY controlled affairs, argued instead that societies such as America were controlled by alternating and rival elites representing different interests. As power was disaggregated in this way, and, according to the theory, all legitimate groups got some say in decision-making, the essentially 'democratic' nature of the societies was claimed to be upheld. One version of this theory has come to be known as POLYARCHY, and later writers have tried to show that the realities of power in most societies, including supposedly TOTALITARIAN states like the USSR are essentially pluralist. The most important rival theory of power in capitalist societies, apart from the MARXIST theory, is that rather broad set of theories described as 'Power Elite' theories, often associated with writers like C. Wright MILLS and R. MILIBAND. The pluralist thinkers seem to be a development of the earlier ELITIST thinkers, and are connected with a parallel development in the theory of elections associated with such economist-oriented theorists as SCHUMPETER and DOWNS.

Police

The police are the specialist corps recruited to keep the law—especially the criminal law—in a state. Most countries began to develop such forces at the beginning of the 19th century and their precise role in any political system naturally varies with the character of that system. Two political issues have always been controversial with respect to the role of the police. The first relates to the extent to which the police are accountable for their actions and to which level of government is thought appropriate to control the operations of a country's police force. In Britain, where the political role of the police has been relatively minor, it has always been thought preferable to place responsibility for the police in local authorities, although since 1964 the number of police authorities has been reduced. In the 20th century also central government has acquired additional responsibilities for training and recruitment which to some extent balance the local nature of policing in the United Kindom.

By contrast European systems have generally assumed that a centrally organized police force would be more efficient. As a result the police in such countries as France have been seen as much as an arm of the state as a neutral instrument for upholding the laws and protecting the individual citizen.

The second issue which recurs in any discussion of the police is the extent to which they may use force or are constrained by the rules of law or CIVIL LIBERTIES. In the United Kingdom for example the police are generally unarmed, although the experience of the street riots in the 1980s forced them to experiment with new techniques of crowd control such as water cannon. (And in Northern Ireland policing is on a quite different basis). By comparison the United States, France and many other countries allow their police to be armed and to use a variety of modern methods of a para-military kind.

Police State

A Police State is a political system where those in power use naked force by police, secret police, military and even private armies to control and dominate the population. At its root a police state is identified by its contempt for ordinary notions of the rule of law, as well as by totally ignoring any idea of civil liberties. It is the immediate power of the executive, or whomever controls the repressive forces to inflict punishment, even death on particular individuals or groups, without having to show them guilty of breaking formally constituted law that characterizes such a state. As an inevitable consequence of such political behaviour, the police themselves come to wield unchecked power on their own behalf, as well as on behalf of their political masters, with consequential corruption and an even wider spreading of terror.

The two best known and most fully developed police states in modern times have been Nazi Germany and the USSR under Stalin where respectively the Gestapo and the KGB exercised such direct power over anyone even suspected of opposing or even disapproving of the political system. Often in these examples the external forms of judicial process were held to, but using the courts which would not have dared anything but to support the police. Equally often not even a sham of legal respectability was put up. The whole concept of a 'police state' refers, of course, to a technique of ruling, and either to the structure of a state or its justifying political ideology. It is not impossible that a majoritarian democracy could operate, at least vis-à-vis some unpopular minority, by police-state tactics, and both Britain when governing Northern Ireland and some Southern states of the USA on questions of racial politics have been accused of such behaviour. In general though, only a dictatorship of some form will be likely to be a thorough-going police state. The converse is not, of course true—dictatorships, totalitarian systems, or such like do not have to be police states.

Polis

Polis is possibly the most important concept in Classical political theory, and is vital for understanding the politics of the whole ancient world. Usually inadequately translated into English as 'City State', a 'polis' was the basic unit of political organization throughout the ancient world, but was especially important in Greece from the Dark Ages until the Hellenistic period at least. For the leading Greek political theorists like PLATO and ARISTOTLE, living in a polis was a constituent of being human, hence Aristotle's famous definition of man as a 'political animal', where political actually meant, the inhabitant of a polis. The polis was a relatively small self-contained state centering round a city, though the agricultural hinterland was seen as equally a part. Citizenship in this unit was the main political bond, the main identity on which a Greek could fall back, and was vastly more important than the much less formal notion of being a Greek, or even of being part of the various federations of city-states that existed from time to time. It was to the small, almost 'face-to-face' community of the polis that loyalty went, and from which protection and benefit could be hoped for. Theorists varied in their accounts of the reason for the vital nature of the polis, but, especially during democratic periods, the main idea was that participation in the life of the polis gave moral development to the citizen, organized his religion, provided his culture, and was the overriding duty of the citizen or even the metic (non-citizen but legally resident alien.) It is particularly important when contrasted with the 'STATE OF NATURE' or 'SOCIAL CONTRACT' thinkers of the ENLIGHTENMENT, because few Greeks would have thought that someone living in a state of nature was even truly human, so important was the collective bond and shared identity of fellow members of a city state. This was more powerful, both in theory and practice, than the patriotism expected later of a subject in a European nation state, in part because of the difference in scale and the impossibility of genuine participation. Even during periods of what the Greeks called 'tyranny', when actual participation in decision-making was denied, the sense of collective interest and identity was stronger than has been possible in subsequent political organizations. Even later, not only during the Roman Empire when lip service at least was paid to the importance of Roman citizenship, but in, say, Italian medieval city states, this focus on very local loyalty was to prove a major barrier to building national communities.

Politburo

Technically the Politburo, the Political Bureau of the Communist Party of the Soviet Union (see CPSU), is just a committee in permanent session of the irregularly meeting Party Congress, no more than, say, the National Executive Committee of the British Labour party. In practice the Politburo is as near as the Soviet Union comes to having a 'Cabinet', a body continuously directing policy and making all urgent, and many day to day, decisions. Its exact role and power, as well as its make up, have varied enormously over the years since 1917. Under STALIN it hardly met, while under KHRUSHCHEV it was more or less a rubber stamp for his decisions, being packed with his men. (When Khrushchev was overthrown, this was achieved by a majority forming against him not in the Politburo, but in the Central Committee of the party, a much larger and less controllable body.) Since Khrushchev's time it has become more representative of the various forces and interests in the Soviet State, and subsequent leaders have had to make sure they had a majority in the Politburo for any policy. It was the fight in the Politburo that Andropov won in 1982 to make him undisputed leader of the Soviet Union. Although officially a party body, rather than a constitutional organ of state, the party and the state are so intertwined in the Soviet Union that the distinction is largely without meaning. Nonetheless the men who head the vital state ministries (and who will, of course, be senior party members) will be on the Politburo, thus linking the two pillars of the political system in one decision-making body. It is a small body, and in 1976, for example, had only 16 full members, notably smaller than the British cabinet, and is thus more easily able to agree upon and then enforce policies. Its membership in that year, typical of post-Khrushchev Russian politics, had six people there purely because of holding party offices at the centre of the party, four who held vital regional party leaderships, as well as representatives of the most important state organs, principally the ministers of defence and foreign affairs, and the head of the KGB. (At the time, this was Andropov, whose power base for the rest of his life depended largely on his previous control of this body.) Most Eastern European Communist regimes mirror this form of organization, and politburos, in their purely party sense, exist in Western European communist parties. In modern political discussion, the easiest way of describing the Politburo is just to think of it as 'The Government'.

Political Culture

Political culture was a popular technical term in political science during the BEHAVIOURAL revolution, and, though less often referenced, is still of some importance. Roughly a 'political culture' is the totality of ideas and attitudes towards authority, discipline, governmental responsibilities and entitlements, and associated patterns of cultural transmission, like the education system and even family life. The importance of all these factors, and the reason for linking them together into one portmanteau concept, is that they give an overall profile of how people are likely to react to political matters. Thus a classic study into political culture across several countries, The CIVIC CULTURE, showed that some societies seemed to transmit a general distrust for authority, and to create very low levels of political hopefulness in their citizens, whilst others, rightly or wrongly, bred citizens who felt they could trust politicians and that they themselves had a fair say in determining policy and political decisions. All sorts of matters can be relevant in applying this concept, from the discipline systems in schools to, in one perhaps extreme case, child-rearing patterns in Burma. While no one, arguably, has ever managed to define or measure the concept sufficiently precisely to make it theoretically testable, it is clear that some general set of views about the nature and utility of government and authority can plausibly be seen as prevailing in all societies, and may well be a more important determinant of the decisions and shape of government than more obviously contemporary events.

Political Development

Political development was a major research topic in POLITICAL SCIENCE in the 1950s and 1960s, but has of late become somewhat less fashionable. The basic idea, operating on an analogy with economic development, was that there existed a fairly objective path of political progress through which societies moved towards further political sophistication, just as there is, arguably, a trend towards greater economic capacity which all economies can at least hope to take. Political development had obvious serious problems in avoiding a purely ideological bias in which nations were seen as more developed the more they came to look like either Western Liberal Democracies or whatever else one took as one's ideal. Particularly in America a great deal of effort was put into COMPARATIVE GOVERNMENT studies with a developmental approach, and much of this was organized round the popular sociological theories of the day, which were all forms of FUNCTIONALISM. The idea that there is a developmental path towards greater political complexity and more efficient problem-solving is not new, however. All of the major social theorists of the 19th and early 20th centuries, COMTE, Spencer, MARX, WEBER, DURKHEIM, and arguably the English UTILITARIANS, believed in some sort of regular developmental sequence in the changes that political systems underwent. In a less theoretical mode the policies of former colonising powers in Europe often implied such a notion too, with the idea that the local inhabitants of, say, India, had to be led slowly towards a capacity for independence by stages of taking more and more responsibility as their economic and educational systems improved. In a similar way much of the propaganda of the non-democratic nations of the Third World rests on an idea of slow development of political capacity, usually going hand in hand with economic development. Thus the ideas of DIRECTED DEMOCRACY and justifications for one-party states often start from the argument that fully-fledged LIBERAL DEMOCRACY is incompatible with the stresses arising from the need to build national unity and to organize a productive economy. Too much importance, however, tends to be placed on the fact that Western Democracies followed a roughly similar path from FEUDALISM to DEMOCRACY, and that newer nations can be expected to follow a similar developmental sequence.

Political Obligation

Political obligation is the theory of why, and when, a person is morally obliged to obey a government. There are a series of alternative theories to account for our requirement to obey governments. Probably the most commonly referred to is the idea of CONSENT, but arguments ranging from DIVINE RIGHT to FORCE MAJEURE have been canvassed. There is, of course, no general argument that can satisfy everyone, but the operating convention on political obligation seems to be, roughly, that obedience is better than anarchy, and that only some laws, for example those against racial integration, may be disobeyed without one being regarded as a criminal or a traitor. To some extent the very asking of the question is problematic because it assumes a STATE OF NATURE approach in which it is plausible to imagine men as not already under governmental control.

Political Participation

Political participation is usually defined as the extent to which citizens avail themselves of those ordinary democratic rights of political activity to which they are constitutionally entitled, and the measure is held by political sociologists to indicate the nature of the country's POLITICAL CULTURE. However there is no reason to apply the concept only to LIBERAL DEMOCRACIES. Participation can be usefully measured in other contexts, and can tell one a good deal about the political nature of that society. Thus varying rates of attendance at party meetings in the USSR, or at rallies for ruling parties in Third World states and so on, indicate the legitimacy and popularity of the state.

Political Science

Political Science is one of a number of titles for the academic study of politics and political behaviour. As an academic discipline the subject is very old. ARISTOTLE refers to it as the 'Queen' of sciences, but for many centuries thereafter it lost a separate identity. Until perhaps the 19th century such intellectual work as was carried out on politics was done by political philosophers, theologians, journalists, but seldom by full-time professional political analysts. (Although the first Chair in the subject was, in fact, set up in Sweden in the 17th century.) Gradually by a process of intellectual separation of powers the discipline became specified out of the previous conglomeration of law, economics and philosophy, so that by the turn of the last century most American universities and many German ones had chairs and departments of politics or political science. Britain was relatively late adopting this trend, and despite the creation earlier of the London School of Economics and Political Science, any widespread study and teaching of the subject is a post–1945 phenomenon. Political Science as such has no collective corpus of knowledge, or even commonly agreed methodology, but is somewhat of a 'holding company' for a series of subdisciplines, the workers in which do not necessarily accept others as really sharing a common discipline except in terms of subject matter. Thus 'POLITICAL THEORY', 'Comparative politics', POLITICAL SOCIOLOGY', 'international relations', and perhaps 'political history' are rather separated sub-disciplines (and indeed contain further often incompatible subdivisions within themselves). Broadly, though, political science is the study of the nature, distribution, and dynamics of power, usually at the national or international level, but sometimes a very 'micro' level. The techniques of the discipline vary all the way from highly mathematical and statistical analyses of objective data (most commonly found in political sociology), via rather journalistic descriptive accounts of political institutions, or almost ethnographical accounts of foreign political cultures to logical and conceptual analysis of political morality. Increasingly the rather artificial distinction between the sub-disciplines is being eroded, as empirical researchers realize the need to be 'guided by' theory, and as theorists see that they must seek to explain and generalize about real political phenomena as well as worry about moral implications. At the same time the technical training of the profession, especially in terms of quantitive techniques is getting steadily better and considerable progress is being made in developing empirically founded generalizations, and powerful analytic models, as with, for example, economics.

Political Sociology

Political Sociology is a sub-field of POLITICAL SCIENCE and, as its name suggests concentrates both in terms of subject matter and research technique on political analogues to the typical subject matter of Sociology. Political sociologists tend to concentrate very much more on the behaviour, beliefs and formation of the masses of political actors, whilst other branches of political science look much more to the behaviour and attitudes of political elites. Thus a major area of political sociology (and perhaps the best developed area in the whole of political science) is the study, by survey research and statistical analysis, of electoral behaviour in Western democracies. Outside those who specialize in political theory itself, political sociology is also probably the most 'theoretical' of the empirical research divisions of political science, mainly because of the influence of the great founding fathers of sociological theory, MARX, WEBER and DURKHEIM, all of whom made serious attempts at theoretical explanation of political phenomena.

Political Theory

Political Theory really falls into two broad alternative disciplines, though many of the past practitioners of the subject would have to be seen as belonging on both sides of the divide. On the one hand it tends nowadays to connote a philosophical examination of the meaning and logic of political values, to concern itself with the 'ought' questions at the heart of political belief, as, for example, with the perennial topic of the basis of one's obligation to obey the state. On the other hand increasingly political theory is coming to bear the same relationship to empirical political research as does say, theoretical physics to applied physics. That is, political theory is trying to weld together the insights, data and understandings of those who study the actuality of political life into a coherent, explanatory theory or theories of political behaviour capable, even, of generating predictions. Traditionally the classic political theorists like HOBBES or PLATO in fact did both jobs. Ideally political theory should probably be defined as trying to combine the empirical truths about human political reactions with the moral truths of what is politically desirable by designing institutions and consti- tutions which will generate the desirable by harnessing human political nature. That is clearly a massive job, perhaps never capable of more than limited achievement, but it is increasingly the goal of a united and coherent political science.

Polyarchy

Polyarchy is a concept invented by Robert DAHL, and taken up by other PLURALISTS, to describe modern self-described democratic states. In this theory society is controlled by a set of competing interest groups, roughly along the lines of Bentley's GROUP theory, with the government as little more than an honest broker in the middle. The derivation is, of course, from the Greek along the Aristotelian lines, meaning the rule of the many, though not, democracy, the rule of the people. The best description and analyses of this notion come in the COMMUNITY POWER studies where details of influence and power in small social settings are shown to involve this sort of group competition.

Popular Front

Popular Fronts in general are alliances, either just for electoral tactics, or as would-be governing conventions between all left-wing (and sometimes liberal-centrist) parties in a political system. Typi- cally they involve some form of co-operation with a Communist party which would otherwise be left 'out in the cold' of political life. The most famous popular front, and the one usually meant by the phrase was the alliance formed in France in the mid-1930s between the Socialists and the Left-Radicals (who were in fact a centrist party of the lower middle classes and richer peasants). In 1936 this coalition took office, supported by the French Communist party, which had received orders from the Third International to co-operate, though it refused actually to enter office. It was the first left-wing government that France had experienced in the 20th century, and was brought to power partly because of the effect of the international economic depression, the effect of which on France had been delayed longer than in Britain and America. The second reason for its success was that both the centre and the far left in France had become badly frightened by an upsurge of extreme right-wing, at times openly fascist strength and agitation inspired by Hitler's Germany. Thus an alliance that might plausibly have occurred much earlier, and solved many of the problems and deep divisions in French society, was delayed until much too late.

The government, which lasted until 1938, made a brave attempt at social reform. Its most important reforms were increasing industrial wages, shortening working hours and carrying out long needed welfare programmes. But by then the economy, which had long needed modernization, could not sustain the demands made on it, and French financiers deserted the franc forcing the government to moderate much of its programme. External threats and the whole problem of defence added to burdens that were exacerbated by the hostility of the trade unions who felt the pace of change was much too slow and staged crippling strikes. The popular front coalition fell as a direct result of its leader, Daladier's, appeasement of Hitler at Munich, which the more left-wing members could not accept. Had the THIRD REPUBLIC not been destroyed soon after by the war, some revived form of the government would probably have returned to office, but nothing quite like it was to re-appear on the French political scene, unless one counts the contemporary socialist government, with its small Communist ally. Popular Fronts appeared at roughly the same time in Spain (losing the civil war to Franco) and Chile. The first Chilean popular front government, elected in 1938, was probably the only truly successful one, staying in office until 1947 and achieving lasting social reform. However, Chile's second popular front, elected in the early 1970s under Allende's leadership was too far to the left to allow the centre and right parties to help it against the brutal coup d'etat of General Pinochet, and led straight to military dictatorship. Popular fronts are less and less likely to emerge as the non-Communist left in most developed countries increasingly gains ground over the Communists, and become electorally popular in their own right through presenting an efficient and united alternative to the centre and right.

Populism

Populism is a political tradition especially prevalent in Latin America, though various European and North American movements (Nazism, McCarthyism) have been described as populist. Its essence is that it mobilizes masses of the poorer sectors of society against the existing institutions of the state, but under the very firm psychological control of a charismatic leader (see CHARISMA). Populism tends to have no precise or logically consistent ideology, but to be a rag-bag of attitudes and values chosen, perhaps cynically, to appeal to alienated and deprived members of a mass society and to direct their fury and energy against existing rulers, without actually committing the populist leaders to any very concrete promises about the likely reforms. It attacks traditional symbols of prestige, in the name of popular equality, but not usually by promising the creation of a normal LIBERAL DEMOCRACY. Thus populist rhetoric tends to be a collection of strands of both left and right-wing thought, with a heavy stress on leadership on the one hand, and popular equality on the other, often with a highly illiberal and intolerant stand on traditional civic liberties. The most famous post-war populist is probably Juan Peron of Argentina. Typically he was originally one of the Generals who staged a coup d'état in 1930, and characteristically of populist movements in general, he studied and admired Italian FASCISM in practice. Populism tends to be over-used, being applied to almost any unorganized mass protest movement whose leadership comes from a higher social class than most of its membership, and it is doubtful whether it has, as a concept, enough analytic capacity or concrete scope to be useful. Those who fear populism as a danger to the stability of the democratic state, such as W. Kornhauser in his *The Politics of Mass Society*, make much of the alienated and drifting marginality of the followers of typical populist leaders, and advocate social systems where multiple ties to class, family, ethnicity, and ordinary organized political groups can give a sense of identity and meaning to the individual, thus making him immune to the often irrational and emotive forces that populism both uses and inspires. In another sense populism simply means having mass popular backing, or acting in the interests of the mass, the people, hence the derivation from Populus. In this, decreasingly common usage, one finds 'popular' or 'populist' democracy carrying none of the overtones of this definition.

Positive Law

Positive law is a term found at least as early as Thomas HOBBES, and used to describe a concept apparent much earlier. Basically it is often necessary to distinguish, when talking about laws, between those that exist in some theoretical or moral sense, as with the 'laws of nature', and those which exist in a practical sense. These latter are considered as 'positive' laws, and the term refers to actual duly legislated rules that are observed and enforced in a particular society. There may, but need not be, overlap: a particular statute (or diktat of a ruling elite) may also be seen as morally or theoretically desirable or necessary, but equally the two realms may be totally opposed. Whether or not some rule is a positive law is an empirical question. There is no inconsistency, for example, in holding that Hitler's laws depriving German Jews of their property were certainly laws in the positive sense, but were 'illegal' in terms of moral or natural law. The more extremely pragmatic of legal theorists, especially the school founded in Britain by Austin in the 19th century and called 'legal positivists' wanted to restrict the whole of legal study, and the whole legitimacy of law to positive law. A law, for Austin, was simply the command of a sovereign (i.e., anyone powerful enough to enforce it), and no other sort of law was anything more than metaphysical speculation. Until fairly recently a modified version of this doctrine was probably the majority view in Britain and in some American law schools, but increasingly it is losing out to a revivified 'natural law' school.

Positivism

Positivism is a term found generally in the social sciences to indicate a particular approach to the methodology of study. Broadly it indicates a 'scientific' approach in which human behaviour is to be treated as an objective phenomenon to be studied in a purely 'value free' manner. At its crudest this means that beliefs, attitudes, values of human actors are to be dismissed as insufficiently concrete or objective to become data for scientific study. Thus DURKHEIM, the leading exponent of positivist social science would not accept that what an actor thought he was doing was a relevant part of any social science description. Even so personal an act as suicide could only be measured 'externally', and suicide rates, as statistics, rather than the accounts of would-be suicides, were the appropriate subject matter. Although there is no logical necessity, positivism tends to go hand in hand with a preference for statistical and mathematical techniques, and with theories which stress the 'system' rather than the individual in explaining political phenomena. Positivism sees as its enemy those who would study political values, either as political philosophers or as, say, political psychologists, the one because it is 'metaphysical', the other because it is concerned with individuals and their perceptions, rather than systems and the externally measurable. Though very popular in the immediate post-war development of political science, few today hold to such an extreme position, and the label is increasingly a vague and general way of indicating the main thrust, rather than the detailed methodology of a social scientist. This is partly because the naive view of what it is to be a 'scientist', or the attraction of being one has declined considerably with the development of more subtle philosophies and sociologies of scientific activity, and partly because anyone interested in empiricism and its related theoretical and research techniques has much in common with another such in the face of the fundamental split that now dominates social science, between Marxists and non-Marxists.

Power

Power, by which we mean here social, economic, or political power, is at the heart both of actual political conflict, and of the discipline of POLITICAL SCIENCE. Despite this it is extremely hard to give any useful definition, and not only are most definitions contentious, but some theorists hold that there cannot be a value free (see VALUE FREEDOM) account either of what power is or when it exists. The safest definitions are, typically, formal, and perhaps vacuous. Thus one very common definition of power in modern political science is 'the ability of A to make B do something B would not choose to do'. The trouble is that such definitions raise almost more questions than they answer. For example, if I get B to want something he 'would not otherwise want', which I want, am I not exercising power? Or, suppose two people both try to get B to do (different) things he does not want, which is to be seen as the more powerful? How does one deal with 'potential' power, the power I might well have, but choose not to use, to make you do something? What are the sources of power? Above all, there is a problem of measuring power. This is not simply an erudite quibble, because important modern theories about the nature of politics, especially ELITISM and PLURALISM depend on answers to these questions. It is held against Pluralism, especially in the version represented by the COMMUNITY POWER studies, that only open conflicts between identified interests are taken as the evidence for the theories of power distribution, while a secret élite who managed to ensure that no one ever got the chance of attacking them, would be regarded as powerless. Clearly no one definition can be satisfactory to all needs, and no use of the concept of power can guarantee to be value free. Nonetheless we have an intuitive understanding of power as something that may indeed come out of the mouth of guns, but also of people, which can be wielded evilly, but also for good, and which ultimately does depend on changing peoples' preferences. The preferences may be between obeying or dying, or they may be much earlier preferences for, say, one toothpaste over another. To use 'power' as a concept at all involves assuming some basic possible human autonomy, some set of preferences that would 'naturally' exist. Whilst this is obviously sometimes no problem (we would naturally prefer not to tell robbers where our jewels are, and pulling our fingernails out is an effective use of power to change our preferences) sometimes the arguments become highly metaphysical. It is the belief that power relations are endemic to all human interaction and largely determine the quality of human life that makes the concept central, and justifies political science as an academic discipline, because politics is, ultimately, the exercise of power.

Pragmatic

Pragmatic has been used almost as often in a pejorative sense of politicians as in a commendatory way by a politician of himself. Whatever its technical dictionary meaning, the best way of characterizing its use in political argument is to say that, in its commendatory usage it is the political equivalent of 'common sense', and when used as opprobrium, it means 'lacking in ideas', or possibly, 'just muddling through'. On the whole it is the conservative side in politics who wish to think of themselves as pragmatic, and in so doing they are seeking to draw a distinction between 'ideologues', those who are committed to some social theory which they feel will solve everything and to which they will stick at any cost, and the 'practical' or common-sense approach of those who consider each problem separately and all solutions 'on their merits'. Despite the almost 'knock-about' way the term and its opposites are used, there is a serious point of rival political theory underlying it. It has been an article of conservative faith in most Western countries since the ENLIGHTENMENT that human reason is not powerful enough fully to understand the complexity of politics and society. As a result conservatives distrust all general theories which purport to give blueprints for policy or social reconstruction. The argument, as put classically by BURKE, is that given our incapacity to theorize and understand, we should, on the whole, change little, and change only slowly. Instead we should, on the whole, accept that any institution that has lasted for some time should stay much as it is. Instead we should go in only for what a later writer, Karl Popper, has called 'Social Engineering'. This entails a gradual, piecemeal and 'practical' orientation to reform, guided at least as much by precedent, instinct and above all caution as by any theory. It is this concatenation of values that 'pragmatism' is meant to convey, and thus 'pragmatic' suits the conservative temperament. The opposition is from those who are committed to a general theory, who believe in the possibility of radical and systematic reform and change. To this position pragmatism all too easily slips into opportunism, and is a synonym for mindless short-term expediency. The distinction, in fact, between pragmatists and ideologues is probably false, if only because pragmatism, with its dogmatic insistence on the impossibility of far-seeing deliberate reform, is itself a deliberate 'ideological' standpoint on human nature. But taken at face value, from the point of view of political science, the distinction between those who would welcome the two labels may well be more useful than the more convential 'LEFT' v 'RIGHT' characterizations.

Presidential Government

Presidential government is a system which gives a strong role to a President who heads the EXECUTIVE and participates in its actual decision-making processes. It is therefore to be contrasted with systems where the President is simply a ceremonial head of state or has merely the function of appointing a prime minister or other official to head the government. Forms of presidential government vary but in many countries, including the United States and France, the President is elected separately.

Presidential government in systems which are marked by a SEPARATION OF POWERS (for example the United States) is sometimes seen as a constitutional distortion because power is meant to be balanced between the various institutions. In the United States such terms as 'imperial presidency' became common after the period of American involvement in the VIETNAMESE WAR and Watergate and there has latterly been a reassertion of congressional power there.

Presidents

Presidents are Heads of States in Republics, where, lacking a monarch, there is still a need felt to have a single individual who can represent, legally and symbolically, the entire state. Usually Presidents do only carry the symbolic and emotional powers of a modern constitutional monarch, with the added limitation that they must in some sense be elected and do not inherit by blood-right their role. Some, and the US President is the leading example, are also powerful political figures as heads of the EXECUTIVE as well. Still

273

more complex are situations like that in the French FIFTH REPUBLIC where the Presidents have somewhat usurped direct head of government powers from Prime Ministers when they might be argued constitutionally only to have the Head of State role.

Like Monarchical Heads of State the ultimate power that nearly all Presidents still have is to be influential, and possibly determining, in the selection of who should be the head of government after any election where the results are unclear. They usually have, in addition, emergency powers, though these are very seldom used. Though this entry has talked of Presidents as though they were figures only of electoral democracies, the need to identify some one person as the single leader of the people has meant that most dictatorships and one-party systems also have a presidential role, which may not equate with true power.

Pressure Groups

Pressure groups are voluntary organizations formed to defend a particular interest in a society or to promote a cause or political position (see INTEREST GROUPS). These groups can operate in a number of different ways and seek to exert pressure at a number of different points in the political system but normally they do not themselves directly seek elective office nor put forward a programme covering the whole range of governmental activities. The sanctions which pressure groups have vary from the strike, which is used by trade unions, and direct action, frequently used by movements which feel marginal to the political system as a whole, to the withdrawal of co-operation.

Primaries

The primary is a way of allowing the electors themselves to select who shall run for office under a particular party label. As a device it became extremely popular in the United States in the early years of the 20th century when the Progressive Movement was seeking to break the hold on the political process of what were often seen as corrupt party machines. Primaries vary in form but a distinction is usually drawn between the so-called open primary, where any qualified elector can vote in any party primary, and the closed primary where there has to be some formal evidence of party membership before an elector can participate in his party's selection of the candidate. In the United States two developments with respect to primaries have occurred in recent years. First the parties have taken steps to abolish the open primary and the courts have generally upheld them in this. Secondly the number of states using the primary to express their preference in relation to the presidential nomination has grown so that the primaries now virtually determine the outcome of the presidential selection process well in advance of the conventions. This development has been criticized as costly (because the candidates have to campaign across the states) and inflexible because it may mean that a party will find itself bound to a candidate who has become inappropriate or unpopular after the primaries but before the presidential election. Nevertheless it will be difficult to reverse the trend and return the nominating process to the older mix of primary selection, party caucus and behind-the-scenes manoeuvring.

The idea of introducing a primary system into Britain has often been mooted but it would be resisted as a transfer of power from the activists to the ordinary electors who in theory are less knowledgeable than the party workers about the merits of individual candidates. In favour of such a move is the fact that in some constituencies selection as a Labour or Conservative candidate is tantamount to election and that it is undemocratic to allow a very small group of perhaps unrepresentative partisans to make such an important choice.

Prime Ministers

The prime minister emerged as a distinct figure in Britain in the early 18th century and Sir Robert Walpole is generally credited with having been the first prime minister. Originally the term was one of abuse since it carried the connotation that the politician in question was in some sense arrogating power that ought properly to belong to the monarch. As the 18th century passed the office became more defined and the prime minister became accepted as the channel for the communication of advice from the cabinet to the monarch, as the chairman of cabinet meetings and—in the 19th century as parties developed—as the leader of the party (see CABINET GOVERNMENT).

In Britain the office of prime minister remained almost informal until 1937 when a Ministers of the Crown Act recognized the term in law for the first time. Otherwise the official style of the prime minister was 'First Lord of the Treasury'. The older Commonwealth countries which modelled their constitutions on Britain's—for example Canada, Australia and New Zealand—had little difficulty adapting the office to their own political systems. Some countries such as Australia and Canada, however, have allowed the office to develop slightly differently and in Australia, for example, there is a prime minister's department which serves the prime minister alone and supports him in the central policy-making process. In Britain such a department, although suggested from time to time, is thought to be a dangerous step towards the personalization of power and to undermine collective cabinet responsibility.

Although the idea of a prime minister and the term itself emerged in Britain, continental countries adopted it in the 19th century. Here however the powers of the prime minister have sometimes been at odds with the claims of the president. In France for example, where the office of prime minister emerged after the restoration of the monarchy the balance of power between prime minister and head of state has fluctuated. In the present French polity (see FIFTH REPUBLIC) it is clear that the prime minister is subordinate to the President who is the real determinant of government policy. In earlier republics, however, the President had occupied a much weaker role akin to a constitutional monarch and the prime minister had accordingly been the true head of the executive.

Proletariat

Proletariat, a term popularized but not invented by MARX, refers to the ordinary, propertyless working class in a capitalist society, those at the bottom of the power and wealth distribution, the ones, the mass, exploited by the bourgeoisie (see BOURGEOIS). The origin is from classical Rome where the unpropertied mass, the poor 'proles' were seen as a useless and demanding mob, living off state charity. So the emotional loading has changed considerably to the idea of the deserving and exploited mass of humanity. In MARXIST theory the proletariat will be the last class in history, because the revolution they will raise, under the leadership of the Communist party, specifically identified as the 'VANGUARD OF THE PROLETARIAT' will neither wish nor be able to exploit anyone. There is, in Marxism, an exact technical definition of the proletariat, as those who neither own nor control the means of production. More loosely, though, it is used simply to mean the poor, and often with the implication that it is the urban or industrial poor, because those employed in agriculture are seldom seen as being part of the proletariat. One often finds the adjectival form 'proletarian' used by those on the left as a very general commendatory modifier, not infrequently in usages that are mildly ludicrous as in 'proletarian theatre'. In such cases it is neither that the theatre is run by, nor attended by, actual members of the industrial working class, but that it enshrines values the Marxist intelligensia believe are in the interest of the proletariat.

Proportional Representation

This is a method of election which seeks to ensure that minorities as well as majorities and pluralities are adequately represented in the legislature and which distributes seats or units of legislative 'representation' in accordance with the proportion of the vote recorded in the whole electoral division. There are many different methods of translating votes into such units and indeed an infinite variety of redistributional formulae. Two major distinctions may however be made. In some countries (for example Ireland) the voting and allocation of seats is done on a constituency basis with individual candidates. In others (for example Israel) voting occurs on the basis of a party list. In Israel a voter may not indicate a preference for an individual candidate since the voting is entirely on a list system and indeed there are no constituencies since the whole country is treated as a single constituency. (See ELECTORAL SYSTEMS.)

Public Interest

Public Interest, like COMMON GOOD and GENERAL WILL is one of a family of related terms which are used to distinguish the selfish or personal interests or cares of individuals or groups from the best interests of society as a whole. The Public Interest refers to some policy or goal in which every member of a society shares equally, regardless of wealth, position, status or power. Most political theorists today are sceptical of the existence of more than a very few goals that might, in the long term, really be seen as 'in the public interest'. Partly this is because there is almost always the possibility of arguing that, were society reformed or changed in some fundamental way, then it would be obvious that most people did not benefit from the relevant policy, or that the policy is only solving a problem that need not exist at all were such reform to be carried out. Thus a major drive on crime, for example, otherwise a fairly obvious example of a public interest (we are probably all equally likely to be mugged) is not in the public interest in the long term if one takes the view that violent crime is the result of ALIENATION caused by an exploitative society. Even military defence, often used as the single clearest example of a public interest, can be attacked on the grounds that it is not in the interest of those badly treated by society that the political system should be protected from its enemies. However the basic idea that one can distinguish between policies that are equally useful to all citizens *qua* citizens, and those that are only for the good of a few is clearly analytically useful.

Part of the logic of the argument depends on being able to strip away the particular details of someone's life and position, and treat him simply as a member of 'the public'. So one might, when considering, say, industrial pollution, wish to claim that it is in the public interest, even though there are some, the shareholders in a factory, perhaps, who will lose money by having to pay for pollution controls. The argument is that Mr X, *as a shareholder* may lose money, but as an ordinary man walking down a street and having to breathe, he will gain equally with all other oxygen breathers.

R

Racism

Racism is any political or social belief that justifies treating people differently according to their racial origins. In fact, since the arrival of the notion of 'positive discrimination', by which people of certain racial or 'ethnic' background may be given special advantages to make up for historical patterns of racial discrimination, this definition cannot be taken literally. Racist doctrines have existed in world history since our earliest evidence, and have only been thought of as inherently wrong and scientifically absurd during this century. There is no reliable scientific evidence at all for any form of inherent inferiority of any racial group, though from time to time apparent evidence emerges. Thus in the 1970s some psychologists claimed to be able to show that certain racial groups, notably blacks in the United States and Irishmen systematically scored less well than other groups on I.Q. tests. Apart from other unreliabilities in the testing, it is generally accepted that environmental factors, and the possible 'culture-boundness' of such tests can account for any apparent racial differences.

In fact, not only is there no evidence of racial inferiority, but the very notion of racial types is scientifically at best obscure and at worst entire fiction. It is sometimes hard to grasp just how crude the tests used for racial stereotyping in those countries, notably South Africa which operate a formal racial segregation policy can be, and how much of the pseudo-science that characterized Hitler's anti-semitic theory of racial types is still taken seriously. Babies whose parentage is unknown can be characterized into race categories on no more evidence than a microscopic examination of whether a head-hair curls more than 'normal' for a white person. There are really two different aspects to racism. One is a theory of innate differences between racial types which is held to and used or advocated by those who would come out as superior on the scale to justify economic and political inequality. The other, and much more common, is based on cultural differentiation, and simply asserts that people of such and such a background are 'different', and should not be allowed equal competition for jobs or other rewards with the indigenous members of the nation's culture. Without doubt this is still a potent force in the mass cultures of Western societies, and from all available evidence racism of this type is not lacking in the Soviet Union. Discrimination against non-European Soviet citizens is reported as quite intense at times.

Why and how particular groups become the targets of racial hatred and discriminatory behaviour from time to time is unclear. The social science theories that attempt to deal with it, often as a sub-category of a general problem of ethnicity in politics, are unsatisfactory. It is a natural problem for Marxist theorists, as racial groupings seldom fit neatly into the expected lines of class conflict, and the tendency is for Marxists to see racism as a FALSE CONSCIOUS-NESS deliberately or otherwise implanted into the masses to divert them from seeing their common brotherhood as workers facing the true class enemy. But non-Marxist social scientists have no more convincing approach, and tend in the end to assume that racism, as a form of xenophobia, rises from social strains, especially in contexts where there is considerable status-anxiety.

Just how widespread racism, the hating of others because of surface and visible physical differences is, is surprising, and of course hard to estimate. But the idea that there is some dichotomy between white and non-white, or that only 'caucasians' indulge in racist feelings is palpably false. Much of the old caste system in India, for example, rests on the racial distinction between the original Tamil inhabitants and the 'Aryan' invaders from the north during the pre-Christian era. One of the most striking examples of the power of racism is the tension, often violent, between European immigrant Jews in Israel and the indigenous semitic Jews. That racism can overcome the common Jewishness of fellow citizens of a threatened Jewish state is remarkable testimony to its power.

Radical

Radical, as a political epithet has two general meanings, through purists may wish to insist only on its primary derivation meaning. This, from the Latin for 'roots', means anyone who advocates far reaching and fundamental change in a political system. Literally, a radical is one who proposes to attack some political or social problem by going deep into the socio-economic fabric to get at the fundamental or root cause and alter this basic social weakness. As such it can be contrasted with a more 'symptomatic' policy cure.

For example, the problem of crime could be dealt with by more or less draconian or soft policing, or it could be seen as resulting from very basic economic and socializing forces. To attack crime rates by changing the latter would be a 'radical' approach. To try to deal with crime either by severe penal sanctions, or by intensive 'community policing' might be more or less politically extreme, but would not be radical. It is important to keep this distinction clear. Extremeness of policy is highly relative. To deal with a crime wave by increasing the number of offences for which the state might execute someone would not be extreme in the early nineteenth century, but to introduce a probation service would be. Neither policy, properly speaking would be 'radical', though reacting to a crime wave in 1825 by introducing unemployment benefit would be both radical and extreme.

The secondary meaning of radical has come to mean someone on the 'left' of the political spectrum. It makes perfect sense, however, to talk, as is done of the 'radical centre', or even the radical right in political terms.

Raison d'état

Raison d'état is used to describe an overwhelmingly important general social or state motive for an action. There may be, it is argued, problems of such utter importance to the entire well-being of a state, or interests so vital to the entire population, taken as a whole, that all ordinary moral or political restrictions on government actions must be dropped. It derives from debates on international law in the seventeenth century, and has become somewhat discredited. It is not so much that we have dropped the idea that there might be an overwhelming state interest in some policy that would have to override other obligations, as that we are uneasy with the way of stating the claim.

In a sense, of course, it is only an extreme version of the idea that some policy or other is in the PUBLIC INTEREST, or is for the COMMON GOOD. But there are two differences between public interests and raisons d'état. The first is that most liberal political theory will want to maintain that there are some rights or freedoms that cannot be curtailed for the common good. The doctrine of raison d'état, if adopted, would deny this. It might, for example, be held that in general one had an absolute right to due process of law before being executed, yet martial law might be declared in a city on the grounds that a terrorist threat was so intense that, for raison d'état, the rights had to be abrogated.

Secondly the 'state' itself is very much to the forefront when one invokes a raison d'état argument—it is the continued existence of the very basic structure of authority and legitimacy that have to be at stake. This argument arose, though the language was not used, when the restoration of the death penalty was urged in Britain for terrorist crimes only.

By its nature the raison d'état argument is more often used and found in international politics than in domestic politics, and its slight discredited feeling probably has to do with the undue ease that nations have experienced in finding raison d'état for abrogating international agreements.

Ratification

The process of ratification is the formal approval required by many constitutions which set up elaborate systems of checks and balances and which seeks to make certain kinds of constitutional change difficult to achieve without a substantial measure of political unanimity. Thus in the United States for example treaties negotiated by the President must be ratified by a two-thirds vote of the Senate and in some cases—for example the Treaty of Versailles and the Salt II Treaty—Senate support was not forthcoming. Similarly constitutional amendments in the United States need to be ratified by a vote of the State legislatures.

Rawls

John Rawls, the Harvard philosopher, is without doubt one of the very few creative and influential writers of political theory in the contemporary West. His major book *A Liberal Theory of Justice,* published at the beginning of the 1970s, was a major attack on the prevailing 'utilitarian' theories of political obligation and social order, and constituted a brilliant attempt to revivify the 'SOCIAL CONTRACT' approach to political and social theory. His work has started a re-thinking of accepted positions in many related subjects, especially jurisprudence, where legal philosophers have followed him in attacking the 'positive law' theories which were the legal counterpart in jurisprudence. It is impossible to summarize Rawls' work in an entry like this. The most one can do is to try to give the atmosphere of his approach. The essential points of Rawls' work are twofold. He wants to re-establish some form of 'NATURAL RIGHTS' arguments, so that there will be some values we hold as absolute, principally the right to liberty, and secondly, but only secondly, a right to equality. He also wishes to change the methodology from the sort of cost-accounting approach held dear by utilitarians, to a more absolute form of argument. In pursuit of the latter he relies heavily on what he calls the 'justice as fairness' argument. One technique for making these points is his 'veil of ignorance' technique. Essentially this calls on us to try to pretend that we do not know certain basic social facts about ourselves. Thus we are to imagine a person who is ignorant of his sex, age, class, period of history. What social institutions would such a person think were fair? The point is that if you do not know whether you are to be a slave or ruler, man or woman, twentieth or twenty-first century, you could not opt for 'unfair' rules, lest you ended up on the wrong side of the bargain. Once stated, it is a very simple test of whether an institution is 'fair' or not, but no one before Rawls had thought of this way of modernizing the traditional social contract methodology. Rawls has reinstated a particular form of liberal political theory, and whether it lasts or not, has been one of the very few creative and original thinkers in the field this century.

Reactionary

Reactionary is one of those political terms invariably used pejoratively, though there is nothing in its basic meaning that requires this. A reactionary is, literally, one who reacts against some development or change, or opposes some proposed change in society. It is normally used almost interchangeably with 'Conservative', though it is highly relative. Thus propaganda inside communist societies often refers to 'reactionary' movements, those who are holding up true socialist progress, though even the propagandists would not seriously hold that those they are attacking are actually conservative. The term came to popular usage through liberal thinkers in the nineteenth century, whose idea of the inevitability and desirability of progress was so strong that they felt it was possible to identify groups or institutions who were clearly attempting to hold back an unarguably good process. In as much as conservatism does imply a resistance to rapid change, and a doubt that there is necessarily any particular path of social progress for humanity to follow, the connection between reaction and conservatism has a surface plausibility. The implication however is that a reactionary has nothing but a negative opposition to trends or ideas, or a desire to 'put the clock back', and as such is politically anachronistic. Outside some theory that tells its exponents what progress really is, the term reactionary has little use, because most policy making is a matter of reacting to circumstances, and many trends in a society clearly should be resisted.

Realignment

Realignment is a concept in political science usually referring to the change of basic voting loyalties by groups in the electorate. Political sociology has demonstrated that most electorates consist of socio-demographic groups with strong long-term identifications with a particular political party. Although not everyone who is, say, a young, urban, Protestant middle class male will always vote for the Conservative party in Britain, the odds are strongly in favour of him doing so. Similarly nearly all blacks in the US will vote Democrat. These loyalties, often inherited in a fairly automatic way from parents, and reinforced by peer group pressure, last for decades and result in a high predictability in electoral behaviour.

From time to time, however, social change, major events like wars, or economic disruption cause often sudden breaks in these semi-automatic electoral regularities. When this happens a realignment may occur, shifting the bulk of whole socio-demographic groups to new party loyalties. It is often argued, for example, that the economic collapse in America after the Wall Street crash, and Franklin Roosevelt's recovery policies made the 1932 Presidential election a realigning election in which new voting loyalties, known as the NEW DEAL coalition, were formed and which lasted until very recently. Similarly the elections after the First World War in Britain, when the Labour party was first able to present itself as a viable socialist alternative party, set up new working class loyalties, taking voters from the Liberals, and realigning electoral politics in Britain in a way which lasted until the 1970s at the earliest.

Realpolitik

Realpolitik is a German political concept dating from the mid-nineteenth century and often thought to be especially characteristic of Bismarck's policies both at home and in foreign policy. Literally it means nothing more than the politics of realism, an injunction not to allow wishful thinking or sentimentality to cloud one's judgement. It has taken on more sinister overtones, particularly in modern usage. At its most moderate 'realpolitik' is used to describe an over-cynical approach, one that allows little room for human altruism, that always seeks an ulterior motive behind another actor's statements or justifications. At its strongest it suggests that no moral values should be allowed to affect the single-minded pursuit of one's own, or one's country's self-interest, and an absolute assumption that any opponent will certainly behave in this way.

Whilst realpolitik in either of its current meanings is clearly characteristic of a good deal of modern political behaviour, the fixed assumption that people do only act in this way is probably itself an illusion that would not be acceptable to a practitioner of realpolitik under its original meaning. Perhaps a more useful modern definition of realpolitik is that it is, in GAME THEORY terms, a loss minimizing strategy or 'fail-safe'—a way of conducting politics which, though it may occasionally involve one in getting a sub-optimal result when one might have trusted to another or taken an optimistic assumption, will minimize the catastrophes that would happen were one regularly to calculate on a 'best-case scenario'.

Recall

Recall is a method for securing greater ACCOUNTABILITY of officials and elected personnel by providing a procedure by which the electorate may vote to terminate an appointment before the normal retirement date or before the normal date on which the need for re-election would occur. This device became popular in the United States in the Progressive era (i.e. in the last decade of the nineteenth century and the first two decades of the twentieth century) and it now exists in a number of American states—usually alongside two other methods for producing DIRECT DEMOCRACY, the INITIATIVE and REFERENDUM. Because it can be abused by parties, factions and single issue groups, American state constitutions tend to put severe restrictions on access to the ballot—normally by requiring a large percentage of the eligible electorate to petition for recall prior to the question being placed before the electorate as a whole. Recent developments in America suggest, however, that direct mail soliciting may have made such restrictions less effective than in the past because the technique facilitates the process of acquiring the necessary signatures. In the U.S.A. recall is generally used for elected officials but there is no theoretical reason why it could not be used for appointed ones also.

Referendum

The referendum is a method of referring a question or set of questions to the people directly as opposed to allowing them to be settled by the people's representatives in the legislature (see DIRECT

DEMOCRACY and REPRESENTATIVE DEMOCRACY). It was used frequently in the United States from the revolutionary period at the state level and was also often used in Switzerland. The policy question may originate from a group of electors directly via an INITIATIVE or from an offical body such as a state government, legislature or constitutional council. It has been used to determine basic constitutional questions (e.g. in Greece to decide whether to retain the monarchy after the restoration of democracy and in France in 1962 to decide whether the president should be directly elected). The referendum is also frequently used to determine issues of morality which divide a government or party (as with the questions of legalizing divorce and abortion in Italy) and to settle local matters which it is thought are best left to individual areas to decide (for example, the sale of alcohol on the Sabbath in Wales). Sometimes also referendums have been manipulated and exploited to enhance the personal power of an autocratic ruler as occurred in France in 1851 after Napoleon Bonaparte's coup d'état and in Germany after Adolf Hitler obtained full political power in 1934. In these cases the referendum is seen as conferring legitimacy and popular approval on an individual and sanctions unconstitutional or extra-legal activity.

The form which the referendum takes and its legal effect varies with political systems. The referendum may be purely advisory; or it may be binding in the sense that either a measure requires approval to be registered in a referendum before it can be valid or in the sense that a referendum result places an obligation on the executive or legislature to act in conformity with the popular decision within a specified period (see PLEBISCITORY DEMOCRACY).

Representation

Representation is a political concept that arises in a variety of contexts, with subtly but importantly shifting meanings. Technically it means simply a system in which the interests or beliefs of many are 'represented', are argued for, given audience before, some decision-making body by only one or a few people working on behalf of the many. In parliamentary terms representation refers to the constitutional system for electing members of the legislative body who will work for the interests of those who elected them, for whom they are 'representative.' In other political contexts representation may mean the mass *or* some governing élite choosing a few people from the many not normally allowed access to decision-making to come to meetings to pass on the views of those they 'represent'). It does not follow, either in theory or practice, that representatives have any share in the making of decisions. Anyone can 'make representations' to a decision-maker, and may or may not seriously be listened to. So, for example, as a result of student activism in the 1960s, many universities have elaborate systems to provide 'student representation' on university senates, but very few have allowed students an equal, if any, voice in policy making.

Representative Democracy

Representative democracy is a form of 'indirect' rule by the majority of the electorate. In this system (the only widespread form of democracy in actual practice), political decision-making is done by a small number of people elected by the whole electorate. Typically the elected 'representatives' will number only a few hundred, while the electorate may approach 200 million. The usual system is to divide the nation into geographical constituencies, each sending one or more representatives to the legislative assembly. In each constituency several will compete to be elected, and, depending on the details of the electoral laws, the person or persons most popular with the voters will be elected. It may also be the case that the political executive will also be directly elected by the people, especially as in a presidential system like that of France or the U.S.A.

There are two problems that lead critics sometimes to challenge the 'democracy' claim of representative democracy. The first is that the vagaries of electoral laws and voting patterns may well result in the control of the legislative assembly lying in the hands of a group representing very much less than a majority of the population. It is common in the UK, for example for a government to be formed by a party which, though having a majority of members of the House of Commons, was supported at the polls by perhaps only a third of the total electorate. Nonetheless, because of party structure and discipline, this highly 'unrepresentative' group may be able to force the passage of laws bitterly disliked by a majority of the population for the whole term of a parliament. The second point relates to the whole doctrine of representation. There are really only two models of how the mass of the individuals can be represented by a few people. One, usually called the 'delegate' model, involves the elected member being instructed by those he represents exactly how he should vote in the legislative assembly. In this way the majority of preferences of each constituency are directly transmitted to the assembly, and the mass of the population can be said, in some sense, to have their views turned into law. The other model,

287

Republic

most ably and famously defended by Edmund BURKE in his addresses to his own constituents in 18th-century Britain, rejects the idea of binding delegation. Instead the representative is seen as chosen for his qualities, and perhaps for the general principles on which he stands for election. Once chosen, however, he is a free agent, entitled to cast his legislative vote as he believes best, regardless of the opinions of his constituents. At *best* this latter model is what is practised in actual representative democracies. In fact the usual system does not even give the voter the chance of selecting a man who will at least stand by his own convictions. Instead most systems operate with tight party discipline, and in a political system where only those nominated by major political parties can be elected. Thus the voters are in fact choosing amongst rival party-teams, and the character of the man they elect is largely irrelevant. Exactly who is being represented, and exactly how democratic representative democracy actually is, can therefore be sometimes in doubt.

Republic

Republic is unusual amongst political terms in being one that is actually very easy to give an ostensive definition to, but of which it is rather hard to explain the history. A Republic is, very simply, a system of government that does not entail MONARCHY, nor, at least officially, aristocratic or oligarchical rule. But this does not necess-arily mean that Republican government must be democratic, because there is a large gap between abolishing OLIGARCHY and insisting on manhood suffrage. The Roman Republic is, for example, the original precedent for republicanism, but had a clear class structure where only the higher orders of the society had any rights to participate in government. Despite this the ordinary working definition of a republic nowadays is any society that is both democratic and non-monarchical, and a huge number of the states in the world have 'Republic' somewhere in their official title. The fight over monarchy is long dead, the title means little, and the political questions it used to raise are now pointless.

Republican

The term has two common meanings in political discourse. The first and most general one signifies someone who openly advocates the abolition of a MONARCHICAL or imperial system and the substitution of a republican system. Thus in the United Kingdom the reign of Queen Victoria (1837–1901) saw the growth of republican sentiment

288

when the monarch went into mourning; and in contemporary Britain, while republican sentiment is generally weak, there are some such as William Hamilton M.P. who advocate the replacement of the monarchy by a republic—largely on grounds of cost and because monarchy is thought to entail an ossified class system.

The term 'republican' can also be used to refer to a member of the American Republican Party which developed in the 1850s and has survivied as one of the two major American political parties. The Republican Party's original distinguishing feature was its opposition to slavery but in the 20th century, especially after the NEW DEAL, it became the party associated with the support of free enterprise, general suspicion of government intervention in social welfare, and a more conservative foreign policy.

Responsibility

Though this can be seen as a philosophically awkward notion, its political meaning is fairly clear, if legalistic. An officer of the state, whether elected or appointed, whether a senior civil servant, cabinet minister, or policeman on the beat, has responsibilities. These may be clear-cut and precise, directly involving his own acts, or very diffuse and relating to a duty to oversee or share blame with others. In the first of these senses there is clearly no definitional problem at all. The difficulty with the political notion of responsibility is in the latter area. Here one may be held responsible for something done, or not done, by another actor. A Chief Constable is responsible for the actions of a junior constable whom he may never have seen or heard of. The head of a department of state may be responsible for an administrative error by a junior civil servant he could not, in practice, conceivably have controlled.

The point of the political notion of responsibility is that if government is to be accountable to the people, there must be some clearly identifiable individual who can be blamed and punished for an abuse or failure of power, or a mistake or casualness in policy-making. Hence, at least according to orthodox British constitutional law, a civil servant's mistake is answered for before parliament by the member of parliament, who, as a minister of the crown, is his nominal superior, and that minister may have to resign to make up for that mistake, however little an ordinary judgement of guilt could be applied to him.

Though sometimes harsh, the doctrine is vital to ensure ACCOUNT-ABILITY, and, more brutally, to prevent those who are elected from hiding behind the anonymity of the public bureaucracy. The political doctrine is linked to that of COLLECTIVE RESPONSIBILITY. A related though nowadays seldom important doctrine is that of 'responsible government'. This, which used to be paired with the idea of 'representative government' referred to stages in the development of self-government in colonies. As a first stage on the road to independence local citizens would be invited or selected to form a government under the general supervision of the colonial power, that government to be given gradual responsibility for increasing areas of public affairs. This would usually, however, come some time before they were allowed representative government, that is, before the native population would be allowed themselves to choose and sanction which of their number would be given these responsibilities.

Revisionism

Revisionism is usually a term in MARXIST or SOCIALIST debate, indicating a falling-away from a previous, and 'purer' form of a theory. Thus left-wing thinkers like ROSA LUXEMBURG or, for that matter, TROTSKY, were accused of 'revisionism' for suggesting methods alternative to LENIN's for communist revolution. Most modern forms of Marxism might be accused of 'revisionism' in this way, and it remains a highly selective and value-laden concept. Non-Marxist writers have taken over the concept to describe any later, and alternative, theory or account where there had previously been a generally-accepted version. So now we have, for example, 'revisionist' theories about the 'COLD WAR', by Americans who are less convinced than previous writers of the purity of the US foreign policy in the 1950s. This indicates the way in which 'revisionism' is used not only to indicate later alternative theories, but especially those which serve to pour doubt on comforting original certainties.

Revolution

Revolution may be the most dramatic of all political terms, but increasingly becomes used so loosely that the original drama is vanishing. A revolution, properly so called, is a violent and total change in a political system which not only vastly alters the distribution of power in the society, but results in major changes in the whole social structure. As such it is quite different from a COUP D'ÉTAT which simply replaces one set of rulers with another, with no crucial ensuing alteration of the overall political and social scene. Given the full-blooded definition of revolution (which also excludes similarly great socio-political change as a result of defeat in war or success in an anti-colonial uprising), revolutions are almost by definition class conflicts. They are also very rare. The great revolutions in world history are few: the French revolution, which led to the creation of a middle-class controlled republic instead of an aristocratically controlled monarchy; the Russian revolution, replacing a tyrannical monarchy with an authoritarian and even more totalitarian populist élite; the Chinese revolution which replaced a corrupt oligarchical republic with a dictatorship, and only a handful of others. Revolution is, of course, often used allegorically to refer to any wide-ranging change in society, one instituted, perhaps, by scientific or technological change, but in political science the primary meaning must be the deliberate, intentional, and most probably violent overthrow of one ruling class by another which leads the mobilized masses against the existing system.

Right

Right, or 'Right Wing', like 'Left' derive as terms of political description from the French Estates-General which sat immediately before the French revolution. Those who were neither aristocratic nor clerical, and therefore most prone to be radical were traditionally seated on the left of the chamber, the others on the right. Hence right wing has come to stand for forces of privilege and traditional authority. The term has absolutely no fixed semantic content, and can only ever be used relatively. It would be a mistake to see 'right' as a synonym for 'conservative', and, indeed, in many contexts Conservatives themselves will protest against the label. The nearest one can come to a definition is that the 'right' are those least in favour of socio-political change in any context, unless that change be regressive to an (often imaginary) past age.

Further aspects of being right-wing, which really follow from that definition are that the 'right' tend to believe in authority and obedience rather than participation and liberty, that the 'right' tend to stick to values that fit ill with their contemporary societies, and that the 'right' tend to defend whatever system of privilege exists in their society. (Sociologically, it is of course also the case that the more one benefits from the existing system, the more likely one is to be right-wing). It is not at all uncommon, for example, to hear analysts of Communist politics talk of the 'right wing' of the party, and this does not mean those whose ideology is more pro-Western, but rather those who wish to retain the Soviet system as it is, rather than risk experiments with a more liberal socialism. The relativity must be stressed.

Roman Catholicism

Roman Catholicism, one of the largest of all world religious sects, and with more adherents than any other Christian denomination has in the past been enormously important in Western politics. As the original faith of mediaeval Europe the Roman Catholic church was built deeply into the developing political systems of the FIRST WORLD, and though the Reformation led to a considerable diminution in its importance in those areas, mainly Britain and Northern Europe, where Protestantism prevailed, the politics of countries where the Counter-Reformation succeeded remain deeply imbued with Roman Catholic influences. As Latin America, settled by the most determined of the Counter-Reformation states, Spain and Portugal, is almost entirely Roman Catholic, and as the church there plays a crucial role in unstable and often repressive political systems, its importance would in any case be guaranteed. Although there can be no doubt that Roman Catholicism is politically most influential, the nature and direction of its influence varies greatly as the actual history of Roman Catholicism varies. In those societies (Latin America, France, Italy, Poland and Ireland, for example) where it is unrivalled by Protestant or non-Christian religions, the church has often been closely allied either with governing parties and classes, or has been the major opposition to governing secular elites. Elsewhere Roman Catholicism has tended to correlate with social class and reinforce voting patterns. In the USA and Britain, for example, Roman Catholics have tended to be of lower social class, and to have voted strongly for left-wing parties, although religion *per se* has not been the basis for social CLEAVAGES. Yet in The Netherlands the Roman Catholics have been of great political importance as one of three basic political sectors which cut across class lines, the others representing, respectively, the Protestants and the 'secular' (basically socialist) sectors. Religious cleavages of this form, however, tend to become less important over time. The proportion of Roman Catholics voting for the Labour party in the UK is now not much different from the proportion of members of the Church of England doing so, while the MRP (*q.v.*), once a vital party in French politics, has more or less vanished as a political force, and in The Netherlands the two Protestant parties have allied with the Roman Catholic party to become a predominantly middle-class non-denominational Christian party like the German CSU (*q.v.*). In those countries where Roman Catholicism is not only the dominant religion but also has special ties with, or influence over, the state, Italy and Ireland being the most obvious cases, many details of policy are affected, especially those, like abortion, divorce and birth control, which relate to family life and private morality.

Finally, the sheer size of the Roman Catholic congregation world-wide, combined with the highly authoritarian and hierarchical nature of the church, has made its leader, the Pope, Bishop of Rome, a major figure in world politics at times, with little power but with the sort of influence seldom held by heads of even the biggest states. As reforming movements such as that in Dutch Roman Catholicism reduce the internal church political power of the Roman hierarchy, this role may well decline.

Rousseau

Jean Jacques Rousseau (1712–1778) was the leading French political thinker of the eighteenth century, a man often credited, though by then dead, with inspiring the French Revolution, and still perhaps the principal inspiration for the whole 'PARTICIPATORY DEMOCRACY' movement. His work, which covered many areas, as was typical of the ENLIGHTENMENT 'Philosophes', who were happy to number him amongst them, is best portrayed in three works. Of these, *The Social Contract* is by far the best known, if only by its title, but *Discourse on the Origins of Inequality* certainly, and arguably *Emile* (his treatise on education) are equally important for an understanding of his political theory. In *The Social Contract* Rousseau argued that democracy was only possible, and could only guarantee freedom (his principal concern), when people lived in small 'face-to-face' communities such as all citizens could and would fully join in the making of all laws in some form of participatory assembly. For Rousseau, REPRESENTATIVE DEMOCRACY as usually practised in the West was meaningless, making citizens free only for a few minutes every few years when they went to the polls. He insisted that freedom involved being subject only to those rules one had intentionally 'willed', hence his concept of the 'GENERAL WILL', a joint and communal intention which came about only when the whole society met together, ignoring their private desires and voted for what they felt was the public interest. Rousseau, though on the one hand obviously a champion of an extreme if impracticable democratic freedom, has also been seen as a dangerously authoritarian writer, whose views anticipate FASCISM. This opposition comes about because of his very great concern for equality, and his belief in mass meetings and mass influence, both of which seem to threaten liberal individualism. What is usually forgotten in such attacks is that Rousseau himself was so aware of the limiting social conditions for his theories to apply, especially that they could only work in very small communities where everyone knew each other, that he despaired of them ever being implemented in his contemporary Europe. Although his major book is called *The Social Contract*, and although he is usually considered along with HOBBES and LOCKE as a social contract thinker, his own views are much closer to the classical Greek political thinkers, in that he regarded mankind as essentially social in nature, and dismissed the idea of man living in a state of nature, except, perhaps, as a 'noble savage', one without the hallmark of humanity, the use of language.

S

SALT

SALT is an acronym for Strategic Arms Limitation Talks, of which there have so far been two rounds. The first round of talks began in Helsinki in 1969 and were designed to place numerical limits on strategic nuclear weapons (i.e. intercontinental nuclear weapons) and to curb the development of anti-ballistic missile systems (see ABMs). Both rounds of talks have been bilateral rather than multilateral and have been undertaken in the hope that agreement on the most expensive nuclear weapons could lead to a general slowing down of the arms race and a better international environment.

Between the first and the second round of talks, however, opinion in the West began to harden with respect to the intentions of the Soviet Union and to doubt the genuineness of the USSR's commitment to disarmament. Partly this was because of the USSR's refusal to permit any real observation of Soviet missile sites and partly it was because of the other international activities of the Soviets. As a result of the difficulties of verification of the limits on the development of new missiles and of the fear that the USSR was using the opportunity to build a position of military superiority, President Carter's Treaty with the USSR—which was based on the second round of talks—failed to be ratified by the Senate. It was not actually rejected but withdrawn when it became clear that passage was virtually impossible. The campaign against SALT II constituted one of the most vigorously-waged foreign policy battles in recent times in the United States with both the pro-Salt and anti-Salt forces spending very large amounts of money on the campaign. Despite this, both sides have stuck to the limitations in SALT II.

Scenario

Scenario, which has become a much used, even abused word, not only in social science but in political journalism, originates in strategic theory. A 'Scenario' is an imaginary description of a possible future strategic problem, in the terms of which complex equations dealing with matters of (usually nuclear) strategy and force requisites can be calculated. Thus one might posit a scenario in which an uprising in East Germany leads to a clash between the East German army and the Soviet Union, into which might be dragged first the West German forces and then the whole of NATO. Against this background one can then study the political, diplomatic and military consequences of varieties of defence postures that might be adopted by the West. At its most technical, a scenario can be the basis for extremely complicated and even computerized simulations. More generally it has come to mean any plausible future turn of events against which one can test out ideas, or check one's assumptions. So a purely domestic political 'scenario' might be the result of an election in which no party held a majority in the House of Commons, and where the previous Prime Minister, though now the leader of a minority party, refused to resign. The 'scenario', especially if built with sufficient realistic detail, would allow one to examine the adequacy of our understanding of, for example, the constitutional position of the crown, and perhaps to develop theories about the need for a written constitution. It is no different in principle from a technique sometimes used by physical scientists called a 'thought-experiment'.

Schumpeter

Joseph Alois Schumpeter (1883–1950) was born and educated in Vienna, though he emigrated to the USA to avoid the Hitler regime, and worked in Harvard for most of his career. His principal academic discipline was as an economist, in which role he gained great prestige, but his work is probably now most important in political science. Schumpeter's great work, *Capitalism, Socialism and Democracy* (1942) mainly concerns a rather WEBERIAN analysis of how the sheer scale of modern industry is likely to force a convergence between CAPITALISM and SOCIALISM as modes of production, because of the tendency towards a bureaucratic form of management in both societies. At the same time he argued that the scale of industrial units might well require some form of NATIONALIZATION if they were to be controlled at all.

The part of his theory that is still vitally important to political sociology is his discussion of DEMOCRACY, where he developed aspects of the earlier power elite theories, and where his arguments form the basis both for later American PLURALISM, and for the

DOWNSIAN Economic Theory of Democracy. His main contention was that democracy could only sensibly be seen as a procedure for government, a decision-making mechanism, and did not entail specific values in itself, thus putting him at odds with the classical tradition of democratic theory descended from ROUSSEAU and John Stuart MILL. To Schumpeter democracy was no more than the periodic elections during which voters chose one or other of a set of teams of competing leaders, the political parties. That done he felt that the ordinary citizen not only could not, but should not, have any further role in the shaping of policy.

In part this latter aspect flows from his very pessimistic assessment of human rational capacity, and his belief, borrowed from earlier works on crowd psychology, that man, in the mass, lost whatever rational capacity he had and became subject to mass hysteria, and to manipulation by political demagogues. It is noticeable that Schumpeter's own life, lived in Austria and Germany until he was nearly fifty, made him acutely conscious of the dangers of unstable mass democracy. His experience, however brief in government (he was, amongst other things, Minister of Finance for the Austrian Republic in 1919) clearly also contributed to his view of economics and policy-making.

Secession

Secession means the attempt by some region in a political system to become independent of the rest of the state and rule itself as an autonomous nation. Numerous civil wars have been fought over attempted secession moves, the most famous being the American Civil War when the southern states declared themselves a new nation as the Confederate States of America and fought for that independence. More recently secessionist moves in the largely artificial post-colonial countries of Africa have led to civil war, most notoriously in the former Belgian Congo and in Nigeria. Secessionist movements are much more likely in federal or confederal states, partly because by their very nature they keep alive the idea and symbolism of autonomy, partly because they seldom have a lengthy history of unity sufficient to overcome separatist tendencies.

Though attractive, where a region has a strong sense of local identity or of shared interests that conflict with the rest of the society, secession seldom succeeds. Almost nowhere is the idea of secession seen as legitimate, though there are exceptions, notably in the 1936 (Stalinist) Constitution of the USSR where the right to secede was formally granted to all constituent republics.

297

Second Ballots

Second ballots are devices used in ELECTORAL SYSTEMS which require that candidates secure an overall majority of votes before they can be elected. Thus in France for example after a first ballot for the legislature a second ballot is held in which parties with less than 12½% of the votes withdraw and thereby are free to vote for a candidate likely to be elected. At the presidential level after the first ballot there may be a run-off between the top two candidates.

Second Chambers

Second chambers are legislative bodies which are composed on a different principle to that of the first or most important chamber of a country's parliament. Thus the second chamber may be an appointive or hereditary chamber (as in the United Kingdom) or it may be representative of the states or regions rather than individual voters *per se*. This is especially likely to be true in federal systems (for example the US Senate or the Australian Senate.) The powers of the second chamber will usually differ from those of the lower and more politically representative chamber, although—as in the United States—it is not always the case that the second chamber will see itself as politically subordinate. Typically, lower chambers regard themselves as paramount in financial matters; second chambers often concentrate on the revising of legislation or the conduct of foreign policy. In some countries the boundaries of power between the two chambers remains unclear. Second chambers have frequently been seen as conservative bodies which could check the excesses of the more popular chamber. While sometimes true it need not be so. The French Senate, for example, in the early years of the Fifth Republic was a liberal force critical of the government and the American Senate has often been more liberal than the House of Representatives.

Second Strike Capacity

Second strike capacity is one of the many technical terms developed by strategic theorists after the development of nuclear weapons, and as part of the overall doctrine of nuclear deterrence. It means that a country must have sufficient nuclear weapons, or weapons sufficiently well hidden and protected that, even if an enemy successfully launched a nuclear attack with total surprise, the defenders can guarantee to have, after bearing the attack, enough

298

nuclear capacity to inflict guaranteed damage on the attacker. This level of guaranteed damage must be enough to make the original attack not worth the inevitable cost. Typically, second strike capacity involves the special protection of the defender's nuclear weapons, either by siting them in almost invulnerable silos, or putting them to sea in nuclear submarines. The problem with the doctrine is that it refers not to a static concept but a dynamic one, because what was an invulnerable silo, or an undetectable location at one time can cease to be if the potential enemy improves the power of his weapons, or the sophistication of his reconnaissance. Thus the search for the, essentially defensive, second strike capacity, can in itself lead to an arms race. The calculation of what is an effective second strike capacity involves the idea of MUTUAL ASSURED DESTRUCTION.

Secular State

A Secular State is one which has no official ties to any religious movement or position at all. Britain, therefore, cannot technically be regarded as secular because there is an officially established religion, the Church of England, just as the Scandinavian countries have established Lutheran churches whose ministers are very nearly civil servants. The USA, however, with an article of its constitution expressly forbidding the creation of an established church, is a secular state. In practice the term has more to do with the extent to which governing parties are really independent of religious affiliation. With this alternative definition, Britain, America and Scandinavia are essentially secular. In contrast, Italy could not be so regarded, because the major party of government since the Second World War, the Christian Democrats, has vital and close ties to the Roman Catholic Church. Some states, the Netherlands being a good example, are ambiguous on the issue, having clearly identified parties with close religious connections, (often in government), but a general acceptance of the need to ensure religious freedom nonetheless.

Senates

Senates are SECOND CHAMBERS of a legislature. In most political systems they are elected on a different FRANCHISE from the lower house and have different powers within the legislative process. In Italy and France the role of the Senate is secondary to the more important lower house which is seen as the embodiment of the popular political will. By contrast in the United States where the Senate is the institution representing the 50 states the Senate has frequently been seen as the more important legislative body. Certainly the Senate has retained formidable powers in such areas as foreign policy and the confirmation of major presidential appointments and its members have a great deal more political prominence than the 435 members of the House of Representatives. An American Senator is elected for a 6-year term and thus enjoys more security of tenure than his counterpart in the House.

Senates are frequently used in federal (see FEDERALISM) systems where it is thought constitutionally desirable to see that the territorial units of the federation are represented as well as the individual citizens and where safeguards against simple majority rule need to be built into the system.

Separation of Powers

Separation of powers, a classic doctrine of liberal politics, is associated with both John LOCKE and MONTESQUIEU, and is supposed, amongst all other countries, to typify the structure of the US constitution. The idea is that the dangers of political power overcoming the public interest will be minimized if the different sorts of legal power are distinguished and handed to separate bodies for exercise. The three forms of power that are usually identified are the legislative or rule-making power, the executive power, to apply rules and policies, and the judicial power, to try alleged offenders against these rules (see LEGISLATURES, EXECUTIVE and JUDICIARY).

If these three types of power are rigorously separated, with checks against the usurpation of one type of power by another agency, it is thought that the utilization of power will be kept in hand. Furthermore it is seen as inherently likely that abuse of power will arise if, for example, the same body both makes a rule and decides if someone has broken it. Few political systems operate, even in theory, by a strict separation of power—the role of the judicial power in the UK, for example, is less than clear, and both parliament, the legislative body, and the cabinet, as the executive, interpenetrate each other's areas. However the distinction is valid, and keeping at least roughly to it not only reduces the dangers of abuse of power, but probably makes for more efficient government. One of the major problems with totalitarian political systems, or with one-party states and military dictatorships is that the desires of one major group are not only politically dominant, but are exercised in all three fields. The doctrine is closely linked to the idea of the 'rule of law', which absolutely requires a separation between at least the executive and judiciary.

Single Party Systems

A single party system is usually one where there is an actual constitutional ban, or an effectively enforced unofficial ban on the number of parties allowed to stand in elections. Alternatively, as in some THIRD WORLD countries, there may not even be elections at all, and the party is deemed permanently to be in power. However, single party systems often in fact hide considerable degrees of internal conflict, with power struggles capable of resulting in major changes of policy going on inside the party. In other cases there may be legal alternative parties tolerated by the ruling party but with no chance of election, or several theoretically separate parties welded into one tightly controlled organization. The latter is the case in East Germany, for example, whilst in Mexico the ruling party, in office ever since the Mexican revolution, takes care to arrange the elections of a token handful of members from the opposition to give a safety valve to public feelings. Finally, effective single party systems can come about by the sheer preponderance of public opinion in some areas. Until recently many of the southern states in the USA were effectively single party systems because there was absolutely no chance of a representative of the Republican party winning office. In such a situation the Democratic party primary, where the choice of who should be the Democratic candidate was at issue, was the only effective election. The whole business of counting how many parties there are, in any meaningful sense, in a party system is more complicated than it seems, and is discussed under the heading of 'MULTI-PARTY SYSTEMS.'

Single Transferable Vote

This is a form of PROPORTIONAL REPRESENTATION voting system for multi-member constituencies in which each voter lists candidates in order of preference. If any candidate gets a certain quota of votes, he is elected. In order not to 'waste' votes, however, any votes he got above this necessary minimum are transferred to the candidates his first preference voters liked second best. This process goes on until enough candidates have reached the quota, taking account of second and lower preferences, to fill all the seats. It is one of the more intuitively appealing and simplest of the many versions of proportional representation, and as such is used in many elections to clubs and institutions as well as in national elections.

Social Contract

Social Contract theory is a form of political theory which was especially important around the time of the European ENLIGHTEN-MENT, the most famous exponents being HOBBES, LOCKE and ROUSSEAU. The main aim of these theories was to provide a sound logical base for the particular polity most favoured by the individual theorists on the basis of an appeal to the rational self-interest of ordinary men. Historically the tradition arose because, with the Enlighten-ment, the possibility of justifying a political system by reference to tradition or to some theological argument in terms of God's Will or the DIVINE RIGHTS of Kings vanished. The basic argument always took the same form: assume that men are living without any government at all. That is, they are free and autonomous individuals, but also subject to all the difficulties and dangers of living in a state of anarchy. Would such free men wish to have a government? What sort of government would they wish to see set up, and under what conditions would they give up just what proportion of their inde-pendence for the benefits of such a government? The answers one gets out of this particular thought-experiment depend very much on the description of the anarchical set-up (usually called The STATE OF NATURE) that one puts in. Hobbes, for example, painted the state of nature as so awful that he thought it likely that men would freely consent to the most authoritarian and draconian of governments. Locke, however, argued that the state of nature was only mildly awkward, and thus derived a very liberal and weak state from his social contract. It was not necessarily assumed that the social contract had ever been an actual historical event; the emphasis was much more on a logical defence of a hypothetical state by suggesting what would happen were men free to make such a choice. The method of theorising became unfashionable for a long time, being replaced by UTILITARIAN arguments which tended to get to much the same conclusions from a different approach. In the last twenty years modified versions of Social Contract theories have reappeared, especially in the work of the most important of all modern political philosophers, John RAWLS.

Social Democracy

Social Democracy is a label used to indicate a reformist and non-Marxist left-of-centre party, one which differs from moderate Con-servativism only in relatively marginal ways. A typical social demo-crat party, for example, will probably espouse some degree of NATIONALIZATION, but do so more in terms of the capacity for

302

organized planning of the economy, or the guaranteed production of public utilities than from any theoretical opposition to private property *per se*. Again, a social democrat party is likely to opt for higher and more proportional direct taxation, for taxes on industry and commerce, on the grounds of social justice. Such a party will, in general, prefer to balance towards redistribution, especially through an organized welfare state, but will not make equality a primary goal in its own right. The British Labour party, the German Socialist party (SPD), the French Parti Socialiste, are all social democrat parties, although they do not bother, or need, to put that into their titles. The prototypes, or paradigms of Social Democracy are the more or less identical and so named Social Democrat parties of the Scandinavian countries, who presided over a mixed (i.e., capitalist but partly nationalized and highly planned) economy, and a tax-expensive welfare state for most of the period between the end of the First World War and the early 1970s. Occasionally, as in the West German Constitution (*Bundesgrundgesetz*) the phrase 'Social Democracy' is used to identify an entire system of government. If this usage means anything at all, it is a combination of the political theory concept of a 'LIBERAL DEMOCRACY' combined with some general sense (as does pervade the *Grundgesetz*) of a semi-legal right to the protection of a WELFARE STATE. There are political parties elsewhere that explicitly call themselves Social Democrats, Britain since the early 1980s being an example. In this, and in most cases, the explicit use of the title is an attempt to establish a special identity to a more 'right wing' version of what is in fact a generally unrevolutionary and un-radical form of socialism, and does not usually connote any specific theoretical or ideological position.

Socialism

As with communism, socialism can mean a variety of different things, not because of ambiguity or vagueness, but because it is a concept that operates in several different ideological vocabularies. For its technical meaning inside Marxist-style theories, see the entry on Communism. Outside that debate, socialism does become extremely vague, and is best differentiated, as elsewhere in this book, between brands, such as CHRISTIAN SOCIALISM, SOCIAL DEMOCRACY, and so on. At its simplest, the core meaning of socialism is that it is a politico-economic system where the state controls, either through planning or more directly, and may legally own, the basic means of production. In so controlling industrial, and sometimes agricultural plant, the aim is to produce what is needed by the society without regard to what may be most profitable to produce.

At the same time all versions of socialism expect to produce an egalitarian society, one in which all are cared for by society, with no need either for poverty, or the relief of poverty by private charity. A famous dictum of Marx's may summarize socialism at its best: "... from each according to his ability, to each according to his need." Socialism has gone through many variations, and dating its origin is next to impossible. Certainly it stems most seriously from the industrial revolution, and many who are not Marxists would probably agree that socialism arose as a reaction to CAPITALISM, and could not become a popular theory until the development of extensive industrial private property with a society based on contractual relations rather than semi-feudal status relations. Nonetheless the essential ideas of equality and the effective abolition of private property, combined with the need for social protection against the chances of fate can be found much earlier in political theory. The basic varieties of socialism today can be arranged fairly easily on a spectrum according to just how much control of the economy, and just how much equality are seen as necessary or desirable. To some extent this coincides with the more broadly used LEFT/RIGHT spectrum, on which, for example, the British Labour party is only mildly left or socialist, and the Communist parties of Western Europe are very far to the left, and very 'socialist'. An alternative principle for differentiation would be the extent to which a basically Marxist 'economic determinist' view is taken, as opposed simply to a fairly untheoretical demand for a more just and equal society, with more state impact on the economy. In this sense, for example, the German Socialist party (SPD), the earliest in Europe, started far to the left, and became less socialist, more 'right wing' in the late 1950s when it officially gave up Marxism and became a 'reformist' party acceptable even to the conservative CSU-CDU in the grand coalition government of 1965–1969.

Solon

Solon was an Athenian statesman who was made chief archon (magistrate) in 594/3 BC. In the early part of the 6th century BC there was considerable economic distress and political unrest among the poorer classes, who, if they had no property to offer as security, were liable to be sold into slavery for non-payment of debts. Solon appears to have been trusted by all classes and was therefore appointed to deal with the unrest and to draw up suitable legislation for the future. He cancelled all debts for which land or liberty was the security, and prohibited all future borrowing on the security of the person. He endeavoured also to stimulate trade and industry to help reduce the economic problems.

His reform of the constitution involved the division of the citizen body into four classes according to their economic status, and giving each class a degree of political responsibility in proportion to this economic status. By so doing he broke the stranglehold on politics of the traditional elite class of rich landowners and made the process of government more democratic, while other reforms gave individuals the right of appeal and thus weakened the previously unrestrained power of magistrates. He also initiated a more humane code of justice. Although he did not succeed in pleasing all parties simply because he set out to strike a reasonable balance that he felt all parties would be able to accept, his work provided a sound basis for later economic and social reforms.

Sovereignty

Sovereignty means the right to own and control some area of the world. It has, nowadays, nothing to do with MONARCHY, which might seem to be implied by the connotation of sovereign, but entirely depends on the idea of independent rule by someone over somewhere. Thus a country might dispute the sovereignty of some island where another country had established control, claiming that they had the right to rule. It is a curiously important concept because it tends to connote colonial ideologies, but can, at the same time, be used inside one country. One can talk about the sovereignty of the people, as against *de facto* rule by an élite, for example. Its basic meaning is legitimate rule, as opposed to actual power. As a result, those who actually control a country, even though they may have done so for a long time, may face denial of their sovereignty over that area.

Soviet Bloc

The Soviet Bloc is a shorthand for those Eastern European states under more of less firm control of Moscow, and governed by Communist parties. It includes for certain the major East European powers of East Germany, Hungary, Poland, Czechoslovakia and Romania. It can also cover Bulgaria, Albania and Yugoslavia. However the first two are increasingly under Chinese communist influence, and the latter has been so notably independent of Moscow since President Tito's taking of power that they cannot be seen as certain to side with the Soviet Union on all issues, this being the

305

effective test of membership of the bloc. An alternative definition might be to take membership of COMECON (technically Council for Mutual Economic Assistance) set up by Moscow in 1949 and which has developed into the Soviet Bloc's alternative to the EEC. Such a definition would also place Cuba in the bloc which, though geographically odd, makes fairly good political sense. As COMECON was originally intended by Stalin to be used as a force to bring the over-independent Yugoslavs to heel, this definition would exclude the most autonomous of Russia's wartime acquisitions.

Stalin

Joseph Stalin (1879–1953), born Joseph Vissarionovich Dzhugashvili, was a Georgian peasant by origin who rapidly rose to power in the BOLSHEVIK movement before and after the Russian Revolution. By the early 1920s he was close to the centre of power, then wielded by LENIN, and benefited by Lenin's suspicion of other Communist leaders, like TROTSKY, so that he was able to take ultimate power, originally as General Secretary of the Communist Party, on Lenin's death. Stalin ruled the Soviet Union, his power increasing all the time, from then until his death in 1953. For the latter part of his reign, especially after the mid-1930s, he was a total dictator, whose paranoia led to a huge bloodletting in countless purges of party military and administrative leaders. The estimates of death resulting from his reign have been put as high as twenty million, and the major source of his power was his use of the secret police, especially the NKVD, later re-named as the KGB. His main policies were to force the 'COLLECTIVIZATION' of agriculture, this itself requiring the forced mass migration of millions of peasants and the deaths of all those who resisted, and the development of heavy industry at the expense of immediate living standards. He controlled the whole social, economic and cultural world in the Soviet Union brutally and totally. His major motivation seems to have been a desperate fear for the security of the revolutionary society once it became apparent that other Western societies were not likely to follow the revolutionary path; indeed he transformed the originally internationalist orientation of Soviet theory and policy into his own doctrine of 'Socialism in One country'. This led to his originally trying to arrange an anti-capitalist mutual protection treaty with Hitler, though on Germany's invasion in 1941 Stalin's energies and efforts led to the costly but ultimately successful war effort, and the conquering of most of Eastern Europe as a Soviet Empire.

Stalinism

Stalinism is a word used to describe a particular brand of COMMUNISM, often used of European Communists or Communist parties. It means the most hard-line, inflexible and undemocratic version of Marxist-Leninism, and is associated with the style of policy and practice adopted by Joseph STALIN in the 1930s and 1940s. Stalinism places particularly heavy stress on the duty of rank and file members of Communist movements to obey the hierarchy, denounces internal debate, and requires the strictest adherence to the Moscow line in any policy. Unquestioning support for the Soviet Union, and the total denial of the possibility of a non-revolutionary road to socialism are parts of the Stalinist's position. For most of the post-war period the French Communist party (see PCF) has been seen as especially Stalinist, in contrast, for example, to the EURO-COMMUNISM of the PCI (q.v.). One also finds the concept used of the Russian-dominated Eastern European states, where relatively 'liberal' societies like, for example, Yugoslavia or Czechoslovakia (before 1968), are contrasted with the more 'Stalinist' regimes in East Germany and, at one time, Poland.

State

The State may be the most commonly-used and the most opaque term in the whole of political vocabulary. Even the derivation of the term is obscure, and in many cultures, (including early medieval European society, to take one example) it would be hard to specify what word should be translated as 'State'. It is easier to define it negatively; the State is, for example, opposed to the mere 'government'. Governments come and go, at least in democracies, without changing the State. In a different way the State is often opposed, by political theorists, to what they call the CIVIL SOCIETY, where civil society means the whole range of organized and permanent institutions and behavioural practices, like the economy, churches, schools and family patterns that make up our ordinary life under the ultimate control of the coercive force of politics. The State means, essentially, the whole fixed political system, the set-up of authoritative and legitimately powerful roles by which we are finally controlled, ordered, and organized. Thus the POLICE, the ARMY, the CIVIL SERVICE, are aspects of the State, as is PARLIAMENT and perhaps local authorities. But many institutions with a great deal of actual power, TRADE UNIONS, for example, are not part of the State, because they are voluntary organizations which we could, at least hypothetically, do without, and especially because they directly represent one section of society against another. At least in theory, state organizations are neutral in any such sectional conflict. For this reason political parties are not part of the State (and in most constitutions are totally ignored), and the governments formed and supported by them are not quite seen as part of the State. The trouble comes when one has to recognize that the offices of, say, Prime Minister or President, which depend entirely on parties for their filling and operation, are state offices, even though neither the parties that compete for them, nor the actual individuals filling them, are, in their own right, parts of the State, but are, rather, aspects of civil society. As a concept the State has been somewhat overlooked in the political theory and research of the last century, especially in the Anglo-Saxon world, and still creates a good deal of confusion and uncertainty. The easiest way to think of it is as the set of fixed roles and institutions that make up the generally legitimate political institutions within which partisan conflict is combined.

State Capitalism

State Capitalism was a phrase coined by LENIN, and used briefly by him to describe the nature of BOLSHEVIK economic policy during the brief period between the revolution and the creation of the NEW ECONOMIC POLICY (NEP). What he meant by it was that Russia had not fully experienced the transformation from feudal to capitalist society, which MARX has seen as a necessary stage in social progress, and which he saw as being carried out by the bourgeoisie. This point was generally accepted by all parts of the Russian left, but the moderate Menshevik party and their centrist allies felt that it meant the revolution should go no further than the abolition of Tsarist feudalism, and that true SOCIALISM would have to wait on the ultimate breakdown of bourgeois CAPITALISM. Instead, Lenin argued, the building of a developed industrial infrastructure could be carried out directly by the state under the control of the leaders of the proletarian revolution. This still implied a period, perhaps a lengthy one, before the 'withering away of the state' and the arrival of true egalitarian socialism, but at least one where exploitation was minimal and socialist goals expressly sought. Even after Lenin had dropped the idea (or the phrase, at least) it continued in common left-wing parlance. It is now used, usually pejoratively, by Western left-wing groups anxious to insist that comparisons with the Soviet Union are irrelevant as criticism of Marxism because the Soviet Union practises not COMMUNISM but 'merely' state capitalism.

State of Nature

State of Nature is a powerful concept in many brands of political theory, especially SOCIAL CONTRACT theory, and its modern versions such as that developed by John RAWLS. The State of Nature is an imaginative reconstruction of how human life and interpersonal relations might have been before the creation of organized political society. Theoretically such an image is used to deduce what the major drawbacks of living in a pre-political environment would be, and thereby to decide what rules for organized political life would recommend themselves to the men in a position to make such a choice. Naturally much depends on the original description of how people unconstrained by political authority behave. If one takes a very pessimistic view of human nature, as does HOBBES, then the recommendations for the best form of political organization are going to be very different from those given by a political theorist like LOCKE, who thinks that men would be able to cooperate fairly well without government, and would thus only agree to a rather limited form of political control. The obvious trouble is that we have, in fact, no evidence at all about non-political social systems, and the arguments about the nature of the State of Nature are entirely hypothetical. Nonetheless, given some basic views about human nature, it can be a theoretical technique of great analytic power, even though we now accept that man has never lived outside of at least a rudimentary state.

Strategic

Strategy, as opposed to tactics, involves longer term, and farther reaching preparations and planning. Primarily strategy and tactics are military terms, though they can be and are applied in any conflict situation. Thus one can contrast politicians who are concerned only with, say 'electoral tactics' (how best to win the imminent general election), with those who have a political 'strategy' (how to restructure the economy, say). In contemporary military terms it is probably best to think of strategy as inherently political, and tactics as the purely technical decisions of military men about how best to achieve the strategic goals set them by their political masters. Thus vital questions on the nature of NATO's overall policy for the use of nuclear weapons, or whether Britain should retain a military capacity to intervene in conflicts outside Europe are strategic questions. What exact forces to deploy, armed with what, with what precise orders, are tactics. In terms of nuclear warfare there is a slightly different distinction. Strategic nuclear forces consist of major intercontinental missile systems intended to massively destroy the homeland of the enemy. Tactical weapons (sometimes called 'battlefield' nuclear weapons) are intended for use against enemy military formations, and have much lower yield warheads. NATO has systematically refused to promise never to be the first to use 'tactical' nuclear weapons, but always allowed it to be thought that it would only use 'strategic' missile forces in defence against a Soviet FIRST STRIKE.

Strategic Arms Limitation Talks (see SALT)

Stratification

Stratification, usually more fully 'social' stratification, refers to the way in which a social system is hierarchically ordered. The most common and obvious form of stratification is a CLASS system, but race, and, at times, religion or even language, can be forms of stratification. Because political parties tend to form around layers in a stratification system, the basics of social stratification have much to do with the nature of politics and partisanship in a society.

Structural Functionalism

Structural functionalism is one variant of a general theoretical approach to the analysis of political systems, and is not easily distinguishable from FUNCTIONALISM or SYSTEMS THEORY. It has principally been used by students of comparative government who needed a way of making intelligent comparisons between very different societies at different levels of political or socio-economic development. Essentially the theory consists of identifying a set of necessary functions or 'tasks' that any social system must fulfil for survival, and then researching what institutions or structures seem capable of satisfying these needs. Thus one may be in the position of being able to show that, say, tasks carried out by political parties in a developed Western democracy are still carried out in a primitive tribal society, but by other structures. At this stage important questions of relative efficiency, and of the fit between political culture and political institutions can be asked. Though increasingly abandoned, the theory seemed at one time to hold great hope for an exact, generalized, and perhaps even quantified science of comparative politics.

310

Superpowers

Superpowers in the modern world are those few nation states with huge economic resources far transcending the next division in such a league table. The exact number varies with different analyses. The most common view would allow only two superpowers, the USA and the USSR, with the possible addition of China. But this is to combine a series of variables together—actual economic wealth, population size, and, above all, the extent to which these qualities have been used to produce military strength, especially in the possession of sophisticated nuclear armaments. Ignoring the nuclear aspect might more easily allow China into the club, although her actual economic strength is much less. Alternatively, taking merely economic capacity and wealth would certainly entitle Japan, with no nuclear capacity and very limited conventional forces a position as a superpower.

Syndicalism

Syndicalism is a version of trade unionism, which was mainly important in the years before the First World War, though it remains a potentially explosive strand in the thinking of organized labour everywhere. Inspired largely by the writings of Georges Sorel (1847–1923), and especially his *Reflections on Violence*, syndicalism seeks control of society by direct strike action leading to co-operative worker control of industry. Strikes, and especially the strategy of the general strike, supposed to be able to collapse a capitalist industry in just a few days, were seen as the only useful and legitimate tactic for organized labour to take in pursuit of SOCIALISM. The main country affected by syndicalism was France, and even today the French union movement has traces of syndicalism in its make-up.

There were two important consequences of unions accepting a syndicalist position, one tactical, and one theoretical. The tactical impact was that the highly syndicalist French union movement refused to make political alliances with socialist parties, or to form their own parliamentary party. Electoral reform was seen as a dangerous REVISIONISM, and thus the path that socialism took in Britain, where the unions formed the Labour party specifically to get representatives of workers elected was ignored. As a result no broadly based working class political alliance was possible, and none of the funding and organizing experience of the unions was available to French parliamentary socialists. The consequence was the inability, save briefly during the popular front, of a socialist government to take office in France until 1981. The second consequence, more theoretical, was to force a breach with orthodox communist parties, because syndicalist insistence on worker control and ownership of their own factories and workplaces clashed with the democratic centralist and 'VANGUARD OF THE PROLETARIAT' ideas that Lenin used to build modern international communism. There was always far more of an anarchist flavour about the syndicalists, not only in France but in Italy and during its brief periods of importance in Britain during the period 1911–1914 and in inter-war America. In the shorter and more pragmatic run French trade unionism, as a result of this aspect of its past, has tended to use its efforts much more in pursuit of often symbolic political goals than in more mundane bargaining for wage and work condition improvements.

Systems Theory

Systems theory is a version of FUNCTIONALISM, popular in the 1950s and 1960s, especially associated, as far as political studies go, with the works of the American academic David Easton. It concentrated on the idea of a political system as being a mechanism by which popular demands, and popular support for the State were combined to produce those policy outputs that best ensured the long-term stability of the political system (or STATE). Along with Functionalist and STRUCTURAL FUNCTIONALIST theories Systems theory was often seen as unduly conservative because of its stress on stability rather than change. The basic idea, that political systems could be seen as analogues to operating mechanical systems with feedback loops and clear goals has continued to be useful in some areas of political science.

T

Tactical Nuclear Weapons

In one sense tactical nuclear weapons, or 'battlefield' weapons as they are sometimes misleadingly called, are not easily distinguishable from other 'conventional' munitions, except in power. They are, or were originally, intended for short-range use against purely military targets such as troop concentrations, vital supply or communications centres and so on. The 'yield' measured in the standard units of megatonnage is small, and they are not intended as 'counter-value' weapons, that is, weapons used against civilian or industrial targets. Originally they were deployed mainly by the NATO forces, and NATO doctrine has come to rely increasingly on a first and early use (perhaps within two to three days of hostilities beginning) in order to offset the WARSAW PACT'S superiority in conventional forces. However, this SCENARIO, which makes tactical nuclear weapons no more than more devastating versions of ordinary warfare mechanisms is increasingly inaccurate. For several reasons the Soviet Union has started to deploy its own version of short range nuclear missiles, the SS20. As these can be fired from inside the borders of the Soviet Union, effective counter-attacks by Western powers, especially with their own new generation of such weapons, the Cruise missiles, could not easily be distinguished from more purposive and deliberate strategic strikes against the Soviet homeland, considerably increasing the risk of escalation to all-out nuclear war. In addition, what is known as the 'collateral' damage to civilian centres in the vicinity of the military targets cannot be limited. As a result much of current NATO doctrine is faulty, and is weakening political unity in the Western alliance. There have always been serious problems of command and control in the theory of tactical use of nuclear weaponry, and much of the fear comes from doubts about the actual political situations under which they would be used, and the degree of central control by Washington, London and Paris that could be maintained.

Terrorist Groups

Terrorist groups are political groups which use violence as a matter
of policy to pressurize a government to support radical social
change. Terrorist groups may be motivated by a number of different
ideologies. NATIONALISM is a frequent cause of terrorist activity so
that the IRA in contemporary Ireland may be seen as waging what
it regards as just war against British COLONIALISM. Or terrorist groups
may be engaged in a struggle for changes in the internal political
system. In this category may be placed the Italian Red brigades, the
West German Baader Meinhoff gang and the Uruguay Tupama-
ros—all of which have used assassination and bombings to attempt
a radical change in the social order. Although many terrorist groups
have MARXIST ideologies many are opposed by the official Communist parties. Thus the PCI in Italy has condemned the Red
brigades' activities. In recent years right-wing anti-semitic terrorist
groups have also appeared again in France and have achieved some
publicity from their attacks on Jewish synagogues and other property. In West Germany such groups achieved notoriety from a bomb
outrage at the Munich *Oktoberfest*.

Although most terrorist groups—especially in Europe—have not
in fact achieved their political ends, in the Third World many
former terrorist groups, which began as opponents of colonial
regimes have become the post-colonial government. Only a successful terrorist war defeated the Smith regime in Rhodesia where
Robert Mugabe, a terrorist leader, came to power following an
attempt to maintain a so-called 'internal settlement' in which Bishop
Muzorewa held power with support of both black and white
Rhodesians.

Theocracy

Theocracy is any political system run by priests, or by and along
the tenets of any organized religion. There are few modern examples, though the state of Iran since the overthrow of the Shah could
be an example. Sometimes the notion is used extravagantly to
indicate a state where religious ideas, or religious institutions, have
what is seen as an undue influence. Thus a political system such as
modern Italy, where the Roman Catholic Church has considerable
political influence, having a privileged position in the constitution,
and with the dominant political party being Catholic-oriented and
led, could be seen by some as verging on theocracy.

Theocratic values were in the past more important, and more
common, than in the present world. Medieval political society, for

314

example, was suffused by political doctrines supporting the rule of established religious order, because the political authorities relied on CHRISTIANITY as a justifying ideology. Societies even earlier, Classical Athens for example, could have made little sense of the notion of theocracy because it assumes a distinction between political and religious rule and obligation. Yet these societies were so structured that the functions of the priesthood were connected to those of political leadership. In much later primitive societies this pattern can still be seen. In European terms it was the Reformation which forced a division between politics and religion by establishing the principle of religious toleration. Thus the constitution of the USA actually carries a prohibition on the 'establishment' of any religion as a guard against any theocratic tendencies. There are still countries in the developed world, including Britain and the Scandinavian countries, where ESTABLISHED CHURCHES exist.

Third Republic

The French Third Republic lasted from its creation after the defeat of the Second Empire during the Franco-Prussian war of 1870 until France's defeat by Germany in 1940. Although it was permanently troubled by political unrest and apparent instability, its seventy-year rule is in fact the longest of any French régime since the revolution, and the Republic's ability to withstand the shock of the First World War testifies to its strength. It was very much a parliamentary regime, with a President who never dared use even what few powers he constitutionally had. Originally intended only as a provisional government, with a first elected assembly that actually had a majority of monarchists amongst the deputies, the deep divisions in French society, exacerbated by a fragmented and irresponsible party system, prevented it from ever developing powerful political institutions. From the start a vital sector of the traditional French ruling class, the Catholic and aristocratic right wing was excluded from real participation, partly because they still could not easily accept the original republican notions of the French Revolution. At the same time the parties of the centre, who formed most of the coalitions, were almost as hostile to the emerging working class organizations. As a result the republic was very much run by, and for, the middle classes and the peasantry, with the result that the frequently changing governments had neither the ability nor the incentive to help modernize what was probably one of the most backward economies in Europe. Scandal after scandal rocked the republic, starting perhaps with the infamous Dreyfus case which led to deep suspicion and conflict between the military and the

315

republican forces at a time when France's need to avenge its 1870 defeat was symbolically vital. Not until after the First World War were any efforts made to ameliorate the conditions of industrial workers, and even then the opposition to serious income tax by the supporters of the ruling centrist parties forced the governments into relying on state borrowing rather than more efficient means of raising revenue. The republic might have fallen earlier, under the combined threat of German-inspired Fascist movements from the right and hostility from the developing and Moscow-inspired Communist party on the left. It was saved, temporarily, by the formation of a 'POPULAR FRONT' government in the late 1930s, resulting from a switch to a leftwards orientation by the Radical party. But by the time of the German invasion of 1940 the regime which had done so little for so many Frenchmen fell largely because there was no reserve of LEGITIMACY left to a state that had started almost by accident. Few were prepared to die for the protection of a small élite of politicians who had followed each other in and out of office, acting as little more than delegates for conservative entrenched interests in, largely rural, constituencies.

Third World

The Third World is most easily defined negatively, in that it consists of those countries not in the FIRST or second world. The first world consists of the leading Western industrialized countries of Europe, North America, and the old British Colonies which are of the same level of economic development. It is, in fact, the world of the industrial revolution, whilst the second world (a term very seldom used) covers the rest of the industrialized nations, mainly the Soviet Union and its European satellites. Thus the third world is the less industrialized, non or under-developed world, much of it consisting of ex colonies of the European powers before 1939.

Despite its popularity as a media label, the third world has very little homogeneity, exhibits vast social and economic differences, and has little in the way of common political or economic interests and policies. It is not even certain whether any particular country not in the first two worlds will always count for membership of the third world. Is India, for example, a third world country? Despite its poverty, its status as an ex colony, it is a nuclear power in terms of energy and possibly weapons, and manages to run a political system not always very different from a Western parliamentary democracy. Other countries, notably the oil-producing states of the Middle East have enormous international political influence whilst otherwise being obvious candidate members. The label is probably too deeply entrenched to be avoided, but in fact there are very few statements that can be made with any reliability about the third world (and increasingly about the other two worlds) and any degree of precision requires so many qualifications as to render the tripartite categorization largely useless.

Thought Reform

Thought reform is the idea that a man's political and social attitudes and views can be radically altered to fit in with a particular ideology with which he lacks sympathy. Indeed, so thorough is the idea of thought reform that not only evaluations, but supposedly factual beliefs are seen as alterable. The exact history of the concept is hard to trace, and its use in political discourse is confused by its extensive discussion in fictional literature, and especially in science fiction. Probably the first systematic non-fictional usage arose from treatment by the Chinese of American and British prisoners of war during the Korean war. It seems that some of these prisoners were subjected to intensive conditioning, partly by torture but mainly by psychological means, to persuade them of the entire truth of the Chinese Marxist interpretation of the war and of the relative merits of the East rather than the West in international conflict. It is entirely unclear how successful, and if successful how long-lasting these conversions were. Certainly the Chinese later, during the 'Cultural Revolution', adopted intensive processes of political re-education to persuade those whom the Red Guard saw as 'deviationists' to adopt the more radical views and to confess and seek absolution from their sins and failings. By talking of thought 'reform', rather than of 'change', one is of course accepting a premise buried deep in the process itself, that deviating views are actually not only wrong but a species almost of mental illness, which can be cured, the victim being brought to see reality properly rather than in a distorted way. In the same way the Soviet Union uses psychiatric medicine and mental health clinics on leading dissidents, to alter their beliefs and attitudes towards what is regarded as a correct ideologically, and therefore 'normal' political position. Probably the ancestry of thought reform goes back to the Roman Catholic Inquisition, where the leading Inquisitors were genuinely concerned to re-convert heretics, even if by brutal means, and not simply to kill them to stop the spread of a heresy.

Totalitarianism

Totalitarianism is a political concept often either combined with, or even confused with other notions like that of AUTHORITARIANISM

317

or DICTATORSHIP. The confusion arises because there tends to be an empirical connection such that authoritarian or dictatorial societies are often also totalitarian. There is, however, no necessary connection. To call a society totalitarian means that the political rulers control every aspect of private and social life in the society, as well as having so extensive a political power that virtually no liberty or autonomy in decision-making is left to individuals or groups outside the political power system. Thus the Soviet Union is often described as totalitarian, but this is not because it is a one-party state where only the Communist party wields power. The Soviet Union is totalitarian because of the way it uses power. The whole of the media, of the educational system, the whole of the social, sporting, and other leisure activities, are controlled by, and used to propagate the ideology of, the Communist Party of the Soviet Union (see CPSU). All industrial decisions, including activities of trade unions are under direct control of party appointed officials. Even the military organizations are controlled and ideologized directly by the party, via the system of making the deputy commander of each unit, of whatever level, a party 'Political Commissar'. It is this character of complete permeation of a society by the personnel and ideas of the ruling group that makes for totalitarianism. Other forms of society could, and at times have been, equally totalitarian. A thorough-going THEOCRACY, for example, where the church had the ability to penetrate and organize all aspects of life would be totalitarian. Some writers have even tried to claim that the exponents of radically PARTICIPATORY DEMOCRACY, like, for example, ROUSSEAU in his *Social Contract* were 'totalitarian democrats.' This latter example arises from the way that Rousseau insists on as much communal activity, and as much homogeneity as possible amongst citizens in order to minimize conflict and to aid the production of a publicly-spirited 'GENERAL WILL' amongst all citizens. It is similar to the fears of writers like John Stuart MILL and DE TOCQUEVILLE about the 'TYRANNY OF THE MAJORITY'. In practice few political systems can wholly penetrate a society, and some form of underground LIBERTARIANISM usually flourishes, as with the dissident movement in the Soviet Union, or the capacity to combat some aspects of Nazism by the churches in the Third Reich.

Trade Unions

Trade Unions are organized collectives of working people, usually but not invariably in industrial and commercial rather than agricultural organizations. Until relatively recently they have been predominantly of working class, that is, skilled and unskilled manual worker, membership. In the last decade however, certainly in Britain, and to some extent elsewhere, traditional middle class professions have become unionized. Britain and Germany have the oldest trade union organizations of a legal nature, though in both countries the fight for legal recognition was prolonged. In Britain it was not until legislation following industrial unrest and violent state coercion at the beginning of this century that modern legal protection for the right to strike and to picket (absolutely essential ingredients of union activity) was granted, in 1906. German unions gained similar protection at roughly the same time, and, except for a period of repression during the Nazi regime, the two union movements have been very similar.

The main set-back for British unions came with the failure of the only-once-attempted general strike in 1926, but in the post-war economy unions have been strong, and usually accepted by governments. The only serious post-war attempt at state or legal restriction of union activities was the Industrial Relations Court set up by the 1970–1974 Conservative government, but this was so violently rejected by the unions that it was quickly abolished by the 1974–1979 Labour government. (Indeed it was conflict with the unions by the Tory government that effectively lost them power.) The British Trade Union movement has always been closely tied to the Labour party, which it helped set up, far more closely than unions elsewhere in the Western world are linked to their left wing parties. Unionism in France, though existing as an underground force from around 1830 was never strong until the post Second World War years, if then. In part this was due to the low degree of industrialization in France, but also to the syndicalist political views that led them both to eschew formal parliamentary links or co-operation, and to advocate direct general strike action to force social revolution. In the USA the union movement was split into two bodies, the AFL and the CIO until the mid-1950s, and although individual unions are important in their own industries, the federal level joint union organizations are of little political importance. Unions tend to be divided amongst themselves as much as they present a common front to the government or industrial leadership, and Britain's highly organized and powerful TUC (Trades Union Congress), organized since 1868, may be unique. The other Western nations with important union movements are mainly the 'Old Commonwealth' countries, where Australia and New Zealand follow the British, and Canada the American pattern. Probably something in the region of 50 to 60% of the British work force are unionized, but it must be remembered that most members are passive, joining either as a condition of holding their job, or out of social pressure, and take almost no part in union politics.

At least in the last decade the phenomenon of trade unionism has been unpopular in British public opinion, with regularly 70% of opinion poll samples thinking they have too much power. (A figure that is not notably different amongst members themselves.) Unionism tends to be strongest everywhere either in craft or large scale industry, and weak in distributive, white collar, or very unskilled trades. Various attempts are made by governments from time to time (and of all political colours) to restrain union power, but the whole principle of unionization, to establish somewhat more equal bargaining power between employers and employees is so well-established that, despite the surface unpopularity of unions, little can be done to curtail their privileges under law. Unions exist, and membership is compulsory in all Communist countries, but the right to strike is usually withheld, and, with the exception of the Polish Solidarity movement during the early 1980s, these unions are so totally controlled by the local Communist parties as to be mere facades. Perhaps the most important theoretical, as well as practical question about union membership is the problem of what is known, in Britain, as 'the closed shop'. This is a system where no one is allowed to keep a job in a factory or other workplace unless he or she joins the relevant union. Although a constant target of criticism by conservatives in both America and Britain, it is a practice that employers themselves quite often approve of, if only because it simplifies their own negotiating strategies. The union's argument is quite simple—the benefits they gain by concerted action should not be enjoyed by those unprepared to share the effort, and it is certainly true that unions operating in a non-closed shop environment tend to be less effective. This, again, is not a phenomenon restricted to working class movements—some university libraries in the UK, for example, operate a closed shop rule even for academic level staff.

Trotsky

Leon Trotsky (1879–1940) changed his name from Lev Davidovich Bronstein after escaping from exile in Siberia in 1902. He, along with LENIN, was one of the great leaders of the Russian revolutionary forces both before and after the 1917 revolution. Also like Lenin he was a revolutionary long before he was a MARXIST. Trotsky was arrested and exiled when only 19, for trying to foment revolution amongst industrial workers, though his own family was relatively prosperous. On his escape he fled to London where he met and worked with Lenin and rapidly became a leading member, especially as a propagandist, of the then more or less united Russian Social Democrat movement, most of which was similarly in exile. During the period from the turn of the century to 1917 the Social Democrat movement was badly split between factions with very different interpretations of how SOCIALISM could be achieved in Russia. One wing, later to be known as Mensheviks, took a version of Marxism which required Russia to go through a full industrial revolution of a capitalist nature, and thus felt that, even if a revolution set up a democracy, a lengthy period of co-operation with Liberal BOURGEOIS parties would be necessary. The opposition, Lenin's BOLSHEVIKS, argued instead that an alliance between what there was of an industrial proletariat, and the peasantry could force the pace of industrial transformation, making it unnecessary to put up with the transition phase of liberal capitalism. Trotsky however could never quite make up his mind about this split, floated back and forth in the endless congresses of the exiles, and thus created ill will and suspicion on both sides. He returned to Russia briefly in 1905 to help the abortive revolution of that year, and he was back in Russia much earlier in 1917 than Lenin, playing a vital role in organizing the extreme Communist opposition to the original moderate government.

His own analysis was, in fact, even more revolutionary than Lenin's, when he worked it out, because he denied that the support of the peasantry was needed, and argued for what he called 'permanent revolution'. This was a strategy in which the first revolution, to overthrow the autocratic Czarist regime should be immediately followed by a purely proletarian revolution, and one which should be 'exported' to all Western countries, as he believed that under-developed Russia could not long sustain a socialist society. Though he co-operated ultimately with Lenin, he was always unhappy with the latter's stress of the leadership of the party. He held a variety of vital posts in the Bolshevik government set up in October 1917, the most important of which was the creation and running of the Red Army with which he successfully, though brutally, won the civil war against the traditionalist 'White' Russian army. He lost power, after Lenin's death, to STALIN and his faction, who advocated 'Socialism in one country', and because he opposed the central authority and the ignoring of the Russian masses which Stalin took to even greater lengths than had Lenin. Expelled from the party, he was exiled yet again, this time permanently, in 1929, and ultimately murdered supposedly on Stalin's orders in 1940. He spent the last few years of his life in propaganda against what he saw as the corruption of the revolution, even attempting, with no real success, to create a rival International Communist movement (the so-called Fourth International). In recent years self-styled 'Trotskyist' political groups have proliferated on the left in many Western countries. All that is meant by this appellation is that these movements deny the acceptability of any non-revolutionary strategy, or of any compromise with other parties. Trotsky remains perhaps the theoretically most interesting character of the whole Russian revolutionary movement, but the one whose ideas are least acceptable to orthodox Communists on either side of the iron curtain.

Trotskyism

Because Trotsky had disagreed with LENIN, and even more with the STALINIST group in Russia after 1917, and was exiled and ultimately murdered by the Stalinists, he is a vitally emotive symbol for extreme left wing MARXIST groups who wish to distance themselves from what they see as the discredited 'STATE CAPITALISM' of the modern Soviet Union. Two aspects of Trotsky's thought particularly appeal to these left wing splinter groups who call themselves Trotskyist and are found throughout Western (but not Eastern) Europe. First, Trotsky had a notion of what he called 'permanent revolution.' In fact this doctrine is usually misunderstood by these self-styled groups, who tend to see it as a semi-anarchist call never to accept or support authority at all, seeing it as similar to some of the elements in the Maoist cultural revolution. All Trotsky meant by it was that, in contrast to the Russian social democrats, he did not believe that there would have to be a lengthy period of BOURGEOIS capitalist rule in Russia after the revolution against semi-feudal Tsarist autocracy. Instead he felt the first, anti-Tsarist revolution could immediately be followed by a full scale revolution by the urban proletariat against the new reformist bourgeois government. (As, indeed, it was.) The second point is Trotsky's opposition to Lenin's stress on the need for a highly disciplined and authoritarian party organized on the principles of democratic centralism. This, of course, is highly attractive to far left splinter groups in Western political systems, because their major enemy is as likely to be an orthodox Communist party as a Conservative party. Whether Trotsky would particularly have approved of such groups is somewhat unclear. At the end of his life he was working for the creation of international and national co-operation by all left wing parties in popular front governments. In any case plenty of other Marxist leaders, notably Rosa LUXEMBURG, were equally opposed to Lenin's views on centralized party authority. At the moment Trotskyism is a useful general term, though increasingly debased. To be called 'Trot' in modern British politics probably means nothing more definite than that one's views are slightly to the left of the centre of the Labour party.

Two-Party Systems

Two-party systems are actually very rare, if one is to be exact. The classic examples have always been held to be the Anglo-American democracies, and the USA, at least on the Federal level, is as near as exists to a genuine two-party system. (Though even American Presidential elections usually have several more candidates, and in the 1980 election the third party candidate, though ultimately getting a very poor vote, was seen by some commentators as a serious threat earlier in the campaign.) Britain has never been a true two-party system since the early years of this century; there have always been MPs from several parties, and always, especially, some sort of parliamentary liberal party. As the de-alignment of voters from the traditional two-class, two-party model has developed, especially with a liberal upsurge and the rise of the Scottish and Welsh nationalists, parliament cannot any longer be described as bi-partisan. Rather as is the case with one-party systems, the 'two' parties in a two-party system tend to be so broadly based as to be almost holding companies for a set of ideologically conflictual elements. The point is that unless the social CLEAVAGE structure of a society is very simple indeed, there will always be more points of view, and more sectional interests than can properly be represented by one or two united and homogenous parties. The existence, or apparent existence, of two-party systems owes more to a combination of the greater salience of one cleavage than of the others and an election system that is, as in the Anglo-American polities, extremely unproportional in its representative effects.

Tyranny of the Majority

The tyranny of the majority is a phrase found in John Stuart MILL'S *Essay on Liberty*, but is representative of a general fear found amongst many liberal political thinkers in the 19th century, notably in the works of DE TOCQUEVILLE. The idea is that liberal values, especially values of freedom of expression of opinion, and the freedom to exercise a life style of one's own, however unconventional, as long

323

as it hurts no one, will be seriously at risk in majoritarian democracy. For Mill the uneducated working class majority was seen as peculiarly prone to intolerance of opinion and behaviour, and likely to persecute, at least informally if not legally, anyone who did not 'fit in' with common trends. He certainly believed in at least restricted democracy, but held to such a strong notion of the limitations on rightful government interference with private liberty that he had reason to doubt that freedom would be protected as well in a popular democracy as in some forms of enlightened despotism. A similar, though somewhat more pragmatic view was held by DE TOCQUEVILLE, mainly in his classic work on the emerging political system of the USA, *Democracy in America.* Here his argument was that there were tremendous pressures towards conformity, and therefore mediocrity at work through the combination of egalitarianism and popular democracy, and furthermore, that the mass of ill-educated citizens were prone to exploitation and being misled by talented but corrupt demagogues. He was hardly alone in this view, as the authors of the *Federalist Papers,* and the founding fathers of the American constitution had argued for intervening layers of electoral colleges to insulate the Presidency and the Senate from direct influence by the masses. Much later a version of this fear of intolerance to minorities on the part of masses whipped up to fury by unscrupulous demagogues formed part of the PLURALIST thesis common to most American political scientists post war. In particular Kornhauser's *The Politics of Mass Society* argued that vicious dictatorships of the Nazi type could easily arise unless the social structure prevented direct access of leading political figures to the emotions of the masses. In many ways the tyranny of the majority is a version of the standing tension between the two halves of the prime Western goal of creating 'Liberal-Democracies' (see LIBERAL DEMOCRACY).

U

Unilateralism

Unilateralism is a term born of the protests against nuclear weapons which first became politically important in the Britain of the mid-1950s. It is the doctrine that the UK government should immediately abolish all of its nuclear weapons, whether or not any other country agrees to do so. During the 1950s this movement, under the organization of the Campaign for Nuclear Disarmament (CND) attracted considerable mass support, as was especially demonstrated during its annual symbolic march from the town of Aldermaston (the site of the nuclear weapons research establishment) to London. It also attracted politically important support in the Labour Party and certain trade unions. Briefly in the late 1950s the Labour party's annual conference adopted unilateralism as official policy, though this was swiftly reversed by the leadership of Hugh Gaitskell. Until the 1970s the movement was quiescent, but it re-emerged in the mid-1970s, initially in opposition to the basing of American owned and controlled missiles in the UK, especially the Cruise missile. Thus in its second version unilateralism has come to be not only the doctrine that the UK should not own nuclear weapons, but that it should not allow them on its soil either.

The unilateralist position is not, in principle, restricted to nuclear weapons. Clearly any fully-fledged pacifist, who holds that it is wrong in any and all circumstances to use force, would logically be required to be in favour of total unilateral disarmament. What makes unilateralism special is that it is not necessary to be pacifist to adopt it, and many unilateralists insist that they support at least the current, and possibly a considerably increased, level of defence spending on conventional weapons. The arguments of unilateralism are diverse, as is the motivation of its supporters. They break down roughly into two aspects. The first, more often prominent in the 1950s than in the later period, is that it is wrong in general to use weapons of such power, and which can only cause massive destruction to non-combatants. The second strand of argument is that the proliferation of nuclear weaponry makes all-out nuclear war more rather than less likely. It is thus held that abandoning Britain's nuclear weapons is, amongst other things, a policy most likely to protect the UK from attack. It is further argued, in this direction, that abandoning nuclear weaponry and removing US nuclear forces from UK territory will ensure that the Soviet Union has no reason to use similar weapons on the UK. As such the unilateralist argument essentially conflicts with the general defence of nuclear weapons, which is that they are held as deterrents, to ensure the safety of the UK. There is no doubt that the unilateralist argument commands a good deal of public support, and is the official policy of the British Labour party, which in part fought the 1983 election on the issue. Much sympathy for it also lies in other parts of the political spectrum. Unilateralism has the odd nature of being a policy that can only exist in two countries, Britain and France, because, for the third Western nuclear power to go unilateralist, the USA, would effectively be for the entire Western alliance to trust entirely to the good intentions of the Soviet Union, which has repeatedly scorned any idea of full nuclear disarmament. In France the thesis appears to command very little public support, and critics of the unilateralist position have, as a result, suggested that British unilateralists are consciously or otherwise, sheltering under the American nuclear umbrella.

United Nations

The United Nations Organization (UN) replaced the inter-war League of Nations in an attempt to ensure world peace and secure the economic, social and political conditions under which this can be achieved. It started as an agreement between the allies fighting Hitler's axis powers in the Second World War, and much of its structure and subsequent problems follow from this. Its charter originated from discussions held at Dumbarton Oaks (Washington DC) in 1944, between the USA, UK, USSR and later China, and some fifty nations originally signed the Charter in June 1945, with this number increasing to well over 120 by the early 1970s. There is some problem about counting the real membership, as a series of political compromises had to be made early in its history to retain the joint membership of both the USA and the USSR, given that the first vital few years of the UN coincided with the worst of the early COLD WAR days. Thus, for example, the Ukraine is counted as an independent member state, although in fact it is totally under the control of Moscow as a constituent republic of the USSR.

Similarly until 1971 the 'China' that was shown on the membership roles was not the major world power led by Mao tse Tung, but the tiny American puppet government of Taiwan, the USA refusing to recognize the communist mainland government.

The mark of its 1944 wartime birth shows also in its basic organization. The most important organ of the UN is the Security Council, in permanent session and charged with maintenance of international peace and security, including calling on the armed forces of member states to put together a peace keeping force and to intervene in disputes. This body has 15 members, of which five are permanent. They are, in effect, the main victorious allies of the Second World War, the USA, USSR, UK, France and China. Until the People's Republic of China replaced Taiwan in 1971, therefore, this insignificant island was actually a permanent member of the Security Council. Even now second-rate powers like Britain and France are ensured permanent membership whilst equal or superior powers like West Germany and Japan can only get on for two years every now and then when elected. As the five permanent members each have an absolute veto on Security Council resolutions, the international power balance is frozen into an image almost 40 years out of date.

The other main organ, the General Assembly, consists of all members and can debate and pass resolutions on any matter covered by the Charter, except for disputes already on the agenda of the Security Council, though it is largely a propaganda arena and ideological battlefield to which few nations in conflict pay any attention. The most important work of the United Nations is done, other than the peace keeping of the Security Council, by the specialist agencies, and by the direct personal diplomacy of the administrative heads, the Secretaries-General. These latter have nearly all been extremely widely respected international statesmen whose personal interventions have often been of great help. The specialist agencies like the World Health Organization have, along with other agencies affiliated to the UN like the International Labour Organization (which actually began under the League of Nations), made major contributions to international social welfare and economic development. Others, like the United Nations High Commission for Refugees, or the International Court of Justice, though dependent on political consensus for their work, have often been able to minimize the human suffering that would have been consequent on political conflict that the UN has not actually been able to avoid. There are fifteen of these special agencies, many of which have associate members who are not full members of the UN itself. That apart, the Charter of the United Nations, and its associated Declaration on Human Rights, while hardly lived up to by the membership, serve at least to keep a general standard of aspiration which was lacking on the international scene before, and perhaps even during, the existence of the League of Nations.

The greater effectiveness of the UN compared with the League of Nations is shown mainly in its ability on several occasions to put military forces in the field which have either stopped international aggression (the success of the UN in the Korean War) or minimized it, as with the peace keeping forces in Cyprus and the Belgian Congo. This competence, and its general ability to function as an international safety valve is due to the fact that whilst the League of Nations lacked the most important conflicting powers, the USA and Germany, the UN has both the USA and the USSR firmly entrenched in the Security Council. (Though it must be noted that the greatest single achievement, the expulsion of invading communist North Korean forces from South Korea by the UN forces, was only possible because the USSR was, at that time, boycotting the UN. It would otherwise have had to use its veto in support of North Korea.) No major power is very happy with the UN, especially the USA which ends up paying nearly a third of its total budget compared with the USSR's 14%, yet tends to find its causes unpopular with the General Assembly dominated by a coalition of non-aligned and Communist nations, yet its positive value as a neutral ground has made it the longest lasting and most universal international political body yet.

Utilitarianism

Utilitarianism is the moral, social and political theory originated by BENTHAM and James MILL, and further developed by John Stuart MILL. At its core is a simple equation between 'the good', and 'happiness' or pleasure. The basic thesis states that whatever measure, policy, choice or decision maximizes the positive balance of pleasure over pain across a population, or for a single individual if only he is concerned, is what is 'good' and therefore 'right'. The theory expressly denies, in its earlier versions, any ordering, moral or otherwise, of the sources of pleasure. In Bentham's own words, 'pushpin is as good as poetry'. Except for the distribution principle, 'that each man should count as one, and none for more than one' utilitarianism allows no other moral or political criteria of decision. Bentham argued that it ought, in principle, to be possible directly to quantify and sum the positive and negative consequences, in terms of pleasure, of any act by what he called the 'Felicific Calculus'.

Policy-making for a society, as much as private moral decision-making for an individual, would then become essentially an auto-matic process. Naturally there have been many adjustments and refinements to this basic utilitarian theory over the years. Two may be picked out especially.

J.S. Mill attempted to get away from the over-hedonistic emphasis by suggesting that there were, in fact, hierarchies of desirability. Those who had experienced, as it were, both 'gross' and 'refined' pleasures would always opt for the less basic or gross. He also attempted, though somewhat unconvincingly, to demonstrate how our other basic politico-moral values, a desire for justice, say, or a high value on freedom, could be derived from the utility principle. The other broad area of development, mainly the work of modern moral philosophers, has been occasioned by some unfortunate consequences of utilitarian argument when applied as a public political philosophy as well as a private moral code. The problem has tended to be that what maximizes the interests or happiness of a single individual might, were everyone to act in the same way, be disastrous as a public policy. Thus there has come about a distinction between 'Rule' versus 'Act' utilitarianism. An 'Act' util-itarian requires that each individual ensures that his every act maximizes his own utility, whereas the more plausible 'rule' utili-tarian requires that laws and regulations be decided so that, on balance across the population, the rule maximizes the sum of individual utilities, even though in particular cases individuals would not, as selfish utility maximizers, choose to act as the rule requires. The whole aim of utilitarianism is to escape, as much as possible, from reliance on any source of moral authority, whether it be religion, another metaphysic, or appeal to such abstractions as 'natural law'. Although it is not obvious on the surface, nearly all parties and governments in the Western world do in fact operate now according to a utilitarian approach. Most of economic theory, and the whole of 'Welfare Economics', and many of the theoretical models and justifications for democracy are frankly utilitarian. Policy analysis, especially as developed by civil servants and aca-demic specialists in the 1960s is equally based on a utility calculus, and until recently the prevailing theories of law and jurisprudence were derived from utilitarianism. Only in the 1970s did political theorists of a non-Marxist kind even begin to develop non-utilitar-ian general political philosophies, so total was the hold of the Benthamite tradition over Western intellectuals. Even then it is instructive to note that the new approaches, by writers like RAWLS, NOZICK, and DWORKIN were based on a return to the tradition of political theory, mainly that of John LOCKE, which was the original

329

competitor to the writers from whom utilitarianism itself derived, such as HOBBES and David HUME. In a secular society, and one without the intellectual armoury of 'scientific socialism', which has to operate with a minimum coercion in a more or less democratic manner, there is really little alternative to an appeal to rational self interest, which is what utilitarianism amounts to.

Utopianism

Utopianism is a social theory designing a perfect political system, a Utopia, after the most famous classical utopia sketched in Sir Thomas More's description of an imaginary island of that name in 1516. Earlier writers had, of course, had elements of utopianism in their work. The most obvious are the political systems designed in PLATO'S *Republic* and *The Laws*. The point of difference though is that Plato, and most political theorists, either expect that their systems could actually be put into operation, or admit that they are second best precisely because of the impossibility of carrying out an ideal design in reality. More, and subsequent works of utopian writing, stress the ideal as a measuring tool for reality, rather than as an empirical possibility. Utopias, if intended as such, are really thought experiments, political theory's equivalent to the perfect frictionless bearing, or perhaps an economist's model of the perfect competition model.

We stress the idea that utopias are impossible, and that writings in the field might not intentionally be utopian because the concept of utopianism has largely become derogatory. MARX was one of the earliest writers to use the concept as a criticism, when writing of some early socialist blue-prints. By not taking enough notice of the brutal facts of material restrictions and class warfare, Marx thought these socialist writers were being purely utopian, operating in a fantasy land. Thomas More did not believe that his island political paradise could ever exist; later ROUSSEAU was to stress in his writings, especially *The Social Contract*, that hardly any existing society could be transformed to his specifications. This is why, indeed, the conditions of political life are so much more pleasant on the island of Utopia than in, say, HOBBES' *Leviathan*. The latter is if anything the opposite of a utopia, a system designed to fit with the worst possible realities of human nature and political incompetence, and thus practicable but hardly desirable. At the same time, whilst Hobbes might help us set up a state that might work, as might, say, MACHIAVELLI, it requires a Thomas More or a ROUSSEAU to inspire our political judgements and ambitions.

V

Value Freedom

Value freedom is a methodological requirement of a useful social science, and would be treated as one of the primary requisites in judging most POLITICAL SCIENCE, though not POLITICAL THEORY, writing. It consists in the effort to carry out one's analyses in the most impartial manner possible, and in not allowing one's own preferences to colour or bias the research, data collection, or the conclusions one draws. The model being invoked is, of course, that of the natural sciences. By the advocates of value-freedom it is belived that a physicist, for example, has no private preference for any one theory of nuclear particles rather than another, and therefore produces unbiased work. Similarly, it ought to be possible to study the causes of social stability, or of voting behaviour, or efficiency of Presidential rather than Prime-Ministerial governments without any bias resulting from personal conviction. As such it is a goal both long established as ideal, (WEBER wrote extensively on the problem and COMTE thought he had achieved it), and hotly contested by various schools of the philosophy of science. There are two major points that raise doubt about the possibility of such value freedom in social science research. The first is the general argument that all men, everywhere, are subject to the dominant ideology of their societies. As a result truth, and especially truth about social reality, is inevitably relative. A Marxist like Lucacs, for example, argues that an economist working inside the framework of a capitalist society simply cannot grasp that CAPITALISM is doomed to collapse through its internal contradictions and because of its exploitative nature, because to accept this would be incompatible with his entire outlook. A second, more subtle argument denies the utility of analogy with the physical sciences, because they too are seen as less than impartial. A physicist, because of his training, career expectations and his own creative limitations is stuck inside a 'paradigm' in which he does indeed have a preference for one theory over another. He will prefer the theory that fits into his overall view, and will attempt to prove that, rather than to prove one that would force a general re-thinking. Thus the political sociologist may be forced into working towards, say, a rational choice theory of voting both because such a theory defends the LIBERAL DEMOCRACY he has been socialized to believe in, and because the intellectual apparatus he has been trained in is only efficient given such assumptions. There is no ultimate solution, and perhaps it does not really matter. What is important is not so much that values do not enter into the choice of theory or research method, but that they be explicit and open, so that those who oppose them can criticize the work. Some political theories of LIBERALISM, like UTILITARIANISM, seek for value freedom in a different sense; they seek to create a constitutional framework in which as wide a variety of human values as possible can be achieved. This sense of value freedom could be said to pervade most justifications for democracy.

Vanguard of the Proletariat

The Vanguard of the Proletariat is a MARXIST notion made more famous, and relied upon very much more, by LENINISM. It refers to the Communist party in any society, and especially in a revolutionary or post-revolutionary situation. The basic Leninist thesis is that the ordinary mass of the industrial proletariat cannot come to a true consciousness of their situation, and cannot develop a fully revolutionary spirit spontaneously and without leadership. Consequently there must be formed a party of professional revolutionaries, those who do have the capacity to escape from FALSE CONSCIOUSNESS and ideological manipulation. This party will raise the revolutionary consciousness of the masses, and lead them in the revolution, hence being the 'vanguard'. The more important extension of this doctrine, in itself plausible, is that, after the revolution, there will still be a need for direction and control of the efforts of the proletariat in building the truly socialist society. Thus the initial revolutionary leadership becomes institutionalized into a 'DICTATORSHIP OF THE PROLETARIAT' via the rule of a single dominant Communist party. Here there is a considerable strain between the original thought of MARX and ENGELS, and the subsequent interpretation of how a post-revolutionary society should be run, as developed by Lenin and taken to extremes by STALIN.

Vichy

The Vichy regime (named after the town where it was set up in 1940) was the collaborationist civilian French government of unoccupied France set up with German support after their invasion in the Second World War. The assembly of the THIRD REPUBLIC gave full power to the emergency Prime Minister, Pétain, who had been perhaps France's greatest military leader in the First World War. However he rapidly declared himself Head of the French State, and organized, or acquiesced in the organization of, a semi-Fascist state along authoritarian lines. The Vichy regime was by no means as unpopular as post-war French propaganda has suggested. There had always been a strong element of distaste on the right for the Third Republic, and indeed, amongst many sectors, a refusal quite to accept the principles of the French Revolution and its democratic republican spirit. Pétain himself, and he was old and feeble before the war even started, came under the influence of deliberately pro-Nazi leaders, especially Laval, a third republican politician, and Admiral Darlan. These men and their followers co-operated actively with the Germans, even when in 1944, the German army occupied the area of France officially under Vichy control. Their police force, the Milice, was hardly less enthusiastic than the Gestapo in carrying out anti-resistance, and at times anti-semitic measures. To many industrialists, Vichy, unhampered by free trade unions, and supported by a strong and resourceful administration and civil service was a positive improvement on the semi-anarchy of industry under the third republic. The essence of the Vichy regime, with its authoritarian and reactionary ideology is well represented by the symbolic replacement of the traditional revolutionary slogan of the Republic (Liberty, Equality and Fraternity) with one of Pétain's devising, 'Work, Family, Country.' The Vichy regime was entirely discredited once France had been liberated, and its leading members tried for treason. However their counter argument, that they were trying to preserve at least some vestige of French autonomy and were essentially patriots forced to accept and moderate the consequences of a military defeat for which they were not responsible cannot entirely be dismissed.

Vietnamese War

The Vietnamese war was a struggle between North and South Vietnam in which the USA was directly involved in the defence of the South and which had severe repercussions both on the politics of South-East Asia and on America's domestic politics. Civil war in Vietnam had been developing since the French withdrawal from Indo-China in 1954 following the military defeat of the French forces in a humiliating battle at Dien Bien Phu. Military aggression by the Communist North led to President Kennedy's 1962 decision to send American military aid to the South. During the Johnson and Nixon presidencies the escalation of the American commitment to defend the independence of South Vietnam caused the United States losses estimated at 57,000 dead. Widespread opposition to the war in the late 1960s and the polarization of American opinion on the issue weakened American commitment. The deterioration of the military situation in favour of the North Vietnamese and mounting Congressional opposition to the war forced President Nixon to withdraw American troops and to conclude a 1973 peace treaty with the North. The treaty proved illusory and in April 1975 the North Vietnamese army successfully invaded the South and captured the capital—Saigon.

Apart from the tragedy of the war for the Vietnamese themselves the war dominated American political life for nearly a decade and cast doubt on the willingness of the United States to intervene again in a military confrontation with communist forces. It also contributed to the abuses of executive power which culminated in the WATERGATE crisis.

Voting

Voting is an act of choice amongst a set of alternatives, by a free individual, and is at the heart of modern democracy. People have, of course, voted for candidates for office, or for policy alternatives, in every social system ever experienced. The recorded history of voting goes back, at least, to the Greek polis. Our modern word for the study of voting behaviour, psephology, derives from the classical Greek Psephos, the piece of pottery on which certain votes, mainly about the banishment of those seen as dangerous to the state, were inscribed. Voting is no more than the voicing of individual opinions—the problems arise in counting the votes, and in deciding for whom, or for what alternative, the votes have been cast.

As far as voting in election, in choosing a candidate amongst others goes, the great point is the secret and individual ballot, which alone allows the impartial measurement of opinion. This is actually quite recent, at least in its fullest form. The secret ballot did not appear in the UK until the late 19th century, for parliamentary elections. Allowing candidates to put party labels on their ballot slips, the minimum necessary to avoid wasted votes, did not happen until the late 1960s. Even now, in many vital sub-political units, trades unions, for example, the individuated secret ballot does not necessarily exist.

The vote has been restricted, throughout history, for a variety of reasons. Probably the most common qualification, in national politics, has been a wealth or property qualification. Since the late 19th century there has been a series of developments on the suffrage, each giving way slightly on voting rights. The average modern standard in the late 20th century is that all citizens, over the age of 18, should be allowed the vote.

W

Warsaw Pact

The Warsaw Pact is the Russian dominated opposition grouping to NATO, signed in 1955, and theoretically initiated as a response to West Germany joining NATO in 1954. Its membership includes most of the Communist bloc, though Albania, which had come more and more under Chinese influence, left it in 1961, and both Hungary and the Czechs tried to leave, unsuccessfully, at the times of their anti-Russian risings in 1956 and 1968. The Warsaw Pact set up a unified military command structure under the control of Moscow, and is largely armed by the Soviet Union. In practice it forms nothing more than an extension of the Soviet Union's military forces, and accounts for perhaps 20 of the 70 or more divisions the pact forces have ready in non-Russian Europe. Many doubts exist among Western defence analysts about the reliability of the armies of most members of the pact should a confrontation occur between the pact and NATO. Furthermore the Soviet Union makes a practice of always equipping these forces with less modern weapons systems. The only time the pact has actually engaged in military operations was the crushing of the Czech uprising in 1968. Even this, however, was mainly a propaganda exercise to demonstrate a spurious East European solidarity, with the real offensive entirely carried out by troops from the Soviet Union. No member other than the Soviet Union has any access to nuclear weapons, and the only seriously effective other member is the East German force.

Watergate

The Watergate is a hotel in Washington DC where a suite of rooms had been rented by the Democratic Party National Committee for the Presidential election campaign of 1972. These rooms were burgled by a group of people working under the orders of senior members of the Republican party, including some holding important positions on President Nixon's staff in the White House. The aim of the burglars appears to have been to gain information about Democratic campaign plans. The discovery of the burglars and their subsequent trials unleashed a massive burst of investigative reporting which ended by incriminating a host of major and minor figures, not so much for having been involved in the initial crime, but for attempting to cover up the White House connections, and generally to impede the course of justice. Amongst these were men as senior as the Attorney-General and the President's Chief of Staff.

At that level the scandal would have been serious but, as most of it became public only after Nixon had won the 1972 election, it was not fatal to him. It became increasingly clear however that the President himself had been involved in the cover-up, and members of the House of Representatives began to move for his impeachment. At the same time secret tape recordings the President had made of conversations in the White House came to be revealed, and court proceedings were instigated to force him to disclose them as vital evidence. Nixon attempted to prevent this move, claiming that they were covered by a doctrine of executive privilege, but this was finally overthrown by the Supreme Court. The culmination of these twin moves, as impeachment began to seem inevitable, led to his resigning office, to be succeeded by the Vice-President, who shortly after gave him a presidential pardon. The crisis shook American politics; faith in executive leadership, already weakened by Nixon's style of government and his secret extension of the Vietnamese war in Cambodia, collapsed. The following years saw Congress rise in power, relative to the Presidency, and a series of attempts to curtail presidential prerogatives and control financial corruption in electoral campaigns. The name Watergate has lingered, and become a journalistic cliché so that almost any political scandal, especially if it involves the theft of documents or the leaking of confidential information, has '-gate' tagged to the end of it.

Weber

Max Weber (1864–1920) was a German academic and politician and one of the three or four founding fathers of sociology. In contrast to DURKHEIM and MARX he argued for a sociological position in which the inner feelings and self-perceptions of the actors themselves were part of the explanation of human behaviour. His most famous sociological work is *The Protestant Ethic and the Spirit of Capitalism*, in which he argued for a natural affinity between certain views of how heavenly salvation was to be earned and the technical requirements of capitalist economic development. As far as politics is concerned he is important for two major doctrines. The most important is probably his theory of BUREAUCRACY, which has been widely copied and developed, and still inspires most social science research on this vital phenomenon. But he was also the creator of a developmental theory of political change which suggested a move from CHARISMATIC authority, via Traditional authority to Rational-Legal authority, which has informed much of subsequent studies in political and social development.

Weimar Republic

The Weimar Republic was the official name for the German political system between the end of the First World War and the coming to power of HITLER with his 'Third Reich' in the early 1930s. It was quite unstable, attempting to operate a competitive party-based democracy in a country which had not only no tradition of such politics, but was also deeply divided by internal social and political cleavages, especially between the Communists and the Fascists. The period, though short-lived, has remained one of great importance and fascination to social scientists, historians, and indeed novelists, because it was the breeding ground for Nazi politics, and because it represents one of the best cases for theories of revolutionary activity and democratic stability.

Welfare State

Welfare State is a term that came into general use during the Second World War coalition government in Britain, largely as a result of the influential Beveridge report of 1944. This set up a plan for a comprehensive set of services, financed largely out of national insurance contributions levied both on workers and employers. The scheme was to ensure not only the previously acquired right to an old age pension, but to put unemployment pay, sickness and injury benefit, and a variety of other financial protections against hardship on to a regularized basis. In the past such matters had either not been attended to at all, or were covered by ad hoc and usually inadequate legislation. The Welfare State, while having no detailed content, is the general idea that misfortunes that have financial consequences to those unable to manage should all be dealt with by the state, through its taxing power. Arguments raged, and still do, about how extensive welfare should be. Should it cover only the small number of the almost destitute, or should it be a safety net for many, or should everyone in society be granted an automatic protection against potential disaster? In some cases, as with the British National Health Service, the entire population is covered by a system of free, or extremely highly subsidized medicine. In other cases means tests are used to direct special benefit payments, for example to families with low incomes and several children, to those particularly in need. The spirit, if not the content, of the Welfare State has never been seriously challenged in Britain since the 1945–1951 Labour governments implemented the basis of the Beveridge report. No one need now rely on private charity to sustain a basic, if low standard of living, whatever ill fortune in terms of unemployment, illness, industrial injury, family breakdown or whatever may happen. At times, though probably wrongly and misleadingly, the idea of the welfare state is extended to cover the social services, so that the general principle outlined above is coupled with the rather less unanimously popular existence of a large bureaucracy of social workers of various kinds.

In recent years the proportion of GNP spent on the various social services has caused concern in a number of Western political systems and ways have been sought to curb expenditure on these services.

Welfarism

Welfarism is a vague, and often pejorative political reference to the principles behind the welfare state. It does no more than indicate that the person so characterized believes that the state should take responsibility for the financial security of those in society unable to manage on their own resources. As a result it is perhaps more often used by Conservative politicians, especially in the USA, who themselves adopt a much more LAISSER-FAIRE approach, to attack others who they feel are over-solicitous to the poor. Alternatively it is a general statement that society should take such responsibility, and a denial of the reactionary 'Let them stand on their own feet' position.

Z

Zionism

Zionism is the political creed, dating from early in the diaspora, that the old Jewish national homeland of Palestine should be regained by Jews and run as a national home and centre for world-wide Jewish solidarity. Although Zionism grew with increasing fervour from the early 20th century, the rise of vicious ANTI-SEMITISM in Europe during the 1930s gave it its major boost in support. For a long time the area demanded, Palestine, was governed under a mandate from the League of Nations and then the United Nations by Britain, because, whatever international Judaism might argue historically, it was a fully populated Arab country which could not be evacuated or suddenly flooded with European Jews, and tight immigration controls were applied. After the European holocaust however it became both morally and practically difficult for Western powers to maintain their protection of the area, and after a terrorist campaign and the pulling out of British troops, militant Jewish groups founded the state of Israel as the official Zionist homeland.

The doctrine of Zionism has increasingly become suspect even amongst Jews, in and out of Israel, because of the problem of the Palestinian people and the activities of their political and military organization, the PLO (q.v.). Nowadays Zionism principally refers to a HAWK versus DOVE orientation towards Israeli policy. Zionists support at least the retention of the land gained in the various Arab-Israeli wars since 1947, and possibly a further military expansion. Non-zionists, whether Jewish, Israeli or neither, increasingly believe that some sort of accommodation, almost certainly involving the creation of a Palestinian state somewhere inside the current de facto Israeli borders is both right and politically necessary.

A secondary meaning sometimes given to Zionism refers to the internal politics of Israel, and especially to the extent to which the theological rather than purely ethnic and cultural aspects of Judaism should be enforced or encouraged by the state. Zionism still retains considerable support, often amongst financially and politically powerful Jews in Western countries, and especially in the USA.